GOD AND THE PHILOSOPHERS

God

AND

THE

PHILOSOPHERS

the

reconciliation

of faith and reason

Edited by
Thomas V. Morris

OXFORD UNIVERSITY PRESS
New York   Oxford

Oxford University Press

Oxford   New York
Athens   Auckland Bangkok   Bombay
Calcutta   Cape Town   Dar es Salaam   Delhi
Florence   Hong Kong   Istanbul   Karachi
Kuala Lumpur   Madras   Madrid   Melbourne
Mexico City   Nairobi   Paris   Singapore
Taipei   Tokyo   Toronto

and associated companies in
Berlin   Ibadan

Library of Congress Cataloging-in-Publication Data
God and the philosophers / edited by Thomas V. Morris.
p.   cm.
ISBN 0-19-508822-0
ISBN 0-19-510119-7 (Pbk.)
1. Christian philosophers—United States—Biography.
2. Philosophers, Jewish—United States—Biography.
3. Philosophy and religion.   4. Theism.
I. Morris, Thomas V.
BR102.A1G63   1994
210′.92′2—dc20
[B]   93-38656

10 9 8 7 6 5
Printed in the United States of America

CONTENTS

CONTENTS

GOD AND THE PHILOSOPHERS

INTRODUCTION

Most of the great philosophers in Western civilization have been people who believed in God. And a number of the most influential proponents of a religious world view throughout history have been recognized as great philosophers. It is the job of a philosopher to seek the deepest levels of understanding possible for human beings, to penetrate the veil of appearances in our world, and to discover the underlying realities with which we most ultimately have to deal. Religious philosophers are individuals who claim to have found that the most fundamental of those realities is spiritual. Theistic philosophers identify the ultimate spiritual reality as God.

Over the past few years, I have asked a number of active, creative, theistic philosophers who are at various stages along life's way, as well as in their own intellectual and scholarly careers, whether they would consider writing an essay "from the heart," speaking of their own spiritual journeys, explaining how they personally see the relationship between the spiritual and the philosophical in their own lives, or else showing with their own stories how a person of faith can grapple with some of the problems and prospects of religious belief from a philosophical point of view. Nearly everyone I approached with this project wanted to give it a try, appreciating the potential importance of such an exercise for themselves as well as for their readers. But all saw it as a challenging request.

We philosophers aren't accustomed to writing from the heart. We are more practiced at doing intellectual combat head to head. Abstract analysis and rigorous debate is more our style. And, as a result, philosophical writing has, for the most part nowadays, become as technical and difficult to read as any other specialist literature in the academic world. Care, precision, and intellectual responsibility demand no less within the covers of the professional journals. And autobiography is out. We deal in ideas, not personalities, in arguments, not in the histories of individuals' inner lives. The tone of most writing by contemporary philosophers is, further, more that of at least approximate *objectivity,* and not at all forthright *subjectivity.* So, what I sought from most of the contributors to this book, and what I have attempted myself, is well outside our typical scholarly comfort zones. But for a long time, I have been convinced that it is important for some of us to push ourselves outside those comfort zones and contemplate the rich, underexplored realm of our own personal experience as philosophically reflective human beings who seek to center our lives on God. Those who have provided essays for this book have shared my conviction and have fought the constraints of extremely busy schedules, along with the scholarly habits of style inhospitable to what we all hope to accomplish in offering to each other, as well as to others, these first fruits of our personal reflection. I thank my adventurous colleagues from the bottom of my own heart for joining me in this pioneering effort.

Even as recently as two or three decades ago, a project like this might have been thought an impossibility. To many people, it certainly would have seemed an incongruity. The twentieth century had appeared to witness the divorce of faith and philosophy after a long and fitful process of separation. Reason and religion were thought by many to dwell in different worlds. God and the philosophers, it seemed, were no longer on speaking terms. Philosophy in its modern forms had acquired a reputation for being the enemy of religious belief.

When I was an undergraduate at the University of North Carolina at Chapel Hill in the early 1970s, my first philosophy professor, a man well known in academic circles, announced to the class with great enthusiasm and self-assurance that he was an atheist. I remember that his look and tone seemed to imply that if we didn't want to be intellectual embarrassments to ourselves, or at least to the philosophy department, we'd better be atheists too. This was quite a surprise to the 250 students in the room, counted among whom were probably 200 native Southern Baptists, a selection of Methodists and Presbyterians, and a few Episcopalians (out-of-state students from pricy prep schools). Two wild-looking hippies in the room seemed extremely pleased at this declaration, and positively glowed when the professor went on to remark that if he ever took up anything remotely like a religious practice at all, it would have to be Zen Buddhism. In this predominantly freshman class, most of us had never heard of Zen Buddhism, but we figured that if the hippies liked it, it must be something pretty strange. Everyone in the room was affected by these announcements of such a personal nature, coming as they did from a person not otherwise inclined to engage in autobiographical revelation. We were led to believe, and much subsequent experience in the study of twentieth-century philosophy seemed to confirm, that the best modern philosophers had no patience whatsover with that old-time religion of our upbringing. Philosophers in our time, it was easy to conclude, had utterly dismissed the existence of God, along with such other nonsense as faeries, ghosts, goblins, and elves.

This seems to be the general impression held by most relatively well-educated people in America today. Philosophers are assumed to be enemies of faith. Reason and religion are thought to be diametrically opposed.

What many people, even within academic circles, do not realize is that there have been tremendous changes within the world of philosophy over the past couple of decades. In that short time, we have seen a dramatic and unexpected resurgence of religious belief and commitment taking place among the ranks of some of the most active practitioners and teachers of philosophy on college and university campuses all over America, a development found extremely perplexing by many onlookers. More than a decade ago, for example, a professional organization was formed by several senior members of the American Philosophical Association as a sort of support group for Christian philosophers, who at the time were increasing in number and prominence, and yet were still clearly swimming against the main currents of philosophical thought in our time. Since its inception, this organization, the Society of Christian Philosophers, has grown to about 1,000 active members and has launched a professional journal, *Faith and Philosophy,* that in the years of its existence has become a focal point for exciting new philosophical work on religious topics.

At the Center for Philosophy of Religion at the University of Notre Dame, now the editorial headquarters for *Faith and Philosophy,* I have been privileged to work in the midst of these new developments, getting to know people from around the world who philosophize from faith perspectives and who are producing important new insights concerning the human quest for spirituality, our idea of God, and the divine economy governing our world. Drawing on the work of the best religious philosophers in previous centuries and appropriating the most helpful aspects of contemporary thought, the many philosophers now devoting their efforts to the concerns of faith are making significant intellectual headway and are coming up with new insights into many branches of traditional philosophical inquiry, from ethics and epistemology to metaphysics.

Most nonreligious philosophers find these recent developments within the philosophical world surprising. Even some religious people find it a bit confusing—especially within the Christian faith. For after all, they point out, we do find in the New Testament, in the book of Colossians the following admonition:

> See to it that no one take you captive through philosophy and empty deception, according to the tradition of men, according to the elementary principles of the world, rather than according to Christ. (2:8)

It is unfortunate but true that this passage has often been read as intended to steer the Christian believer away from philosophy. What it attempts to warn the Christian against, however, is *false* philosophy.

Recalling that *philosophy* is etymologically "the love of wisdom," consider some of the preceding context of that well-known verse from Colossians. The author has just said:

> For I want you to know how great a struggle I have on your behalf, and for all those who are at Laodicea, and for all those who have not personally seen my face, that their hearts may be encouraged, having been knit together in love and attaining to all the wealth that comes from the full assurance of understanding, resulting in a true knowledge of God's mystery, that is, Christ himself, in whom are hidden all the treasures of wisdom and knowledge.

The religious believers to whom the letter is addressed are to be knit together in love, and they are to attain together the wealth of understanding and wisdom that is properly theirs as Christians. They are to philosophize together as *believers*. It is only philosophy based on nothing more than the traditions of autonomous human thought and the elementary principles of this world, a pattern of world-view construction not informed by or answerable to divine revelation, that they are to avoid serving. They are not being instructed not to use their intellects to the utmost in understanding their lives as Christians. Quite the contrary. They are to seek understanding and wisdom. The religious person's philosophical abilities can and should be put to work in service to the journey of the spirit.

The Jewish, Christian, and Muslim communities have all produced philosophers of penetrating intellect and profound wisdom over the centuries, philosophers who have centered their own world views on God and drawn deeply on the resources this has provided. Rather than being in tension with their religious commitments, this activity of philosophizing, at its best, has, I believe, most often enhanced their own spiritual lives, as well as that of their communities. It is my hope that the philosophers who have contributed the essays to be found here will thereby extend their already considerable impact as thinkers within their own faith communities, as well as within the academic world and the world at large.

Francis Bacon once said of some of the intellectuals of his time:

> Their discourses are as the stars which give little light,
> because they are so high.

In this book, we have gathered a group of philosophers capable of the highest flights of intricate reasoning who have sought to bring their reflections down to earth. They write as human beings who are people of faith seeking to understand and to share their understanding.

These are of necessity interim reports. But we hope they will help others to grapple better with issues of faith and thought in their own lives.

I

SUSPICIONS

OF SOMETHING

MORE

Thomas V. Morris

My first experience inside a church did not at the time seem to bode well for my ecclesial future. The memory is still vivid. Pandemonium. I'm three years old, and a very large female Sunday school teacher is holding me upside down by my ankles and shaking me as the class gathers around us, shouting and shrieking. I'm choking on a forbidden piece of hard candy, unable to breathe, and she is determined to shake it out of me. After a good deal of jostling and back whacking, it pops free. Breathing again, I'm restored to the upright position, and the crowd of onlookers is dispersed. In many ways, this little episode inside the Westwood Baptist Church of Durham, North Carolina, is a metaphor for the role of the Christian faith in a number of my more mature struggles, even without the expected observation that it has on occasion turned my little world upside down.

Most Sundays as a child I was taken to church, both for Sunday school and for the worship service. My father was treasurer of the Sunday school, and my mother helped as teacher or assistant for whatever class I was in, graduating with me from year to year throughout my preteen years. I have many memories of those times, but most are social more than spiritual. Even as a small boy, I think I was often more aware of the cute girls in the class than of the lessons I was supposed to be learning. And the only act of theft I can recall ever performing involved taking home a toy from a Sunday school classroom. I still remember the fear of discovery, the burning ambivalence, and the inevitable sense of humiliating guilt on being caught. But that was an aberration. Deep down, from the very beginning, I resonated with the moral and spiritual lessons I was taught, primarily from the pages of the New Testament, and I began developing a religious view of the world. Church was for the most part a happy, accepting place, with pleasant music and good food to eat outdoors on special occasions.

In my traditional Southern Baptist church, every service ended with an invitational hymn. The pastor called for anyone to come forward who wanted to accept Jesus Christ as their personal savior for the forgiveness of their sins. We sang quietly, heads slightly bowed, as people in the congregation struggled within, trying to decide whether they should make a public profession of faith as new Christians or as a rededication to an old commitment that had waned over the years. Often, between the penultimate and last stanzas of a hymn, the singing would stop on cue while the minister spoke to us and prayed for us to have the responsiveness and courage to come forward as the organ or piano played on. With head lowered and eyes shut, I could not contain my desire to peek every few seconds to see if there was any response. Sometimes one or two people made their way across the pews and down the center aisle to the front, where I would catch a glimpse of the minister embracing them or shaking hands and praying with them in thankfulness. On occasion, a crowd would stream forward, especially during revival services, to the extent that I worried whether I was going to be the only one left in the pews with a hymn book. I wasn't prepared to do the closing verse solo.

I think I was the last one my age to make the public profession. Officially, this was a free decision to be made from the heart at the prompting of the holy spirit, and yet it seemed to be understood that by the age of ten, eleven, or twelve, everyone would do it. Inwardly shy and not very comfortable with public displays of this sort, I was a bit of a holdout. I knew what I believed and desired, and yet for the sake of everyone else, it seemed, I was supposed to take the plunge. Sunday after Sunday the pressure built. I could almost feel everyone wondering when I would finally take the expected walk. My ears sometimes burned from the embarrassment of not moving from where my feet were firmly planted during that part of the service. But finally, one bright day during the playing of the most dramatic, most traditional invitational hymn, the altar call theme song of the famous Billy Graham crusades, "Just

As I Am," a hymn sung at least once every few months at my church, as late in the song as I could possibly wait, I came forward, told the minister I wanted to accept Jesus into my life, and felt a great sense of liberation. A short time later I was baptized "in the proper way" by total immersion. Not a swimmer, I thought I was going to drown. Although I was a pretty big boy and flailed around fairly vigorously while underwater during that symbolic and sacramental second or two, the minister somehow managed to keep his feet and return me to the upright position, snorting and gasping for air.

In junior high school, I became a rock-and-roll guitar player, formed bands, and played at big parties and dances around town. As the years passed, this became a more and more serious involvement, as I hit the road with rock and Southern soul bands. The Baptist church did not believe in the propriety of rock and roll, wasn't very favorably disposed to parties of any kind, countenanced no music for the soul other than hymns, and strongly discouraged any form of dancing among the young people. This, of course, was bad for my business. I began to feel a growing distance between myself and the church, started skipping services more and more frequently, and found that, although my core beliefs had not changed, they had begun to mean much less to the rhythms of my daily life. In the lingo of the faithful, I "fell away" from the church for a number of years, as is fairly common for that age in life.

In high school, after a big football game, I was in a crowd of revelers outside the top hot spot in town, Anna Maria's Pizza Parlor, listening to the juke box blaring "Twist and Shout" and "Double Shot of My Baby's Love," when a friend pulled up on a motorcycle and yelled out an invitation to what I thought was another party. He was actually asking me if I wanted to go to "Young Life," a high school Christian fellowship and outreach program meeting in people's houses in the evenings. I thought he had asked whether I wanted to go to something called "*Wild* Life." That sounded interesting, so I went along.

The house was crammed with people. The cheerleaders were there, the school sports stars, the rock and rollers, and the intrinsically cool people whose presence, for no specifiable reason, was important. I felt that I fit right in. There was lively music, hilarious comedy, and a short lesson from the Bible told with verve and energy. Imagine my surprise at this point. It was the social event of the month. And it ended with a prayer. Astonishing. I went to the next scheduled Young Life meeting as well, still not quite sure what I was attending. Soon I was recruited to play guitar. A great chance to show off, meet girls, have fun, and laugh a lot. And in the midst of all this, I was hearing from the college student leaders about the practicality of a faith perspective on life. At their urging, I bought a J. B. Phillips translation of the New Testament, which I was surprised to find I really enjoyed reading in bed at night. I had never been exposed to anything other than the elevated, reverential, remote, and yet admittedly evocative language of the King James Version of the Bible. Some fellow Southerners of a more rural sort, it seems, had even come to think of that language as the original spoken tongue of the biblical characters. In a debate over the teaching of foreign languages in the public schools, one Tennessee state legislator of the time was reported to have capped his adversarial argument from the floor with the exclamation that "If the King's English was good enough for our Lord and Savior Jesus Christ, it's good enough for our kids." But J. B. Phillips's modern English was my language. It came alive to me as I read it, and I grew eager to talk to someone about the insights I believed I was getting from it left and right.

In a very short time, I was attending a Bible study group made up of the most spiritually dedicated young men in the high school, together with a collegiate Young Life leader. It was pleasant. It was enlightening. But I learned very quickly that I had no firm commitment to group meetings that did not involve loud music, the other gender, and raucous hilarity. I craved the energy any of those three could generate.

The peak experience of my Young Life years involved an appropriately high-energy road trip to a summer camp in Colorado filled with a cast of characters fit for the big screen—a former NFL lineman with the New York Giants, the beautiful daughter of a wealthy Brazilian industrialist, who had not heard from her family since a recent military coup, some of the most talented storytellers and musicians I had ever met, and a rambunctious, wacky group of multisport team members calling themselves "The Kickapoo Joy Juicers." It was an altogether amazing religious retreat, the pinnacle of which involved juggling two new girlfriends and finally choosing the more glamorous of the two, a tall, stunning blond model from a highly visible Chicago family. Ah, the joys of youthful spirituality. My love of life, love of God, and love of love, or at least of the teenage variant thereof, were all woven together in a sometimes complex tangle. I was a pack animal, loving the communion with my fellow soul mates; a guitarist loving the creation and experience of music; a still chaste but erotically attuned young romantic, embracing the magnetic, electric wonders of male–female attraction; an emotional sponge to the world, taking in all the grandeur, pathos, tragedy, and joy I could find; and, finally, a budding thinker on all these things. I found that animality, musicality, sensuality, emotionality, and intellectuality could all be apertures to spirituality, openings in my life for that deep energy and insight I have come to recognize as the proper province of the spiritual.

One close Christian friend in those high school days was a bit worried about what he considered to be my materialism. When we talked of the future, he noticed that I often spoke about beautiful houses and fine cars, with an occasional mention of tennis courts and swimming pools. In a friendly but pointedly jocular way he chastised me for my values. He counseled me on being more spiritual. I listened. I laughed at his worries and then worried at my laughs. Not long afterward, I entered the University of North Carolina as a business major heading toward law school, with an eye on an eventual corporate presidency. No sense in planning small. But as it turned out, I finished up my undergraduate years with a religion major instead and went to Yale for a Ph.D. in philosophy and religious studies. My concerned friend followed family tradition and matriculated at Harvard, where he graduated with an engineering degree and later took an MBA, entering the world of big business. The difference in our respective career paths seemed to become one of life's little ironics, except for the fact that he remains, by all standard criteria, the more spirtual of the two of us, which I consider an even more ironic twist.

When I arrived at North Carolina in the fall of 1970, Chapel Hill was something like a Disneyland of the 1960s, with all the social, political, musical, and psychological rides you could imagine. In class, there were guest lectures by whatever nationally known radicals and revolutionaries happened not to be in jail. There were constant parties. There was an exuberance of ideas, of relationships, of possibilities. It was all new for a Southern Baptist boy, but I loved every minute of it.

It was also the time of the Jesus Movement on college campuses across the country—counterculture Christianity with rock music rallies, holy hootenannies, and bumper stickers that shouted "HONK IF YOU LOVE JESUS!" Invited by a friend in my dorm to attend a Bible study/discussion group, I went along and found myself in the midst of Campus Crusade for Christ International, a sort of Young Life at the collegiate level, replete with great music, beautiful people, and charismatic leaders who, in a talk before a small group or a large campus rally, could segue among gripping drama, inspiring vision, and uproarious humor in a flash. The energy of these meetings was unbelievable. But they needed a better guitar player. I was hooked. My faith was rekindled, my social life took off like a skyrocket, and I learned a catalogue of new songs. Before I knew what was happening, I was wearing ONE WAY T-shirts and "witnessing" in the dorms, going door to door with a Crusade-trained group leader to try to initiate conversations about religious faith with other students.

I dreaded the act of "going witnessing." But I was told by everyone around me at the time that it was a necessary part of the Christian life. I preferred not to bother people who were studying, relaxing, or, more likely, partying, preparing to party, or recuperating from too much partying. And despite my ability to perform in front of thousands of people with a guitar in my hands, I was still in many ways a very shy person who dreaded this sort of forced, artificial social encounter, conversationally dragging the Great Beyond into the here-and-now.

But once a conversation started, I was entranced. People would share with a stranger their hopes and fears, their most personal worries, and often their confused anger about life, the lack of direction they felt, the lack of satisfaction, all their uncertainties. If there is a God, why isn't it more obvious? Why is there so much evil in the world? Why are some religious people such jerks? If Christianity is true, then how could so many atrocities have been committed throughout the centuries in the name of Christ? Isn't it all a beautiful myth from the ancient past? And what about Judaism? Hinduism? Buddhism? Does science leave any room for religion at all?

I tried to come up with answers to all these questions. And in the process, I discovered questions of my own. I was intrigued by talks I heard on the historical reliability of biblical texts, on historical evidence for the resurrection of Christ, on prophecy and miracles, and on arguments for the existence of God. I had always been a questioner, an empirically minded debater, and I could not contain my excitement over the opportunity to think and talk about such big issues with the Crusaders who so clearly seemed to care about all these things. I began to read about and then to master the philosophical and historical arguments I was coming across. From what I could tell, in the arena of open debate, it looked pretty good for a fundamental belief in God, as well as for the core of the Christian faith.

A religion course with a dynamic lecturer on Old Testament themes won me over to the academic study of those issues I so vigorously discussed around the dorms at night. Six courses with this popular professor, Bernard Boyd, a dapper man late in life with a flair for drama, and I was firmly grounded in biblical studies. Another professor, a forceful and very funny philosopher of science who was also an Orthodox Jewish rabbi, George Schlesinger, hooked me on philosophy. In three courses and in a great many private conversations, he began to show me how formally developed philosophical techniques could be deployed in defense and analysis of traditional religious belief. And I began to appreciate the true power of ideas in the life of a person who really uses his mind.

Known as an outpost of liberal thought, Chapel Hill had also become a hotbed of evangelical Christianity. The Chapel Hill Bible Church, started with only a few founding members toward the beginning of my time at North Carolina, grew to a membership of 500 students, faculty and townspeople in only a couple of years. Its growth has continued apace since then. The pastor, Jim Abrahamson, was one of the best public speakers and teachers I had ever heard. A graduate of the conservative Dallas Theological Seminary, he was an extremely open-minded and well-balanced representative of traditional Christian thought, capable of uniting people of disparate theological commitments. His church brought together all the campus Christian groups like Campus Crusade, the Navigators, and the Inter-Varsity Christian Fellowship, with whom I was more involved toward the end of my undergraduate years, a group that seemed to put more stress on intellectual, cultural, and broadly philosophical issues as they related to Christian faith.

This lively, well-read minister had an important impact on me, showing me in more ways the tremendous effects a great teacher can have. Another influence was church elder Wright Doyle, at the university my professor of New Testament Greek. Perhaps more than anyone else, he encouraged me to become a thinker, to develop my nascent philosophical skills, and to seek to have a positive impact on the world. But he also worried about my rock-and-roll tendencies. On occasion, as I walked to the front of the church to accompany a special hymn on the acoustic guitar, he would lean over and whisper loudly, with a look of near desperation, "Don't jazz it up!"

I was a welcomed insider to many religious groups, yet I always felt like something of an outsider. Many of my friends erected walls with their theologies; I wanted to build bridges. While most nurtured religious certainties, I was more inclined to explore possibilities. I was always a bit on my own frequency. I was awakened to Christian philosophy by the writings of Francis Schaeffer, C. S. Lewis, and others whose books I enjoyed, but no one of these popular contemporary Christian writers seemed to me to be operating at the most careful and penetrating philosophical level. I could not become the wholehearted fan of any of them that many of my friends had become. I couldn't accept easy answers, but at the time, I could find no guidance for digging deeper into so many of the issues these writers addressed. Moreover, for all these campus groups, spirituality seemed to be something distinctive, somehow set apart from the rest of life, and yet something that we were supposed to take and then apply to everything else. But I kept sensing that the sources of spirituality might be more numerous and more pervasive in life than was canonically acknowledged in these circles. And from the sparkling energy in a young woman's eyes, I could not help but feel a connection between *eros* and *theos,* the erotic and the theological, sex and God. But no one even whispered about anything like this, so who was I to bring it up?

I married a wonderful young woman with sparkling eyes whom the reportedly psychic grandmother of a high school friend had once described to me many years before as my future wife, although we were not to meet until my junior year at college, and then I set myself to prepare at Yale for the sort of vocation this same remarkable older woman had told me I would follow, despite all my plans for a business career. For someone unfamiliar with modern, logical, analytic philosophy of religion, her description of my future vocation in context was striking—"something like science, only spiritual," she had said. During my graduate years, I studied the techniques of science to pursue topics of the spirit. But at Yale, despite any appearances of having my world view well put together, and deep beneath all my developing facility in arguing that view, I was at many times and in many ways confused, uncertain, and troubled.

The problem of evil in particular gnawed away at my theism. How indeed could a good and loving creator allow all the horrible suffering in this world? If I could just meet with the right philosopher or theologian and discuss this problem, I though at the time, surely it could be answered to my satisfaction. I even had a particular scholar in mind. When I did finally come to meet and talk with this renowned intellectual, I came to the shocking realization that, in the end, he really didn't know any more than I did about the questions that most mattered to me, and that, ultimately, we're all in the same boat. We'll never make sense of it all by just finding a piece of information or an idea heretofore elusive to us but long known by some philosophical expert. That's not how the most important things work. Like it or not.

I had to make my own way in philosophy of religion at Yale. I had to make my own way in life. On either level, I was flying by the seat of my pants, as old pilots say, with the help of an occasional, but frustratingly rare, piece of good advice from a fellow traveler. In the Yale Divinity School, I took as many classes with Paul Holmer as I had as an undergraduate with Bernard Boyd, and I was inspired but never quite satisfied. Holmer introduced me to a feast of Wittgenstein, Kierkegaard, and finally, more indirectly, Pascal. It was in those days that I became close friends with another budding Christian philosopher, a fellow graduate student, Jorge Garcia, whose background, ethnicity, catholicity, and education were about as different from mine as possible, and yet who was the best dialogue partner I've ever had. We would often walk the sidewalks of New Haven and talk philosophy for hours, occasionally saving each other at street corners from fallacies and oncoming cars. His probing questions helped me to see what it really takes to develop and defend a philosophical position plausibly. And his example inspired me in my explorations of a Christian world view.

Excited by the seminal work of Saul Kripke, I began to consider how I could apply the new developments in philosophical logic and the philosophy of language to an understanding of the most difficult and central Christian doctrines, such as the doctrine of the Incarnation, the foundational Christian belief that in the life of Jesus, God had taken on human form. I decided to write my doctoral dissertation on identity statements and the Incarnation. None of the faculty could figure out what exactly I was doing and why in the world I was doing it. What hath Jerusalem to do with Athens? Doctrine and modern logic seemed to some of them to mix like snake oil and holy water. The theologians were perplexed at the ins and outs of arguments about Leibniz's law—the identity of indiscernibles, the indiscernibility of identicals, and the principle of substitutivity—that cluster of logical and metaphyical principles I was bent on applying to incarnational contexts, and the philosophers were just plain dumb founded by my interest in understanding and resisting the theological heresies of Nestorianism, Appollinarianism, psilanthropism, and patripassionism. These are not interests everyone has. An unusually large group of faculty came to attend my dissertation defense the way a crowd tends to gather at the scene of an accident. Curiosity got the best of them.

I learned some important lessons from all this. First, philosophizing about religion with the best techniques of contemporary logic, epistemology, and metaphysics was not a practice widely established in the contemporary academic world, and it was not strongly encouraged either in the domain of contemporary philosophy or within the province of current academic theology. Both sides expected the application of philosophical tools to have a detrimental effect on religion. Philosophers thought it wasn't worth the trouble. Theologians thought that trouble was all it was worth. Both were wrong. I learned that the more deeply I explored traditional theistic and Christian thought, the more I could make sense of initially problematic and mysterious ideas. Yet, at best, I found that I was typically explicating and defending possibilities, not establishing or demonstrating truths in any way guaranteed to convince the doubter or decisively answer the questioner. I was often working more in the area of plausibility than in that of certainty. Still, I found that tremendous intellectual progress can be made in dealing with fundamental religious questions. On the surface, many intellectual objections can be raised against a religious point of view, and some of these problems, such as the problem of evil and the problem of the hiddenness of God, can appear quite daunting. But the more deeply I dig in response to such problems, the more resources I discover within a theistic view of the world, and within the rich texture of Christian theology, in particular, for illuminating a great number of the otherwise apparently intractable questions we can ask. The more I probe, the better a religious picture of the world looks to me, however subtle some of its strengths might be.

However, it was no amount of philosophical reasoning that originally gave me this picture of the world. Even apart from my formal religious training, I have long had a suspicion that there is much, much more to reality than meets the eye. One of my most vivid memories of childhood is that of hearing my mother tell of the death of her father when she was still a small girl. His last words to the family before he died, uttered in a voice of amazement, were, "It's beautiful." From a very young age, I wondered what he saw and what this statement meant.

There were other intriguing events in family lore. My father's mother was said to have special abilities to bring nearly dead plants back to life and to train, and even more deeply communicate with, animals. When my father as a young man lived in Baltimore, Maryland, he would arbitrarily, with no patterned regularity, make surprise trips back home to the farm in North Carolina. His mother would always have his place set at the table and food cooked for him, saying she knew he was coming that day. When my father first met the young woman I would later marry, he announced to my mother with no clues from me, from her, or from the circumstances, and long before I had a clue, that he had just met my future wife, a revelation he passed on to me only after the friendship had taken a new turn and commitments had been made. On board ship in the Pacific Ocean during the Second World War, he once lived through a bizarre evening of shooting dice all night, somehow knowing before each throw what he would get, feeling his wins before they came, a vivid, alternate-state-of-consciousness experience, never to be repeated, which left him stunned, perplexed, and fascinated with what could have transpired. More recently, on a visit to a ministerial friend, as he raised his arm to knock at the man's front door, he "heard" the words "Don't disturb him, he's dead"; lowered his arm; turned around; got back in his wagon; and drove back home. Not much more than an hour later, he received a call from the man's son conveying the news that he had just been found dead in that house of a heart attack.

My father never made much of these and similar unusual experiences, but they clearly meant a great deal to him. He often recounted them to me, but he never tried to explain them. In fact, he sometimes wondered aloud what they meant, how they happened, and even why they occurred. But he did recall them as important, and this was clearly communicated to me.

One professor I got to know well at Yale once told me that he was an atheist and that he did not accept the reality of anything like a soul or a spirit in the human domain, but that one thing worried him: Enter a room full of intelligent and sincere people, loosen them up a bit so that they're comfortable talking about personal matters, and you'll often hear some strange stories along these very lines, stories that it's terribly hard to make sense of, apart from something like a religious view of the world. I've already mentioned the older lady who once "saw" me almost twenty years down the road in my life, a deeply religious woman reticent to talk about her reputed psychic powers. And my old high school friend who worried about me, when he visited from Harvard, brought back stories from the Harvard–Radcliffe Christian Fellowship that made me listen transfixed—stories about penetrating prophecies, "speaking in tongues," and healing miracles he claimed to have witnessed firsthand, such as a grotesquely broken bone being restored instantly in the midst of a pickup football game in response to group prayer. What do you do when people you respect, admire, and otherwise completely trust tell tales such as these? You begin to be suspicious, despite any inclinations you might have to the contrary, that there may indeed be a great deal more to life than meets the eye.

And I have felt it. One day as an undergraduate walking in front of the math building at North Carolina, I had a small epiphany unexpectedly, an intimation of my future calling, an experience that lasted no more than a few seconds but that has resounded in my life for decades since. It came on me quite suddenly and emphatically that I had a mission in this life, a calling within an overarching scheme of things—that I belonged in this world and that I had a job to do. No visions, no auditory phenomena, nothing paradigmatically mystical or overtly paranormal, yet it was an experience as of a message delivered, unexpectedly and powerfully. I resonated within with its content, and at once felt both personally addressed and intimately comforted. I told no one of this experience but have carried its memory with me vividly since that day. In its own distinctive way, it was for me a clearly and profoundly religious experience.

Philosophers often discuss the relation between religious experience and religious belief. What is it about an experience that generates or even suggests a religious interpretation? What is it to have an experience properly described as religious? And how do such experiences relate to the big-scale, overarching beliefs that together make up a religious world view? Are they *evidence* for beliefs about the divine? Or is there some more immediate and intimate relation than a merely evidential tie?

It is clear to me, first of all, that it is not just discrete and dramatic, extraordinary experiences of a limited duration and a memorable nature that function in one's coming to have and then both maintaining and maturing in a religious world view. I have had a few fairly dramatic experiences—nothing it would take George Lucas or Steven Spielberg to re-create on the Big Screen, yet dramatic nonetheless—but it seems to me that the job has been done in my own life primarily by a lot of little experiences, insights, intuitions, feelings, adumbrations, and convictions I have sensed forming within myself. These have provided fertile soil for the testimony of others, who report similar, and more dramatic, experiences. And all this has then provided a context within which the more powerful and memorable experiences have had their impact. I am a Christian because the deep resources of Christian theology resonate with and make sense of both the contours of my experience and the lineaments of my thought as I seek to gain a better theoretical understanding of the world metaphysically, morally, aesthetically, and epistemologically. I realize that with this brief claim I am abstracting from over forty years of experience processed in myriad ways, and that without an exhaustive cataloging and description of the many modalities of that experience, such a claim will necessarily remain quite enigmatic. And not even the more comprehensive task of my trying to spell it all out would do the job for any other person. My testimony can serve for others as the word of others has served for me. As clue and as support. But it cannot do more.

The great seventeenth-century scientist and mathematician Blaise Pascal once had a religious experience that changed his life. But he did not talk about it. In his notes for a book on the truth of the Christian faith, the perennially best-selling *Pensées,* he makes no mention of his "night of fire," as it is referred to by historians. We know about it only by the discovery, after his death, of a memorial written on parchment and sewn into the lining of his coat, a silent reminder he carried with him every subsequent day of his life.

But unless Pascal's life and faith were very different from anything in my own experience, my guess is that this night of fire was not just a single oasis of contact with something more, isolated in an otherwise desolate experiential landscape. He wrote too much about reasons of the heart, about instinct, feeling, and intuition, for me to be able to believe that. I think there is a spiritual dimension to our existence that breaks through many apertures within the natural flow of our experience. There are special revelations, but we would not know what to do with them unless there were more subtle, more frequent sparks and incursions of the spiritual into our lives, small aspects of more ordinary experience that allow us to recognize and appropriate the extraordinary when it comes our way. Not everyone claims to have such experience. Many claim not to have it. And maybe they don't. But it was Pascal's conviction that they need not be bereft of it. And it's mine that they should not be. I've come to believe that any serious attempt to cultivate the moral and spiritual dimensions of life will yield a texture of experience that, while it may not lead to answers to all our ultimate questions, and is not guaranteed to result in detailed agreement on spiritual issues, will nonetheless begin to generate and nourish growing suspicions of something more, that something more to which religious faith is both a response and a call. Much of what I have experienced to this point in my own life has elicited this response and has encouraged this call, despite any obstacles I have encountered along the way.

2

A PHILOSOPHER'S

WAY BACK TO

THE FAITH

William P. Alston

I must begin by confessing that I
am quite unaccustomed to testifying,
which is what I have let myself in for
by agreeing to write this essay. Abstract reasoning is more my line.
Therefore, I must ask you to bear
with me if I sound like a fish out of
water.

If I am to speak of my way back to
the faith, I must say something about
where I was coming back from. And
for this, a little background is needed.
I was raised as a Methodist in the
South—Shreveport, Louisiana, to be
exact. My undoubtedly imperfect recollection of this particular religious
ambiance is that it was perfunctory
and lacking in warmth of conviction.
No doubt, a lot was going on there
that was not getting through to me.
But when, many years later, I came to
learn something about John Wesley

and the origins of Methodism, I was surprised to learn that great store was set on personal religious experience. It is a plausible conjecture that the fact that I have spent a large part of the last fifteen years working on the epistemology of religious experience represents a development of seeds that were planted during my childhood as a Methodist in Shreveport. However, as I say, none of this made any strong, conscious impression on me at the time (to the best of my recollection), and on attaining the age of reason (or what I thought of as such in early adolescence) and becoming acquainted with atheistic arguments and attitudes, I readily abandoned ship.

After being unchurched for a number of years, I was drawn into the Episcopal church during my first year out of graduate school, my first of twenty-two years on the faculty of the University of Michigan. Why did I come back to the church? It is easier for me to understand why I came to the Epsicopal church in particular than why I returned to the church at all. I chose Episcopalianism over Methodism, Presbyterianism, and so on, partly because I was drawn to the liturgy and partly because I found the intellectual climate of Anglican thought congenial. Moreover, I generally find myself a middle-of-the-roader in philosophy, theology, and most other things; and so I was a natural for the *via media*. But why get involved in any Christian church or any other? It was certainly not that I had become convinced of the truth of Christianity by philosophical, theological, or historical arguments. It was largely a matter of feeling a church-shaped hole in my life and having sufficient motivation to fill it. I believe that I went into the Episcopal church with the idea that "I'll give it a fling and see what's there" rather than "I am thoroughly convinced that this is the right story, and therefore the thing to do is to sign up." The process was inaugurated by attendance at a memorial service at the local Episcopal church for a late colleague in the philosophy department. Thus this 1950 move to the church was triggered in a way similar to my 1975 return, to be narrated later.

In any event, I was duly confirmed in the Episcopal church in 1950, and during the 1950s I was rather active in St. Andrew's church, Ann Arbor—singing in the choir, for example—and also in the Episcopal Student Foundation at the University, participating in discussion groups at Canterbury House. Moreover I was making a real effort to lead a Christian life. But looking back on it from this vantage point, I can see that something was fundamentally amiss. I was seeking to use the church and the Christian faith as a refuge from life. I was seeking a relation with God as a substitute for facing and resolving the problems in my life—problems concerning interpersonal relations, as well as various emotional tensions and conflicts. In condemning myself for this orientation, I do not mean to make a negative judgment on the institution of monasticism. Quite the contrary. To be sure, people can also enter monastic orders for the wrong reason, and they can use the religious life as an escape in the way I am deploring in my own case. But not all monastic vocations are like that. In any event, I certainly was not entering a monastic vocation. I was staying in the world and enjoying the delights thereof, or attempting to, while at the same time trying to use religious devotion as an escape from the task of working out a satisfactory relation to my work, to other people, and to myself. I want to do everything possible to avoid misunderstanding here. I am by no means suggesting that God cannot or should not be a help, a comforter, a source of consolation and strength. But I wasn't trying to get God to help me face my problems; I was trying to get Him to help me forget or evade those problems. One way of putting this is to say that I was trying to live the first and greatest commandment—to love the Lord your God with all your heart, and with all your soul, with all your strength, and with all your mind—without making any serious attempt to live the second commandment, which is like unto it—to love your neighbor as yourself. This program had predictable results: I made no progress with either. The commandments are inseparable, as St. John tells us so pithily ". . . if a man says 'I love God', while hating his brother, he is a liar. If he does not love the brother whom he has seen, it cannot be that he loves God whom he has not seen" (I John, 4:20).

When in the late 1950s I came to appreciate the situation for what it was, I jumped ship again. On looking back, I can't believe that I made the wrong decision. I realized that I was playacting, and playacting at something I really didn't have my heart in. I had no real relation to God and no real reason to believe in God, much less believe anything more specifically Christian. I have already said that I went into the church with a "I'll give it a try and see what happens" attitude, and so far it was clear to me that nothing worth mentioning was happening. And with the basic orientation I described above, I was in a position to move toward a genuine Christian faith. I needed to get away from the whole thing and gain a different perspective, just as it is often useful for students to drop out of college for a year or so and come back with a different attitude toward the educational process. God works in mysterious ways, and I believe that He is sometimes leading us to Him when we seem to be running in the opposite direction.

For about fifteen years I led what seemed to be a purely secular life, though I now believe that things were going on under the surface of which I was not clearly aware at the time. Then in a year of leave, 1974–75, most of which was spent in Oxford, these things began to surface. I had never been completely at ease in my attempt to live without God. I was never an enthusiastic atheist. By the mid-1970s, the sense that I was missing out on something of fundamental importance was beginning to crystallize. Furthermore, I was rather a different person from the dropout of the late 1950s. For one thing, I had had a lot of psychotherapy, and with some of the internal tensions resolved, I was in a better position to make a realistic assessment of the problems. Moreover I was able to hear the gospel message straight or more nearly straight, at least in a position to hear it and not distort it into something wildly different. You may resist the idea that God should have had to wait until I had gone through a variety of life experiences and profited in various ways from psychotherapy before He could get His message across to me. Can't God deliver His message to anyone at any time and make sure they get it right? Of course He can. But quite clearly, He doesn't do this with everyone all the time. Why He doesn't I don't presume to say. In any event, one thing He does instead is to make use of various indirect ways of preparing the ground, and I believe that my experience is a case in point.

Psychotherapy, and modes of thought from that quarter, had more to do with my case than I have thus far brought out. During my years of exile the main intellectual bar to taking Christianity as a live option was not a rejection of classical proofs for the existence of God or a rejection of historical arguments for the veracity of the Scriptures. I don't have a radically different assessment of all that in my revivified state than I did when I was wandering in the wilderness. The main bar to faith was rather the Freudian idea that religious faith is a wish fulfillment—more specifically, an attempt to cling to childish modes of relating to the world, with the omnipotent daddy there presiding over everything. A powerful case can be made for the view, which is not necessarily tied to the complete Freudian package, that the most important psychological root of religious belief is the need that everyone has for such a childish relationship with a father figure. Be that as it may, I had been psyched into feeling that I was chickening out, was betraying my adult status, if I sought God in Christ, or sought to relate myself to an ultimate source and disposer of things in any way whatever. The crucial moment in my return to the faith came quite early in that year's leave, before I had reexposed myself to the church or the Bible, or even thought seriously about the possibility of becoming a Christian. I was walking one afternoon in the country outside Oxford, wrestling with the problem, when I suddenly said to myself, "Why should I allow myself to be cribbed, cabined, and confined by these Freudian ghosts? Why should I be so afraid of not being adult? What am I trying to prove? Whom am I trying to impress? Whose approval am I trying to secure? What is more important: to struggle to conform my life to the tenets of some highly speculative system of psychology or to recognize and come to terms with my own real needs? Why should I hold back from opening myself to a transcendent dimension of reality, if such there be, just from fear of being branded as childish in some quarters?" (Or words to that effect.) These questions answered themselves as soon as they were squarely posed. I had, by the grace of God, finally found the courage to look the specter in the face and tell him to go away. I had been given the courage to face the human situation, with its radical need for a proper relation to the source of all being.

This opened things up, but it didn't point in any particular direction. Then my daughter, Ellen, showed up in Oxford for a brief visit. She had been raised an Episcopalian but had, in her turn, jumped ship in late adolescence. Now she was being drawn back, and she gave my wife, Valerie, and me the nudge we needed. (My daughter is now an Episcopal priest, co-rector with her husband of a parish in Connecticut.) Valerie, thanks be to God, was groping her way back into the faith at about the same time and at about the same rate as myself, after having been out in the wilderness for about the same period. Ellen suggested that we attend services at the Anglican cathedral in Oxford, which doubles as the chapel of Christ Church College and boasts a world-famous choir. This was literally the first religious service, apart from weddings and funerals, that I had attended in about fifteen years. Something happened, which I still find it difficult to put my finger on. But I had definitely made a positive response to the proclamation of the gospel and to the sacramental presence of our Lord, and we began attending services regularly. Oxford is a marvelous place for being drawn back into the church if music plays a large role in one's communication with the divine, as is true in my case. Three of the colleges have choir schools, and to give the youngsters something to do with all that expertise, evensong is (or was at that time) sung in all three college chapels every weekday.

When we returned to Princeton in the fall of 1975, I was still a long way from thinking of myself as a full-blooded Christian believer. I didn't feel much more disposed to make an intellectual assent to Christian doctrines than I had before all this started. Insofar as I had any expectations of my religious future, I supposed that I would adopt some sort of watered-down Christianity in which I would participate in the services of worship, supposing the doctrinal elements to be symbolic of some ineffable supreme reality. But I had opened myself up where before I had been closed, and something was coming in through that opening and working unmistakable effects. I wasn't yet prepared to give a traditional Christian explanation of what was going on, but I had no doubt that something highly significant *was* going on. The most striking demonstration that something was happening was that now I was attuned to precisely what was fatally lacking in my earlier adult fling with Christiantiy—the second commandment. I found myself, incredibly, with a quite different orientation to the people around me. I began, for the first time in my life, to get a glimmer of what love means. It was a most exhilarating experience. Just to make sure that I was not imagining all this, I checked with my wife, my main contact with external reality. She assured me that I was, indeed, quite different.

In the fall of 1975 we had been attending services at the beautiful old Episcopal church near the center of Princeton—Trinity Church. But in January we happened to wander into a newer Episcopal church on the outskirts of town—All Saints, a fine example of "Japanese Gothic," as the rector put it. All Saints had a remarkable choir, directed by the man who was Gian Carlo Menotti's chief assistant for the Festival of Two Worlds, then held each summer in Spoleto in Italy. But the main thing we discovered at All Saints was the rector, who bore the unusual name, for an Episcopal rector, of Orley Swartzentruber. Insofar as I have become, or am becoming, a Christian, I credit it to Orley, or to God working through Orley. I am sure that Valerie would say the same. Orley had an unusual background, as well as an unusual name, for an Episcopal rector. His father was a Mennonite missionary, from Canada, in South America. He grew up there and received his higher education in the United States. He became a Mennonite minister and had a variety of experiences, including the founding of an Alsatian Mennonite church in Paris. At a later stage he was a graduate student at Princeton Theological Seminary, where he received a Ph.D. in the Old Testament. While there he became drawn into the Episcopal church and, in the fullness of time, was ordained an Episcopal priest. Perhaps partly as a result of his Mennonite background, he preached the gospel in a way I have rarely heard elsewhere among the "frozen people of God," as an exasperated Episcopalian once referred to his brothers and sisters in the faith. Indeed, I have rarely heard the gospel preached that way anywhere, under any circumstances. One not only heard the gospel being interpreted in a way that had direct application to one's situation then and there, but one could, as it were, literally see the gospel being lived out in front of one. All this without any obvious histrionics and with the aid of profound scholarship. I may be making Orley sound too good to be true, but why shouldn't God work through someone in that way? Orley is a living example of what Christian spirituality can be in late-twentieth-century America.

When we began attending All Saints, I discovered that there was a charismatic prayer group within the parish. At that time I didn't even know the distinctively theological meaning of the term *charismatic,* and I was blissfully unaware of the recent efflorescence of the charismatic movement across Christendom. On the "I'll try anything once" principle, I decided to attend. This was a very muted and proper Anglican-style charismatic group. The singing was from the Episcopal hymnal, rather than folksy-jivy stuff, and speaking in tongues and the like was rarely heard. But clearly, something was happening there. I must confess that I was badly turned off at first, especially by people giving thanks to God for finding them a parking place. But I forced myself to persevere out of sheer doggedness, and eventually I began to get drawn in. I began to see that these people were really in touch with God as a more or less continual living presence in their lives, and that this influenced, to a greater or lesser degree, every facet of their existence. This meant that I had a whole bevy of role models for the Christian life, and that I had the opportunity to expose myself to them once a week and to try out these roles myself under their tutelage. The Eucharist was celebrated at the end of these sessions, and I found that it took on a new meaning in that context.

Unfortunately, or perhaps in God's grand design fortunately, we left Princeton for Urbana, Illinois, in August 1975. We had been at All Saints for less than a year. But we were incredibly fortunate in having happened on to that parish at a time when we were just groping our way back into the faith but were still essentially on the outside looking in. By the time we left Princeton we were definitely hooked. We had, and still have, a long road to travel, but we had unequivocally embarked on the journey, and we had been pointed in the right direction.

In our first year in Urbana I began attending an ecumenical charismatic prayer group at the Newman Center at the University of Illinois. This was hard-core stuff—including speaking in tongues and other such manifestations. Furthermore, the Roman Catholics, who, as usual, had things beautifully organized, had an eight-week course of preparation for baptism in the Spirit. I signed up for this and did, at the culminating session, receive the gift of tongues, along with a new and more vivid sense of the presence of the

Spirit. That sense has never really deserted me, though, of course, it waxes and wanes, as does any mode of human experience. I am rather ashamed of not having remained active in the charismatic movement. There just seems to be too much of a cultural gap between myself and most charismatics in terms of approach to the scriptures, musical taste, and general lifestyle. I am rather ashamed of my dropout status, because I feel that I have taken a great deal from the movement and given nothing in return. I will be eternally grateful for the vivid sense of the presence of the Holy Spirit that I was privileged to receive, and I honor the movement for its continuing witness to the overriding importance of the work of the Spirit in our lives. Perhaps one day I will find my way back to the movement. In the meantime I hope that I am able to give something back in other contexts.

This ends the narrative of my way back. From here on I am within the faith, trying to understand it, to live it, to grow in the spiritual life. As I said earlier, I have been blessed by the fact that Valerie was drawn back into the church at about the same time, and by the fact that we have had the opportunity to find our way together, to embark on the endless task of growth in the Christian life together, and to encourage and sustain each other in that task. That is God's grace indeed. Since coming to Syracuse in 1980 I have, God help me, become increasingly involved in ecclesiastical affairs in both St. Paul's Cathedral, where we are members of the congregation, and the Diocese of Central New York. Heavy church involvement can serve to deaden one's response to the Holy Spirit, just as it can be a way of contributing to the work of the kingdom. I suppose that both have been exemplified in my case. For most of the time, at any rate, I have been trying to "give something back" in this church work, as well as to keep myself moving forward in the new life of the Spirit, so far as in me lies, with the help of that same Spirit.

IF THERE HAS been any point in my rehearsing these not very remarkable events from my life, it is that there are things to be learned from my experience that are of relevance to people other than myself. And given the emphasis of this volume, it is to be hoped that something can be gleaned from this case about how a philosopher might be involved in the Christian faith and the Christian life. I will organize what might be learned under three headings: (1) why I left the church, (2) how I came back, and (3) what I came back to, the shape of the faith within which I find myself at present.

1. Under the first heading, the simple moral is that one can be attached to Christianity for the wrong reasons, for radically wrong reasonss, and that when that is the case, the best thing to do may be to get out and give yourself a chance to make a fresh start under new circumstances at some later time. I am *not* offering this as a general recipe. With respect to all or most of us, there is *something* wrong in our appropriation of the faith. I am certainly not suggesting that everyone leave the church periodically and stay away for some minimum period of time. I can only report my conviction that this was the

thing to do in my case, and that when someone you know does something similar, don't forget the possibility that God may be at work there in ways you cannot see for the moment.

2. As for the way back, there are points as to what was involved and, equally important, what wasn't involved. Before launching into this I want to stress that I am not presenting my case as a model of what conversion should be, or what it is when it is most authentic or most complete, or anything of the sort. I believe that there are many roads to the faith. I am describing one route out of many, one possibility that might get overlooked since it is less dramatic or less easily categorized than others.

At this point I must make another confession. I chose the title of this essay in the hope that my readers would entertain false expectations. I anticipated that many of you would suppose that anything advertised as a philosopher's conversion would feature an intellectual process of coming to realize the cogency of arguments for the existence of God, for the historical accuracy of the Scriptures, or whatever. If a philosopher is to find his or her way back to the faith, he or she should do it in a manner befitting the profession. Right? Well, if that's what it takes to be a respectable combination of philosopher and Christian, I must plead guilty. My narrative has been conspicuous for the absence of any presentation of arguments, any account of trains of reasoning leading up to an intellectual assent to this or that doctrine.

Before attempting a general characterization of what was in the center of the picture, let me qualify the above remarks somewhat. Although I didn't move from unbelief to belief by a process of reasoning myself into an intellectual assent to the articles of faith, I don't wish to suggest that philosophical views and philosophical reflection played no role. At a minimum, I never would have taken Christianity seriously had I firmly held a naturalistic or a materialist metaphysics. For those who have philosophical positions, a position that is open to the truth of Christian doctrine is a necessary condition of acquiring a full-blooded Christian faith. Moreover, my intellectual wrestling with Freudian and other reductive accounts of religious belief provided, as I have already made explicit, an essential preparation for an openness to the Spirit. But all of this is by way of background. It opens up the possibility of a discovery of God in Christ in the church, but it doesn't make that discovery itself. I take this to be generally true of the role of philosophy in the religious life. It has an ancillary role, a very important one, but ancillary nonetheless. Philosophical thinking can enable us to see through objections to Christian belief; it can exhibit the faith as something plausible and intellectually respectable; it can show the faith as something that can command the assent of an educated, intellectually sophisticated, and knowledgeable denizen of the late twentieth century. But it rarely, if ever, propels one into a condition of faith. Consider the classic arguments for the existence of God. I believe they have an important role in the religious life. They can reveal connections between God and various aspects of the world. They can show Christian faith to be a not unreasonable stance. But it must be extremely rare for them to play the major role in a move from unbelief to belief. Again, philosophical thinking can play a crucial role in coming to a deeper understanding of the faith. "Faith seeking understanding" is a motto by which I try to live. Philosophy always has been, and continues to be, a primary tool in the ongoing attempt to gain a more penetrating grasp of the import of the basic articles of faith: the nature of God, creation, sin, the Incarnation, the atonement, the work of the Spirit, and so on.[1] But when faith is seeking understanding, the faith is already there, and philosophy comes on the scene too late to produce it. To be sure, one who is still on the outside might seek a better understanding of what's on the inside, and that understanding might remove blocks to faith or otherwise move one in that direction. That would be analogous to the other preparatory roles I have mentioned. The general upshot of all this is that although philosophical reasoning has very important roles to play in the religious life, producing faith where it had been absent is not one of them. Certainly it was not in my case.

Returning from this digression, I will try to give a general characterization of what was most centrally involved in my movement from unbelief to belief. So far as I am aware, it was primarily a process of responding to a call, of being drawn into a community, into a way of life. That can sound as if I had embraced one of the well-known naturalistic or humanistic substitutes for Christianity, in which one adopts a certain stance or orientation or commitment without seriously believing that one is thereby related to an infinite source of all things that has revealed Himself in Jesus Christ. And, as I have already made explicit, at an early stage of the process that would have been a not wholly inaccurate characterization. But that is certainly not what the process led to in the fullness of time. In saying that what was most centrally involved was my being drawn into a community, into a way of life, I do not mean to imply that the "horizontal" was substituted for the "vertical" dimension of the Christian life. I am saying, rather, that I found the vertical dimension through the horizontal. I found God as a reality in my life through finding a community of faith and being drawn into it. That's where the message was being proclaimed, and if I had not been able to see, eventually, that He Who was being proclaimed was Himself at work in those proclamations and in those proclaimers, I would, no doubt, have continued to turn a deaf ear.

It should be clear from what I have just been saying that I take the church very seriously. I am as keenly aware as anyone of the many failings of institutionalized Christianity, and I cannot sincerely claim that everyone (or most people) who regularly attends an Episcopal church, or any other Christian church, displays the love of God in every word and deed. Nevertheless, the new life of the Spirit is being lived there, and my experience, for what it is worth, confirms the New Testament picture of the new life as essentially a life lived in the community of the faithful. One of the significant milestones in my way back came when the words of the postcommunion prayer took hold of me one day. I am thinking particularly of the passage in which, after thanking God for feeding us with the "spiritual food of the most precious

Body and Blood of thy Son our Saviour Jesus Christ," the congregation goes on to thank God "that we are very members incorporate in the mystical body of thy Son, which is the blessed company of all faithful people." In concluding this point, I cannot do better than to quote G. K. Chesterton: "In the last analysis, the reason I am a Christian is that the church is a living and not a dead teacher."

So, to descend to slogans, my way back was not by abstract philosophical reasoning but by experience—experience of the love of God and the presence of the Spirit, as found within the community of the faithful. I didn't reason myself into the faith. Rather, my entrance into the faith gave me new materials, new data, new premises for my reasoning, and, of course, new problems as well. It was more like having one's eyes opened to an aspect of the environment to which one had previously been blind; more like learning to hear things in music that one had been missing; more like that than coming to realize that certain premises have an unexpected implication. But though mine was an experiential way into the faith, it did not follow the evangelical pattern of an overwhelming conviction of sin, followed by an equally overwhelming sense of release when one commits oneself to Christ and accepts the forgiveness of that sin offered in Christ's atoning act. I hope that all of us will eventually attain a balanced, inclusive, well-rounded faith, one that has room for all the main elements of Christianity. But most of us don't start with that. Each of us approaches the infinite complexity of the faith through one or another of its aspects. Mine was as just indicated. And perhaps as a result of my experience of gradually getting drawn in, rather than undergoing the one-shot ZAP after which one's life is completely changed, I think of the Christian life more on the Catholic model of a gradual progress—a gradual sanctification of the person, a process that will presumably be continued after death as well as throughout this life—rather than as a once-and-for-all being *saved*, after which one is with the sheep rather than the goats, and that's that.

3. Finally, a word about the shape of the faith to which I found my way back. Let's get at this by asking the perennial question, "What is it to be a Christian?". Here too my attitude is that there is much room for legitimate diversity in the emphasis we place on particular facets of the infinitely rich totality of the Christian faith. Different persons and different groups will seize on different aspects as the one that is most central in their experience. At least this is legitimate so long as it does not lead to ostracizing those with other emphases. To oversimplify greatly, we could say that the Catholic story on what it is to be a Christian is "to have been baptized, to have been received into the church, the body of Christ," while the evangelical Protestant answer is "to have accepted Jesus Christ as one's savior." My answer, in a nutshell, is this: To be a Christian is to be open to the revelation of God in Jesus Christ; to stand within the community that is bound together by the fact that it derives its ultimate commitment from that revelation; to take that revelation as the supreme guide for one's life; to seek to relate oneself to God and to one's fellows as indicated by that revelation. Needless to say, the openness and

commitment of which I am speaking is a matter of degree, and I don't want to get into legalistic arguments as to where one has to be along this continuum in order to count as a Christian. I merely want to suggest that what is distinctive about being a Christian is such openness and such commitment. I also seek to be as inclusive as possible in my conception of the Christian life. It involves the attempt to grow in one's understanding of the faith through study of the Scriptures and the theological tradition and through thinking about the issues they raise. It involves prayer and contemplation. It involves the reception of the sacraments. It involves joining with one's fellow Christians in the worship of God, in study and prayer, in helping each other to lead the Christian life. It involves trying to carry out the law of love in all one's relationships. It involves witnessing to such light as one has received. And so on.

I also want to mention one thing I do not take to be required for being a Christian. I do not accept the idea that in order to be a Christian one must adopt a certain view as to the way in which God has revealed Himself in the Scriptures, nor do I accept the idea that a certain set of theological propositions must be assented to. I think there is room for honest differences of opinion on such matters within the Christian community. To be sure, there are limits. I am far from suggesting that anyone who thinks that love is very important in human life is properly called a Christian just on those grounds. If one does not believe that the universe depends for its existence on a transcendent source of being that can be thought of in personalistic terms, or if one does take Jesus Christ to be a supreme revelation of God, one is not a Christian in the proper sense of the term. But just how all the fine print is set up is, for my money, an internal family matter, a problem to be discussed, worked out, quarreled about if necessary, within the family, and discussed, one hopes, without rupturing the bonds of the family. I think of theology as related to the basic Christian faith somewhat as high-level scientific theories are related to our basic commonsense awareness of the physical environment. In both cases we can share the same picture of the major outlines of the environment while disagreeing on the fine structure and the ultimate explanation of that common reality.

TO SUM UP: My way back to the faith was not primarily through philosophical reasoning, or any other form of argumentation, but through an experience of God at work in the Christian community. Naturally, as a philosopher who carries out philosophical reflection on religion, including his own religion, I believe that philosophy has important roles to play in the Christian life. I have already briefly set out what I take some of those roles to be. But I don't feel that philosophy's job description includes bringing us to faith. That job, on the human side of the interaction, is reserved for more intuitive, less discursive activities. Philosophy has a crucially important role in clarifying, systematizing, and defending the faith, but that role presupposes that there is a faith there on which to exercise it.

Note

1. For a recent application of contemporary philosophy to the understanding of these issues, see *Philosophy and the Christian Faith,* ed. T. V. Morris (Notre Dame, Ind.: University of Notre Dame Press, 1988.).

QUAM DILECTA

Peter van Inwagen

3

> Yea, the sparrow hath found her an
> house, and the swallow a nest, where
> she may lay her young; even thy altars,
> O Lord of Hosts, my King and my God.
>
> Ps.84:3

Three of my grandparents were un-churched Protestants, and one (my father's mother) was a devout Roman Catholic. As a consequence, my mother was, and is, not much of a churchgoer, and my father was a lapsed Catholic with pretty strong feelings on the subject—an enthusiastic reader of Paul Blanshard and similar authors. When I was seven, my parents briefly sent me to a Presbyterian Sunday school. Our lessons were from a little textbook with the excellent title *The King Nobody Wanted,* which I still occasionally come across in secondhand bookshops. I recall learning that we Christians believed that Jesus was the Messiah and that the Jews did not. (I remember wishing that I could have a chance to tell the Jews about Jesus;

I was sure that they would be reasonable about his messianic status if someone were to inform them of it.)

I must also have absorbed the idea that Jesus was the Son of God, for after my family had joined a Unitarian congregation, my father sternly informed me (presumably in response to some casual theological remark of mine) that we Unitarians did not believe that Jesus was the Son of God. Well, I was shocked. I had thought that everyone believed *that* (except, of course, the Jews, but it was pretty clear that Unitarians weren't Jews). I have a memory of walking through a hallway at my school—I think we've got to about age thirteen—and saying defiantly to myself, "I can believe that Jesus is the Son of God if I want to." I must have been wanting in what Roman Catholic theologians used to call heroic faith, however, for I was soon enough a good little Unitarian boy. I learned in Sunday school that the feeding of the multitudes was really a miracle of sharing, and how much more miraculous that was than a magical multiplication of loaves and fishes would have been if it had occurred, which of course it hadn't. (Twenty years later, in the early 1970s, Peter Geach told me how shocked he had recently been to hear the same story from a Roman Catholic priest. I was able to tell him that the Unitarians were at least twenty years ahead of Rome.)

My attachment to Unitarianism (and its three pillars: the Fatherhood of God, the Brotherhood of Man, and the Neighborhood of Boston) did not survive my going away to college. That sort of thing is, of course, a familiar story in every denomination, but it's an easier passage for Unitarians, since it does not involve giving up any beliefs. My wife, who is one of my most useful critics, tells me that this is an unkind remark and ought to be omitted. It seems to me to be an important thing to say, however. I did not experience the crisis of conscience so common among Evangelical or Roman Catholic university students who leave the church. And the reason is that if Evangelicals or Roman Catholics stop going to church, it is hard for them to avoid the question how they can justify not going to church when they believe what they do—if, indeed, loss of belief was not their reason for leaving the church. It is, however, simply a fact that a Unitarian can sever his connection with Unitarianism without changing any of his beliefs.

If you had asked me about my religious beliefs when I was an undergraduate or a graduate student (a period that covered roughly the 1960s), I suppose I should have said I was an agnostic, although there was a brief period when I was in graduate school during which—under the influence of some version or other of the Argument from Evil—I should probably have said I was an atheist. This was a position of the head, not the heart, however; it had no more connection with my emotional life than, say, my belief (also briefly held in graduate school) that Quine had shown that quantified modal logic was impossible. My emotional life in the late 1960s, insofar as I had one, had entirely to do with the concerns of everyday life—although, to be sure, everyday life for a graduate student in philosophy is a little different from the everyday life of most people. A very important feature of my life as a graduate student was a growing conviction that I was a better philosopher than any of my fellow graduate students and most of my teachers. Vanity in this area—wounded vanity, because little attention was paid to me or to my work during the early years of my career—was a dominant feature of my inner life in the 1970s. (Professional vanity may well continue to dominate my inner life, but it would be harder for me to tell these days, since I now feel, rightly or wrongly, that my philosophical talents are adequately recognized by the profession. Wounded vanity is a rather more salient feature of one's inner life than self-satisfied vanity.)

When I was a graduate student, I began to read the apologetic works of C. S. Lewis. There were (under God) two reasons for this. First, I had loved his "space trilogy," and I was looking for "more Lewis." Secondly, I recognized him as a master of expository prose and thought—rightly—that I could learn a great deal from him about the art of expressing a line of argument in English. Like many other people, I first discovered what Christianity *was* from reading Lewis. The discovery was purely external, a matter of being able to use the right words when talking about "Christianity," but it was no small gain to have a *correct* external understanding of Christianity. I saw that the picture I had been given of Christianity by my Unitarian Sunday-school teachers and various teachers of philosophy (no great difference there) was self-serving, frivolous, and wildly inaccurate. I saw that Christianity was a serious thing and intellectually at a very high level. (I was thinking, of course, in terms of propositions and distinctions and arguments.) I lost at that time, and for good, any capacity for taking any liberalized or secularized version of Christianity seriously. I could read Lewis. I could try to read Harvey Cox or William Hamilton. I could see the difference. To this day, I cannot see why anyone disagrees with my judgment that academic theologians of their stripe have nothing of interest to say. I have to admit, however, that some very learned people do disagree with this judgment.

The only thing was, I didn't believe it. I could see that there was an "it" to believe, and if I did not really see how much there was to being a Christian beyond having certain beliefs, I did see that the beliefs must come first, and that a Christian life without those beliefs is an impossibility. One day in the late 1960s, I fell to my knees and prayed for faith, but faith did not come. I do not know what led me to make this gesture, but presumably there must have been some sort of felt pressure, and presumably this pressure did not long continue. I expect that I had been setting God some sort of test: If You don't give me faith on the spot, I'll conclude that You do not exist or are not interested in me, and that these pressures I've been feeling have some sort of purely natural explanation and can be ignored till they go away. We all know how well that sort of thing works.

I married, spent two years in the army (at the height of the American military involvement in Vietnam; but I was safe in Germany), became the father of a daughter, and began to teach philosophy. I was entirely immersed in the secular world. Sunday was my day of rest and my day of nothing else. Although I continued to be interested in Christianity in an intellectual sort of way, it would no more have occurred to me to take up churchgoing—even as an experiment—than to take up hang-gliding or bookbinding. In 1973, I spent six delightful weeks on the campus of Calvin College at an NEH Summer Institute in the Philosophy of Religion, which was directed by Alvin Plantinga. As far as I am able to tell by introspection and memory, this had nothing to with my religious development, although it had a great deal to do with my philosophical development. (Plantinga's lectures—roughly, *The Nature of Necessity*—became for me a model for doing philosophy.) Besides my family, my only interests were philosophy and my career in philosophy. Perhaps my former wife and my daughter would say that the qualification "besides my family" is unnecessary. I certainly was taken up both with my researches and with my desire to be recognized and admired. My researches, I think, went very well indeed, but I haunted my departmental mailbox mostly in vain, and was subject to frequent periods of depression and spasms of anger because of my lack of professional recognition. The anger was directed at certain of my former teachers (the more famous ones), who, I believed, were in a position to advance my career and yet were doing nothing for me. I believed that they just didn't see how *good* I was and wasted their influence in advancing the careers of people who were less good than I. (I was never jealous of these other people, only envious: I didn't want them *not* to get what they got, but I wanted some too.) When Al Plantinga wrote to Hector Castañeda, suggesting that a paper of mine be published in *Noûs,* and when Tony Kenny wrote to the Oxford University Press, telling them that I had a manuscript that they ought to try to get hold of, this made me even angrier with my teachers: "There," I said to myself, "that proves it. It *can* be done. Comparative strangers do it, but *they* don't." I sometimes wonder whether my teachers knew about this anger. My relations with them were entirely friendly whenever we met. This friendliness was not exactly hypocrisy on my part, since, as I say, the anger was not continuous but spasmodic, and I am not very good at being angry with people who are actually in the same room with me. (But I never once in a calmer moment repented these spasms of anger, which I always considered appropriate and fully justified.)

I can remember pretty well one feature of this period that is particularly relevant to my topic: what it was like not to have any religious beliefs. That is, I can remember pretty clearly certain episodes of thought that are possible only for the secular mind, but the memory is not "sympathetic"; it is a sort of looking at the past from the outside. Here is an analogy. Suppose that you now love someone you once hated. You might well be able to remember an episode during which your hatred manifested itself—say, in the writing of a letter in which you said terrible things to that person. You might remember very clearly, for example, hesitating between two turns of phrase, and deciding that one of them was the more likely to wound, and choosing it on that account. But since you now love that person, and (presumably) cannot feel the way you felt when you hated, there is a good sense in which you cannot remember what it was like to write the letter. You are looking at your past from outside.

I shall try to describe three of these "episodes of thought."

First, I can remember having a picture of the cosmos, the physical universe, as a self-subsistent thing, something that is just *there* and requires no explanation. When I say a "having a picture," I am trying to describe a state of mind that could be called up whenever I desired and was centered on a certain mental image. This mental image—it somehow represented the whole world—was associated with a felt conviction that what the image represented was self-subsistent. I can still call the image to mind (I *think* it's the same image), and it still represents the whole world, but it is now associated with a felt conviction that what it represents is *not* self-subsistent, that it must depend on something else, something that is not represented by any feature of the image, and must be, in some way that the experience leaves indeterminate, radically different in kind from what the image represents. Interestingly enough, there was a period of transition, a period during which I could move back and forth at will, in "duck–rabbit" fashion, between experiencing the image as representing the world as self-subsistent and experiencing the image as representing the world as dependent. I am not sure what period in my life, as measured by the guide-posts of external biography, this transition period coincided with. I know that it is now impossible for me to represent the world to myself as anything but dependent.

The second memory has to do with the doctrine of the Resurrection of the Dead. I can remember this: trying to imagine myself as having undergone this resurrection, as having died and now being once more alive, as *waking up* after death. You might think it would be easy enough for the unbeliever to *imagine* this—no harder, say, than imagining the sun turning green or a tree talking. But—no doubt partly because the resurrection was something that was actually proposed for my belief, and no doubt partly because I as an unbeliever belonged to death's kingdom and had made a covenant with death—I encountered a kind of spiritual wall when I tried to imagine this. The whole weight of the material world, the world of the blind interaction of forces whose laws have no exceptions and in which an access of disorder can never be undone, would thrust itself into my mind with terrible force, as something almost tangible, and the effort of imagination would fail. I can remember episodes of this kind from outside. I can no longer recapture their character. I have nothing positive to put in their place, nothing that corresponds to seeing the world as dependent. But I can imagine the resurrection without hindrance (although my imaginings are no doubt almost entirely wrong) and assent, in my intellect, to a reality that corresponds to what I imagine.

The two "episodes" I have described were recurrent. I shall now describe a particular experience that was not repeated and was not very similar to any other experience I have had. I had just read an account of the death of Handel, who, dying, had expressed an eagerness to die and to meet his dear Savior, Jesus Christ, face to face. My reaction to this was negative and extremely vehement: a little explosion of contempt, modified by pity. It might be put in these words: "You poor booby. You cheat." Handel had been *taken in*, I thought, and yet at the same time he was getting away with something. Although his greatest hope was an illusion, nothing could rob him of the comfort of this hope, for after his death he would not exist and there would be no one there to see how wrong he had been. I don't know whether I would have disillusioned him if I could have, but I certainly managed simultaneously to believe that he was "of all men the most miserable" and that he was getting a pretty good deal. Of course, this reaction was mixed with my knowledge that the kind of experience I tried to describe in the preceding example would make Handel's anticipation of what was to happen after his death impossible for me. I suppose I regarded that experience as somehow veridical, and believed that Handel must have had such experiences, too, and must have been trained, or have trained himself, to ignore them.

In 1980 or thereabouts, I began to experience a sort of pressure to become a Christian: a vast discontent with *not* being a Christian, a pressure to *do something*. Presumably this pressure was of the same sort that had led me to pray for faith on that one occasion ten years earlier, but this was sustained. This went on and on. My mind at the time is not readily accessible to me in memory. I wish I had kept a journal. I know that sneers directed at God and the church, which— I hope I am not giving away any secret here—are very common in the academy, were becoming intolerable to me. (What was especially intolerable was the implied invitation to join in, the absolutely unexamined assumption that, because I was a member of the academic community, I would, of course, regard sneering at God and the church as meet, right, and even my bounden duty.) I perhaps did not have anything like a desire to turn to Christ as my Savior, or a desire to lead a godly, righteous, and sober life, but I did have a strong desire to belong to a Christian community of discourse, a community in which it was open to people to talk to each other in words like the ones that Lewis addresses to his correspondent in *Letters to an American Lady*. I envied people who could talk to one another in those terms. I know that I was becoming more and more repelled by the "great secular consensus" that comprises the world view of just about everyone connected with the universities, journalism, the literary and artistic intelligentsia, and the entertainment industry. I knew that, confused as I might be about many things, I was quite clear about one thing: I could not bear the thought of being a part of that consensus. What made it so repulsive to me can be summed up in a schoolyard *cri de coeur*: "They think they're so smart!" I was simply revolted by the malevolent, self-satisfied stupidity of the attacks on Christianity that proceeded from the consensus.

I remained in a state of uncertainty for some time. During this period, I described my state of mind by saying that I didn't know whether I believed or not. Eventually I performed an act of will. I asked Bill Alston (to his considerable astonishment) to put me in touch with a priest. The priest I was put in touch with was—at that time and in relation to that particular need—of no help to me, but my interview with him took place in his study, which was in a church building. While I was talking with him, it became clear to me that a large part of my difficulty with the church might be churches. It became clear to me that one fact about me that was of relevance to my condition was that I didn't want to start going to church. Well, I thought, at least that's a fact I can do something about. I decided to start going to church—simply to attend an early Eucharist—every Sunday morning as a sort of observer, with no more commitment involved than five dollars for the collection plate. I began doing this. The first effect was that it put my wife into a fury, despite the fact that I was always home from church before she was awake. But I soon found that I liked going to church, and that an unconscious fear of churchgoing was no longer a barrier between me and the church. This would have been in September 1982, at just about the time of my fortieth birthday. The following May I was baptized. (I have just noted, while setting out the sequence of dates in my mind, that this took place nine years ago to the day.) Following my baptism, I received my first communion. Since then, the Sacrament has been the center of Christian devotional life for me. It is no more possible for me willfully to forego Holy Communion on a Sunday than for me, say, to slander a colleague or to refuse to pay a debt.

And since then I have been an Episcopalian. I regard myself as a Catholic, and the Anglican communion as a branch (separated from other branches by historical tragedy) of the Catholic church that is mentioned as an article of belief in the Creeds. I cannot easily see myself as a member of any other denomination, although I believe that the Episcopal Church is among the best possible illustrations of Robert Conquest's Second Law: Every organization appears to be headed by secret agents of its opponents. Eventually, I suppose, the high-minded progressives who control the denomination at the national level will do some truly appalling thing and I shall at last have to leave, but I hope I have a while left in the Episcopal Church, because I really do like the place. (An Anglican joke: "Why is Rome called the Eternal City? Because there's always Rome.")

As a Christian, I, of course, believe that conversions are the work of God and are thus largely invisible to the convert, save in their effects. Nevertheless, I believe, the convert must have turned to God and, in some fashion, have asked for His help. I have no useful memory of what I did to ask God for His help or of the form in which that help came. Naturally, I prayed—conditionally—but what it was about those prayers that was different from my prayer in the 1960s, or what it was that I did besides prayer, is unknown to me.

I was allowed the usual honeymoon. The counterattack occurred in 1985. As might be expected with a person like me, it was an intellectual counterattack. At least, it was an intellectual counterattack in the sense that it had to do with propositions and evidence and arguments, and not with personal tragedy or sexual temptation or distaste for liturgical innovation or disillusionment with the behavior of my fellow Christians. But it was not an intellectual counterattack in the sense that it had much respectable intellectual content. A great deal of its content, in fact, was simply ludicrous, and I was perfectly well aware of that at the time, but that did not make it any less effective. One part of the counterattack was a real intellectual difficulty: I was extremely worried by Jesus' apparent prediction of the end of the present age within the lifetime of some of the witnesses to his earthly ministry. Nowadays I would say that I don't expect that the New Testament always gives an exact account of Jesus' words, and that the passages that worried me are probably a conflation of his prediction of the destruction of Jerusalem and his description of the End Times; I would say that this conflation was natural enough, given the beliefs of the early church. And I would add to this that I am not sure it is inconsistent with a robust and orthodox theology of the Incarnation to hold that Jesus himself believed in an imminent Parousia (although I am not entirely happy about that idea). And not only would I say these things nowadays, but I said them (to myself, just about daily) for several years in the mid-1980s. The difference is that now I am perfectly comfortable with these arguments, and then they seemed like a wretched subterfuge to me. It's not that I perceived some flaw in them that I was unable to deal with. I perceived no flaw in them. They simply seemed like a wretched subterfuge to me, and that is all that there was to say about the matter.

The other parts of the counterattack are so flimsy that I am ashamed to record them. One derived from a newspaper report that a certain biblical scholar (a man who I later learned had written a book the central thesis of which was that Jesus was a hallucinogenic mushroom) maintained that unpublished material from the Dead Sea Scrolls contained prototypes from which the Gospels were derived, prototypes that antedated the birth of Jesus. The other had its basis in the claims of some physicists and cosmologists to be able to show (or to be about to be able to show) that the cosmos was somehow a thing that had come into existence literally out of nothing—that is, without any causal antecedents whatever, either temporal or ontological. I knew what to say in response to these arguments, of course. Anyone who thought about it would. I knew that this scholar did not claim to have *seen* these Gospel prototypes; rather, he inferred their existence from scraps of information about the unpublished Dead Sea Scrolls material by an elaborate Rube Goldberg (or Heath Robinson) chain of reasoning; I knew that he was demonstrably regarded by many scholars as a crank and that his theory was endorsed by no one; I knew that he was fanatically hostile to Christianity. As to the physicists and cosmologists, their claim was philosophical nonsense, tricked out to look like sense by games played with the word 'nothing'. These things I knew then as well as I do now, but I could not make them real to myself. There was always a voice that whispered, "But this is not philosophy. You are not a biblical scholar or a physicist. You are out of your element here, and they are in theirs. Your criticisms are without value, you amateur."

The net result of my state of mind was fear. I was unable to read the Bible or to look at a newspaper article reporting the latest public pronouncement of some cosmologist about where the universe came from. And I was ashamed to seek help from my fellow Christians, since I knew that the things that were troubling me were nonsense, and I didn't want to look a fool. (And, at the same time, there was this quite inconsistent fear: Suppose that I did ask and was told, "You know, that's always worried me, too. I don't know what to say about that. And those counterarguments you keep rehearsing to yourself are worthless, and I'll tell you why.") Perhaps the best way to describe my state of mind would be by an analogy. You don't believe in ghosts, right? Well, neither do I. But how would you like to spend a night alone in a graveyard? I am subject to night fears, and I can tell you that I shouldn't like it at all. And yet I am perfectly well aware that fear of ghosts is contrary to science, reason, and religion. If I were sentenced to spend a night alone in a graveyard, I should know beforehand that no piece of evidence was going to transpire during the night that would do anything to raise the infinitesimal prior probability of the hypothesis that there are ghosts. I should already know that twigs would snap and the wind moan and that there would be half-seen movements in the darkness. And I should know that the inevitable occurrences of these things would be of no evidential value whatever. And yet, after I had been frog-marched into the graveyard, I should feel a thrill of fear every time one of these things happened. I could reason with myself: "I believe that the dead are in Heaven or Hell, or else that they sleep until the General Resurrection. And if my religion is an illusion, then some form of materialism is the correct metaphysic, and materialism is incompatible with the existence of ghosts. And if the church and the materialists are both wrong and there are ghosts, what could be the harm in a ghost? What could such a poor, wispy thing do to one?" And what would the value of this very cogent piece of reasoning be? None at all, at least in respect of allaying my fear of ghosts.

Possibly, if one were subject to an irrational fear of ghosts, one would eventually lose it if one were forced to spend every night alone in a graveyard. Something like that seems to have happened to me as regards the irrational fears that underlay what I have called the counterattack. Eventually, they simply faded away. I am now unclear about what the time frame of all this was. I know that the full force of it lasted for several years and that it was horrible. I am sure that I could say nothing that would convey the horror of it to someone who had not had a similar experience, just as someone who was "afraid of ghosts" (without believing in their existence) could do nothing to convey to someone who was free from this fear what was so horrible about spending a night alone in a graveyard or an abandoned and isolated house. The fears, while they lasted, were tireless and persistent. (At one time I called them—to myself; I never spoke of these things, out of pride and shame—the barrage.) Reason is impotent in such situations, since one is already intellectually convinced that there is nothing to fear. (Fear replies, Ah, but you have reasoned wrong. "How have I reasoned wrong?" I said; you have reasoned wrong.) And prayer, whatever its objective benefits, brings no immediate psychological comfort, as it can do in many kinds of affliction; on the psychological level, prayer merely aggravates the fear that there is No One There by making the question whether there is anyone there momentarily inescapable, and letting the fears loose on it.

Somehow, with God's help, I got through this period. (I often wonder whether it was some kindergarten version of "the Dark Night of the Soul," but I have never really understood what that phrase means.) I hope it never returns. I hope that the part of me on which it operated is dead, swallowed up in that death into which we are baptized. But God has, as is His usual practice, given me no guarantees, and, for all I know, it could all start again tomorrow.

There is not much more to tell about my life that is relevant to my topic. In 1987, my first wife, for reasons that I do not understand, insisted on a divorce. (This is perhaps the only bad thing that has ever happened to me, at least as the world counts bad things. I do not think I should make much of a martyr; I have not had the training.) The divorce was granted the following year, and the year after that I married Elisabeth Bolduc. Several years earlier, her husband had moved out and left her with a three-week-old baby and two older children. We met and were married in the church in which I had been baptized and confirmed.[1] Lisette, as my wife is usually called, is—besides being a deeply Christian woman—an extrovert with a very strong personality and a vigorous emotional life. She thinks I am too intellectual and introverted and is determined to draw me out of myself. She may be succeeding. And then again, I may be too old a dog to learn new tricks.

At present, my religious life is in what is sometimes called a dry period. I have trouble praying and "finding time" to read the Bible. I have almost no sense of myself as a sinner who needs the saving power of Christ, although, of course, I fully accept the *proposition* that I am a sinner who needs Christ. I can see perfectly well my pride and anger and sloth and lust and self-centeredness and callousness. I can see perfectly well that pride and anger and sloth and lust and self-centeredness and callousness are sins. What I cannot do is to make the obvious logical consequence of these two objects of intellectual awareness real to myself. All of the particular acts that fall under these general headings (pride, etc.) "feel" all right to me because they are done by me—that is, in *these* mitigating circumstances, which only I appreciate. (Of course it was excusable for me to answer him in those words after he looked at me like *that*.) Nevertheless, whether I should be or not, I am not greatly troubled or uneasy about this. I am somehow confident that God, having brought my intellect (at least to some degree) under His control, is patiently working inward and is beginning to achieve some sort of mastery over my passions and my appetites. I believe that parts of me that were diseased but vigorous ten years ago have been killed and replaced with grafts of living, healthy tissue. But it is obvious from my behavior and the shameful inner thoughts that I reveal to no one but God (and I sometimes catch myself thinking in ways that seem to presuppose that I can hide these thoughts even from Him) that the process has a long way to go. I often feel as if God is saying to me (when I have formed, say, some shameful plan of revenge and humiliation), "You know, if it weren't for Me, you would actually carry out that plan. Don't suppose that you are really capable of resisting the temptation to do things like that. In letting you have these thoughts, I am showing you what you would do if I ever left you to yourself, even for a moment."

"YES, YES autobiographical narrative is all very well, but we want to know how you can possibly believe all that stuff."

A couple of years ago, I wrote a paper about New Testament criticism, which contained the following passage:

> I am a convert. For the first forty years of my life I was outside the Church. For much of my life, what I believed about the Church was a mixture of fact and hostile invention, some of it asinine and some of it quite clever. Eventually, I entered the Church, an act that involved assenting to cetain propositions. I believe that I had, and still have, good reasons for assenting to those propositions, although I am not sure what those reasons are. Does that sound odd? It should not. I mean this. I am inclined to think that my reasons for assenting to those propositions could be written down in a few pages—that I could actually do this. But I know that if I did, there would be many non-Christians, people just as intelligent as I am, who would be willing to accept without reservation everything I had written down, and who would yet remain what they had been: untroubled agnostics, aggressive atheists, pious Muslims, or whatever. And there are many who would say that this shows that what I had written down could not really constitute good reasons for assenting to those propositions. If it did (so the objection would run), reading what I had written on those pages would convert intelligent agnostics, atheists, and Muslims to Christianity—or would at least force them into a state of doublethink or intellectual crisis or cognitive dissonance. Perhaps that's right. If it is, then among my reasons there must be some that can't be communicated—or I lack the skill to communicate them—, like my reasons for believing that Jane is angry: something about the corners of her mouth and the pitch of her voice, which I can't put into words.[2]

I read the paper that contained this passage at a conference on philosophy and New Testament criticism at Notre Dame University, and Bas van Fraassen, who was in the audience, told me afterward that he did not think that I could find it as easy to write down "my reasons for assenting to these propositions" as I supposed. I had to admit that it was possible that he was right. To this day, I am not sure. But I am now going to put the matter to the test.

Let me begin with a fact about philosophy. Philosophers do not agree about anything to speak of. And why not? How can it be that equally intelligent and well-trained philosophers can disagree about the freedom of the will or nominalism or the covering-law model of scientific explanation when each is aware of all of the arguments and distinctions and other relevant considerations that the others are aware of? How can we philosophers possibly regard ourselves as justified in believing anything of philosophical significance under these conditions? How can *I* believe (as I do) that free will is incompatible with determinism or that unrealized possibilities are not physical objects or that human beings are not four-dimensional things extended in time as well as in space when David Lewis—a philosopher of truly formidable intelligence and insight and ability—rejects these things I believe and is aware of and understands perfectly every argument that I could bring in their defense?

Well, I *do* believe these things. And I believe that I am justified in believing them. And I am confident that I am right. But how can I take these positions? I don't know. That is itself a philosophical question, and I have no firm opinion about its correct answer. I suppose my best guess is that I enjoy some sort of philosophical insight that, for all his other merits, is somehow denied to Lewis. And this would have to be an insight that is incommunicable—at least *I* don't know how to communicae it—for I have done all I can to communicate it to Lewis, and he has understood perfectly everything I have said, and he has not come to share my conclusions. But maybe my best guess is wrong. I'm confident about only one thing in this area: The question must have some good answer. For not only do my beliefs about these questions seem to me to be undeniably *true,* but (quite independently of any consideration of which theses it is that seem to me to be true), I don't want to be forced into a position in which I accept no philosophical thesis of any consequence. Let us call this unattractive position "philosophical skepticism." (Note that I am not using this phrase in its usual sense of "comprehensive and general skepticism based on philosophical argument.") I think that any philosopher who does not wish to be a philosophical skeptic—I know of no philosopher who *is* a philosophical skeptic—must agree with me that this question has some good answer. Whatever the reason, it must be possible for one to have good and sufficient reasons for accepting a philosophical thesis when there are philosophers who, by all objective and external criteria, are at least equally well qualified to pronounce on that thesis and who reject it.

Will someone say that philosophy is a special case? Perhaps because nothing really hangs on philosophical questions, and a false or unjustified philosophical opinion is therefore harmless? Or because philosophy is in some sense not about matters of empirical fact? As to the first of these two suggestions, I think it is false that nothing hangs on philosophical questions. What people have believed about the philosophical theses advanced by—for example—Plato, Locke, and Marx has had profound effects on history. I don't know what the world would be like if everyone who ever encountered philosophy immediately became, and thereafter remained, a philosophical skeptic, but I'm willing to bet it would be a vastly different world.

The second suggestion is trickier. Its premise is not that it doesn't make any difference what people believe about philosophical questions; it's rather that the world would look exactly the same whether any given philosophical thesis was true or false. I think that that's a dubious assertion, but rather than address it, I will simply change the subject.

Let us consider politics.

Almost everyone will admit that it makes a difference what people believe about politics, and it would be absurd to say that propositions like "Capital punishment is an ineffective deterrent" or "Nations that do not maintain a strong military capability actually increase the risk of war" are not about matters of empirical fact. And yet people disagree about these propositions (and scores of others of equal importance), and their disagreements about them bear a disquieting resemblance to the disagreements of philosophers about nominalism and free will and the covering-law model. That is, their disagreements are matters of interminable debate, and impressive authorities can be found on both sides of many of the interminable debates.

It is important to realize that this feature of philosophy and politics is not a universal feature of human discourse. It is clear, for example, that someone who believes in astrology believes in something that is simply indefensible. It would be hard to find a philosopher who believed that every philosopher who disagreed with his or her position on nominalism held a position that was indefensible in the same way that a belief in astrology was indefensible. It might be easier to find someone who held the corresponding position about disputed and important political questions. I suspect that there really are people who think that those who disagree with them about the deterrent effect of capital punishment or the probable consequences of unilateral disarmament are not only mistaken but hold beliefs that are indefensible in the way that a belief in astrology is indefensible. I can only say that I regard this attitude as ludicrous. On each side of many interminably debated political questions—it is not necessary to my argument to say *all*—one can find well-informed (indeed, immensely learned) and highly intelligent men and women who adhere to the very highest intellectual standards. And this is simply not the case with debates about astrology.

Everyone who is intellectually honest will admit this. And yet, few will react to this state of affairs by becoming political skeptics, by declining to have any political beliefs that are undisputed by reputable authorities. But how can this rejection of political skepticism be defended? How can responsible political thinkers believe that the Syndicalist Party is the last, best hope for Ruritania when they know full well that there are well-informed (even immensely learned) and highly intelligent people who argue vehemently—all the while adhering to the highest intellectual standards—that a Syndicalist government would be the ruin of Ruritania? Do the friends of Syndicalism claim to see gaps in the arguments of their opponents, "facts" that they have cited that are not really facts, real facts that they have chosen not to mention, a hidden agenda behind their opposition to Syndicalism? No doubt they do. Nevertheless, if they are intelligent and intellectually honest, they will be aware that if these claims were made in public debate, the opponents of Syndicalism would probably be able to muster a very respectable rebuttal. The friends of Syndicalism will perhaps be confident that they could effectively meet the points raised in this rebuttal, but, if they are intelligent and intellectually honest, they will be aware . . . and so, for all practical purposes, ad infinitum.

I ask again: What could it be that justifies us in rejecting political skepticism? How can *I* believe that my political beliefs are justified when these beliefs are rejected by people whose qualifications for engaging in political discourse are as impressive as David Lewis's qualifications for engaging in philosophical discourse? These people are aware of (at least) all the evidence and all the arguments that I am aware of, and they are (at least) as good at evaluating evidence and arguments as I. How, then, can I maintain that the evidence and arguments I can adduce in support of my beliefs actually justify these beliefs? If this evidence and these arguments are capable of that, then why aren't they capable of convincing these other people that these beliefs are correct? Well, as with philosophy, I am inclined to think that I must enjoy some sort of incommunicable insight that the others, for all their merits, lack. I am inclined to think that "the evidence and arguments I can adduce in support of my beliefs" do not constitute the totality of my justification for these beliefs. But all that I am willing to say for sure is that *something* justifies me in rejecting political skepticism, or at least that it is *possible* that something does: that the conclusion that one is not justified in holding any "controversial" political beliefs is not a necessary truth.

Now let us turn to questions of religion. Is religion different from philosophy and politics in the respects we have been discussing? It is an extremely popular position that religion is different. Or, at least, it must be that many antireligious philosophers and other writers hostile to religious belief hold this position, for it seems to be presupposed by almost every aspect of their approach to the subject of religious belief. And yet, this position seems never to have been explicitly stated, much less argued for. Let us call it the Difference Thesis. A good example of the Difference Thesis at work is provided by W. K. Clifford's famous essay "The Ethics of Belief."[3] One of the most interesting facts about "The Ethics of Belief" is that nowhere in it is religious belief explicitly mentioned.[4] It would, however, be disingenuous in the extreme to say that this essay is simply about the ethics of belief in general and is no more directed at religious belief than at any other kind of belief. "Everyone knows," as the phrase goes, that Clifford's target is religious belief. (Certainly the editors of anthologies know this. "The Ethics of Belief" appears in just about every anthology devoted to the philosophy of religion. It has never appeared in an anthology devoted to epistemology.) The real thesis of Clifford's essay is that religious beliefs—belief in God; belief in an afterlife; belief in the central historical claims of Judaism or Christianity or Islam—are always or almost always held in ways that violate the famous ethico-epistemic principle: It is wrong always, everywhere, and for anyone, to believe anything upon insufficient evidence. If, moreover, he is of the opinion that beliefs in any other general category are always or almost always (or typically or rather often) held in ways that violate his principle, this is certainly not apparent.

Let us call this principle—"It is wrong always, everywhere, and for anyone . . ."—Clifford's Principle. It is interesting to note that Clifford's Principle is almost never mentioned except in hostile examinations of religious belief, and that the antireligious writers who mention it never apply it to anything but religious beliefs. (With the exception of illustrative examples—like Clifford's example of the irresponsible shipowner—that are introduced in the course of explaining its content.) It is this that provides the primary evidence for my contention that many antireligious philosophers and other writers against religion tacitly accept the Difference Thesis. The fact that they apply Clifford's Principle only to religious beliefs is best explained by the assumption that they accept the Difference Thesis. The cases of Marxism and Freudianism are instructive examples of what I am talking about. It is easy to point to philosophers who believe that Marxism and Freudianism are nonsense: absurd parodies of scientific theories that get the real world wildly wrong. Presumably these philosophers do not believe that Marxism and Freudianism were adequately supported by the evidence that was available to Marx and Freud—or that they are adequately supported by the evidence that is available to any of the latter-day adherents of Marxism and Freudianism. But never once has any writer charged that Marx or Freud blotted his epistemic escutcheon by failing to apportion belief to evidence. I challenged anyone to find me a passage (other than an illustrative passage of the type I have mentioned) in which any devotee of Clifford's Principle has applied it to anything but religious belief. And yet, practically all philosophers—the literature will immediately demonstrate this to the most casual inquirer—subscribe to theses an obvious logical consequence of which is that the world abounds in gross violations of Clifford's Principle that have nothing to do with religion.

An explanation of the widespread tacit acceptance of the Difference Thesis is not far to seek. If Clifford's Principle were generally applied in philosophy (or in politics or historiography or even in many parts of the natural sciences), it would have to be applied practically everywhere. If its use became general, we'd all be constantly shoving it in one another's faces. And there would be no comfortable reply open to most of the recipients of a charge of violating Clifford's Principle. If I am an archaeologist who believes that an artifact found in a Neolithic tomb was a religious object used in a fertility rite, and if my rival, Professor Graves, believes that it was used to wind flax, how can I suppose that my belief is supported by the evidence? If my evidence really supports my belief, why doesn't it convert Professor Graves, who is as aware of it as I am, to my position? If we generally applied Clifford's Principle, we'd all have to become agnostics as regards most philosophical and political questions, or we'd have to find some reasonable answer to the challenge: "In what sense can the evidence you have adduced support or justify your belief when there are many authorities as competent as you who regard it as unconvincing?" But no answer to this challenge is evident, and religion seems to be the only area of human life in which very many people are willing to be agnostics about the answers to very many questions.

It might, however, be objected that what I have been representing as obvious considerations are obvious only on a certain conception of the nature of evidence. Perhaps the Difference Thesis is defensible because the evidence that some people have for their philosophical and political (and archaeological and historiographical . . .) beliefs consists partly of the deliverances of that incommunicable "insight" that I speculated about earlier. This objection would seem to be consistent with everything said in "The Ethics of Belief," for Clifford nowhere tells his readers what evidence is. If "evidence" is evidence in the courtroom or laboratory sense (photographs, transcripts of sworn statements, the pronouncements of expert witnesses, tables of figures), then "the evidence" pretty clearly does not support our philosophical and political beliefs. Let such evidence be eked out with logical inference and private sense experience and the memory of sense experience (my private experience and my memories, as opposed to my testimony about my experience and memories, cannot be entered as evidence in a court of law or published in *Physical Review Letters,* but they can be part of my evidence for my beliefs—or so the epistemologists tell us), and it still seems to be true that "the evidence" does not support our philosophical and political beliefs. It is not that such evidence is impotent: It can support—I hope—many life-and-death courtroom judgments and such scientific theses as that the continents are in motion. But it does not seem to be sufficient to justify most of our philosophical and political beliefs, or our philosophical and political beliefs, surely, would be far more uniform than they are. If "evidence" must be of the courtroom-and-laboratory sort, how can the Difference Thesis be defended?

If, however, "evidence" can include "insight" or some other incommunicable element—my private experience and my memories are not necessarily incommunicable—it may be that some of the philosophical and political beliefs of certain people are justified by the evidence available to them. But if evidence is understood in this way, how can anyone be confident that some of the religious beliefs of some people are not justified by the evidence available to them? If evidence can include incommunicable elements, how can anyone be confident that all religious believers are in violation of Clifford's Principle? If "evidence" can include the incommunicable, how can the Difference Thesis be defended?

All that I have said so far in this section amounts to a polemic against what I perceive as a widespread double standard in writings about the relation of religious belief to evidence and argument. This double standard consists in setting religious belief a test it could not possibly pass, and in studiously ignoring the fact that almost none of our beliefs on any subject could possibly pass this test.

I ask the reader to abandon this double standard. I ask the reader not to demand that my arguments meet standards modeled on courtroom rules of evidence or the editorial requirements of the *Journal of Molecular Biology.*

In the sequel, I will present some arguments for the Christian faith. To set out these arguments, in my judgment, is to present those who attend to them with good reasons for accepting that faith. The arguments will almost certainly not convince anyone, but then such arguments as I might give for the truth or falsity of nominalism or regarding the deterrent powers of capital punishment would almost certainly not convince anyone either. It is often said that you can't argue people into faith. Well, I don't want to *dispute* that statement, but I do want to deprecate the idea that it is something worth saying. What *can* you argue people into? Faith—Christian faith, that is—is believing what the church says (and continuing to believe it even when it is under the sort of "night in the graveyard" attack that I tried to describe in the preceding section). Would anyone say that you can't argue people into believing Plato's account of the trial of Socrates or into believing what the Democratic Party says about the superiority of its platform to that of the Republicans? I suppose that there is an element of truth in these two statements—argument is rarely coercive; in most areas of life, the best argument does not guarantee converts, even among the ideally rational—but argument is hardly irrelevant to the question whether one should believe the statements of Plato and the Democrats. In point of fact, no one ever does say things like this. The fact that people go about saying that you can't argue people into faith, and saying this as if it were an intelligent thing to say, is simply one more example of the double standard that I have been attacking.

There are several things I am not going to discuss that I might be expected to discuss in connection with arguments for the Christian faith.

I am not going to discuss "arguments for the existence of God." Although I think that some versions of two of these arguments—the Design Argument and the Cosmological Argument—are as good as any philosophical argument that has ever been presented for any conclusion, I don't think that they have any more to do with my religious beliefs than, say, arguments for the existence of other minds have to do with my belief that my wife would never lie to me or my belief that democracy is a good thing. (I am going to touch on some matters related to the Design Argument, but I am in no sense going to *defend* that argument.)

I am not going to discuss "the problem of evil." I have said what I have to say on this topic elsewhere.[5] I have always regarded the problem of evil as simply one more philosophical problem: Every important system of belief raises philosophical problems, and the problem of evil is one that is raised by all religions that are founded on belief in a loving and all-powerful God. I think, of course, that what I have said in response to this problem is right. But that's a mere philosophical opinion. On a religious level, my belief is simply that there are good reasons for the evils we see in the world—and that this would be true even if everything *I* have said on the subject is worthless. If I may interject an autobiographical note at this point, I will mention that I have never had the least tendency to react to the evils of the world by saying, "How *could* there be a loving God who allows these things?" My immediate emotional reaction has rather been: "There *must* be a God who will wipe away every tear; there *must* be a God who will repay." (Or this has been my reaction as a believer. I don't think that as an unbeliever I had any sort of emotional reaction to the evils of the world.)

I am not going to discuss Christian mysteries—the Trinity, the Incarnation, the Eucharist, the Atonement. I have discussed two of these elsewhere,[6] but, on the religious level, my belief is that these apparently impossible things are real and are therefore possible. Christian mysteries are News, and the recipients of news are not always in a position to understand it perfectly. I believe that in relation to the Christian mysteries, we Christians are like people who have never seen a mirror, or even a reflection in a pond, trying to grasp the nature of a mirror from listening to one of their fellows who has been shown a looking glass by a traveler. Perhaps the closest analogy the observer of the mirror can find is provided by pictures scratched in the sand: "A 'mirror' is a kind of flat plate that shows pictures like the ones we scratch in the sand, but they're three-dimensional—looking at a mirror is almost like looking through a window, even though the mirror has hardly any thickness and you just see an ordinary surface if you turn it round and look at the back—and they're in color, and they're absolutely perfect pictures (except that they're backward), and they change and move just the way real things do, and the mirror always shows pictures of the things right in front of it." One can easily imagine the conceptual havoc a skeptical philosopher among these people could wreak on this attempt at description. Nevertheless, considering the situation of the speaker and his audience, it's a good, practical description of a mirror. (It would, for example, almost certainly enable someone who had never seen a mirror to recognize a mirror on his first encounter with one.) In my view, creedal descriptions of the Trinity and the Incarnation are good, practical descriptions of real things, descriptions that will do till we no longer see through a glass darkly. I am confident that they are at least as good as descriptions of curved space or the wave-particle duality in works of popular science.

I do not propose to say anything about religions other than Christianity. I have discussed this topic elsewhere and I have nothing more to say about it.[7]

I do not propose to discuss miracles and questions about the believability of reports of events that are contrary to the laws of nature. This is an important subject and one that I certainly should say something about, given the nature of my topic, but I do not have the space. If I had had sufficient foresight, I should already have written an essay on miracles that I could refer you to. Sorry.

Now, finally . . .

Each of us accepts certain authorities and certain traditions. You may think that you are an epistemic engine that takes sensory input (that "fancifully fanciless medium of unvarnished news") and generates assignments of probabilities to propositions by means of a set of rules that yields the most useful (useful for dealing with the future stream of sensory input) probability assignments in most possible worlds. In fact, however, you trust a lot of people and groups of people and—within very broad limits—believe what they tell you. And this is not because the epistemic engine that is yourself has processed a lot of sensory data and, in consequence, assigned high probabilities to propositions like "Dixy Lee Ray is a reliable source of information on ecological matters" or "Most things that the *Boston Globe* says about the homeless are true." You may have done some of that, but you haven't had time to do very much of it.

As regards questions about the nature of the world as a whole and the place of humanity in the world, it is statistically very likely that you trust one or the other of two authorities: the Church or the Enlightenment. (But some readers of this essay will trust the Torah or the Koran or even—I suppose this is remotely possible—a person or book that claims access to some occult, esoteric wisdom.) What I propose to do in the sequel is to explain why I, who once trusted the Enlightenment, now trust the Church.

There is, I believe, an identifiable and cohesive historical phenomenon that named itself the Enlightenment in the eighteenth century and which, although it long ago abandoned the name, still exists. Like the Church, it does not speak with one voice. Like the Church, it has no central government. Like the Church, it is made up of many groups, some of which heartily detest many of the others—some of which, indeed, regard themselves as its sole true representatives and all others who claim to be its representatives as wolves in sheep's clothing. Like the Church, it has a creed, although, unlike the Church's creeds, its creed has never received an official formulation.[8] But that is a minor point. Its creed can be written down, and here it is:

> There is no God. There is, in fact, nothing besides the physical cosmos that science investigates. Human beings, since they are a part of this cosmos, are physical things and therefore do not survive death. Human being are, in fact, animals among other animals and differ from other animals only in being more complex. Like other animals, they are a product of uncaring and unconscious physical processes that did not have them, or anything else, in mind. There is, therefore, nothing external to humanity that is capable of conferring meaning or purpose on human existence. In the end, the only evil is pain and the only good is pleasure. The only purpose of morality and politics is the minimization of pain and the maximization of pleasure. Human beings, however, have an unfortunate tendency to wish to deny these facts and to believe comforting myths according to which they have an eternal purpose. This irrational component in the psyches of most human beings—it is the great good fortune of the species that there are a few strong-minded progressives who can see through the comforting myths— encourages the confidence game called religion. Religions invent complicated and arbitrary moral codes and fantastic future rewards and punishments in order to consolidate their own power. Fortunately, they are gradually but steadily being exposed as frauds by the progress of science (which was invented by strong-minded progressives), and they will gradually disappear through the agency of scientific education and enlightened journalism.

Various Enlightenment "denominations" such as Marxism or Positivism or Freudianism or Social Darwinism would insist that this statement of the Enlightenment creed omits certain extremely important propositions—even propositions that are absolutely crucial to an understanding of the world and humanity's place in the world. But I have tried simply to capture the highest common factor of the various schools of thought that compose the Enlightenment—the Apostles' Creed of the Enlightenment, as it were.

The Enlightenment has had its chance with me, and I have found it wanting. I was once one of its adherents, and now I am an apostate. On the level of intellectual argument and evidence, it leaves a lot to be desired. And its social consequences have been horrible.

I am going to compare the attractiveness of the Church and the Enlightenment. I will group my comparisons into three parts. First, it seems to me, the teachings of the Church are, as I shall say, "congruent" with the facts of science and history in a way that the "creed" of the Enlightenment is not, and I shall discuss this. Secondly, I shall compare the "fruits" of the Church with the fruits of the Enlightenment. Thirdly, I shall compare the effects of adherence to the Church and to the Enlightenment in the lives of individuals.

The first matter for discussion is congruency.

The preferred universe of the Enlightenment was constructed in the eighteenth and nineteenth centuries. It is infinite in space and time, and it consists entirely of matter in motion. This universe was incompatible with the content of nineteenth-century science, even at the beginning of the century, and science became less and less hospitable to it as the century progressed. Nevertheless, this universe—that is, this picture of the universe—persisted in the popular imagination (which is what it was designed for) throughout the century, and it can be found in some circles even today. Today this picture is simply impossible. Present-day science gives us a universe that began to exist a specific number of years ago and may well be spatially finite; it is, moreover, governed by laws that contain a lot of apparently arbitrary numbers, and if these numbers were only a bit different, there would be no life: Only a vanishingly small region in the space of all possible sets of physical laws is occupied by sets of laws that permit the existence of life, and the one universe there is is governed by a set of laws that falls within that minuscule region. It is, of course, possible to explain these things in terms other than those of theism. My point is that the Christian is right at home in such a universe, whereas the adherent of the Enlightenment would much prefer the universe of nineteenth-century popular science. That, after all, is the universe that was constructed by the imagination of the Enlightenment when the facts still allowed that imagination free play. But it is the universe that was constructed to fit the imaginations of Christians (unless its source was actually in divine revelation) that turned out to be consistent with what science has discovered. (Let's hear nothing about "fundamentalism." Some Christians are fundamentalists, and are consequently unhappy with the universe of modern cosmology. But fundamentalism is one of the accidents of Christianity, not a part of its essence. If St. Thomas Aquinas was a fundamentalist in the current sense of the word, St. Augustine was not. And Aquinas, when he discusses Augustine's thesis that the "six days" of Genesis are a figurative description of six aspects of the created world, simply says that Augustine was wrong; he does not say that Augustine's views were heretical. A fundamentalist-turned-logical-positivist once called me a wishy-washy theological liberal because I read the book of Genesis in a way that was compatible with modern cosmology. I asked him whether he thought that Augustine was a wishy-washy theological liberal. "Yes," he said.)

Coming down to more modern times, cosmologically speaking, what the Enlightenment would really like is a universe bursting with life and chock-full of rational species.[9] But no one knows anything to speak of about the origin of life on the earth except that it is at present one of the great scientific mysteries. There is, therefore, no scientific reason to think that life is something that happens "automatically." It is pretty certain that there is no life elsewhere in the solar system, and the gleanings of the "Search for Extra-Terrestrial Intelligence" have not been very encouraging to those who would like to think of the Orion Spur (our own little galactic neighborhood) as festooned with technological civilizations like ornaments on the Christmas tree it rather resembles. When these facts are combined with the fact that rationality has evolved only once on the Earth (as opposed to forty times for vision and four for flight; and each of these evolutionary inventions is spread over hundreds of thousands of species, while rationality's meager score is one), and the fact that this event would not have happened if a comet or asteroid had not happened to cause the mass extinctions of 65 million years ago, it begins to seem unlikely that the Enlightenment will get what it wants in this area. The Christian, on the other hand, is right at home in a universe in which humanity is the only rational species, or is one of a small handful of them.

The Enlightenment would like it if humanity were continuous with other terrestrial animals, or at least very much like some of them. The Enlightenment would like this so much that it has actually managed to convince itself that it is so. It has even managed to convince itself that modern science has proved this. I remember reading a very amusing response made by David Berlinski to Stephen Jay Gould's statement that modern science was rapidly removing every excuse that anyone had ever had for thinking that we were much different from our closest primate relatives.[10] Berlinski pointed out that you can always make two things sound similar (or "different only in degree") if you describe them abstractly enough: "What Canada geese do when they migrate is much like what we do when we jump over a ditch: In each case, an organism's feet leave the ground, it moves through the air, and it comes down some distance away. The difference between the two accomplishments is only a matter of degree." I am also put in mind of a cartoon Phillip Johnson once showed me: A hostess is introducing a human being and a chimp at a cocktail party. "You two will have a lot to talk about," she says, "you share 99 percent of your DNA." I'm sorry if I seem to be making a joke of this, but . . . well, I *am* making of joke of this. I admit it. Why shouldn't I? The idea that there isn't a vast, radical difference, a chasm, between human beings and all other terrestrial species is simply a very funny idea. It's like the idea that Americans have a fundamental constitutional right to own automatic assault weapons. Its consequences apart, it's simply a very funny idea, and there's nothing much one can do about it except to make a joke of it. You certainly wouldn't want to invest much time in an argument with someone who would believe it in the first place.

The Enlightenment has, historically speaking, felt a certain affection for European civilization. (Admittedly, this affection is not what it used to be.) After all, European civilization produced the Enlightenment, so it can't be all bad. Nevertheless, the single greatest factor in the development of European civilization was the Church, so it can hardly be all good either. Best, perhaps, to stress its similarities to other civilizations (no doubt we'd find native "Enlightenments" bravely struggling against the local superstitions in those other civilizations if we looked closely enough) and to ascribe its bad aspects to the Church and its good elements to the Enlightenment or to such "Morning Stars of the Enlightenment" as Roger Bacon and Copernicus. The main problem confronting this Enlightenment strategy is science.

Modern science—the kind of science of which Newton's derivation of Kepler's law of planetary motion is a paradigm—has arisen only once in history. Oh, there has been some observational astronomy here and some attempt at systematic medical knowledge there. The achievements of the Greeks in taking the first steps down the path of science were magnificent, particularly in descriptive astronomy and statics—that is, in scientific studies that were essentially applied geometry. But the Greeks took a few steps down the road of science and faltered.

Here is the story the Enlightenment tells. There would have been a scientific revolution like that of sixteenth-century Europe in the classical world if the biblical literalism and otherworldliness of Christianity had not stifled ancient science and created the Dark Ages. Over a millennium later, science and the scientific method were reborn in the mind of Galileo (or maybe Copernicus had something to do with it). The Church persecuted Galileo, but it failed to kill the infant he had fathered and has been steadily losing ground to science ever since. (If you would like to see this story set out in more detail, consult A. D. White's *History of the Warfare of Science and Theology*.)

I don't want to get into an historical argument. I will simply tell another story, a story that is, in my view, better supported by the evidence. (This view is, of course, the view of an amateur, but I have, I suppose, as much right to it as any follower of the Enlightenment who was not a trained historian of science has had to the story told in the preceding paragraph.[11])

Ancient science discovered very little after about the time of the birth of Christ—which amounts to pretty quick work if Christianity stifled ancient science. The modern growth of science did not begin suddenly in the sixteenth century but was continuous with the natural philosophy of the High Middle Ages. (This has been well documented by Pierre Duhem.) There has been little persecution of science by the Church. There is nothing in the history of the relations of science and Christianity that can be compared with the Lysenko era in Soviet biology or the condition of science in Germany under the Nazis. When one looks carefully at the persecution of Galileo, the debate between Huxley and Bishop Wilberforce, or the Scopes trial, one finds that most of what one thought one had known about them isn't true, and that the real episodes do little to support the Enlightenment picture of a perpetual "warfare of science and theology."

Just as rationality has "happened" only once in the history of terrestrial life (unlike vision or flight), so science has "happened" only once in the history of humanity (unlike writing or the calendar). And the unique occurrence of science—*real* science, which does not stop with precise and systematic descriptions of phenomena but goes on to probe their underlying causes—happened in a civilization that was built upon the Church. The task of explaining why there was no science in India or China developed into something of an industry in the eighteenth century. To someone who shared the values of Voltaire, it was extremely puzzling that "rational" Confucian China, an ancient and settled civilization with a long history of scholarship and a demonstrated capacity for mechanical invention, should never have developed science. The failure of the much admired classical world to develop science in the modern sense could be blamed on Christianity, but what was it to be blamed on in the case of China? After all, science had flowered in monk-ridden Europe, and it could hardly, therefore, be a particularly frail blossom[12]; why, then, not in China? The question was never satisfactorily answered. It has since been largely ignored. Two devices contribute to this. First, there is a tendency to use the word 'science' so broadly that at least some "science" can be found practically anywhere. If this does not solve the problem, it helps to sweep it under the carpet. Secondly, there is a tendency to identify the history of the world with the history of Europe. While this tendency has lately been much deplored by some of the current representatives of the Enlightenment (and rightly so), it has been useful to the Enlightenment, for it enables one to think of the birth of science as something that belongs to the history of "the world" rather than to the history of a particular civilization; since there is only one world, this makes the unique birth of science seem somehow less puzzling.

I would suggest that science is an outgrowth of Western Latin Christianity, connected with it in much the same way as Gothic architecture. (That is, the connections are historical and causal, not logical, and the causation is not inevitable.) I would suggest that the Christian world view of the High Middle Ages produced a mental climate that made the birth of science possible.[13] (The suggestion has sometimes been made by representatives of the Enlightenment that a belief in miracles is inimical to science. Well, those who actually were responsible for the birth of science—Galileo and Newton, for example—believed in all the miracles of the New Testament. It really is very hard to see how those who believe that, in the normal course of events, nature works by mechanical causes are going to be less effective scientists if they believe that miracles occur at special junctures in what Christians call salvation history—or even that they happen frequently at Lourdes. The real conceptual enemies of science are astrology and magic. There was a very dangerous outbreak of serious interest in astrology and magic during the Renaissance, which the Church worked very hard to suppress.)

The fact that the single birth of science occurred in Christendom is, therefore, a fact that is not congruent with the creed of the Enlightenment. It must, therefore, either be ignored or explained away by the Enlightenment. Christians, however, will be comfortable with the fact that the single most powerful instrument for understanding the world developed in a culture that had been shaped by (as they believe) a unique revelation of the mind and purposes of the Creator of that world.

I have left what I believe to be the single most important congruency for last.[14]

All humans beings are deeply, radically evil. (Are there no exceptions to this generalization? If there are, they are so rare that it is extremely unlikely that you or I have ever met one.) This evil may be only potential, but it is real. (In some cases, it may be comparable to an as yet asymptomatic but deadly and inoperable cancerous tumor.) This fact can be hard for the citizens of a truly civilized society to realize, for it is the business of civilization to train people from birth not even to deliberate about certain acts. (We do not want our fellows to regard murder as a matter for rational deliberation.) It is, moreover, the business of civilization to attempt so to arrange matters that if any individual *does* regard rape or murder or fraud or bearing false witness as a matter for deliberation, the contemplated act be fairly obviously unprofitable. But human history shows that the viewpoint of civilized people is parochial. It shows, moreover, that civilization is not necessarily a stable condition and that people who live in a civilized society have no right to expect that their great-grandchildren—or they themselves in their old age—will live in a civilized society.

The Christian doctrine of original sin comprises an etiology, a diagnosis, and a prognosis. I will mention only the diagnosis and one-half of the prognosis: We are deeply, radically evil, and this condition is unalterable by any natural means. The Enlightenment, of course, does not accept this thesis. The Enlightenment holds either that human beings are naturally good or that they are neither good nor bad but simply infinitely malleable. In either case, the horrible way that human beings treat one another is regarded as a social artifact, and as therefore eliminable, or at least reducible to tolerable proportions, by some form or other of social reorganization. This reorganization (whose nature representatives of the Enlightenment discover by thinking very hard about how society should be organized) will, as the case may be, allow the natural goodness of human beings to flourish or mold them into a form in which they will behave only in desirable ways. The reorganization is humanly possible, and when it has been achieved, it will be stable. Rousseau and B. F. Skinner represent this point of view in its purest, most innocent form (innocent, that is, of contact with reality). But there are much shrewder thinkers who hold it in some recognizable form. It is not clear to me how anyone could ever actually have held such a position, but that anyone could hold it in the late twentieth century is believable only because there it is, right before our eyes.

The Christian is able to have a realistic view of the human past and present. The representative of the Enlightenment cannot. (At any rate, most of them *don't*. I concede that a few of the people who have described themselves as "humanists" have had a realistic view of human nature. But they have never been listened to by the body of the Enlightenment.) It is extremely unfortunate that some Christians have abandoned the doctrine of original sin. As someone, Chesterton perhaps, remarked, they have abandoned the only Christian dogma that can actually be empirically proved. (True as regards the diagnosis and one-half of the prognosis, at any rate.)

The Christian is also able to have a realistic view of himself or herself. As one Christian writer of the present century remarked, "We are none of us very nice." When I look back on the days of my allegiance to the Enlightenment, I discover that this allegiance was primarily a device to assist me in admiring myself. I still admire myself, I'm afraid, but at least I have silenced the voice of one flatterer. ("How intelligent you are," the Enlightenment would whisper in my ear, "how progressive, how, well, *enlightened.*") It may well be that not every adherent of the Enlightenment has used it that way; I do not claim to be able to look into the souls of the living, much less the long dead. But to read such Enlightenment figures as Hume or Voltaire with Christian eyes is to see every possible opportunity for self-admiration taken; and Voltaire and Hume, like me in my own Enlightenment days, do not seem even to be able to get on with the business of self-admiration without perpetual sneers at "milkmaids" (Voltaire)—that is, at the great mass of people who keep the wheels turning while the Enlightenment sips its chocolate and peers at them through its quizzing glass. (The eighteenth-century Enlightenment—the Enlightenment proper, so to call it—no doubt hated kings and priests just as it said it did, but its real driving negative emotion was contempt for subjects and churchgoers. This is still true of the current representatives of the Enlightenment, *mutatis mutandis.*) I must admit, however, that I am not in a position to feel too terribly superior to Voltaire and Hume and my own past self. In theory, I accept the words of the hymn: "Foul I to thy fountain fly/Wash me Saviour, or I die." In practice, of course, I mostly think I'm a pretty fine fellow. (I mean, I not only have all my native niceness, but I'm *religious* as well.[15]) But I'm sorry. Or I'm sorry I'm not sorry. And this is simple realism, however disinclined my heart may be to follow my head in this realism. The Enlightenment seems to be incapable of such realism.

I will now turn to my second kind of argument. "By their fruits ye shall know them," said Jesus. He was, perhaps, referring only to preachers and the doctrines they preached, but the saying has usually been taken in a more general sense (possibly under the influence of St. Paul on the fruit of the Spirit), and that is the way I shall take it.

I have mentioned one of the "fruits" of the Church: modern science. (I remind the Christian reader that I am at this point discussing only things whose existence would be admitted by a non-Christian.) There are others. One might mention democracy (we must remember that no Greek *polis,* if it existed today, would be described as a democracy), the concept of universal human rights and its embodiment in working constitutions, and the rule of law (law as opposed both to the momentary will of the sovereign and to unalterable custom). Like science, these things are, according to the Enlightenment, inventions of the Enlightenment. But they arose in Christian nations, and the individuals who contributed to their development were mostly Christians. I concede that the debt owed by all who cherish these things to certain representatives of the Enlightenment is very great. Thomas Jefferson certainly comes to mind. (If anti-Christians can admire certain Christians—St. Francis, for example—despite the fact that they were Christians, I suppose it is allowable for me to admire certain representatives of the Enlightenment like Jefferson, despite their allegiance to the Enlightenment.) In fact, however, those Enlightenment figures who actually contributed to the development of those benign social institutions that are among Europe's greatest inventions were very imperfectly and selectively de-Christianized. If you want to see the social fruits of the Enlightenment in their pure form, you must look at the contributions to history of those who had consciously and decisively separated themselves from the Christian tradition and who based their political activities solely on Enlightenment theories. There is no point in looking at people like Tom Paine and Karl Marx, who never actually held the reins of political power, for there is no way of determining how they would have used the forces of coercion that power places at one's disposal when they were faced with recalcitrant political reality. I would suggest Robespierre and Lenin as instructive examples.

The Enlightenment makes much of the suffering and death caused by the awful things Christians have done—the Crusades and the Inquisition seem to be the standard examples, although if I were to give the Enlightenment advice on how to conduct its case, I would suggest that it pay more attention to the Thirty Years' War. But with whatever justification these things can be ascribed to the Christian religion, such episodes as the Terror of the 1790s, the Great Terror of the 1930s, and Pol Pot's experiment in social engineering in the 1970s can with the same justification be ascribed to the Enlightenment. And these caused thousands of times as many deaths and incomparably greater suffering than all of the pogroms and religious wars in the history of Europe. The Crusades et al. were quite ordinary episodes in the immemorial string of crimes that mainly compose what the world calls history and what St. Paul called this present darkness. The French Revolution was, as Burke was the first to realize, something new, a new kind of horror. The new kind of horror did not, of course, really hit its stride till about seventy years ago. Let no one say that I have blamed the great post-Christian horrors of the last two centuries on the Enlightenment. My claim is this: Lay out an argument for the conclusion that responsibility for the crimes of the Crusaders and the Inquisition is to be laid at the door of Christianity, and I will produce a parallel argument of about equal merit—not very great, in my opinion—for the conclusion that responsibility for the crimes of the Committee of Public Safety, the Soviet Communist Party, and the Khmer Rouge is to be laid at the door of the Enlightenment.

Whether or not the Enlightenment is responsible for the French Revolution and Pol Pot, it has nothing positive to offer humanity. It cannot legitimately claim to be the author of science or democracy, and its creed leaves only an aching emptiness at the spiritual level. In matters of the spirit, it bakes no bread. In its attempts to undermine Christian belief, it has opened the door to all manner of substitutes that are, by its own standards—standards it has borrowed from the Church; it cannot create standards, but can only edit the standards that the Church has made common currency—even worse than Christianity. The cult of nation-state, Naziism, Satanism, "the jargon of authenticity," New Age fluff, and what is this year called "theory" in literature departments have rushed in to fill the vacuum in the human heart that the Enlightenment has created. As Chesterton remarked, when people stop believing in God, they are not going to start believing in nothing; they are going to start believing in everything. In the end, the Enlightenment cannot survive; even if (by the standards of the world) it should destroy the Church, what replaces the Church at the social and cultural level will destroy the Enlightenment. Saturn's children will devour him. Those who doubt this should reflect on the actual fate of liberal humanism under Hitler or on the probable fate of liberal humanism under a politically established Age of Aquarius or under a triumphalist reign of "theory" in the universities.

Finally, I wish to consider the effects of the Church on individual lives. Here I must be brief, for there is no way that I can convey the evidence I am in possession of to you. I am, therefore, not talking about things whose existence is uncontroversial, although it is also true that I shall not be asserting the existence of anything that is in principle incompatible with the Enlightenment world view.

There are many atheists I know, old-fashioned atheists of the Enlightenment type, who are singularly impressive people, people whose lives and behavior are worthy of the highest admiration. ("How, then, can you, as a Christian believe that without conversion and repentance these admirable people are lost?" That question is not to the present point, but I will make one brief remark. I would look at the issue raised by this question from the other end: In the fact that even these admirable people cannot justify themselves before God, we see why it is that conversion and repentance are all the more necessary for the rest of us.) But each of these people is impressive in his or her own way. There are Christians I know, however, who are very impressive people, and their impressiveness is of a distinctively Christian sort. A common thread runs through their very diverse lives, and it is a Christian thread. I have never been able to discern an "Enlightenment" thread that runs through the lives of the admirable atheists of my acquaintance. There are five or six Christians I know who, for all the rich individuality of their lives and personalities, are like lamps, each shining with the same dearly familiar, uncreated light that shines in the pages of the New Testament. I can no more doubt this judgment than I can doubt many of my much more everyday sorts of judgment to the effect that this or that person is kind or generous or honest or loving. When one is in the presence of this light—when one so much as listens to one of these people speak—it is very difficult indeed to believe that one is not in the presence of a living reality that transcends their individual lives. But there is nothing more I can say about this (except perhaps to say that I am sure that the reason I do not see *more* Christians as lamps is to be found in my own limitations; I have no tendency to believe that the people who look this way to me are closer to God than any other Christians are). I mention it only because not to mention it would misrepresent my claims about the reasons I have for being a Christian.

All of the things I have mentioned—congruency, the fruits of the Church, my perception of the lives of some of my Christian friends—are, in the meditation of my heart, woven together into a seamless garment. When I take all of these things into account, it seems to me that I must conclude that the Church speaks with authority. I do not see how anyone could regard the Enlightenment—or any individual Enlightenment "denomination"—as an authoritative voice. Its creed is not congruent with the world we live in, the social consequences of its influence have been disastrous, and it has nothing at all to offer "milkmaids" and nothing but opportunities for self-admiration to offer the intellectual and governing classes. If two voices tell radically different stories about the world and the place of humanity in the world, one speaking with authority and one with a meretricious pretense to authority, it does not follow that the former is right. Maybe no one is right. (The stories are logical contraries, not contradictories.) It is even possible that the meretricious posturer is right. But there is no way to believe only the logical consequences of what is uncontroversial and to believe very much, and no one—unless it were the inhabitants of some asylum—believes only the logical consequences of what is uncontroversial. It seems to me, however, that anyone who believes the Church in the world as it is is in a pretty good epistemic position—at any rate, a better epistemic position than anyone else who is actually capable of functioning in the world. Maybe the only people who occupy a defensible epistemic position are skeptics—political and philosophical skeptics as well as religious skeptics. There is no way to show that that thesis is false. If there were, there would be a philosophically adequate refutation of skepticism. I believe, however, that the epistemic position of the Christian is demonstrably superior to any nonskeptical position, and it is for this thesis that I have tried to argue.

I am fully aware that my arguments will convert no one who is a firm adherent of any system of belief incompatible with Christianity. (If anyone who reads this essay thereupon becomes a Christian, that person was already a Christian—as regards propositional belief—when he began to read it; he just wasn't yet aware of the fact.) As I have pointed out, however, I could do no better with arguments for any controversial philosophical or political thesis—that is, for any philosophical or political thesis that is of any interest or importance.

I do not mean to suggest that my acceptance of the Church as an authority rests on my own unaided rational evaluation of the arguments I have given. No one who believes the Church could take that position, for the Church teaches that without the help of God, no one comes to Christian belief. But, for all that, the arguments I have given may provide sufficient rational support for (or good reasons for accepting) Christian belief. An argument may provide sufficient rational support for a belief and yet be impotent to produce that belief in some (or all) of those who hear and understand the argument. Almost everyone would admit this as a general truth, whatever disagreements there might be about particular cases. I expect that all readers of this essay will grant that there are arguments that provide sufficient rational support for the following propositions: "Jewish blood cannot be distinguished from Teutonic blood under a microscope"; "The earth is considerably more than 6,000 years old"; "The pyramids are not the work of extraterrestrial beings." And yet, there are those who have heard the arguments and deny the propositions. What I would say about the arguments that I have given is that, first, these arguments do lend rational support to Christian belief (but this assertion is not a part of my Christian faith; it is merely one of my opinions) and, secondly, I require God's help to find them convincing—indeed, even to find them faintly plausible. Hume has said, "Mere reason is insufficient to convince us of its [the Christian religion's] veracity: and whoever is moved by *faith* to assent to it is conscious of a continued miracle in his own person, which subverts all the principles of his understanding, and gives him a determination to believe what is most contrary to custom and experience." The Christian who ignores Hume's ironic intent and examines this statement seriously will find that it is very close to the truth in one way and very far from it in another. God's subversive miracle is indeed required for Christian belief, but what this miracle subverts is not the understanding but the flesh, the old Adam, our continued acquiescence in our inborn tendency to worship at an altar on which we have set ourselves. (For this is what Hume, although he does not know it, really means by "custom and experience.") And by this miracle the understanding is set free.

Notes

1. I had considerable difficulty with the notion of remarriage. But there is little doubt that both my wife's first marriage and mine were invalid by the standards of Rome—hers in fact *has* been annulled, in a proceeding instituted by her former husband—and I suppose that there is no point in being more Catholic than the pope.

2. "Critical Studies of the New Testament and the User of the New Testament" in *Hermes and Athena: Biblical Exegesis and Philosophical Theology,* Eleonore Stump and Thomas Flint (eds.) (South Bend, Ind. University of Notre Dame Press, 1993), pp. 159–190. The quoted passage occurs on p. 176f. The paper will be reprinted in my *God, Knowledge, and Mystery: Essays in Philosophical Theology,* forthcoming from Cornell University Press.

3. In *Lectures and Essays* (London: Macmillan, 1879).

4. To be precise, there are a few glancing references to religion in the essay, but the fact that they are references to religion, while it doubtless has its polemical function, is never essential to the point that Clifford is making. Clifford's ship

owner, it will be remembered, comes to his dishonest belief partly because he puts his trust in Providence. Another of Clifford's illustrative cases is built round an actual Victorian scandal (described in coyly abstract terms: "There was once a certain island in which . . .") involving religious persecution. But in neither case is the proposition that is dishonestly accepted without sufficient evidence a religious or theological proposition.

5. See "The Magnitude, Duration, and Distribution of Evil: A Theodicy," *Philosophical Topics* 16, 2 (1988), pp. 161–187, and "The Problem of Evil, the Problem of Air, and the Problem of Silence," *Philosophical Perspectives* 5 (1991), pp. 135–165. The latter will be reprinted, along with responses to some critics of the paper, in Daniel Howard-Snyder (ed.), *The Evidential Argument from Evil,* forthcoming from Indiana University Press. Both papers will be reprinted in *God, Knowledge, and Mystery.*

6. See "And Yet They Are Not Three Gods But One God," in Thomas V. Morris (ed.), *Philosophy and the Christian Faith* (South Bend, Ind.: Notre Dame University Press, 1988), pp. 241–278, and "Not by Confusion of Substance But by Unity of Person," in a *Festschrift* for Richard Swinburne, edited by Alan Padgett, to be published by Oxford University Press. Both essays will be reprinted in *God, Knowledge, and Mystery.*

7. See "Non Est Hick," in Thomas M. Senor (ed.), *The Rationality of Belief and the Plurality of Faith.* The essay will be reprinted in *God, Knowledge, and Mystery.*

8. See, however, the two "humanist manifestos" issued by the American Humanist Association. They are printed together in *Humanist Manifestoes I and II* (Buffalo, N.Y.: Prometheus Books, 1973). They are pretty mealy-mouthed compared with the "creed" in the text, and they are written in the worst sort of academic prose ("the nature of the universe depicted by modern science makes unacceptable any supernatural or cosmic guarantees of human values"), but they come to much the same thing.

9. For evidence that this is what the Enlightenment would really like, see Thomas V. Morris, *The Logic of God Incarnate* (Ithaca, N.Y.: Cornell University Press), pp. 170–181.

10. I am sorry to say that I do not remember where I read this.

11. My amateurish views on the history of science have been deeply influenced by the work of Stanley L. Jaki. I refer the interested reader to his Gifford Lectures, published as *The Road of Science and the Ways to God* (Chicago: University of Chicago Press, 1978).

12. But the story about this is somewhat confused. The Enlightenment believed that the young Church had stifled the vigorous adolescent science of antiquity but that the powerful Church of the sixteenth century was unable to dispose of the infant science of its day.

13. I have said something about the way in which (in my view) the Christian world view made the birth of science possible in a note (number 15) to "Non Est Hick."

14. George Mavrodes has presented a very interesting congruency argument in his essay "Religion and the Queerness of Morality," in Robert Audi and William J. Wainwright (eds.), *Rationality, Religious Belief, and Moral Commitment: New Essays in the Philosophy of Religion* (Ithaca, N.Y.: Cornell University Press, 1986), pp. 213–226. Mavrodes' thesis is that Christianity—or, more generally, a certain kind of theism—is congruent with a belief in the reality of moral obligation and that the creed of the Enlightenment is not.

15. I have borrowed this marvelous sentence from a talk I once heard Eleonore Stump give.

4

SEEK AND YOU

WILL FIND

Michael J. Murray

During the spring of 1983 I began my third semester in college giving serious consideration to the thought of becoming a philosophy major. I had taken a few courses and found the subject intriguing. More influential in my own considerations was the fact that I had recently converted to Christianity and had been encouraged by some early mentors in the faith to read the works of various Christian philosophers, both contemporary and classical. One evening that semester, I was studying for an upcoming exam when a friend, John, came to the door. From the look on his face, I knew he was after something; what, I wasn't sure. I had known John since arriving at college, having met him at the Christian Fellowship meetings on campus. John had grown up in a devoutly Christian home and had cultivated a deep love for and devotion to his faith. However, he had struggled academically and was especially troubled by the fact that his faith seemed to have little amicable contact with the view of the world set forth by his admittedly unsympathetic professors. John began telling me about the professor for his introductory philosophy class, who was, in his estimation, "leaning on" the theists in the class. He felt that every move in the course was calculated to reinforce the confidence of the atheist at the theist's expense. At the end of the most recent lecture, the professor ended the class, as he had each semester, by offering a challenge to his students: "If you can find anyone who is willing to come to offer a philosophical defense of theism," he mocked, "I will give them an entire class to do so."

Upon hearing this, I feared John was going to ask just what he proceeded to ask: "Would you try it?" Not surprisingly, I thought it unwise for someone with the full experience of one semester of philosophy under his belt to challenge a professor of nearly twenty years. Not to mention the fact that the one I would have to confront would likely be determining my future academic fate as one of my major professors. However, I thought there couldn't be much harm in approaching the professor to see how seriously his offer should be taken and what exactly he had in mind.

The next day I showed up at his office. Entering, I took a seat and told him that one of his students had informed me of his challenge. With a chuckle, I mentioned the fact that this student thought he was on a campaign to discredit the theists in the class. With no introduction and no commentary, he looked at me squarely and informed me: "One of my goals is that all of my students leave my class as atheists." I don't remember much more of our conversation that day, but I was haunted by that remark—and I am haunted by it to this day. From that point on, I became painfully aware that most faculty members had an agenda to sell to their students. Don't misunderstand; it was not that purveyors of contemporary higher education are engaged in some collaborative, self-aware brainwashing program, as many of my friends in evangelical churches seem to believe. The fact is that academics have their jobs because they are passionate about their subject matter and their particular views regarding it. It is tough to feign indifference concerning one's deeply held intellectual commitments in everyday life; it is simply impossible to do so when one is forced to lecture on them before an audience of students. As a result, the institution of higher learning has become, to a certain extent, a smorgasbord of the various deeply held perspectives, persuasions, and commitments of those who rise to the top of the various fields of inquiry. Yet, what kept me awake that night was not the reality of these conflicting, deeply held agendas, but the fact that I saw virtually no one representing the agenda of the devout theist, not to mention the Christian theist. It was at that point that I first came to see the importance of Christians in the academic arena.

Unlike many, my embracing of Christianity did not begin in early childhood. My parents were Roman Catholic, but my upbringing was roughly areligious. We occasionally attended Sunday mass during my earliest years, but it was not long after that such observance generally ceased. I am not sure at what point I first began to give serious consideration to the question of whether or not God exists, but I had some sincere convictions about the matter by the time I was thirteen or fourteen years old—and they were not sympathetic with theism. I was enrolled at a Catholic school at the time and used to visit the home of a friend whose mother considered herself devoutly Catholic. For whatever reason, presumably because she felt it to be conducive to my good, she consistently asked me whether I had gone to mass that week. To this I replied, as I always did, "Why should I?" Each time she responded the same way, with a touch of horror in her voice, "Well, Michael, don't you believe in God?" To this I answered, as I always did, "Nope." Unfortunately, our discussions rarely exhibited much more intellectual depth than that.

As I look back on those exchanges, I wish she had pursued the matter further. Why did I believe as I did? Why did *she* believe as *she* did? Even if she did not have the resources to take the discussion further, why didn't she direct me to someone who could? It was not that I was overly anxious to enter into deep philosophical discussions with this person, especially in light of the far more attractive alternatives of swimming or playing basketball with my friends. Yet, her silence always struck me as one more sure sign that there were no considerations in favor of theism. Thus, while I continued to listen to what I considered the nonsense I was taught in catechism classes, I also continued to give my teachers a hard time. It was hard not to enjoy the fact that it seemed so easy to score points for the atheist against these half-wits.

It was not until the summer of 1980 that I met someone who, like me, thought the intellectual integrity of Christian theism needed some defense. Unlike me, however, he thought such a defense existed. For two years leading up to that time I had been working at a landscaping firm that grew its own plant stock. That summer I again drew the duty of repotting the container-grown nursery stock. This entailed standing at a plywood table for eight hours per day until all of the roughly 10,000 to 12,000 plants were finished. Intellectually stimulating as this work was, I thought it best to share it with someone, so I implored the owner of the operation to hire a friend of mine to help manage the task. He consented, and we set to work. By force of monotonous repetition, we found ourselves canvassing just about every topic seventeen-year-old minds could dredge up. What I didn't know then was that Preston was not just a bright friend but a bright theist—and one with a somewhat evangelistic leaning. As a result, I had unwittingly established myself as his next target.

His own representation of his faith began as a personal matter. He simply began telling me what he believed—that God, an all-perfect being, created all that is, including human beings who freely chose to disobey God and bring eternal condemnation on themselves. God in His mercy, however, sought to deliver all humans from their fallen state and thus sent His fully human/fully divine son to earth to surrender his life as propitiation for our sins, providing us an opportunity to exercise faith in him, effecting our reconciliation. Not surprisingly, I had little patience for such talk, but as long as he wasn't trying to sell *me* on it, I was happy to listen.

It was not long, however, before he was no longer happy to simply give me a daily lecture. He began to mention the fact that, by his lights, all of humanity both stood under condemnation and had access to redemption through Christ's atonement. He would regularly repeat to me Christ's words of Revelation 3:20 "Behold I stand at the door and knock. If anyone hears my voice and opens the door, I will come in and eat with him and he with me." After a time he reminded me of Christ's words of invitation by simply knocking on the plywood table when I happened to be looking away. When I turned to look he would look at the sky with a puzzled face, only to ask, "I wonder who that was?"

I would regularly rebuff such advances because I simply could not bring myself to believe that the God of the Christians existed. In light of all the unanswered questions I had raised to the theists who desperately tried to teach me, Christianity just had, for me, the evident light of falsity. My primary intellectual obstacle to belief sprang from my own rendering of the problem of evil. Many people I have spoken with who reject theism do so in virtue of the fact that they, in the company of numerous contemporary intellectuals, are simply unable to reconcile the existence of evil with the existence of the God of Christian theism. For most of them, however, the problem seems to be an abstract, philosophical objection. For me, the pain of evil in the world was all too real. Early in my life, my father became an alcoholic, and as he continued to find solace in the bottle, he became increasingly abusive. Unfortunately, it was my mother who bore the brunt of the abuse. My two sisters and I endured too many endless nights as we helplessly listened to my father mistreat her.

Not surprisingly, their marriage of twenty-five years ended in a painful and tumultuous divorce. This was, of course, a traumatic experience for a ten-year-old, and one that took its toll on me. In addition to a litany of behavioral problems, I developed a case of the shingles described by a dermatologist as the worst case that he had ever seen in any patient of my age. Now, seven years later, as I was confronted with the Christian gospel, thoughts of these early years haunted me desperately. How could a God of this sort allow my mother and family to endure such horrors? These inner struggles exploded one day as Preston and I drove to a job site. My mind was filled with thoughts of my dad, who had recently been released from a rehabilitation program. My suspicion, later confirmed, was that he had been drinking again. Preston was rehearsing some argument for something or other when I let loose. I remember screaming at him that God would never allow the evils that I had experienced and that unless he had an answer to that, he would do well to keep his mouth shut.

There was an embarrassing silence for both of us after that exchange. It was broken only by Preston's humble remark: "I don't know why God would allow such a thing to happen." At the time, I took his silence and his response as a victory on my part; I think most critics of theism would similarly regard such a confession. However, I now think that my own satisfaction in his answer was misplaced. In fact, as I look back on his answer, it seems to me just the answer I would now give if confronted with the same question. One reason I would respond this way is that it's true. I don't know why God permitted me or members of my family to undergo such suffering. But I don't take this response to constitute a concession to the non-theist simply because there is no reason to think that I would know why God might permit a particular instance of suffering. There are at least three reasons for this.

The first reason is that there may be no particular reason why God permits a certain evil to occur. It may shock both the theist and the non-theist that I am willing to entertain such a possibility. For those who cut their theological teeth on biblical verses like "all things work together for good for those who love God and are called according to his purpose" (Rom. 8:28), it can appear heterodox at best to suggest that some such events may occur without reason. Undoubtedly, there is always some sense in which there is a reason for God's allowing any event that occurs. Whatever reason led God to choose to create the world would, by extension, count as a reason for permitting a particular event contained in it. But what I had in mind at the time was this question: Why would God create the world that contains these very evil events as opposed to some other world that does not contain them? The answer to this question may simply be that there is no answer and, further, that this should not trouble the theist.

To see why this is so, consider the following illustration. I need a new car, so I head to the car dealer to buy one. My intention is to buy a sporty, red 1994 Ford Taurus SHO with antilock brakes, a power accessory package, cassette player, and factory-installed security system. While the antilock brakes are very important to me, I judge the other options to be of similar, but secondary, importance. Now, suppose that I go to the lot and find that the cars in stock are the only 1994s available and that no more will be delivered or can be ordered. Of the 1994 SHOs on the lot, three are red and one is white. One of the red ones lacks antilock brakes. But of the remaining cars, each has all of the options I desire except one. One of the red ones lacks the security system; the other, a cassette player. The white one lacks only the red color. Since my preferences leave me indifferent among these three, I pick the red one without the security system and drive it home. I tell my wife what happened, and after admiring the car, she asks why I chose the car that lacked the security system. I respond that each of the three cars with antilock brakes lacked one feature that we wanted, and since we valued all the other options equally, I just picked this one. If she were to press the issue and insist that there must be some *reason* that I chose the one lacking the security system over the others, what more could I say? There was no reason. I had to pick one, and that car's deficiency was as bad as those of the other cars.

It seems to me that the theist might be able to say the same about some instances of evil in the world. If God wants to create a world with free creatures, He is to some extent limited by their whims. God cannot ever create me in such a way that I am free and that I willingly choose to, say, torture myself for fun. I simply would never freely choose to do such a thing. As a result, if there is some reason why God wants to create a world with me in it, He will have to forgo any plans that include my engaging in that activity. But if God is limited in this way it may be that there is no world that God can create that has as desirable a balance of good over evil as this world and that lacks evil altogether. In other words, any world God can bring about with free creatures might be a world with some, maybe even a significant, amount of evil.

Given that this is so, we can see how God's situation vis-à-vis creation is similar to my purchase of the car described above. It may be that all the worlds God can create have some feature that, considered in isolation, God would prefer not to actualize. Surely, some of these worlds have an amount of evil, or a balance of good over evil, that precludes them from being created by any omnibenevolent being. But of those worlds that are not precluded in this way, it seems that God may choose among them the way I would choose among the cars. While I do not want my car to lack any of the features I desire, none of my available choices satisfies all my desiderata. As a result, while the car I pick has a certain deficiency, there is no particular reason why my car has one sort of deficiency as opposed to another; I simply picked one. Likewise, it may be that there is no particular reason why God permits some *particular evil* to occur other than that all creatable worlds possess some defects and this is the one God selected.[1]

Undoubtedly, this account will offend those who think that scriptural texts such as Ephesians 1:11, which proclaims that God "works out *everything* in conformity with the purpose of his will,"[2] rule out God's actualizing features of the world for "no particular reason." Yet, even if that is not the case, there are other reasons why the theist need not feel uncomfortable with confessing ignorance about the reason for the existence of evils. For example, why would we think that the theistic God would reveal to us the reasons for all or even most of the particular evils we encounter? It is hard to see how one might argue that God is obliged to do so. Furthermore, there may be occasions on which it is counterproductive to do so. I have a friend whose teenage son likes to fix cars. But, like many teenagers, he is notorious about not returning his tools to their place. Despite my friend's repeated attempts to get him to change his ways and his warnings that one day the boy will not be able to find what he is looking for, the bad habit continued. One day he learned that his son was to have a friend over to tune up an old car, and he decided to teach him a lesson. He found his timing light and hid it in a little-used drawer in the garage. As the son began work, he discovered that the light was missing and spent two frantic hours tracking it down. When he finally discovered it, he believed it was just another instance of his own bumbling and began to realize the importance of being organized.

While this boy learned his lesson because his father hid the tool, he did so only in virtue of his mistaken belief that *he* had lost it. If, after he discovered the tool, my friend had told him that he had put it there, the boy may have continued in his old pattern, either out of resentment toward the father or because he continued to believe that the bad habit was not responsible for his trouble. It is easy to see how analogous principles may well apply in numerous instances of evil where creatures suffer. The point here is not that God manipulates us as the father did his son, but simply that there can be cases in which our ignorance of the circumstances that led us into a certain difficulty is required for us to learn from it. Thus, as with the case of the teenage son, even if God *could* tell us the reason for our suffering, doing so may well thwart some function it is intended to serve.

Finally, it may well be that for many instances of evil, if God were to reveal the reason for permitting a certain evil, I would not be able to understand it or the connection between it and God's permission of the evil. The Scriptures often portray the relationship between God and His creatures in terms of the relationship between parent and child. And this thought picture provides us with numerous helpful insights into how we might conceptualize our relationship with God. In the case of earthly parents, it is their responsibility, during the child's early years, to see that the child is kept from harms of which the child cannot be aware. If I were at Busch Gardens with my two-year-old and he decided to make a rush for the alligator pond to take a swim, I would be permitted to thwart him, even if doing so caused him the pain of being pulled back by his arm. He might well wonder why I kept him from the perceived good of swimming and why, further I inflicted pain on him. Yet, even if I were to explain it to him, it is easy to imagine that he would have no way of conceptualizing what would have happened to him if I had not restrained him. He might not understand what it means to be "eaten by an alligator" or why being eaten would be a bad thing for him. For whatever reason, he simply lacks the cognitive capacity for assessing what is in his own interests in such a situation. Similarly, an omniscient God may well have reasons for permitting certain evils, reasons that He could even explain to us if we asked. But, as above, His doing so would provide no guarantee that we would be able to understand the answer or how that answer justified God permitting the evil that He did.

Thus, however painful it might be for us to accept at times, we are rarely able to find consolation in our sufferings through our knowledge of the greater good they will bring about. This is either because they will yield no such greater good, since there is no reason for *them* in the first place, or because, for one reason or another, God does not see fit to tell us what goods He intends to bring from them.

A critic might respond here that all of these remarks are well and good but that they sidestep the *real* issue raised by the problem of evil. In the above, I discuss how we can reconcile the theist's ignorance about the cause of particular evils with his belief in the existence of God. But all of this assumes something the critic might deny here: that it is possible in the first place that a perfect being could ever create a world that contains evil. As the argument is so often put: If God is omnipotent, He can prevent all evil; if He is omnibenevolent, He desires to prevent all evil; if He is omniscient, He is aware of all evil; hence, there ought be no evil. But, there is evil, so either God does not exist or He does not have at least one of the characteristics described. This argument is commonly dubbed the *logical* problem of evil in virtue of the fact that it asserts the logical incompatibility of the existence of God and a creation containing evil.

I will not address this problem here, since this argument has been largely put to rest in the recent literature.[3] However, it is worth noting that I have already hinted at one of the more widely employed solutions to this problem earlier. This solution relies on the possibility that there is no world that God can create that (1) contains free creatures and (2) contains a greater balance of good over evil than this world. Again, the reason for this is that God is limited in what He can create by the free choices creatures would make if they were created. It should be noted, though, that this does not entail any limitation of the divine power. God's inability to determine the outcome of a creature's free act does not obtain because of a limitation on God's power, but simply in virtue of the fact that it is impossible to determine the course of the choices of creatures while leaving those choices free. God could no more pull this off than He could create a round square.

But even once I had become satisfied regarding the problem of evil, there was a second, closely related problem that troubled me. Not only was there what I took to be striking evidence *against* God's existence, there was an egregiously conspicuous absence of evidence *in favor* of it. If, as the Christian story claims, ultimate human fulfillment comes by way of a relationship with the divine, it seemed inconceivable to me that this divine being could not do more to bring His creatures to believe in the truth of Christianity, if not at least in the truth of bare theism. Nietzsche put the matter this way:

> A god who is all-knowing and all powerful and who does not even make sure his creatures understand his intention—could that be a god of goodness? Who allows countless doubts and dubieties to persist, for thousands of years, as though the salvation of mankind were unaffected by them, and who on the other hand holds out the prospect of frightful consequences if any mistake is made as to the nature of truth? Would he not be a cruel god if he possessed the truth and could behold mankind miserably tormenting itself over the truth?—But perhaps he is a god of goodness notwithstanding—and merely *could* express himself more clearly! Did he perhaps lack the intelligence to do so? Or the eloquence? So much the worse! For then he was perhaps also in error as to that which he calls his "truth," and is himself not so very far from being the "poor deluded devil"! Must he not then endure almost the torments of Hell to have to see his creatures suffer so, and go on suffering even more through all eternity, for the sake of knowledge of him, and *not* be able to help and counsel them, except in the manner of a deaf and dumb man making all kinds of ambiguous signs when the most fearful danger is

> about to befall on his child or his dog? ... All reli-
> gions exhibit traces of the fact that they owe their
> origin to an early, immature intellectuality in man—
> they all take astonishingly *lightly* the duty to tell the
> truth: they as yet know nothing of a *Duty of God* to
> be truthful towards mankind and clear in the manner
> of his communications.[4]

The problem seems to be an obvious one, and one that has occurred to theist and nontheist alike. What is particularly striking about this problem is the fact that it has received so little attention in the recent literature on philosophy of religion.

Above, I said that I consider this to be a problem related to the problem of evil. The reason for this is that the theist claims that the greatest good one can know is the fulfillment that comes through being personally related to God. Yet, the fact that God's existence is not at all evident to us seems to introduce a significant barrier to our coming to have the knowledge required for entering into that relationship. As a result, the problem here seems to reduce to this: Why does God allow conditions to prevail, divine hiddenness in this case, that seem to lead to such a severe and pervasive evil as unbelief? The problem is only heightened when one considers that much of the Christian tradition has affirmed that failure to believe does not entail merely that the creature misses the temporal benefits that accompany fellowship with the creator, but that the creature also suffers eternal damnation. The theist, it seems, has some explaining to do.

While I do not recall what Preston had to say about this matter at the time, I do remember that I was satisfied with the answer. Since then, however, I have continued to wrestle with this problem. My own conviction is that, as with the general problem of evil, I have no idea why God does not, in fact, do more to make His existence obvious to us. However, I believe that we can show that divine hiddenness is at least consistent with the Christian conception of God. One way of doing this is by arguing that if God were to make the truths of the faith, including His existence, our separation from God in virtue of sin, the availability of redemption through Christ's atonement, and so on fully evident to us, we would lose the ability to make choices that are both free and morally significant.

I have argued elsewhere that if God were to make the truths of the faith evident to us in too forceful a way, it would be tantamount to the coercion one experiences when threatened by a mugger. Just as the mugger coerces us to hand over our wallet by sticking a gun in our back, God could rob us of our freedom by confronting us with threats of temporal suffering or eternal damnation. Of course, God cannot leave the truths of the faith entirely hidden from us either. How could we justifiably be held accountable for a failure to believe something for which there was no evidence? Thus, the epistemic forcefulness of the truth of Christianity must fall somewhere short of what constitutes coercion, leaving creatures free to determine their own course in a morally significant way, but somewhere beyond a total absence of evidence, in order to ensure that the creatures can make a decision responsibly.

How could God mitigate the coercive pressure that is engendered in the central tenets of orthodox Christianity? This question leads us to the heart of the issue of coercive threats and how they impair one's ability to act freely. Seen in this way, there are at least four ways that God might be able to act to attenuate the coercive force of the threats attending Christianity. First, God might reduce the *strength* of the threat. The less significant the threat, the less coerced one is. On this approach, God would have to mitigate among other things the penalty of eternal damnation for failure to believe. However, according to the Christian theist, God has not availed Himself of this alternative. Second, God might mitigate the potential for coercion by making the threat less imminent. This feature of coercion can be limited in three ways. First, God can lead the threatened person to believe that there is some *uncertainty* as to whether the threat can actually be carried out. The less probable it is that a threat will be carried out, the less coerced one is. Second, God can *postpone* the threatened consequence until long after one fails to comply with the threat. It seems to be a general feature of coercive situations that the further we temporally remove the carrying out of the threat, the less coerced one is. In this way the force of coercion is mitigated, as it is when one is, say, less inclined to tackle an opponent in a football game in a way that he knows will immediately dislocate his shoulder, while he will engage in drill techniques that will bring equal or even greater bodily harm to him in ten or twelve years. The penalty for each act is the same, but the temporal distance between act and consequence in the latter case leaves him feeling far less coerced than in cases of the former type.

Yet none of these methods of mitigating the force of the threat are helpful here. Mitigating the threat's strength is not an option since, according to the Christian theist, the penalty for a failure to believe is fixed. Nor will mitigating either of the two types of imminence help in this case. This is so because, first, carrying out the threatened consequence is absolutely certain on the Christian picture and, second, because merely reducing the temporal imminence of the threat does not appear to be a sufficient guarantee that that creature's freedom is not compromised by the sorts of threats portrayed in damnation. Given the strength of the threat involved, it does not seem that merely delaying the carrying out of the threat is sufficient to mitigate compulsion. If it were, it appears that we could allow that God would reveal Himself in a spectacular display of celestial fireworks, issuing the relevant temporal and eternal threats, and yet not have the actions of free creatures be compelled by the issuing of such threats. It appears, however, that the actions of such free creatures clearly *would be* compelled if they were to be confronted by such obvious threats.

There is, however, a third type of imminence that might be adjusted in order to mitigate the force of the threat implied by the Christian picture. It is what I will call *epistemic imminence*. Epistemic imminence is difficult to characterize, but it is this feature of a threat that explains, for example, why massive advertising campaigns against drunk driving prove largely effective. In general, these ads do not provide the viewer with new information about the dangers of drinking and driving. Still, the powerful visual images portrayed in these campaigns make the dangers associated with the practice far more "epistemically forceful" and force us to realize just how bad such actions are. In general, then, the more epistemically imminent the threat, the more coerced one is. Thus, one way to mitigate the force of threats is by mitigating epistemic imminence. My contention is that, given the truth of orthodox Christian theism, this is the only way for God to mitigate the threat in such a way that it allows Him to preserve the freedom and autonomy of His creatures to make morally significant free choices. Furthermore, since some people are simply more susceptible to coercion by threats, God must limit the amount and strength of general revelation to a level that leaves all of His creatures free from this sort of coercion.[5]

While neither of these early worries of mine were addressed in such detailed fashion, it is worth noting that my objections were not as clearly formulated at the time either, a fact that will not surprise anyone who has taught philosophy to first-year undergraduates. Still, in the course of my early deliberations about Christianity, the things that I read convinced me that the resources were at least available for making reasoned, and reasonable, stabs at resolving these difficulties. Of course, clearing the decks of objections against the faith is not equivalent to giving positive reasons for believing its truth. As I reflect on my own early thoughts about Christianity, I now realize that the single most powerful positive consideration raised in favor of Christian theism was, by my lights, one that still has great currency among popular Christian apologists. In fact, it is an argument that I still discuss routinely when I am asked to speak to student groups on various campuses about my own religious convictions. The argument focuses on the historical reliability of the accounts of Christ's resurrection.

There has been a great deal of discussion about the resurrection and its interpretation by theologians in the twentieth century. Many recent liberal theologians have entirely rejected not only the historical reality, but even the possibility, that Christ was bodily resurrected from the dead. Yet, to naive readers, of whom I am confessedly one, the writings of these theologians smack of modernist accommodationism. Such theologians have retreated from the historical position of the church simply because the possibility or intelligibility of miracles has been called into question by certain philosophical arguments of dubious merit. For my purposes, I will ignore this dispute and treat the resurrection as it has been univocally treated by the historical confessions of the church. On this reading, Christ was crucified, buried, and rose from the dead, bodily, on the third day.

Scripture is categorical in its affirmation of the centrality of the historical resurrection to the faith. In his first letter to the Corinthians, Paul makes it clear that the claims of Christianity stand or fall on the historicity of the event:

> and if Christ has not been raised, then our proclama-
> tion has been in vain and your faith has been in vain.
> We are even found to be misrepresenting God, be-
> cause we testified of God that he raised Christ—
> whom he did not raise if it is true that the dead are not
> raised. For if the dead are not raised, then Christ has
> not been raised. If Christ has not been raised, your
> faith is futile and you are still in your sins. Then those
> who have died in Christ have perished. If for this life
> only we have hoped in Christ, we are of all people
> most to be pitied. (I Cor. 15: 14–19)

Paul makes a bold claim here in tying the truth of Christianity to the truth of a particular historical event. Disprove it, says Paul, and Christianity is doomed. Christians have thereby been led to wonder what sort of historical evidence there is to support the resurrection.

The central argument in favor of the historical veracity of the resurrection has traditionally been framed as follows: There is virtual unanimity among historical scholars, Christian and non-Christian alike, about at least the following: that there was a man by the name of Jesus who lived in first-century Palestine, that during a short period of time he preached a message about the coming kingdom of God, that he attracted a small band of followers, that he was crucified by the Roman authorities, and that the same followers later claimed to have witnessed his resurrected body. Nothing is particularly surprising or noteworthy here until we consider that neither the prevailing civil nor religious authorities of the time were particularly pleased with the upstart Christian movement, for obvious reasons. The Jews realized that all of the early converts to Christianity came from among their ranks, and the Romans feared political rebellion and were disconcerted by the early Christians' failure to proclaim allegiance to Caeser as a divinity. In light of the fact that the Christian faith was centrally grounded in the resurrection, the easiest way for the authorities to derail the early movement would have been to produce the dead body of Jesus. But the historical record is conspicuous for the fact that no one ever claimed to have been able to do just this. As a result, it appears that we must conclude that the tomb was empty. For if it had not been, it would have been easy for the church's early critics to refute their claims. How then is the empty tomb to be explained?

More than one explanation has been offered, and my brief treatment here does not permit an examination of all of the proposed alternatives.[6] It will suffice to say that the only alternative that has any historical plausibility is the first explanation ever proposed. It is recorded in Matthew 28:11–15:

> While they were going, some of the guards went into
> the city and told the chief priests everything that had
> happened. After the priests had assembled with the
> elders, they devised a plan to give a large sum of
> money to the soldiers, telling them, "You must say,

'His disciples came by night and stole him away while we were asleep.' If this comes to the governors ears, we will satisfy him and keep you out of trouble." So they took the money and did as they were directed. And this story is told amongst the Jews until this day.

Of course, Matthew here represents the theory as fiction, but the critic might well regard the explanation as the most plausible rendering of the historical facts. On further consideration, however, this explanation seems to have little if any merit. The reason for this is that many of the early witnesses of the resurrection were martyred for their failure to renounce their faith. What is surprising about this, of course, is that while it is easy to imagine someone who would willingly die for what he believes to be *true*, as evidenced by the 1993 mass suicide of the Branch Davidians in Waco, Texas, or, earlier, in Guyana, it is virtually impossible to believe that someone would die for what he knows to be *false*.

Charles Colson, White House Special Counsel to Richard Nixon during his first term of office, noted this fact in his comparison of the situation of the early followers of Christ and those involved in the Watergate cover-up:

> With the most powerful office in the world at stake, a small band of hand-picked loyalists, no more than ten of us, could not hold a conspiracy together for more than two weeks. Think of what was at stake. . . . Yet even the prospects of jeopardizing the President we'd worked so hard to elect, of losing the prestige, power and personal luxury of our offices was not enough incentive to make this group of men contain a lie. Nor as I reflect today, was the pressure really all that great; at that point there had certainly been some moral failures, criminal violations, even perjury by some. . . . But no one was in grave danger; *no one's life was at stake. . . .*
>
> This is why the Watergate experience is so instructive for me. If John Dean and the rest of us were so panic-stricken, not by the prospect of beatings and execution, but by political disgrace and a possible prison term, one can only speculate about the emotions of the disciples . . . they clung tenaciously to their enormously offensive story that their leader had risen from his ignoble death and was alive. . . .
>
> Is it really likely, then, that a deliberate cover-up, a plot to perpetuate a lie about the Resurrection, could have survived the violent persecution of the apostles, the scrutiny of early church councils, the horrendous purge of first-century believers who were cast by the thousands to the lions for refusing to denounce the Lordship of Christ?[7]

Long before Colson, Pascal similarly observed just how unlikely it is that the disciples would continue in such a conspiracy when faced with the penalties associated with it:

> The hypothesis that the apostles were knaves is quite absurd. Follow it out to the end and imagine these twelve men meeting after Jesus' death and conspiring to say that he had risen from the dead. This means attacking all the powers that be. *The human heart is singularly susceptible to fickleness, to change, to promises, to bribery.* One of them had only to deny his story under these inducements, or still more because of possible imprisonments, torture and death, and they would all have been lost.[8]

We are left to decide, then, what the most plausible explanation is for these historical realities. If one rules out miracle from the realm of logical posssibility, or perhaps takes the weaker Humean line that we are never in an epistemic position that justifiably permits the belief that a miracle has occurred, no amount of historical stage-setting will make this argument plausible, much less compelling. But if one does not find arguments for those conclusions sound, and I believe one should not, the competing explanations must be judged on their merits. By my lights, it is simply impossible to believe that the early disciples, who clearly were not anticipating the resurrection, could have been so resolutely emboldened by their belief in the resurrection that they would remain firm in their conviction in the face of death, unless they had been actual witnesses of the resurrected Christ.

After giving these matters all the careful attention a seventeen-year-old could give them, I began to feel God was calling me. Once we are disarmed of the intellectual barriers that we use to shield ourselves from God, the call of God becomes awfully clear. This was never more true than one hot September evening in 1980 when I called Preston to review matters one last time. By the end of the conversation, I told him that I felt God was moving me to repentance, and I hung up and prayed for the first time. This "calling" is surely mysterious to those who are not Christians—it was to me before my own conversion. There was no voice calling "Take up, read" but the subtle call is well expressed as the "still, small voice."

From that point on, I became increasingly interested in the whole gamut of questions that the intellectually curious believer soon latches on to. This curiosity followed me to college, where I learned that the same issues that fueled my own doubts were pervasive among other undergraduates. As I talked with them and they with me, it became apparent that my experience had been theirs—that for most of their years, even those who had been raised in church-going families had never encountered someone who was willing, much less able, to present Christianity in an intellectually appealing way. As a result, they were fascinated that individuals even existed who had thought through their own faith in a rigorous manner.

I soon realized that my attraction to these topics and discussions represented a permanent condition, and thus thought that philosophy would provide me with a way of cultivating both the skills and the knowledge required to approach these matters more clearly. It was no surprise to me to discover that recent philosophical trends had been largely antagonistic to the Christian picture of the world. As a result, I had braced myself for the inevitable onslaught of challenges that I received from my mentors. The experience they provided in this regard was extremely valuable, not only because it allowed me to sharpen my philosophical skills, but also because it brought me into contact, for the first time, with the work being done by contemporary Christian philosophers, many of whom appear in this volume.

Since attending graduate school, I have realized that the Christian academic continues to face formidable and healthy challenges to the faith. As a result, we Christian philosophers face a mandate we are all too conscious of: not only responding to these external challenges but getting the consistency of our internal house in order as well. My own interests have focused primarily on the latter task. In doing so, I have also come to a deep appreciation for the wealth of philosophical and spiritual genius represented by our philosophical heritage, which we have too easily abandoned. For the Christian philosopher, the history of philosophy is in large measure a story of other thinkers who were confronted with the same puzzles and dilemmas we face. My own work in seventeenth-century philosophical theology has convinced me that much recent work in Christian philosophy is not just reinventing the wheel, but reinventing a wheel that is not as good as the original. Of course, this is not always the case. But it will suffice to say that none of us would be worse off for having a far greater acquaintance with the great Christian thinkers in whose wake we stand.

I took my friend up on his challenge to address the Introduction to Philosophy class during my sophomore year. I spent a couple of weeks poring over the notes of some of the more reliable students in the course, trying to pick up on the arguments that had been flying in the class. When the event finally came off, I was unnerved to find out that not only was the philosophy professor there, but two other faculty members as well, a physicist and a mathematician. I had put together a presentation of the cosmological argument intended to bypass the objections that had been raised in the class, and spent some time discussing the problem of evil that had vexed me as an unbeliever. The presentation went well, and the students were particularly receptive—just defending their own, I am sure. While the other two professors asked questions, the professor of the course, by prior agreement, did not engage me in the class. Afterward, the students flocked around him to ask him what he thought and whether or not he was convinced. "Not yet," was his reply. When the students asked me if I was surprised or disappointed that I had failed to change his mind, I said, "No, I'm not surprised. But there is still hope."

Today, my office adjoins this professor's office. He is now not only my former professor but my colleague. We continue to discuss the issues that divide us, and his answer continues to be "Not yet." But I have hope.

Notes

1. A far more detailed, near-relative of this argument is developed by Peter van Inwagen in "The Place of Chance in a World Sustained by God," in *Divine and Human Action*, Thomas V. Morris (ed.) (Ithaca, N.Y.: Cornell University Press, 1988), pp. 211–235.

2. Italics mine. Some have objected that since this verse and the earlier cited Romans 8:28 rule out the first response, the *Christian* theist cannot entertain it. This may be true, although it is far from clear to me that these two verses in fact rule out this response. These two verses only seem to state that God, as it were, works everything out in the end. But this does not entail that each event in creation is directly intended by God, only that He will ultimately bring the totality of events to a conclusion consonant with His purposes.

3. See, for example, Alvin Plantinga's *God, Freedom, and Evil* (Grand Rapids, Mich.: Wm. B. Eerdmans, 1974).

4. Friedrich Nietzsche, *Daybreak*, trans. R. J. Hollingsdale (Cambridge: Cambridge University Press, 1982), pp. 89–90.

5. Further developments of these themes can by found in my "Coercion and the Hiddenness of God," *American Philosophical Quarterly* 30, 1 (1993), pp. 27–38.

6. Further discussions of this argument can be found in William Craig's *Assessing the New Testament Evidence for the Historicity of the Resurrection of Jesus* (New York: Edwin Mellon Press, 1989), and Stephen T. Davis, "Is It Possible to Know That Jesus Was Raised from The Dead?" *Faith and Philosophy* 1 (April 1984), pp. 147–159. An interesting, although somewhat dated, historical treatment of the issue can be found in Frank Morison's *Who Moved the Stone?* (New York: Century Company, 1930).

7. *Loving God* (Grand Rapids, Mich.: Zondervan, 1983), pp. 66–68.

8. *Pensées*, Alban Krailsheimer (trans.) (New York: Penguin Classics, 1966), p. 125.

5

SKEPTICISM,

ROMANTICISM,

AND FAITH

William J. Wainwright

My religious and intellectual life has been devoid of dramatic incident and radical change; looking back, I clearly see that the boy I was is indeed the father of the man. I therefore propose to address the task Tom Morris has set us by speaking of features of my life and thought that have remained fairly constant and have shaped the way I look at things.

One is a certain constitutional skepticism. I have been told that as a preschooler, I expressed doubts as to whether my mother really knew that the refrigerator light went out when the door was closed, cogently pointing out that since she wasn't inside, she could hardly know whether it was on or not. I also remember my chagrin and anger when told at six that Santa Claus didn't exist and my determination to never again let myself be deceived on an important matter.

I was brought up as a Presbyterian, attending Sunday school, Bible school, and church camps in the summer until adolescence. I was also probably influenced by my mother's piety to a certain extent, although my father didn't attend church. Be this as it may, I can't remember a time when religion didn't seem to me a serious business demanding deep thought and calling for serious commitment. (Because of my reserve and fastidiousness, however, I can recall being both embarrassed and put off by some of its more exuberant manifestations—"calls" at church camps, for example.)

Truths that I had accepted uncritically were first called into serious question for me by what I now realize must have been a very bad book. I was fond of a series that contained such titles as *Living Biographies of Great Inventors, Living Biographies of Great Explorers,* and so on. (My favorites were the volumes devoted to poets, novelists, composers, and artists.) When I was thirteen, I was given *Living Biographies of Great Philosophers* and was deeply taken by what I could gather of the ideas of figures like Plato, Kant, and Schopenhauer. (I remember being struck by these in particular.) One of the book's effects, however, was to make me acutely conscious of the fact that a number of highly intelligent people didn't believe what I did and had reasons for their disbelief. Their doubts fanned the fires of my own latent skepticism, and to this day I find it difficult to embrace *any* controversial belief without *some* hesitation. It is easier for me to detect weaknesses in an argument than to construct one and very easy for me to look at my beliefs through the eyes of my critical opponents.

Why, then, am I not a skeptic? Because, for one thing, over the years, the sort of classical theistic metaphysics found in Samuel Clarke or Jonathan Edwards has seemed more reasonable to me, on the whole, than its alternatives. At a fairly early point in my philosophical career, I became convinced that most criticisms of theistic metaphysics are weaker than they are commonly thought to be. (Kant's criticisms of standard arguments for God's existence are a good example.) By my late twenties, I had come to believe that classical theistic metaphysics survives criticism at least as well as, and probably better than, its competitors. Most of my published work has been designed to help show this.

Even so, I continue to be skeptical about the adequacy of even our best metaphysics. My skepticism, in other words, is not so much about this or that proposition—the belief in immortality, for example, or God's providential governance of human affairs—for these doctrines are credible if theism is true. It is both more general and deeper—a sense of the wretched insufficiency of all our reasoning about anything but the most mundane matters. In part, I suppose, this is a kind of Kantian doubt about our ability to grasp the *ding-an-sich*. This doubt becomes particularly acute, however, when thought's object is the ground of all being. Given the latter's transcendence and human reason's limitations, it is difficult to avoid the suspicion that even our best formulations are only "straw."[1] If one is also sensitive to the ways in which reasoning can be distorted by infantilism, wishful thinking, egoism, cultural bias, and so forth, this suspicion can only be deepened. Freud and Marx are instructive on this point, but so is John Calvin:

> Mingled vanity and pride appear in this, that when miserable men do seek after God, instead of ascending higher than themselves, as they ought to do, they measure him by their own carnal stupidity, and neglecting solid inquiry, fly off to indulge their curiosity in vain speculation. Hence they do not conceive of him in the character in which he is manifested but imagine him to be whatever their own rashness has devised. . . . With such an idea of God, nothing which they may attempt to offer in the way of worship or obedience can have any value in his sight, because it is not him they worship, but, instead of him, the dream and figment of their heart.[2]

It is not surprising, then, that I have long been sympathetic to the negative theology of a pseudo-Dionysius and to Luther's, Calvin's, and Pascal's animadversions on the powers of natural reason. Nor is it surprising that I was at one time strongly attracted to Kierkegaard. In spite of my suspicion of reason, however, I have never despaired of it. And, as I have said, theistic metaphysics seems more reasonable to me, on balance, than its competitors. Although its difficulties are well known, the problems with alternatives seem greater.

Then, too, my congenital skepticism couldn't help but make me suspect that I might be duped if I *didn't* trust what James called my *believing tendencies*. In other words, I have never been able to repress the suspicion that (as he says) the heart "may be our "deepest organ of communication" with reality.[3] Something has always seemed right to me about views that (like Pascal's, Coleridge's, or James's) assign a legitimate role to the heart in the formation of our deepest beliefs, and I have been correspondingly suspicious of views that discount it. (I spent a fair amount of time in my late twenties, for example, reading Gabriel Marcel. I was attracted by the way in which he combined analytic skill [see his *Metaphysical Journal*] with an insistence that some real issues can't be resolved by analytic intelligence but must instead be addressed by a kind of thinking rooted in openness to Being.) Only in the last few years, however, have I begun to suspect the extent to which "considerations of the heart" have affected my own development and the development of other philosophers (including atheists), and it is only lately that I have begun to think systematically about the heart's effect on reasoning. (Most of my recent work has been on, or in the neigborhood of, this subject.)

There are other reasons why I haven't succumbed to skepticism. I have always believed that James was right in thinking that the only hypothesis that is capable of satisfying our whole nature—intellectual *and* "passional"—is the religious hypothesis. I have also been particularly sensitive to theologies of sin and grace—acutely conscious of the wretched insufficiency of human effort, thought, and ideals when confronted by what Tillich called the threat of death, meaninglessness, and sin. Since my adolescence, it has seemed to me that either something like the Christian promise of victory over these threats is true or that there *is* no solution to them and that life, so far forth, is a failure.

These convictions are deeply rooted. As a result, I have long thought that even if Christian theism isn't more probable than not, it is still reasonable to embrace it. Suppose, for example, that Christianity is more probable than naturalism, more probable than Buddhism, and so on, through each of its rivals. (Cf.: It is more probable that Joan will get the job than that Bob will; it is more probable than Joan will get the job than that Mary will; and so on.) I believe that this is true. It doesn't follow, however, that Christian theism is more probable than the disjunction of its competitors. Therefore, it doesn't follow that it is more probable than not. My own view of the matter is that "Christianity is closer to the real truth of things (or contains less error)" is more probable than "One or the other of Christianity's rivals (Buddhism, naturalism, or . . .) is closer to the real truth of things (or contains less error)." (Cf.: It is more probable that Joan will get the job than that either Bob or Mary or . . . will.) But suppose that I am mistaken. Assume that Christianity, Buddhism, naturalism . . . (add any world view to the list that seriously impresses you) are the only plausible accounts of experience as a whole. By hypothesis, Christianity is more probable than Buddhism, more probable than naturalism, and so on, but not more probable than their disjunction. When plausible explanations are available, however, it seems reasonable to adopt *some* explanation rather than none. Which, then, shall we endorse? The evidence favors Christianity (though it doesn't make it more probable than not). The disjunction of rival explanations is more probable than Christianity (on our hypothesis) but isn't itself an explanation. It seems most reasonable, then, to adopt Christian theism.[4]

William James's considerations are also relevant. The practical effect of suspending one's judgment, and refusing to choose between rival religious hypotheses, is to reject *all* of them and thus lose the good "if good there be." Nor can one evade the issue by embracing abstract theism, James's religious hypothesis,[5] or some other alleged common denominator, and suspending judgment about the points on which religions differ. Abstract theism and James's religious hypothesis aren't explanations but rather explanatory sketches. They are too thin to guide life or provide it with depth and meaning. In order to *embrace* these hypotheses (by living in accordance with them and trying to shape one's life by them, that is, in order to take them *seriously*), one must adopt them in some concrete form. I am strongly inclined to think that men and women who practice their religion but believe that they are only embracing generic religious hypotheses unwittingly flesh them out with current opinions, private philosophical speculations, and their own imaginations. My own hunch is that versions of the religious hypothesis like these are less likely to be true than those that have stood the test of time and satisfied the intellectual and passional demands of countless thousands. The most reasonable course, then, is to embrace the most probable of the traditional rivals.

But while I think that these considerations are basically sound, putting the matter in this way is too cold and abstract. For why have I found arguments of this kind persuasive? Because the good that religion promises seems to me so great and so splendid that we ought to pursue it with our whole heart even if that good is only possible—like Kierkegaards's Socrates, who stakes everything on the *possibility* of God and eternal life. "He puts the question objectively in a problematic manner; *if* there is an immortality." But "on this 'if' he risks his entire life, he has the courage to meet death, and he has with the passion of the infinite so determined the pattern of his life that it must be found acceptable—*if* there is an immortality."[6]

And this brings me to a strand in my moral and intellectual life that has probably affected me even more than skepticism—romanticism. As a child, I was captivated by the Oz stories, *Curdie and the Goblins*, and similar books. By the age of nine or ten, I was enthralled by sea stories, stories of chivalry, Dumas's novels, and so on. I became deeply interested in their factual background and learned, for example, to name the standing rigging on a ship of the line, how to use a sextant, and a fair amount of medieval cultural, social, and political history. I was also able to live in these worlds in my imagination for days at a time. (I had the good sense, however, not to betray this to parents or to my friends, who were athletic and uninterested in books.) At thirteen, I discovered poetry. I had, of course, read poems before but always for the "story." (I read the *Song of Roland* and some Tennyson, for example, when I was enamored of chivalry.) At thirteen, however, I came across Arthur Waley's translations of Li Po and other Chinese poets and, for the first time, consciously experienced purely aesthetic pleasure—a delight in images and form for their own sake. Poetry, music, and the arts have played a major role in my life ever since.

But why is this significant? For several closely related reasons. In retrospect, I can see that my preoccupation with art and story has been partly (although by no means entirely) an expression of a yearning or longing for something they promise or suggest but can't fully provide. This yearning or longing is akin, I think, to the (often unacknowledged) dissatisfaction with the temporal, which Pascal describes, or the restlessness that Augustine thinks can only be assuaged in God. It is perhaps closer, however, to desire as described by Plato's Diotoma or to the Romantic's sensucht.

Throughout my life, art and story have, then, not only been sources of aesthetic and intellectual pleasure; they have also seemed to me intimations of something deeper that they indicate or point to but can't fully express. It is not surprising, therefore, that in spite of the difficulties that have been so ably canvassed by Bill Alston, Bill Rowe, and others, something has always seemed right to me about the symbol theories of people like Tillich or Ricoeur. I am even more attracted to the accounts of Coleridge and Horace Bushnell.

I have never believed that all religious language is symbolic. I do believe that an important part of the truth is missed or distorted if one isn't sensitive to the nonliteral but *cognitive* significance of symbol and metaphor. (Although I have never been able to articulate this position philosophically to my own satisfaction.)

At the same time, however, the literalism and rationalism of theists like Samuel Clarke or Jonathan Edwards also seem necessary. Without it, thought wanders without clear direction, and the mind falls prey to fancy. (I have in mind Coleridge's distinction between the imagination and fancy. The former is "essentially vital"; in "creating," "idealizing," and "unifying," the imagination answers to something in reality itself. Fancy, on the other hand, "is no other than a mode of memory emancipated from the order of time and space . . . modified by [arbitrary] choice."[7]

In light of all this, my fondness for Plato (particularly the Plato of the middle dialogues) could have been anticipated. The first philosophy I read (shortly after being given *Living Biographies of the Great Philosophers*) was the Modern Library edition of four or five Platonic dialogues. The only text in my first philosophy course was the *Republic*. Plato continues to be my favorite philosopher. (I also read Plotinus with pleasure and am fond of the Cambridge Platonists. One of many features that attracts me to Edwards is his Platonic strand and, in particular, his notion that ordinary beauty is a shadow or image of divine beauty.) What struck me initially, and still does, is the way in which Plato weaves together closely reasoned pieces of analysis and myth and symbol. He clearly believes that the latter are needed to express some truths, or some aspects of the truth, but he employs them only when the resources of argument have been exhausted. This still seems to me to be the ideal way to do philosophy.

I have always believed that the same is true of theology. I suspect that some religious truths—and perhaps some of the most important ones—can *only* be expressed in symbol and myth. Nevertheless, I also believe that there is a nonsymbolic core that is least inadequately expressed by classical theists like Clarke and Edwards. A person who neglects this is in danger of allowing his or her beliefs to degenerate into arbitrary fancies.[8]

There is also another danger. One can succumb to the belief that religious symbols are only poetic supplements of the "real" facts or new perspectives on familiar realities. To think of symbols in this way emasculates them. Symbols adumbrate the object of our longings. What we yearn for, however, is bread, not a papier-mâché facsimile. James has always seemed to me to be right: "Refined supernaturalism" in which the "world of the ideal . . . never bursts into the world of phenomena," but leaves everything as it was, doesn't seriously address the threats posed by sin, meaninglessness, and death.[9] How, for example, is history redeemed if the empirical order is just what it would be if God didn't exist? How is death overcome if consciousness comes to an end at death? Like James, then, I believe that the negative and symbolic theology of a pseudo-Dionysius must be combined with the "materialism" and "empiricism" of a Tertullian. Victories that are only symbolic aren't real victories.

So, in spite of my attraction to theories of symbols like Tillich's, I take exception to them in three ways. I think there is an important nonsymbolic core. Furthermore, I believe that symbols like those depicting God's victory over the powers of darkness have "material" or "concrete" implications; if they are true, the course of empirical events is different from what it would otherwise be. I also differ from Tillich, Ricoeur, and so on in another respect. I think the best theistic metaphysics and key components of traditional Christian theology (an Augustinian theory of grace, for example, and perhaps a satisfaction theory of the atonement) are what Edwyn Bevan called "symbols beyond which we cannot see."[10] Whatever their inadequacies, and however faintly they shadow forth the truth, they cannot (even for purposes of thought) be replaced by other language that is deeper or truer (Tillich's being ontology, for example, or Ricoeur's quasi-Heideggarian metaphysics). They are as close to the truth as we are likely to get.

But why, after all, do I believe that this language has any purchase on reality? Partly because, as I have already stated, theism's account of human experience seems less inadequate to me than its alternatives. Other factors, however, are at least as important. I am deeply impressed by the reports of the mystics (particularly the great theistic mystics like John of the Cross, Ruysbroeck, Tauler, and Rāmānuja). I am also impressed by the lives of such "saints" as Augustine, George Herbert, the Wesleys, and Edwards. Men and women like these strike me as people who have won life's victory. I simply can't believe, when all is said and done, that their lives were based on delusion. The bottom line, however, is probably what James calls "instincts," "divinations," "a sort of dumb conviction that the truth must lie in one direction rather than another," something in us that "whispers . . . 'it must be true'."[11] Augustine argued that a person who lacks wisdom may still be able to judge who has it and can lead one to it.[12] I believe that this is profoundly right. In any case, when everything has been said that can be said, I can only appeal to my "dumb conviction" that more truth is to be found in Christian theism than elsewhere and that something precious would be lost by rejecting it—that here, if anywhere, are the "words of eternal life."

At this point, the reader probably won't be astonished to learn that I found a home in the Anglican church. The Presbyterianism in which I was raised was the tepid sort of liberal Protestantism so common in mainline Midwestern churches in the 1940s. Although I continued to be privately concerned with religious questions, I drifted away from the church during adolescence— partly because it didn't fit my image of myself (my friends and I were more interested in cruising and partying than anything else) but also, I think, because I wasn't challenged by it on either an intellectual or an emotional and volitional level. In any case, with vague aspirations of being a poet and a strong interest in literary studies, I enrolled in Kenyon College. I chose Kenyon because it was a center of the New Criticism (*The Kenyon Review* and the *Partisan Review* were the principal literary quarterlies of the period) and because writers like John Crowe Ransom, Peter Taylor, Robert Lowell, and Robert Frost either taught or studied there or were often on campus. It so happened, however, that Kenyon was an Episcopal college and, at that time, required its students to attend chapel. I am probably one of the few on whom the requirement ever had much effect. What affected me was the Book of Common Prayer, and the church's worship—not only in its order and beauty but also its theological substance. In the service, abstract theological truths and credal formulae acquired resonance, engaged my imagination, came alive. As a result, I was confirmed in my sophomore year and have remained active in the Episcopal church since then, serving many times on the vestry, on diocesan committees, and as warden. I have never had serious second thoughts about my decision. Anglicanism's combination of intellectual tolerance, theological substance, and recognition of the importance of symbol and rite appeals to me today much as it did when I was a young man.

Before concluding, I should say a few words about another feature of my thought and feeling that has probably had some impact on my religious attitudes and beliefs, although I am not sure how much. From the age of about fifteen or sixteen, my intellectual and aesthetic sensibilities have been largely shaped by high modernism—composers like Schoenberg and Webern, painters like Matisse and Mondrian, poets like T. S. Eliot and Wallace Stevens, and novelists like Proust, Faulkner, and Mann. In addition, I am sympathetic to, and value, many products of postmodernism—Nathalie Sarraute, for example, or the poets John Ashbery and James Merrill, or visual artists such as Jasper Johns, Robert Smithson, Richard Serra, Gerhard Richter, and Bruce Nauman. I also take many of modernism's and postmodernism's intellectual products seriously. I have learned something from Sartre and the other existentialists, from Adorno and Habermas, and, more recently, from Foucault.

What do I share with these artists and thinkers and with such predecessors as Nietzsche, Marx, and Freud? Three things, I think. First, a certain skepticism about the powers of reason and its alleged neutrality and objectivity. (Though the real target, I think, isn't so much reason as the Enlightenment's conception of it.) Second, a sympathy with the "hermeneutics of suspicion"— methods of interpretation guided by the idea that systems of belief are (at least partly) ideologies masking unacknowledged desires for power, economic and social exploitation, and psychological and moral inadequacies. And finally, an acute consciousness of the plurality of discourses and intellectual frameworks, and of the attractiveness of many of them. The first two are closely akin to two important strands in Christian thought—the combination of skepticism and fideism best represented by Pascal, and the Augustinian conception of sin with its sensitivity to the pervasiveness of idolatry and the subtle forms it assumes. The third, I think, is an essentially new phenomenon, although some historical precedents can be found in the history of the Jesuits in China and elsewhere. I believe that W. C. Smith and others are right in asserting that any adequate contemporary theology must address this issue. Theologians and philosophers of religion can no longer proceed as if the only serious alternatives were Judaeo-Christian theism and naturalism. Many Hindus and Buddhists, for example, are as knowledgeable, as intellectually sophisticated, and as religiously and morally sensitive as we are. While it may once have been possible for an educated person to dismiss these religions without

thinking too much about them, we now know too much to excuse the carica-
tures, oversimplifications, and distortions that dominated discussions of
other religions in the past. (I have made some attempts to take Buddhism and
Vedānta seriously in *Mysticism* and in *Philosophy of Religion,* although I am
painfully aware of the shortcomings of these efforts.)

I am not, as I have said, sure of the precise extent to which these trends
have shaped my religious attitudes and beliefs. But I am sure of one thing—
the need to think through the relations between theism and modernity without either capitulating to the latter (as I believe Cupitt, and to a lesser extent
Tillich and Bultmann, have done) or largely ignoring it. (Contemporary philosophy of religion seems to me too often to do the latter.) Modernity's
insights into self, world, and society may be right in significant respects.
Insofar as they are, theists should incorporate them within their intellectual
framework. The trick is to do so without emasculating the latter. (It may be
useful to remind ourselves of the way in which Aquinas incorporated and
transformed the insights of Aristotle, or in which Edwards incorporated and
transformed the insights of Locke.) I lack the gifts needed for this task. I am
convinced, however, that until it is performed, theism will remain on the
defensive—not because it is *intellectually* indefensible, for it isn't, but because
it involves too many theists in a kind of noetic schizophrenia—a felt lack of
coherence or fit between their religious convictions and their other beliefs and
attitudes. Though I don't often agree with D. Z. Phillips, I think he is right
about one thing: Disbelief is less often the result of intellectual objections
than of the clash between religious beliefs and attitudes and sensibilities that
have been shaped by an environment that leaves little room for God or the
sacred.[13] For example, it is more difficult to see God's handiwork in the world
when the natural and human landscapes have been transformed by technology and bureaucratic rationalization. Again, modernist attacks on the unity
of the self don't comport well with traditional ideas of the soul. (Although I
would argue that they aren't strictly incompatible, since the disputants are
largely talking about different things—the metaphysical self and our image of
the self.) Analytic philosophers of religion tend to dismiss clashes like these as
pastoral, not philosophical, problems. But this, I think, is a mistake. What
needs to (and I believe can) be shown is that a robust theism isn't forced to
turn its back on modern culture but can absorb much of it without losing its
identity or integrity.

These, then, are some of the important strands in my religious life and
thought. My attitude is in many ways similar to T. S. Eliot's. Eliot appears to
have combined a deeply serious faith with both irony and skepticism. (When
asked why he accepted Christianity, he said he did so because it was the least
false of the options open to him.[14]) I also share his modernist sensibility
(though not his political and social conservatism). I do not regard my stance
as exemplary. If Christianity (or indeed any form of traditional theism) is true,
a faith free from doubt is surely better. I suspect, however, that my religious
life may be fairly representative of the lives of many intelligent, educated, and
sincere Christians in the latter part of the twentieth century.

Notes

1. "In December 1273, after an experience while saying Mass, he [Aquinas] suspended work on the third part of his *Summa Theologica,* telling his secretary that he had reached the end of his writing and giving as his reason the fact that 'all I have written seems to me like so much straw compared with what I have seen and with what has been revealed to me.' " F. C. Copleston, *Aquinas* (Hammersmith, Middlesex, UK: Penguin Books, 1957), p. 10.

2. John Calvin, *Institutes of the Christian Religion,* Vol. 1, (Grand Rapids, Mich.: Wm. B. Eerdmans, 1957), p. 46.

3. William James, "Is Life Worth Living?" in *The Will to Believe and Other Essays on Popular Philosophy* (New York: Dover, 1956), p. 62.

4. Richard Swinburne makes a similar point in *The Existence of God* (Oxford: Oxford University Press, 1979), p. 289f. Whether this should be called believing is doubtful. It shouldn't if "A believes p" entails "A believes p is more probable than not." Swinburne proposes that we use the term *weakly believing. Rational acceptance* might be better.

5. Religion's first affirmation is that "the best things are the more eternal things, . . . the things in the universe that throw the last stone, so to speak, and say the final word. . . . The second affirmation of religion is that we are better off even now if we believe her first affirmation to be true." "The Will to Believe," in *The Will to Believe,* op. cit., p. 25f.

6. Soren Kierkegaard, *Concluding Unscientific Postscript* (Princeton, N.J.: Princeton University Press, 1944), p. 180.

7. Samuel T. Coleridge, *Biographia Literaria,* in *The Selected Poetry and Prose of Samuel Taylor Coleridge* (New York: Modern Library, 1951), p. 263.

8. Ricoeur is more sensitive to this danger than Tillich. He insists, for example, on the importance of a rigorous philosophical thinking that attempts to think through the medium of rational concepts what has already been thought at the level of imagination. (His own attempts to provide "philosophical approximations" of symbolic texts borrow heavily from Kant and Hegel.) I should add that Coleridge and Bushnell seem to me largely immune to the charges leveled against Tillich and Ricoeur in this paragraph.

9. *Varieties of Religious Experience* (New York: Modern Library, c. 1902), p. 511. James's comments can be compared with Augustine's remarks about the Platonists. While he learned many truths about God from them, he didn't learn that God had decisively intervened in history in Jesus of Nazareth (*Confessions* [New York: Modern Library, 1949], pp. 130–132.)

10. Edwyn R. Bevan distinguishes between symbols "behind which we can see" and symbols "behind which we cannot see." In the latter case, "we cannot have any discernment of the reality better and truer than the symbolical idea, and we cannot compare the symbol with the reality as it is more truly apprehended. . . . The symbol is the nearest we can get to the reality." It is "the truest statement of the reality possible in human language," including metaphysical language. The quotations are from the eleventh lecture of *Symbolism and Belief* (Port Washington, N.Y.: Kennikat Press, 1968).

11. The quotations are from "The Will to Believe" and "The Sentiment of Rationality" in *The Will to Believe,* op. cit., pp. 29 and 93, and from *A Pluralistic Universe* (New York: Longmans, Green, 1947), pp. 328–329.

12. William J. Collinge, "The Relation of Religious Community Life to Rationality in Augustine," *Faith and Philosophy* 5 (July 1988), p. 244.

13. D. Z. Phillips, "Belief, Change and Forms of Life: The Confusions of Externalism and Internalism," in *The Autonomy of Religious Belief* (Notre Dame, Ind.: University of Notre Dame Press, 1981).

14. Peter Ackroyd, *T. S. Eliot: A Life* (New York: Simon and Schuster, 1984), p. 160.

6

FAITH HAS

ITS REASONS

C. Stephen Layman

Early in life, I displayed an interest in religion. By the fourth grade, I was listening carefully to sermons and taking them to heart. Our minister said to read the Bible every day, so I began to do so. By the end of the fifth grade, I had read the New Testament from start to finish. Of course, I hadn't understood much of it, but I had made an honest effort. Unfortunately, it wasn't long before I found out that some people thought it was remarkable that a fifth grader had read the entire New Testament. I immediately took the opportunity to indulge in self-congratulation.

Each fall we had revival meetings. The speakers at these events were called *evangelists,* and they employed a highly emotional style of preaching. The preaching on hell was especially vivid, and it had an electric effect on me. I remember trying to imagine what it would be like to burn in a lake of fire for an unending period of time. Rightly or wrongly, I also derived from the evangelists' messages a belief that the vast majority of the human race is going to hell. They often quoted such scriptural warnings as "Broad is the way, that leadeth to destruction, and many there be which go in thereat: . . . and narrow is the way, which leadeth unto life, and few there be who find it" (Matt. 7:13–14, King James Version).

By my early teen years, I began to suspect that I would go to hell. After all, the evangelists had made it clear that only *genuine* Christians would avoid this fate and that *genuine* Christians were in the minority. Moreover, it was clear enough to me that I did not fit the evangelists' descriptions of what a *genuine* Christian is like. Not surprisingly, this realization led to a lot of gloomy thoughts. Without putting the idea explicitly into words, I gradually came to think of God as a being who offered the human race the following option: "Either do my will or burn forever—it's your choice." In short, I had come to think of God as a cosmic tyrant. My faith, laden with guilt and fear, no longer gave me any joy.

In my senior year of high school, I came under the influence of some Christian leaders who stressed God's love. I began to see that the Christian gospel was supposed to be something positive—"good news." But the ideas about hell existed side by side with the positive message of God's love, and both ideas pressed themselves on me in turns. Though I would no doubt have *professed* a belief in God's love, I was inwardly wavering and confused.

Perhaps I am making it sound as if my early life was fully absorbed in explicitly religious thoughts and activities. Of course, this was not so. I was involved in many of the usual activities at school and with my family. But I often felt my religion to be a burden, and I envied the secular kids at school. They didn't have to live with an all-knowing God looking over *their* shoulders all the time. They could sin without feeling guilty or fearful. Under peer pressure I frequently behaved as they behaved, but there was a price to pay later in solitude, when the fear of hell and the knowledge of my own moral weakness would come upon me.

Partly because of the turmoil of my religious thoughts and feelings, I decided to attend a college associated with the denomination I was brought up in, the Christian church or Church of Christ.[1] I had a vague notion that attending this college would help me sort out my spiritual problems. I studied hard and began to take a deeper look at my faith. I read most of the works of C. S. Lewis, and through them I caught a glimpse of the vast sweep and richness of Christian theology. Through the lens of Lewis's theological works, something of the wonder of creation and life came through to me in a way it never had before. Looking back, I think this experience is one of the deep roots of my love of philosophy. For since my college years, it has been theology and philosophy that have again and again renewed my sense of the extraordinariness of existence.

Two courses, one in apologetics and one in philosophy, marked a profound change in my intellectual life. I became much more interested in logic and argument. I became interested in whether "faith" means "believing without evidence," and I decided that, if it did, then faith wasn't for me. I began to see that it would be intellectually dishonest for me to demand evidence for other religious or philosophical views if I refused to acknowledge this demand for my theological views. I was taking the first step in a way of thinking that would change my views dramatically.

At this time, I had an opportunity to spend one year studying philosophy at Cornell University. Some of the courses raised very difficult questions about my faith. What affected me most were books and papers that articulated and defended a materialist world view. It became clear to me that materialism could explain much more than I had previously supposed. This was disturbing. Also disturbing were the numbers of students who regarded Christian theology as unworthy of serious intellectual consideration.

On the advice of a friend, I decided to seek an undergraduate degree in philosophy from Calvin College in Grand Rapids, Michigan. I found Calvin delightful and challenging. There I felt free to explore questions about my faith, but I also felt encouraged to regard my faith as a philosophical asset. Through the writings and teaching of such Calvin philosophers as Alvin Plantinga and Nicholas Wolterstorff, I saw the possibility of combining Christian faith and philosophy. I decided to study philosophy at the graduate level.

Naturally enough, in graduate school I encountered a deeper level of questions about my faith. I soon became convinced that the doctrine of God's love is incompatible with the doctrine that some persons will be punished forever in hell. If a loving being seeks the long-term best interests of those he loves, how could a loving being make anyone miserable forever? Put bluntly, it couldn't possibly be in anyone's long-term best interest to be eternally damned, so a loving God wouldn't damn anyone eternally. It would be more loving to annihilate people than to make them miserable for all eternity. I thus jettisoned my belief in an eternal hell with a certain sense of relief. I was careful to remind myself, however, that the argument did not rule out divine punishment, only *eternal* divine punishment.

I realize that my giving up the doctrine of eternal hell will appear a quaint episode to many. But the episode had far-reaching consequences for me. Having made this step, I felt a new freedom to follow up arguments wherever they might lead. I also felt a combination of exhilaration and dread in regard to the power of philosophy. I saw that philosophy is a serious thing that can alter one's beliefs at a fundamental level. I had crossed a line and wasn't sure where it might lead. But I felt certain then, and still do, that intellectual honesty is the best policy.

Much deeper challenges awaited me. I found that nearly all of my fellow graduate students—even ones who were sympathetic to theism—had a low opinion of the so-called proofs of God's existence. Through a process of dialogue, I gradually came to share this opinion. I began to fear that the Christian faith could not be backed up with adequate evidence. Worse was yet to come as I examined the problem of evil at an advanced level. It was widely admitted, even by Christian theologians, that no one had ever found a convincing reason why God permits certain forms of suffering. A loving parent is not going to stand by and let her child be tortured until it goes insane—not if she can do anything about it. Yet, does not God stand by daily while His children are thus tortured in the prisons of tyrants around the world? So it seems. A neural disease destroys a child's capacity to think. Would a loving parent who is able to prevent this evil stand by without interfering? Surely not. Therefore, is it not straining language beyond reasonable limits to assert that "God is love"?

Several factors combined with these intellectual difficulties to bring me into a period of intense religious doubt. First, early in the third year of graduate school, my marriage of some years broke down completely. While I initially felt a sense of relief to be free of a strained relationship, my divorce administered a series of pyschological shocks. The counseling sessions that preceded the divorce made it clear even to me that my own immaturity was a major cause of my wife's disaffection. I knew that I had failed at one of life's most important tasks. I also felt that a failed marriage was proof of a lack of Christian virtue, and that my moral and spiritual inadequacy had thus been exposed for all to see. Finally, within a few months of my divorce, I began to feel terribly alone and uprooted. Far from family and old friends and under the intense pressure of graduate study, I lost my sense of direction and became deeply unsure of myself.

Second, at this time I decided to stop attending the sorts of churches I had grown up in, namely, those belonging to the Campbellite movement. I made this decision for a variety of reasons. I had moved some distance from the conservative theology these churches espouse. For example, I could no longer believe that the Bible is infallible. I also thought that these churches often evinced a suspicious attitude toward philosophy. The Campbellite slogan, "Where the Bible is silent, we are silent," left too little room for the valuable contributions philosophy had made to theology over the centuries. And, anyway, wasn't "Where the Bible is silent, we are silent" itself a bit of philosophy? Perhaps I should join a denomination whose history included some good philosophers and systematic theologians.

Whatever the merits of these reasons for leaving my old denomination, doing so left me feeling even more uprooted and rudderless. Looking back, I can see that I was really asking for spiritual trouble by abandoning my old church just at the time I was undergoing a divorce. I was increasing the psychological pressures on myself at a time when I was particularly fragile.

Third, I must record an attitude that came over me, and that put psychological distance between me and all churches. Given my negative assessment of the traditional proofs for God's existence, I began to fear that my faith was due simply to my upbringing. How could I know otherwise unless I became an atheist or an agnostic—at least for a period of time? If I became an atheist or an agnostic and *then* regained my faith, I would at least know that my faith wasn't simply due to my being conditioned by authority figures at an early age. And how could I give up my faith if I were involved in the life of a church? I knew I wouldn't be able to do so.

These thoughts seem a bit fantastic to me now, but they didn't then. I seldom made them explicit to myself, but they had a hold on me. I couldn't act on them decisively, so the result was a ridiculous compromise of attending a variety of churches but avoiding any commitment or involvement. I kept this up for several years, and not surprisingly, it did have the effect of greatly attenuating my faith. To the best of my knowledge, I never entirely stopped believing that some sort of personal Power lies behind the world of appearances, but I came to have very deep doubts about God's love.

During this period of doubt, I became interested in the American philosopher William James and, in particular, in his famous essay "The Will to Believe." In that essay James argues that it can sometimes be rational and moral to believe even when the issue cannot be settled by an examination of the available evidence. James is not, I think, endorsing belief *against* a preponderance of evidence. Rather, he has in mind cases in which we find it difficult to assess a complicated range of pros and cons—cases in which we aren't sure where the preponderance of evidence lies. Moreover, it is a crucial part of James's view that believing in such circumstances is rational and moral only if the issue is momentous, that is, only if something important can be gained via belief. Furthermore, James says that "the option" to believe must be "living," and although this can be interpreted in various ways, I think James is trying to pick out a class of cases in which we are *able* to believe—perhaps because we are already inclined to do so.

I continue to think "The Will to Believe" is an insightful essay for several reasons. First, James emphasizes the practical nature of belief. What we believe about religious and moral issues has momentous consequences for the way we live and for the kinds of persons we will become. (Here I came to see a danger in agnosticism. The agnostic says, "We can't, or at least don't, know whether God exists." But people who claim to be agnostics typically live *as if* there is no God; for example, they don't pray or worship God. This amounts to placing one's bets on the side of atheism.) Second, James's view comports well with the fact that few (if any) come to faith primarily because of evidence or arguments. For example, people often come to faith because they feel that their lives are lacking in some important way and because they have the impression, based on their acquaintance with certain exemplary religious believers, that faith may be of help. Third, James rightly challenges the idea that one is always irrational if one fails to proportion one's belief to the evidence. When evidential considerations leave us unable to settle a matter, there is still a sense in which it can be reasonable, in a practical sense, to believe. After all, while well-evidenced truth is one of the goods humans reasonably seek, it isn't the only good. Thus, if I cannot in my own mind settle a given religious issue, such as the existence of God, simply by examining the available evidence, but I can gain greater moral motivation or hope for living by so believing, it may still be rational, at least in a practical sense, to do so.[2]

As for myself, after the years of doubt described above, I found the halfway house of half-believing quite unsatisfying. For me personally, it was truly time to take decisive action: either reject the Christian faith and live a secular life, or else get serious about following Christ. It became clear to me, at this juncture, that both the historical figures I admired most and the persons of my acquaintance whom I most admired were men and women who had tried (or were trying) to follow Jesus Christ. This being so, why hesitate any longer? The option was momentous. I became actively involved in an Episcopal parish and plunged again into the life of the church.

While James's will-to-believe doctrine still seems to me a helpful counter to the plausible but oversimple view that one should always proportion one's belief to the evidence, this doctrine does not now seem to me satisfying as a justification for the belief of most Christians throughout most of their lives. My primary reason for saying this is that most Christians, for most of their lives, do not view central theological issues as undecidable in James's sense. For example, they typically believe (or come to believe) that "God exists" is more probable than "God does not exist."[3] During a period of doubt, even of extended doubt, one may indeed have the opinion that the evidence favors neither theism nor atheism. But this view surely is not typical of theists. Most of them do think, or do come to think, however inarticulately, that theism is more probable (given all relevant factors) than atheism, or pantheism, or any other alternative they are aware of.[4] So, we must ask: Is it reasonable for someone to believe that "God exists" is more probable than the alternatives?

Let me begin by clearing away one common misunderstanding. People often think it significant to assert that "God's existence can't be proved." A proof, I suppose, is something that will convince anyone who is intelligent enough to understand it. If so, very little of interest regarding major philosophical issues can be proved. This goes for issues in metaphysics, morality, political philosophy, and aesthetics. All or nearly all of the major positions under these headings are highly controversial. There are brilliant people on either side of the interesting fences. So, if we demand proofs in philosophy, we will wind up as skeptics on all or nearly all of the important issues. Surely that is not the way of wisdom. I often ask my students to imagine themselves giving an antislavery speech to a group of slave owners. What are the chances of convincing the audience? Slim to none. Surely, then, it is possible to have good arguments for a view even though these arguments are not recognized as such by groups of people who do not share our convictions.

I think the old metaphor of a jury's verdict, though currently unfashionable, is helpful at this juncture. It is noteworthy that in a civil case the standard is that of a "preponderance of evidence" (as opposed to the standard in a criminal case, i.e., "beyond a reasonable doubt"). Furthermore, in a civil case, a verdict can be rendered even though not all the jurors agree (e.g., in a twelve-person jury, two can dissent).[5] Several points about juries and jurors are worth bearing in mind. First, it is surely reasonable for a juror, in many cases, to believe that her view of the case is supported by a preponderance of the evidence. Second, and more important, I believe that most people who have served on juries would allow that individual jurors can have a reasonable assessment of the evidence even when their assessment is in conflict with that of some of the other jurors.

How is it that jurors who disagree on a verdict can *reasonably* regard each other's views as reasonable? The answer lies, I think, in their mutual awareness of the difficulty of assessing a complicated range of evidence. One does not need to be highly intelligent to understand the basic concepts involved in the typical court case. But the sheer number of factors—the variety of witnesses, the speeches of the lawyers, the judge's instructions—can be confusing, and a responsible juror is apt to agonize over the weight to be given to the various bits of evidence. For example, many cases turn centrally on whose testimony is most credible. There is simply no formula for determining that sort of thing, and a reasonable juror is painfully aware of his own fallibility.

Third, even if the disagreements among jurors prevent them from rendering a verdict, those same disagreements do not necessarily make the *beliefs* of the individual jurors unreasonable. Perhaps only nine of twelve jurors agree in a civil case. If so, no verdict can be rendered. But the jurors may still have *beliefs* about what probably happened, and those beliefs may still be reasonable in a given case.

Fourth, a jury's deliberations will usually focus on a few *pivotal* bits of evidence. For example, certain key pieces of evidence may be taken by some jurors to indicate that Mr. Jones probably did strike Ms. Smith with the intent to cause bodily injury. Other jurors may not agree with this assessment, at least initially, and the deliberations will focus on these matters. A juror's assessment of these pivotal bits of evidence often determines her view of the entire case.

I think this point about pivotal evidence helps us to understand how religious beliefs can be rational. The range of factors involved in assessing an entire world view is so vast and complicated that any formulaic approach is bound to be inadequate. We can and should try to be objective, but it will likely be our assessment of certain pivotal lines of evidence that determines our view, so far as the intellectual side of things goes. I hope it is clear that I am not suggesting that just *any* assessment of a given piece of evidence is reasonable. Some assessments are plainly unreasonable. On the other hand, it is clear that equally intelligent and fair-minded people can assess the same evidence differently, and this may lead them to widely divergent conclusions. I now want to illustrate these abstract remarks about pivotal evidence by describing one particular line of evidence regarding materialism and theism. This description is meant to be illustrative, so I am not pretending to provide a decisive argument. One the other hand, I do mean to sketch one key reason why I now assess the evidential situation concerning materialism and theism differently than I did during my lengthy period of doubt.

In graduate school, I tended to see as pivotal those matters that were then receiving a great deal of attention among professional philosophers. At the time, it seemed that the burden of proof was on theism. Is there enough evidence for God's existence? Are there any theodicies that provide an adequate solution to the problem of evil? Is theism logically coherent? I think the general climate of opinion in academic philosophy at that time, in regard to theism and materialism, could be summed up as follows: "Materialism is

pretty clearly defensible, whereas theism at least appears to be indefensible."
(By *materialism* I mean roughly the view that there are no gods or immaterial
souls, that only matter exists, and that matter always behaves in accordance
with the laws of nature.[6])

Two very important changes in my perspective have occurred since those
days. (1) I do not now see theism as having any special burden of proof. The
question "Is there enough evidence for God's existence?" now seems to me
misleading. I think it is much more helpful to think in comparative terms.
Does theism explain the range of relevant phenomena better than (as well as,
or worse than) its rivals do? In my view, the serious philosophical rivals to
theism are few, with materialism being the most impressive. (2) It now seems
to me that materialism is a highly problematic view. I think its difficulties are
more severe than those of theism, so I think theism is more probably true. I
shall now attempt to describe one of the difficulties of materialism.

I am firmly convinced that humans are morally responsible for many of
their actions. Sometimes they are responsible for acting in cruel or unjust
ways. Sometimes they are responsible for acting in ways that are loving or
just. However, there is a connection between moral responsibility and free
will: If a human being is morally responsible for a given act, then she performs the act freely. And if a person does not perform a given act freely—for
example, because she was coerced or drugged—then she is not morally responsible for that particular action.

Does materialism provide an adequate explanation of free action? It seems to
me that it does not. Some materialists have not only admitted this point but
have insisted on it. Thus, B. F. Skinner, in *Beyond Freedom and Dignity*, argues
that the belief in free will is a relic of our prescientific past. However, Skinner's
view is extremely problematic, since it rules out moral responsibility altogether. An anecdote may serve to underscore the philosophical cost of denying
that humans are morally responsible. I once knew an ethics professor who employed a dramatic pedagogical technique with regard to students who professed to be amoralists, moral subjectivists, or moral skeptics. If a student professed such views in class, this professor would give the student a failing grade
on the next paper—regardless of the paper's merits. Inevitably, the student
would complain about the grade. The discussion would go something like this:

> STUDENT: Why did you give me an F?
>
> PROF.: Do I need a reason? I just felt like failing
> the paper.
>
> STUDENT: But that's not fair.
>
> PROF.: Fair? *Fair* is a moral word. You're not
> suggesting that I'm responsible for an *im-
> moral* action, are you?

A serious discussion of metaethics would follow. The point is that it's one
thing to verbalize amoralism or moral skepticism, and it's another to accept

the implications of these views. In any case, I will state my firm opinion that it is entirely reasonable to reject a philosophical view that cannot make room for moral responsibility.

However, the current trend among materialists is not to deny freedom and morality, but to claim that human freedom is compatible with causal determinism. In other words, a given act can be both free and determined at the same time. This view is called the *compatibilist* view of free will. An act is free for a person in the compatibilist sense if and only if she performs the act because she wants to (all things considered). The phrase "all things considered" is an acknowledgment of the fact that a person may have conflicting desires. I may want both to go to the party and to study for the exam. If I can't do both, I will presumably do what I want, "all things considered." Thus, for the compatibilist, "free" contrasts with "coerced." When I am not coerced, but rather perform the act because I want to (all things considered), I act freely.

But we must ask: What accounts for the fact that I *want* to perform a given act, all things considered? On the materialist account, every event is the result of prior states of the physical world together with the operation of natural laws.[7] The way the world is today, right down to the last detail, is a result of the way the world was yesterday (and the natural laws that obtain). Now, I do not have control of the past (e.g., of the way the world was yesterday or the day before). Nor do I have control of which natural laws govern the physical world or, indeed, or whether any natural laws govern the physical world. It thus appears that I do not have control of my "wantings" if materialism is true. For my wantings are entirely the result of factors over which I have no control.[8]

But if I do not have control of my wantings, am I free in the relevant sense? I think the answer is no. Suppose that, via a pharmacist's error, I am administered a drug that makes me want (all things considered) to hit someone. Am I free in a sense that makes me morally responsible if I hit someone while under the influence of such a drug? Surely not. I was unable to choose otherwise.

Perhaps I can make my main line of reasoning more concrete by applying it to one particular type of materialist, the type who claims that mental states are identical to brain states. On this view, a particular choice will be identical to a particular brain process. But brain processes are, of course, physical events, subject to physical laws. Given the laws of nature and the way the world was yesterday, we have the deepest causal account of the occurrence of this brain process, according to materialism. And there is no reason to stop at yesterday. Today's "choice" is a brain processs that is linked via natural laws to states of the physical world prior even to my birth. Again, since I am not in control of the past states of the world, and not in control of which (or whether) natural laws hold, I am not in control of my acts if materialism is true.

Therefore, it seems to me that we must take the *incompatibilist* view of free will, according to which a given act cannot be both free and determined. The details of this conception of free will are controversial, but I hold that an act is free if and only if (1) the agent performs it because she chooses to, (2) she could have chosen to do something else, and (3) nothing other than the agent is the total cause of her choice. But clauses (2) and (3) rule out the materialist picture in which the agent's mental states are fully caused by prior states of the physical world.

It almost goes without saying that materialists have replies to these arguments, but this isn't the place to go into the details.[9] I can only record a firm belief that the materialists' replies don't work. It thus appears to me that to accept materialism is implicitly to reject free will and hence to reject morality. This is something I am not capable of doing.

It is interesting to note that, if my reasoning to this point is on the right track, then materialism confronts a problem of evil analogous to the traditional problem of evil for theism. The traditional problem concerns whether theists can explain the presence of moral and natural evil in the world. It presents the theist with this question: "Isn't it unlikely that a perfectly good and all-powerful Deity would allow certain kinds of moral wrongdoing (e.g., torturing babies) or extreme suffering due to nonhuman causes (e.g., earthquakes, diseases, or hurricanes)? But if materialism rules out free will, it rules out moral responsibility, and hence it rules out what is traditionally meant by the phrase *moral evil*. This seems to me at least as serious a problem of evil as any the theist faces.

Perhaps it will seem to some readers that I have been presupposing, throughout this chapter, that belief in God is rational only if it is based on philosophical arguments. I do not, in fact, think this. Many believers have neither the time nor the inclination to pursue such reasoning, and some lack the mental capacity. Is faith then able to go it alone, without any help from reason or philosophy? I think this is a complicated question, and I shall finish this essay by outlining one answer to it.

First, in the typical case, I think there are potent nonevidential causes of religious belief. For example, many Christians were brought up in the faith, and this sort of upbringing inevitably involves some psychological conditioning. Furthermore, in regard to those Christians who were not brought up in the faith, many decide to practice the Christian way out of a sense of deep psychological need.

It might be tempting to conclude that such causal factors leave no room for reason. But I think such a conclusion would be a serious mistake. There are several ways in which reason can *and typically does* come into the picture.

1. Thoughtful people are apt to recognize the existence of evidence that appears to run contrary to their views. And it is either impossible or exceedingly difficult to believe something if one thinks the preponderance of evidence is against it. So, reason must play at least an ancillary role for many people in enabling them to reconcile their convictions with contrary evidence.

2. We must keep in mind that having evidence and being able to articulate it are two different things. Two jurors may regard a witness as credible, but one juror may be much better at articulating his reasons for this opinion than the other. Yet, surely, both jurors may be said to *have* evidence by virtue of having listened attentively and critically to the witnesses. More generally, many peo-

ple who are good at coming to an intuitive conclusion based on a complex range of factors are not particularly good at breaking that intuition down into arguments. I think that the belief in God is often based on this kind of intuitive assessment of a very broad range of factors about the world and about human life. Furthermore, I think it is a mistake to regard such intuitive assessments of evidence as nonrational. They are, as it were, the well from which are drawn the reasons we can put into words.

3. Both those brought up in the Christian faith and those who come to it out of a sense of need believe that the church is an authority on religious isssues. (By *the church* I mean the community of Christian believers, i.e., those persons, whether dead or alive, who have adhered to the Christian tradition.[10]) Thus, the faith of all Christians is supported by an appeal to authority. And an appeal to legitimate authority is entirely reasonable. Perhaps most of what we believe about the world is accepted on authority.

But is the church a *legitimate* authority on religious matters? This may be doubted for a variety of reasons. Here I can only outline why I answer in the affirmative. When we know little about a matter and are not in a position to sort through all the evidence thoroughly on our own, we do well to listen to some person, or group of persons, who is more likely to have the truth than we are. Such an appeal to authority is reasonable, it seems to me, unless one is aware of (or should be aware of) a superior authority. (Authority A is superior to authority B if A is more likely than B to be correct.) For example, suppose that I am trying to reach a remote location in the wilderness on foot, and I do not know the way. I will do well to take the advice of a person who has had the experience of hiking to that location. But how do I know that a given person has actually had this experience? Initially, I may have little to go on but her word and the impression of her credibility that I receive from listening to her story. Possibly some others can assure me that she is indeed an experienced hiker.

But what if some other experienced hiker contradicts the testimony of the first one? This is analogous to the religious situation, since there are religious traditions that contradict Christianity. Would I then be unreasonable if I still accepted the advice of the first hiker? Not necessarily. The contradictions may be on minor points that need not concern me greatly. But let us suppose that they are on major points. Then what? Well, I may still reasonably believe that the first hiker is the superior authority. Perhaps her account is more detailed and coherent, or perhaps I simply judge her to be a more competent and trustworthy person, even though I am not able to break this intuitive judgment down into convincing arguments.

Consider one example of contradictory religious authorities. The church says that ultimate reality is a sort of mighty Person, that is, a thinking, willing being. But one of the major Hindu traditions, Advaita Vedanta, says that ultimate reality is undifferentiated being. On this view, ultimate reality is not personal, as theists claim, and it is not physical, as materialists claim. Further, since ultimate reality is undifferentiated being, our perception of differences must be illusory. Is Advaita Vedanta as credible as the church on these basic metaphysical issues? I think it is possible to arrive at reasonable answers to such questions. For example, isn't there a real difference between me and you? Our sensory and moral experience tell us this is so, but Advaita Vedanta says that this distinction is illusory. Furthermore, isn't the distinction between illusion and reality itself a real distinction? And since Advaita Vedanta employs this distinction when it says that sensory experience is illusory, Advaita Vedanta seems to presuppose at least one real distinction while insisting that distinctions are unreal. Any view that says that all distinctions are unreal has a serious credibility problem, in my book.

Now, returning to the example of the two hikers, suppose that I cannot judge one hiker to be superior (as an authority) to the other. Is it then necessarily unreasonable for me to accept the advice of either hiker? Well, I can certainly accept those points on which they agree. But what about the points on which they disagree? For example, suppose that one hiker says that I should seek out a certain mountain pass, and the other says that there is no such pass. Should I ignore both hikers in favor of my own uninformed guess? Perhaps I'll be better off if I act on the advice of one of the hikers, even though it may be mistaken. After all, both hikers seem to be better informed than I am. (Naturally, I will remain alert on the trail and revise my plans if error becomes evident.) So, it seems to me that it can be reasonable to place limited trust in authority even when equally trustworthy authorities disagree on some important matters.

Of course, it is not reasonable for persons to place their trust in the church if they have (in hand) good reason to believe that the church is not worthy of this trust. To the extent that the church shows itself to be unconcerned with an honest examination of the relevant evidence, I believe that it presents itself as unworthy of this trust. Serious inquirers should be apprised of the relevant evidence the church has in its possession and on which its authority is based. This is one reason why the Christian community should place a high value not only on theology and philosophy proper, but on a broad range of intellectual disciplines that have or may have a bearing on its central teachings. Thus, it seems to me that reason, broadly construed, plays a vital role in ensuring that the church is a trustworthy authority on matters of faith. In this sense, at least, faith requires the support of reason.

As I look back over my life, I see that I cannot be content with a faith that ignores or scorns reason. But the intellectual part of the Christian life is, like the other parts, a difficult and narrow way.

Notes

1. The stated goal of these churches is to restore the primitive Christianity of New Testament times. Historically speaking, these churches stem from the work of Thomas and Alexander Campbell in the early nineteenth century. The Campbellite movement grew rapidly on the American frontier when Ohio, Kentucky, and Indiana *were* the frontier. Though I have referred to the Christian church or Church of Christ as a

denomination, I am aware that it is not regarded as a denomination by its own members, but simply as a movement to restore New Testament Christianity. I consider this point essentially verbal.

2. This brief summary of James's will-to-believe doctrine may raise a number of questions. For a more complete discussion, see C. Stephen Layman, "The Truth in 'The Will to Believe'," *History of Philosophy Quarterly,* ed. Nicholas Rescher, 4, 4 (October 1987), pp. 467–483.

3. Two technical points about belief and probability arise here. (a) In my view, to say that a person believes a proposition P is to say that she is more confident that P is true than that the alternatives are true (with not-P usually being the salient alternative). This definition of *belief* leaves open whether one's confidence in a proposition P necessarily indicates a confidence that P is *probable on the evidence or grounds.* If a person believes P when the issue is undecidable in James's sense, she believes P without believing that P is probable on the evidence. (b) The word *probable* here should not be taken as *necessarily* indicative of tentativeness. A person who is *certain* of God's existence is simply one who regards the probability of "God exists" as high enough to exclude a reasonable doubt.

4. I am not here ignoring or ruling out the view that belief in God is properly basic, that is, warranted or justified independently of inference, such as "I see a tree." But it should be clear that a person who holds that belief in God is properly basic does not regard the issue of God's existence as undecidable in James's sense. If anyone holds that "God exists" is properly basic, he or she presumably holds that "God exists" is either grounded in some sort of experience or knowable a priori. Such properly basic beliefs have grounds, I take it, even though they are not based on further beliefs. To illustrate, if "I see a tree" is properly basic for me, this is presumably because the experience of seeing the tree somehow grounds the belief.

5. For all I know, these standards vary from state to state, but this is how it is in the State of Washington.

6. I say "roughly" because I do not wish to deny the materialist a belief in certain abstract objects, such as sets, which may be nonphysical. But such abstract objects (e.g., the set of whole numbers between 4 and 7) are not agents and cannot, I take it, initiate events in the physical world.

7. My language here may carry the suggestion that the natural laws are somehow independent of matter and operate on it. Of course, that is not what materialists believe, and my phrasing should not be so interpreted. Presumably materialists believe that those regularities that scientists call *natural laws* are grounded in propensities of the fundamental physical particles—whatever the fundamental particles turn out to be. Furthermore, although some materialists take these propensities to ground deterministic laws, my argument is designed to apply even if natural laws are taken to be statistical (probabilistic).

8. The argument against materialism in this paragraph owes a heavy debt to an argument Peter van Inwagen has given in favor of incompatibilism (the view that free will is not compatible with determinism). However, since I am adapting this material for my own purposes, I must take responsibility for any mistakes in the reasoning. See Peter van Inwagen, *An Essay on Free Will* (Oxford: 1983), p. 56.

9. Readers interested in the compatibilist/incompatibilist debate regarding free will may wish to read Gary Watson, ed., *Free Will* (Oxford: 1982), as well as van Inwagen, op. cit.

10. Some may wonder why I have not spoken here of the authority of the Bible. The Bible is, of course, the major document of the Christian tradition. It is thus a vital

part, but not the whole, of what the church has to offer in the way of evidence regarding spiritual matters. But humanly speaking, it is the church that drew up the biblical canon. And if we are inquiring into the reasonableness of believing in God, we can't very well start with the question-begging assumption that God guided the church to draw up the canon.

ON KEEPING

THE FAITH

Jerry L. Walls

7

I was eleven years old the night it happened, November 27, 1966 (the date is written in my red King James Bible, a gift I received the following Christmas). It was a Sunday night during the Fall Revival at Bethel Chapel Christian Union Church, the small country parish I attended in southern Ohio. The evangelist was my uncle, Woodrow Trainer. His text for the evening was a phrase from I Samuel 20:3, "there is but a step between me and death."

The sermon, as usual, was delivered with passion and a great sense of urgency. The words came rapidly, as if God were transmitting thoughts directly to the preacher, and he could hardly spit them out fast enough. The unpredictable ways of death were detailed. We were reminded of what a crazy world we live in, rife with terrorists, heart attacks, and automobile accidents. The truth of the text had me in its grip, and I was finding it harder to breathe.

Eventually the sermon wound down, and my uncle assumed a more conversational style as he gave the invitation to come to the altar to receive salvation. This was the time I always dreaded. I had heard similar sermons before, in this revival and in previous revivals, but I had always managed to fight back my impulse to go forward. I assumed, however, that someday I would do so when I was an adult, or at least a teenager.

But now my resolve to put the decision off was being severely tested. I knew I did not want to take that fatal step into death's trap and then have to face God with my sins unforgiven. And I couldn't be sure how many more chances I would have to repent.

As the invitation hymn was sung, my brother-in-law, Robert Uhrig, sensed my uneasiness and simply asked me if I was ready to go forward. I did not hesitate. I went to the altar and asked God to save me from my sins. I wept tears of repentance and then tears of joy. I was sure I had met God and that He had granted me salvation. And I certainly knew that I felt much better than I did a few minutes before, when I had the weight of death and hell on my shoulders.

The next day I went to school and reported to my friends that "I got saved last night." They knew what I meant, but they expressed doubts that my religion would last. It was common for persons who were converted during revivals to "backslide" after a short time, so their reservations were understandable. They had a relatively superficial but straightforward test for the reality of my conversion: They would see if I stopped swearing. I failed the test twice that day, and they immediately pointed it out to me.

Despite this shaky start, the experience had a lasting impact on me. I began reading the Bible and taking an active part in our church. My family attended every Sunday morning and night, every Wednesday night, and any other time the church held special services. I listened to the sermons now in order to "grow," as I had been advised to do, and I often "testified" during Wednesday night "testimony meetings." With the benefit of this kind of nurture, carried out under the watchful eye of my parents and other church members, including my uncle, who had become our pastor, I was well equipped to avoid "backsliding." Indeed, my relationship with God was very real to me, and I wanted to keep moving ahead in the path of obedience to Him.

Two years later, when I was thirteen, I faced a crisis in my spiritual life. I started to sense that God was calling me to be a preacher. Now clergymen are common in my family. Both of my grandfathers were preachers, and so are three of my uncles, one of my brothers, and one of my brothers-in-law. I always believed the ministry was a very serious matter and deserving of the highest respect. Several years after this time, my parents presented me with a Bible in which my father wrote: "Always remember that you have one of the greatest callings that is entrusted to man." That pretty much summed up the attitude of my father and mother toward the call to ministry.

In view of this, it would not be surprising if I were attracted to the ministry.

The thought of it, however, caused a great deal of conflict in my young soul. I'm not sure to this day how to articulate why I believed God was calling me. I know the Bible spoke to me as I read it, and I felt an urgent sense of its truth and importance. But on the other hand, I thought I was not old enough to be a preacher, and I was afraid I was imagining God's call. I kept all of this inside and never shared it with anyone.

The crisis came to a head one Sunday evening, when my uncle preached from the text "I can do all things through Christ which strengtheneth me" (Philippians 4:13). As my uncle preached, it seemed that God was saying to me: "If I call you to preach, I will give you the strength to do it. So you cannot use your age as an excuse." I was struggling with thoughts like this as we sang the final hymn:

> Must Jesus bear the cross alone
> And all the world go free?
> No, there's a cross for everyone
> And there's a cross for me.

These words pierced my heart, and I began to cry. I was overwhelmed with the feeling that I must be willing to preach if that was what God wanted me to do.

My brother-in-law, who was an elder in our church, asked me later what was bothering me. I told him about my feelings, and he asked if I wanted to preach some Sunday. I said I would try, so he arranged for me to preach on November 24, 1968, almost two years after my conversion experience.

I never told anyone that I was going to preach, not even my parents. My father sometimes had to work on Sundays, and as it turned out, he was not there for the occasion.

At any rate, I prepared to preach as best I could, selecting for my text Proverbs 3:5–6, a passage I had memorized at a church camp. I was very nervous as I sat in front of the small congregation that Sunday morning. I felt out of place and was not at all sure I was doing the right thing. I remember very little about my first "sermon" other than that it lasted only about five minutes. The congregation was very encouraging and supportive of my effort, however, and my call to preach seemed to be confirmed.

Before long I was being invited to preach in other area churches. By the time I graduated from high school, I had preached well over 100 sermons. At one memorable time, a revival broke out in my school when a group of my friends came one night to hear me preach at a local church. Several of them were converted that evening and at subsequent services.

My spiritual life during high school was greatly enriched by three summers I spent with an organization called Teen Missions. The first summer, I worked with a group that completed a construction project in Mexico. The second, I was part of a phone counseling ministry in Texas directed to other teenagers. Our training for this ministry included attendance at Explo 72, a large rally and teaching seminar sponsored by Campus Crusade for Christ and held in the Cotton Bowl. The thousands of young believers at the rally cheered as enthusiastically for Jesus as any crowd ever cheered at a football game. We were challenged by speakers such as Bill Bright of Campus Crusade, Billy Graham, and musicians such as Johnny Cash. The event helped give momentum and direction to the "Jesus movement" of the 1970s, which gained national media attention as "Jesus freaks" (converted hippies) became more numerous. My third summer, after high school graduation, I went to England with an evangelistic team. We sang and preached in churches, schools, shopping malls, and even on street corners.

These were heady times indeed for me and for many other youthful adherents of the Kingdom of God. We believed that Jesus was the answer for the problems of life, and we were excited about spreading the word. I remember those summers with great fondness and a sense of nostalgia.

I also remember my early years at Bethel Chapel with warmth and appreciation. I owe a great deal to this church for its loving support during my adolescence. My own parents and other family members played a key role in this. They always taught me that the most important thing in life was one's relationship to God. And they modeled their teaching by giving clear priority to the church over other competing claims on their lives and time. Although they never put pressure on me to enter the ministry, or even suggested that I should do so, after I began to preach, they did everything they could to help me follow that vocation.

My mother was more demonstrative than my father, and she displayed an evangelistic zeal that, I must admit, sometimes embarrassed me. She was straightforward and unpretentious and showed by her life that, like the apostle Paul, she was "not ashamed of the gospel." Another aspect of my mother's life, which I recall now with more appreciation than I had at the time, was her concern for the poor and disadvantaged. We were hardly wealthy ourselves, but Mom had a keen awareness that many people had much less than we. And she was always ready to help them in concrete ways. I do not mean to imply that my parents were without fault, either as parents or as Christians. But their consistency impressed me much more than their inconsistency.

I look back, over several years now, at my conversion and call with a sense of wonder as well as gratitude. Even today, it is hard for me to talk about these events without becoming emotionally moved.

CHRISTIANS FROM LUTHER to C. S. Lewis have had their beliefs and experiences psychoanalyzed and explained away. In an age of deconstruction, it is only natural to cast a suspicious eye on accounts of childhood piety and teenage preaching. My conversion experience could be explained easily enough, I suppose, as an emotional catharsis in a frightened little boy looking for security in a scary world. And as for my call, well, the will to power has its adolescent dimensions. It must be an exhilarating thing for a teenager to speak the word of God to adults.

Such thoughts have, of course, occurred to me, and I have reflected on them from time to time. During the experiences, to be sure, I had no doubt that it was God encountering me, speaking to me, forgiving me, and so on. But the sense of certainty does not continue indefinitely. I am inclined to think that if God had reason for doing so, He could reveal Himself to someone in such a way that the person would find it psychologically impossible ever to doubt the reality of the experience. Perhaps God might choose to do this in the case of special revelation to prophets and apostles. But normal religious experience does not seem to have this sort of invulnerability. At least mine has not.

As long as I have had any sense of these sorts of issues, I have believed that the integrity of my faith depended on the truth of certain historical and theological claims. For instance, sometime during high school I heard about Hugh Schonfield's book *The Passover Plot*. This book received a good deal of notoriety for its reconstruction of the events surrounding Jesus's death. According to Schonfield, Jesus planned his own death and "resurrection." The plan was for him to be taken from the cross while he was still alive and then recover, and later appear to the disciples. The plot was foiled, however, when a soldier pierced Jesus's side on the cross and he actually died.

Now Schonfield's account did not seem very plausible to me, and I do not recall that it seriously disturbed my faith. But I somehow felt that I needed to read the book for my faith to remain credible to myself. I did not want a faith that could not face the facts. I'm not sure what I would have done if I had found Schonfield convincing. I know I could not simply have dismissed the argument as irrelevant.

A few years later, when in college, I saw Bertrand Russell's book *Why I Am Not a Christian* in a bookshop in a synagogue. Again, the book had a fascination for me, and I felt I should read it. I remember feeling a certain anxiety, however, about doing so. I suppose I was afraid my faith would be exposed as indefensible by an intellect superior to mine. There was a suppressed fear that, in the arena of reason and honest inquiry, atheism might win. But I thought I needed to confront this fear, so I started to read.

As it turned out, I found the book provocative and even rather enjoyable. Apart from some of Plato's *Dialogues*, which I read in high school, I think this was, ironically, the first book by a serious philosopher I had ever read. I appreciated Russell's emphasis on the point that Christianity makes truth claims, and that honest belief requires commitment to a certain core of these claims. To this day, one of my favorite sayings is from this book, namely: "I can respect the men who argue that religion is true and, therefore, ought to be believed, but I can only feel profound moral reprobation for those who say that religion ought to be believed because it is useful, and that to ask whether it is true is a waste of time."[1]

Russell's arguments that Christianity is neither useful nor true certainly did not bolster my faith, but neither did they shatter it. I did, however, gain a measure of confidence merely by engaging Russell, reflecting on his arguments, and finding I could still believe what he denied.

During the time this occurred, I was attending Circleville Bible College, a small school near my home in Ohio. Circleville was a "holiness" school with a revivalist emphasis. Each year the school held revivals in which students were encouraged to seek *holiness,* or *entire sanctification,* or the *baptism of the Holy Spirit* (more or less synonymous terms) as a "second definite work of grace" subsequent to conversion. I resonated with the call to live a holy life, a life empowered by the Holy Spirit and totally consecrated to the will of God.

At this point in my life, however, I was somewhat suspicious of emotional religious experiences, despite my own background in a revivalist church. I was more engaged with the sorts of issues Russell had raised about the truth of Christianity. Although I was learning a lot about the Bible and Christian doctrine, most of the courses I took were not directed at these kinds of questions.

Sometime during the two years I was at the Bible College, I was initiated, somewhat fortuitously, into the world of Christian philosophy. I was at home at the time, looking for something to read. It may have been during summer break. I came across a book my father had purchased at a secondhand book-store with the title *Pollution and the Death of Man: A Christian View of Ecology,* by Francis A. Schaeffer, an author of whom I had never heard. Now I didn't have much interest in ecology, but I was curious enough about the notion of a Christian approach to the matter to give the book a try.

To my surprise, I found it absolutely intriguing. Schaeffer described the ecological debate as fundamentally a conflict about the ultimate nature of reality. He argued that neither pantheism, naturalism, nor Platonic dualism gives us an adequate view of nature and of man's relation to it. Along the way, he illustrated his points with references to the likes of Camus, Sartre, Huxley, and the Marquis de Sade. Then he showed how the biblical doctrine of creation gives a basis for treating nature with integrity while also recognizing the special significance of man.

During the next couple of years, I read all of Schaeffer's books. In these, he carried out a broad critique of modern culture, highlighting the loss of mean-ing as expressed in much contemporary art, music, film, and literature. What was particularly exciting for me was how he probed the roots of modern culture by laying out sketches of key movements and ideas in the history of philosophy. And as always, he argued that only Christianity provides satisfy-ing answers to the questions and problems of our age.

Reading Schaeffer transformed my understanding of Christianity. He helped me to think of my faith in a much more comprehensive fashion than I had done before. My faith was becoming a more or less complete world view, which embraced all kinds of things I had never associated very clearly with spirituality. God's existence was seen to be a resource for providing very plausible solutions to problems in the big arenas of metaphysics, morality, and epistemology. And on a smaller scale, I liked the way Schaeffer brought all facets of everyday life under the umbrella of Christian spirituality. I was falling in love during this time with a beautiful and vivacious woman named Patricia, who would later become my wife. I was also writing a lot of poetry, which I enjoyed a great deal. I came to see that both romance and poetry are good gifts of a loving, intelligent Creator, and I could best appreciate such things when I viewed them in this light. My faith was not only answering questions for me, it was also firing with new meaning things I already loved and valued.

After two years at the Bible College, I transferred to Houghton College in the State of New York. I was excited by the prospect of studying philosophy in a more formal manner, and I wanted to take as many classes in the subject as I could, despite a friendly warning I received from the registrar. He remarked to me that the new philosophy professor Larry Wood had only recently received his Ph.D. and that he sometimes forgot that he was teaching *under*graduates.

Perhaps so, but my philosophy classes were the highlight of my two very happy years at Houghton. Wood's classes, which I found provocative, emphasized the history of philosophy and how that history influenced theology, especially in the modern period. In my senior year, another new professor came who was more oriented toward the broadly analytic tradition, namely, Brian Sayers. In a seminar on the philosophy of religion, he introduced me to the charm and challenge of works like Alvin Plantinga's "Free Will Defense." I was enthralled by the rigor and subtlety of the argument and inspired by the fact that such impressive machinery could be deployed in defense of Christian belief. Under the influence of Wood and Sayers, I began to form the aspiration of someday doing a Ph.D. in philosophy or theology.

After graduating from Houghton, I enrolled in Princeton Theological Seminary for my master of divinity degree and then took another master's degree at Yale Divinity School. Since my undergraduate training had been in conservative evangelical colleges, I thought it would be beneficial to do my theological studies at more liberal mainline schools.

These years were valuable for giving me a firsthand acquaintance with the remarkable variety of options in contemporary theology. The traditional orthodoxy I had always believed was challenged from a number of directions by many students and faculty alike. Although I had come to Princeton precisely to encounter such views, it was still initially somewhat disconcerting to find myself defending, say, the deity of Jesus as an essential Christian doctrine in conversations with fellow churchmen. These discussions caused me to do a lot of thinking about the whole notion of essential Christian doctrine and about the role of propositional belief in Christian faith.

My reflections on these issues convinced me that the doctrines of the Creeds are the defining boundaries of Christian belief, as well as integral to meaningful worship and other Christian practice. It seemed to me that much contemporary theology had abandoned traditional faith without seriously engaging it or appreciating its true riches. The trendy theology that was offered in its place was often vague in its claims, and when it was clear, it was sometimes hard to see how it even qualified as a version of Christianity. Such theology typically left me with the feeling that it was just not worth believing. I have never understood, for instance, why anyone would want to become or remain a Christian if the supernatural elements of the faith were eliminated or given a merely existential interpretation, as in Bultmann's theology.

My work in philosophy, by contrast, continued to help me conceptualize and articulate my faith. Indeed, I was coming more and more to suspect that orthodox Christianity was getting a better hearing in many philosophical circles than it was in many theological circles. Two events symbolize why this seemed to me to be the case.

The first was a lecture by Alvin Plantinga, who came to the seminary under the sponsorship of a student group in which I was active. The lecture was an analysis and a sharp critique of Gordon Kaufman's book *God the Problem,* which argued that we cannot know anything about God as He is in Himself. The only God we have access to is a mental construct of our own making. Now such views have been theologically fashionable for some time. Plantinga, however, showed no reverence either for these views or for their best-known progenitor, namely, Kant, as he spelled out the philosophical and theological problems in this sort of position. His crisp critique of such theology was a refreshing breeze of clean air for me and many other students who attended.

The second event was more low key. It was my happening on Peter Geach's book *Providence and Evil,* which was newly published at the time. As I thumbed through the book, I was pleasantly surprised to see extended discussion and defense of the traditional Christian doctrines of original sin and hell, among other things. I did not know much about Geach at the time—or I would hardly have been surprised—but I did know he was a distinguished British philosopher. A line on the dust jacket also caught my eye. It said that the book was "in striking contrast, both in style and substance, to the concessive uncertainties of most recent Christian apologetics."

Well, I know the contrast certainly was not lost on me. It was hard to find anyone in contemporary theology who had much interest in those topics, especially hell. Where eternal life was still affirmed, universal salvation seemed generally to be assumed. Most did not think the topic of hell even worthy of serious debate. Geach obviously thought otherwise. I remember well the sense of irony I felt that a noted philosopher should be defending a doctrine so widely abandoned by theologians. By the time I graduated from Princeton and entered Yale, I had pretty much concluded that for my concerns, I should eventually pursue a graduate degree in philosophy.

My year at Yale was a pleasant and productive one, mainly because of the several courses I took with Paul Holmer. His thought had been shaped significantly by Kierkegaard and Wittgenstein, and I read both of them under his tutelage. I found these writers enormously stimulating, although I was uneasy with the fideistic/relativistic flavor of their writings. I was also attracted by the intensity of these figures, which I suspect connected at some level with the intensity of my revivalist heritage. (Perhaps this also explains, more remotely, the affinity I have always felt for Bobby Knight and John McEnroe, two of my favorite personalities in the world of sports!) Appropriately enough, I also took from Holmer a course he called "Emotions, Passions, and Feelings." One of the main lessons I learned here was about the interrelationship between the emotions, the intellect, and the will. I came to recognize much more fully the cognitive dimension of emotion, and this helped me to relate more intelligently the emotional component of my religious life to my more recent quest for an intellectually satisfying account of my faith.

For the next three years I served as the pastor of a rural United Methodist church in northwestern Ohio and was ordained into the ministry of that denomination. The preaching and teaching aspects of the ministry were very fulfilling; administration and visitation were less so. Preaching especially is demanding work, and my own spiritual life was much enriched by the continual attempt to communicate Christian doctrine and teaching to my congregation in a way they found clear and applicable to the experiences of daily life.

I particularly enjoyed preaching during the part of the church year that stretches from Advent through Trinity Sunday. I found that the great doctrines of the church "preach well" because they make sense of our lives and answer to our deepest hopes and aspirations. Our desire for love and our belief in its importance is supported by the doctrine of the Trinity, which maintains that the Father, Son, and Holy Spirit always existed in a relationship of perfect love, even before the world was created. So love and relationship are not relative newcomers in the history of the world, which emerged accidentally from the blind forces of matter. Rather, love and relationship "go all the way down" in the structure of reality.

Incarnation is a majestic story of love and redemption that can transform our lives. When Jesus tells us that we are to love each other as he has loved us, it is remarkable (John 13:34). But it is truly staggering in view of Jesus' further statement that he loved us as the Father loved him (John 15:9). In Jesus, the eternal love of the Trinity was lived out in our midst. And he commands us to perpetuate the same sort of love, and promises to give us the inner power to do so through the coming of the Holy Spirit at Pentecost.

Resurrection likewise stirs deep chords of desire by giving reason from concrete history that love is stronger than death. I know my spirit soars when I sing Charles Wesley's great hymn "Christ the Lord Is Risen Today." And Christ's promise that he will return stirs to life a hope for the pure joy of His coming kingdom, a hope that must lie buried if Christ is not raised.

The power of these doctrines also came into focus for me in the high moments of celebration and the hours of crisis that ministers are privileged to share with parishioners. The strength of the Christian message is evident in the fact that it is not mute in the face of death. I do not mean to deny or trivialize the pain and horror of death. But the crisis of mortality can bring into sharp relief the resilience of the Christian view of life. The same is true of the joyous occasion of a Christian wedding. Trinity, Incarnation, Resurrection, and Pentecost charge matrimony with depth of meaning and provide resources of resolve and confidence that the weighty vows of marriage can be kept.

During the years I was in parish ministry, I continued to read philosophy when I could, and I also wrote a few papers in philosophical theology. I also came to the important insight, from studying St. Paul's teaching on the gifts of the Spirit, that teaching can be as much a form of Christian ministry as preaching. This was significant for me because I had come to feel that my own inclinations and interests were in the area of teaching. Furthermore, my earlier aspiration to do graduate work in philosophy had not waned but had in fact grown stronger. So at the end of three years at the church, I enrolled in the philosophy department at Notre Dame.

I was excited to be going to Notre Dame, for it was developing a reputation as the place to study philosophy of religion, my main area of interest. And indeed, my years at Notre Dame were everything I had hoped they would be. Intellectually, these years were the highlight of my life.

I was challenged afresh by the vision of a thoroughly and profoundly Christian philosophy. The nature, the shape, and the possibilities of such a way of doing philosophy were articulated with compelling force by Alvin Plantinga, Tom Morris, and Fred Freddoso, among others. I saw more clearly than ever that Christian belief can mesh nicely with exacting philosophical thought. I also gained a much greater appreciation of the philosophical resources available for explicating Christian doctrine. My dissertation dealt with a doctrine that raises the problem of evil in a particularly acute form, namely, the doctrine of eternal hell. The idea of hell had haunted my imagination since my earliest religious experiences, and I had been giving it serious thought ever since seminary. My research on the matter convinced me that the doctrine does involve a number of important philosophical and theological issues, and that the problems it raises are not beyond resolution.

After three years in the bright shadow of the Golden Dome, I left Notre Dame for the bluegrass of Kentucky to take a job ideally suited to my background and interests, namely, teaching philosophy of religion at Asbury Seminary, a school in the Methodist tradition. Here I answer my call to ministry by helping train students who have experienced a similar call and who desire, as I still do, a greater understanding of the faith they have embraced.

WRITING THIS PIECE has been itself a spiritual experience for me, and has served to remind me of why I still believe I encountered God when I was eleven years old and have walked in His grace—often very imperfectly—ever since. I am reminded that what I believe about the story of my life is inseparable from what I believe about the history of the world. I continue to believe God has forgiven my sins and filled me with his Holy Spirit, and I reject a Freudian or Nietzschean reduction of these experiences because I believe Trinity, Creation, Incarnation, Resurrection, and Pentecost are true accounts of what is real and what has happened. To perceive the world in these terms not only makes sense of my life to this point but also gives me a hopeful view of the future.

Recently, my eleven-year-old daughter, Angela, was confirmed in proper United Methodist fashion. As she took her vows of church membership, I reflected again on my own visceral conversion experience at the same age, and I was inwardly moved. I found myself hoping and praying that the beliefs she was professing would be deeply rooted in her heart. I want her to grow up believing in a God of love, whose Son died for her sins and was resurrected from the dead. And I want this God of love to preserve her for eternity in his everlasting arms.

For reasons like this, I readily admit that I *want* Christianity to be true. I care about the things it promises, and it is emotionally and morally satisfying to believe those promises will be kept. Too much is at stake for me to feign indifference. And yet, I could not continue to believe if I did not find Christianity intellectually satisfying as well. I did not come to Christ initially for philosophical insight, but such understanding has been vital for my keeping the faith.

I recall here a passage from Kierkegaard in which he maintains that those who truly believe do not need proof or objective evidence:

> But when faith begins to feel embarrassed and ashamed, like a young woman for whom her love is no longer sufficient, but who secretly feels ashamed of her lover and must therefore have it established that there is something remarkable about him—when faith begins to lose its passion, when faith begins to cease to be faith, then a proof becomes necessary so as to command respect from the side of unbelief.[2]

But I believe Kierkegaard misrepresents the role that evidence and rational arguments play in relation to faith. They are not adduced just to gain respect from unbelievers. Rather, their primary role is to address questions that naturally occur to believers themselves.

My faith in the Resurrection, for instance, is not sustained just because my passions are stirred when I sing the great hymns of Easter. Nor is my will, in concert with my passions, sufficient to carry the weight of this belief. I continue to affirm the Resurrection of Jesus largely because I believe a good case can be made for it in the court of rational investigation. If I did not think so, my faith in Christ would lack integrity. My emotions and my will would follow after him; my mind would not.

My explorations in philosophy have convinced me that all three can unite in affirming "that there is something remarkable about Him," that in following Him is salvation.

Notes

1. Bertrand Russell, *Why I Am Not a Christian* (New York: Simon and Schuster, 1957), 197.

2. Søren Kierkegaard, *Concluding Unscientific Postscript* (Princeton, N.J.: Princeton University Press, 1968), p. 31.

8

A LITTLE

PROTECTOR

Robert C. Roberts

*Early Experience:
Years 1–21*

My parents had five children, of whom I am the oldest. My brother Jim is twenty months younger, Margaret is three years younger, and Lissy (who died in childbirth in 1987) was five years younger. When I was fifteen, Nancy was born.

My father, who was a lawyer, searched incessantly for a solution to life's questions and problems, especially the problems of suffering, illness, and mortality. He was curious about some forms of Christianity. In the late 1950s he watched Oral Roberts's healing meetings on TV, and he was later impressed with Billy Graham. But he had little use for the local congregation, which he regarded as promoting an empty, impractical, and powerless religion. He inclined more to movements like L. Ron Hubbard's Dianetics (later called *Scientology*). For some reason, he did go to church for a while in my adolescence and even held the office of deacon in the Presbyterian church. But for the last thirty or so years of his life, his religious aspirations were focused more on health foods, herbal medicines, yoga, and the ouija board.

Dad always seemed to me to need caring for, and I was willing enough to oblige, both mentally and behaviorally. I worried about him, was afraid he would die young, fretted when he didn't come home from work on time, watched for signs of decline, and found a lot of them. (By the time he died at age eighty-one, I had pretty much quit worrying about him, having brought into the world three new little people to worry about.) Behaviorally, I tried to make his life more pleasant. Mom would say, "Why don't you go out and play with your daddy?," and I would go out to the workshop and stand around while he worked on his projects. I think I owe to my father a basic confidence in my own abilities, to which I have sometimes adhered in the face of powerful counterevidence. He never flagged in his conviction, often expressed, that I was up to anything I tried.

Mom is the daughter of a Presbyterian minister. She was the source of the religious instruction we received in the home; she was the stay that kept us going to church. I was probably influenced by a Nazarene Bible class I went to briefly as a child and by my friend Darrell Johnson, whose family were fundamentalists. I wouldn't have known what fundamentalists were in those days, but I did notice that the Johnsons took their religion a lot more seriously than we Presbyterians did. They seemed to believe everything they read in the Bible, and I remember how odd it was that they dutifully called out the selahs when they read the Psalms. When I was twelve or thirteen, we became charter members of the Trinity Presbyterian church, whose founding minister was Hank Andersen. Tall, handsome Hank was a natural leader who always seemed relaxed and in control, preached moderate, practical, and serious sermons, and was adored by the congregation. It was during one of his sermons, preached in the school auditorium before Trinity had a building of our own, that I decided to become a minister. Why? Probably because Hank was so glorious and loved, but also, I think, because I thought that anybody who spent as much time and concentration on eternal matters as a minister does couldn't possibly miss being saved, and Darrell and the Nazarenes had me worried about that. I never did quite lose my desire to be a minister, even to this day. Later, I think I was motivated by a more aesthetic concern, to wit, that I felt there was something deep about what ministers preoccupy themselves with, and I wanted to be in on it and spend my time exploring it. My mother once asked me why I wanted to be a minister, and I told her it was because I enjoyed working with people. She was surprised to hear that. I have learned to enjoy people quite a bit more than I used to, and I attribute the change in part to Christian nurture; but I am still a little bit ambivalent about the critters.

I mustn't give the impression that my childhood was consumed with religious preoccupations. I was a busy child, mostly with business of my own making, most of which was nonintellectual. We lived on the outskirts of Wichita and had enough land to raise animals and vegetables. I tried to sell garden produce to the local grocery store, and for a week at the end of June and the beginning of July, Jimmy, Dad, and I would construct a stand, set it by the side of the road, and Jimmy and I would sell fireworks. Dad built scooters and go-carts and I worked at it with him, but I never became much good at things mechanical. (I remember what a triumph it was when I succeeded in changing the transmission in my 1951 Chevy when I was about sixteen.) At various times I raised chickens, lambs, turkeys, ducks, pheasants, quail, and rabbits. I hunted and fished with my friend Johny Howell, and in the winter ran traplines along the river that flowed behind our house, stretched the pelts, and sold them to Sears, Roebuck. Johny and I took a correspondence course in taxidermy, and we would shoot pigeons in abandoned siloes late at night with our blow darts and then mount the pathetic things, lumpy and leaning. Later, I took up photography, and retouched negatives for portrait studios around Wichita and set up a studio of my own in my Grandmother Roberts's basement. I practiced the guitar a lot and was active in the Wichita Society of the Classic Guitar. As a teenager, I took up with some Mexican and Cuban people and learned Spanish from some of them.

It sometimes came up that I might make a career of photography or music, but I never took such ideas seriously because of the sense of destiny that Dad's confidence in me instilled. I fancied myself an intellectual, though I had achieved nothing, even by local school standards, that would support such a claim. And I had the sense, not entirely distinct from the claim to brilliance, that I was "called" to the ministry, something that I regarded as quantitatively higher than making beautiful pictures and beautiful sounds. I'm afraid I was more than a bit of a snob.

Somewhere around my fifteenth year, I read Will Durant's *The Story of Philosophy* and was especially inspired by what he said about Schopenhauer and Kant. With my exalted opinion of myself, I thought I was quite a lot like both of them—deep and almost mystically sensitive to the darker side of existence, like Schopenhauer, and intellectually brilliant, like Kant. So I chose the topic of "pessimism" for my high school junior research paper. I remember the sense of awe and excitement I felt in the stacks of the Wichita Public Library as I comtemplated the potential for deep spiritual riches hidden in dusty volumes like *The World as Will and Idea* and the *Critique of Pure Reason*. I would read bits of them at the heavy walnut tables of the library, my sense of awe being increased by my near-inability to make anything out of them. During this time I started visiting used-book stores, where I bought books mentioned by Durant, and new-book stores, where I bought Harry Austryn Wolfson's *Spinoza* and Bertrand Russell's *A History of Western Philosophy*. I still have a copy of Herbert Spencer's *First Principles* that I bought in one of those used-book shops. (Sorry to say, I haven't read it yet.) I also bought several copies of the *Critique of Pure Reason*. I don't remember why I thought it would be better to have more than one.

My paper was on Schopenhauer's pessimism, but most of my reading was not from Schopenhauer, but from Durant and encyclopedias that I found in the public library. A chief charm of the topic was its shock value. My mother received with more equanimity and good humor than I expected my announcement that I was a pessimist, but that disappointment was not repeated at school. My English teacher was a very proper and completely humorless single Christian lady about fifty years old whom it was one of my favorite pastimes to scandalize. When I told her of my chosen topic, she obligingly pursed her lips and tried in vain to dissuade me. I remember the sense I had, during the weeks of that research, of being spiritually deep and superior. As I walked down the halls of the high school, passing among all the ordinary people, I knew that I carried within me an exalting secret: As a philosopher, I was in touch (or at least on the verge of being in touch) with Being.

The senior year brought another opportunity for a research paper, and I chose the epistemology of Kant's first *Critique*. This time I did study the book itself, slowly and laboriously, sentence by sentence, refusing to go on until I had achieved some sense of what Kant had said in any given paragraph. I remember setting up the garage a large aluminum table on which I could spread out all my note cards. In memory it seems as though I sat there for hours on end, laboring to master a paragraph or two, but I'm sure my attention span was in fact quite short and my mastery unimpressive. I tried to cover the whole book and did some writing on the Transcendental Dialect, but the text I had really understood, to some degree, was limited to the Introduction, the Transcendental Aesthetic, and the very beginning of the Transcendental Analytic.

While involvement with all this heady stuff was certainly an ego trip, as I have indicated, it seems to me that it was also a search for something beyond or above or underneath the ordinary experiences of gardens and chickens, of houses and cars and the routines of daily life, of photographs and music, of the cycles of life and death and life and death. Looked at from the viewpoint of a Christian psychology, it was the restlessness of the heart that Augustine speaks of, the generic human yearning to find (or be found by) Something utterly worthy of praise, something in which to "rest"—not in the sense of taking one's ease, but in the sense in which a building rests on its foundations. We are foundation seekers and show by our restlessness that we are at present floating unnaturally, detached from the Solidity and Depth to which we were created to be tied. The search for the Foundation cannot, in us, be separated from the search for the understanding of our life, and so it always takes, it seems to me, the form of a search for concepts in terms of which to make sense of ourselves and our world. That is, it's always a philosophical or theological project. The Christian sees, in the midst of all the perversity that attends the search, the hand of God beckoning the soul to himself and the soul reaching, groping, even if it knows it not, for that hand.

With Will Durant's help, I was more aware than most college freshmen of what philosophy is, and so when I went to Wichita State University in the fall of 1960, I declared myself a philosophy major from the beginning. The department at that period was nothing to write home about. The one professor lectured on the history of philosophy by reading especially pertinent passages to us from the textbook, understandably had difficulty keeping order in class, and after my second year took a job as a logician in some company in the Southwest. I remained a philosophy major during those two years but spent them mostly studying French and Spanish and music theory, in addition to general education. It wasn't until I got back from Europe in 1963 that I started studying philosophy in earnest. In one of my classes—I can no longer remember which—I met a student named Conner Sorenson, who was to be instrumental in my religious development.

In late spring 1962 I went to Europe, to study French in the Cours de Civilisation Française pour les Étrangers at the Sorbonne in Paris during the academic year, and spend the summers in Siena studying guitar in Andrés Segovia's master class at the Accademia Chigiana. After flying into Shannon, I stopped in London on my way to Siena. I went to a phone booth and looked up John Williams, who, though already a famous guitarist at that time, was almost exactly my age. I called him, and he was willing to see me. He served me tea, and since I neglected to have my last meal, I ate all his biscuits. I think he was a little dismayed by that, but he was even more dismayed by what came next. We talked about Siena, where he was often showcased as Segovia's star pupil, and he asked me to play something. I played the first movement of Lennox Berkeley's Sonatina for Guitar, and he said, "You know, Siena is for people who *already* know how to play the guitar." But he followed up with the comforting statement that there would no doubt be other people "like you." In a day or two I left for Italy, but having not yet learned the difference between checking one's bags into the train's luggage and checking them into a holding room in the train station, I arrived in Florence twenty-four hours later without guitar or money and only the clothes on my back. It was a complicated business, arranging to have the bags sent across two national borders in my absence, and two weeks was a long time to subsist on panini and wander around Florence unable to afford the galleries and other tourist attractions.

Williams's assessment was borne out when the class started a couple of weeks later. After the audition, I was relegated to observer status when Segovia was teaching, though fortunately for me and others like me, Segovia disappeared within a week or two, and we were all given lessons by his assistant, Alirio Diaz, who himself was no mean guitarist. Unlike Segovia, Diaz rotated democratically through the whole class, giving lessons to all who wanted them. In the second summer, however, Segovia stayed in Siena much longer. Diaz taught people like me separately, but in the main sessions Segovia worked with his favorites by rotation. If there was time left over after they had all had their lessons, he would call for volunteers from among the players who were like me. We were all cowards, of course, and the class would end because nobody volunteered. After this happened a couple of times, I became disturbed that we were missing a golden opportunity to have a lesson from the maestro. So one afternoon when the call for volunteers went out, I screwed up my courage and walked up onto the platform. (We were meeting in a tiny, plush concert hall in the Chigi palace that was designed for a small organ. It had perhaps no more than fifty seats, and a little stage on which sat Segovia in the center, his twenty-one-year-old wife on the left, and Alirio Diaz on the right, with the student guitarist sitting square in front of Segovia.) Segovia didn't have a reputation for gentleness, and I was scared spitless: It had left my mouth and was now coming out of the pores in my fingertips, and my hands felt fat and foreign. No longer part of me, they now seemed to need commanding from afar. "What will you play?" he asked, and my answer was unfortunate. It was a piece by Albert Roussel titled "Segovia." Like the Berkeley Sonatina, it was too hard for me except when I was very relaxed, and I butchered it. "Do you have anything else?" he asked, without commenting on my performance of "Segovia." I offered to play Sor Study No. 12, which was also too difficult (would I never learn?). When I botched it too, he motioned to the class for a guitar, and played a few bars of Sor Study No. 12, with all the mistakes I had made and with his mouth gaping open, as mine had been. (I have a deviated septum and sometimes breathe with difficulty in the springtime.) I took that as my dismissal and returned to my seat. After this, as I remember it, the summer passed without any more volunteers from among the people like me.

Italy brought out the romantic and the quasi-mystic in me. Oscar Ghiglia, who at that time was the star of Segovia's class, would lead a little group out to the steps of the Chiesa dei Servi or to a wine cellar located in the city wall that overlooked the olive groves, and would play exquisitely for us among those ancient stones. We would drink wine whose flavor in the night air seemed metaphysical in its implications, and this combination of beauty and antiquity seemed to put us in the presence of Something great and deep and foundational beyond the senses. The cathedrals of Europe, viewed from inside, had and still have a cognate effect on me. Salient in my memory is an experience of "depth" that I had the morning I left Siena for France at the end of my first summer. It was cool, and the sun was just preparing to rise over the city and the surrounding countryside. The streets were deserted, except for the produce vendors who were entering town and setting up for the day's work. As I walked to the train station with my bags, the glowing sky and the stone city below it seemed to speak of something permanent and profound, which I was on the verge of glimpsing. Precipitating the experience were no doubt factors like sleep deprivation, the nervous excitement of facing anew the unknown, and recent reading of Evelyn Underhill and Aldous Huxley. Like many experiences of romantics, this one had an element of ostentation and self-congratulation: How deep and sensitive *I* am, to experience the world in this way! Yet despite our suspicions of it, the Christian view of the world justifies our treating such experiences as urgings of our eternal nature and as promptings of God. When I got to Paris it was still several weeks before classes started at the Sorbonne, and, of course, I didn't know anybody. So, being the shy person I was, I holed up in a hotel and read books in my native language, one of the most memorable of which was

Evelyn Underhill's *Mysticism,* which filled me with romanticized religious aspirations.

Conversion and Later
Formal Education

During my fifteen months in Europe I had written a couple of times to Conner Sorenson, the student at Wichita State I mentioned earlier. I don't understand how Conner got singled out for this privilege. I wrote to a few people other than my family and didn't know Conner particularly well. In any case, on returning, I found that my letters had precipitated a friendship.

Conner belonged to the chapter of Inter-Varsity Christian Fellowship (IVCF) on campus. He gently urged me to greater Christian commitment and invited me, a few weeks after school started, to a retreat at the Kansas Bible Camp in Hutchinson. There I was struck by the very concrete and personal relationship that the students had with God, and how seriously they took Jesus Christ as mediator and member of this relationship. My own religious-ness, up to this point, had been tentative and searching, and the object of my worship (if what I did could be called worship) was very indefinite. It was as though these students *had* what I was merely *looking for.* But even more crucial was my meeting Richard Burson.

Richard was the closest thing to a pope that the Plymouth Brethren have. He directed the Kansas Bible Camp and traveled far and wide, visiting congre-gations for encouragement, renewal, and problem solving. He was convinced of the importance of a vital intellectual life among Christians, and had a book display at which he sold good Christian books at very good prices. Being the bookworm that I was, I was sniffing around those tables when Richard came by and struck up a conversation with me. I told him I wanted to go into the ministry. He asked me how long I had been a Christian, and I told him I wasn't sure I was one. I don't remember the details of the conversation that ensued, but eventually we crossed the yard to his house, where he had some-thing he wanted to read to me. It was Francis Thompson's "The Hound of Heaven." He read the poem to me and then told me quietly, but very defi-nitely and with no trace of tentativeness, that God was on my trail, that He wanted me for His own, and the He would not stop until I was firmly in His fellowsip. It turned out, in the sequel, that Richard himself was a chief agent of God's resoluteness and perseverance in this matter. I remember one very slow automobile ride between Wichita and Hutchinson during which I said something like "I'm glad to have Jesus save me from my sin, but it's unreal to me because I don't feel like a sinner." Richard wisely told me that feeling like a sinner is also a matter of spiritual growth, and that that would eventually come. We had long conversations in which the work of C. S. Lewis figured importantly. He gave me many books then and in the coming year. I read Lewis at his urging. I learned from Lewis, but found him a bit too jaunty and rather pat and not dark enough. Richard visited me several times in Wichita, and I visited him in Hutchinson. In subsequent years he had me up to the Camp to lead Bible studies and talk to groups. That weekend at the Kansas Bible Camp also marked the beginning of my involvement with the IVCF, which was to continue for the following two years at Wichita State and then again for three or four years at Yale.

The IVCF has been a significant source of sustenance and occasion of growth. It has also been a source of conflict and pain. I have felt guilty, and still do, about my disinclination to collar people, the way Richard Burson collared me, and speak to them seriously and personally about Jesus Christ. Why am I so disinclined to do for others what was such an important contribution to my own life? When I am among non-Christian intellectuals, I make it a point to "witness" in the sense of making it plain to them that I am a Christian, and I am glad to talk to them about Christianity. But I am not aggressive and ingressive in the way that Richard and the best of the Inter-Varsity types are, and I often feel that this failure is a failure of love.

If Lewis wasn't dark enough for my taste, Kierkegaard was. In a religion course and in one on existentialism at Wichita State, we were assigned *Fear and Trembling* and selections from *Concluding Unscientific Postscript*. I was vastly attracted to Kierkegaard's religious passionateness, his intellectual depth, his literary playfulness and brilliance and elusiveness, his Christian orthodoxy combined with an appreciation for a general religiousness in human beings. Here was a Christian philosopher who was also a world-class artist and intellect. He also did what seemed to me essential for any philosophy worthy of the name "Christian," namely, to get beyond merely theorizing about God and creation, and to speak (write) in a manner that transforms, renews, encourages, and builds up the spirit. Kierkegaard seemed to combine the mind of a first-rate philosopher with the rhetorical and counseling skills of a first-rate pastor. He seemed to me the answer, the thinker who could guide me in the ways of mind and heart and spirit.

On returning from Europe, I was greeted by a reconstituted philosophy department with Anthony Genova at the head and Troy Majors teaching history of philosophy and continental, while both worked on their dissertations. Richard Lineback joined the department the following year, as I remembered. My first experience of studying philosophy under a first-rate teacher was Genova's course on Berkeley, Hume, and Kant, for which I wrote a paper comparing Hume's ethics with Kant's. I had never thought so hard or written so scrupulously and slowly. My A+ gained me a certain notoriety in the department and the paper got Genova's attention, though he became disillusioned with me later when I came under the influence of Wittgenstein. I took Genova's seminar on my beloved first *Critique* and Majors's course on Plato's *Dialogues* and Lineback's in analytic philosophy. I didn't do justice to any of them, but they laid foundations in philosophy that have remained with me these many years.

In the fall of 1965 I enrolled in Princeton Theological Seminary in accord with my intention to become a minister of the gospel or something (by this time it was becoming pretty clear that my interests and talents were more intellectual than would be good for the local parish). I chose Princeton because it was a seminary of my Protestant denomination, but also because I supposed it would be a good place to study Kierkegaard, since Walter Lowrie, the first major English translator of Kierkegaard's works, had taught at Princeton. I was also interested in studying with John Hick. As it turned out, there was little interest in Kierkegaard at Princeton, and Hick had recently left. Diogenes Allen had not yet arrived. (I think he was hired the spring that I left.) I learned quite a bit of theology while at Princeton, but for me the most consequential event of the year was a talk given by Paul Holmer of Yale Divinity School. In near-blizzard conditions, I made my way across campus one evening to the common room, where Holmer spoke on "Bonhoeffer and Concepts." I can't remember a single particular of Holmer's talk, but hearing it was an experience of recognition: I heard in that talk something rare, something like what came across in Kierkegaard's writings and in little else, a perfect combination of intellectual power and passionate will or spiritual integrity. I knew then that I needed to study with Holmer. The next morning I found him at breakfast in the refectory. I talked to him about studying Kierkegaard at Yale and asked whether I could come to Yale Divinity School (YDS). He gave me permission and the matter was settled, as far as I was concerned. I told my friends at Princeton that I was going to Yale. But on the way, I spent a year studying Aristotle, Heidegger, and Wittgenstein, among other things, at Wichita State, where Genova had offered me a teaching assistantship.

It was becoming increasingly clear that something was wrong with my family. My brother Jimmy returned prematurely from Peace Corps work in Colombia because of a breakdown connected with his sense of himself. Upon returning from a year's travel in Europe, my sister Margaret became quite depressed and disappeared one night. Dad found her the next day, sitting on a log in the woods up the river from our house, where she said she had been meditating on the problems of life. And Nancy, my youngest sister, was becoming increasingly thin and unmanageable and behaviorally enmeshed with my mother in an episode of anorexia nervosa (as it was to be professionally labeled a couple of years later). I think it was as much the sense that I needed to be near home as the opportunity to be paid for studying that led me to go for the master's degree at Wichita State.

The following fall I went to YDS, more worried than ever about the state of my family, and feeling increasingly that if I didn't do something about Nancy, nobody would. Mom seemed to be willing to give her life for Nancy, but that was only making things worse, and Dad just sat there helplessly, withdrawing more and more. At Yale I studied monomaniacally with Paul Holmer, neglecting, to my loss, many of the rich resources of YDS but profiting enormously from Holmer's inspiration and example. (I've always suffered from a certain narrowness, but I've also felt that, because of native limitations of mind, an effort at greater breadth would probably have resulted in an unacceptable shallowness.) During my two years at YDS, I did take four seminars in Yale's philosophy department on Hegel's *Phenomenology of Spirit* (Kenley Dove),

Kierkegaard's *Either/Or* (Karsten Harries), Kant's first *Critique* (John Smith), and Wittgenstein (Robert Fogelin). Nancy continued to degenerate, and I looked for a way to get back to Wichita without abandoning my work entirely. I found a pastoral internship at Grace Presbyterian Church in Little Rock, Arkansas—not very close to Wichita, but within a day's drive.

On my understanding of philosophy and theology, they aren't completely disconnected from the nurture of souls. So this was not the hiatus in my philosophical education that it might have been for somebody on whose view philosophy is primarily a matter of esoteric theory. I visited the sick, managed the youth group, preached periodically, and conducted a horrific emergency funeral in the absence of the pastor. I came to know, and to feel affection for, all kinds of people I would never have met within the halls of the academy. I got to the point where explaining my desire to go into the ministry as I had twelve years earlier—that I enjoyed working with people—was no longer a lie, though I never got beyond needing to be away from people for a portion of the day. I think the fifteen months I worked under pastor Don Campbell's wise direction not only readied me to be a better churchman and a better teacher of undergraduates, but also gave me a subtler and more realistic basis for making judgments in certain areas of philosophy and theology. Lack of contact with human reality afflicts a lot of theology and philosophy, and always to their detriment.

During the year in Little Rock, Nancy's condition came to a crisis. I looked for an institutional setting for her in Arkansas (in retrospect, a very bad idea), and after a horrendous weekend in which I had her with me in Little Rock, we discovered that one of the best places in the world to be mentally disturbed was Kansas. On admission to Topeka State Hospital in 1969, she weighed about fifty pounds. On release from that hospital in 1972 she weighed twice as much and looked wonderful, but her troubles were by no means over.

When I returned to Yale in the fall of 1969, I was much more at ease about the situation at home and continued my studies under Holmer—Kierkegaard; Wittgenstein; emotions, passions, and feelings; virtues and vices; the nature of theology and its relation to faith. I believe it was at about this time that I became good friends with Richard Olmsted. We endlessly discussed preaching and pastoral work, faith and history, the epistemology of conversion, the nature of doctrine, the virtues and limits of Wittgensteinian theology. Richard insisted, in a way that none of the other theologians at Yale did, on the centrality to Christian thought of the Christian teaching about the atonement of Jesus Christ for sin. This was a time when much of the agenda for my future thinking, teaching, and writing was set, and it was Holmer the professor and Olmsted the fellow student who contributed most to my formation.

If I were to characterize in a phrase the outlook that was emerging, it would be a conviction of the truth and adequacy of orthodox Christian doctrine of a Reformed or Lutheran tint, along with an insistence that that doctrine not become an end in itself, but that it form the background of lives lived in Christian holiness and emotional vitality. Thus we were both ill at ease with doctrinal revision of the sort we saw in Schleiermacher, Bultmann, and Tillich, and also wary of scholasticism and indeed of academic theology generally. Theology was always to be practiced within, and formative of, the life of the church and the life of the individual Christian. We were also very critical of the conceptual sloppiness that characterized most of the theology of that time, and of theology in the service of politics and various social causes of the left or right. During the second semester of 1969–70 I was interim pastor of the First Congregational Church of Westbrook, Connecticut, where again I had a very warm experience of ministry.

By this time, however, I was clearly headed toward a career in the academy and applied to five philosophy departments for admission to their Ph.D. programs. All turned me down, and Holmer helped me arrange hastily to begin D.Phil. work at Mansfield College, Oxford. There I was assigned to John Macquarrie, just the kind of theologian I had learned to distrust. Partly due to my own immaturity and arrogance, our relationship was strained from the beginning, and after three terms at Oxford, which in other ways were quite glorious and instructive, I returned to Yale in 1971, this time to the Department of Religious Studies, to pursue the Ph.D. I took a year of coursework and then, starting with material I had written in a course with David Kelsey, quickly wrote a dissertation on Rudolf Bultmann's theology, using philosophical techniques that I seem to have learned from Wittgenstein, and started looking for a job teaching theology. Finding nothing, I resigned myself to another year at Yale, during which I would compose the final chapter of my dissertation and write articles for publication. But in August 1973, I received a call from Western Kentucky University, wondering whether I'd like to teach philosophy there.

Career

I flew down to Bowling Green and back to New Haven all in the same day, as I had sole responsibility for Paul Holmer's house. During that day I interviewed, signed the contract, and ordered the books for the courses that I would start teaching in a couple of weeks. The first year or more I worked incessantly, often arriving at the office at 4:00 A.M. so that I would have something intelligible to say at 9:15. As one preparing to teach theology, I had not recently been studying the kind of philosophy that one can teach to beginning undergraduates. My courses were Introduction to Philosophy, Ethics, and Symbolic Logic, and I was lecturing, as one of my colleagues put it, "hand to mouth"—that is, no sooner were the notes on paper than they needed to come out of my mouth. Indeed, the lag time was sometimes as little as a minute and a half. I managed to prepare decently well for Intro and Symbolic Logic, but I skated a lot in Ethics. I remember overhearing one student, who had the misfortune to take both Intro and Ethics from me in my first semester of teaching, say to another that the two courses were pretty much the same.

When summer came, I wrote the remaining chapter of my dissertation, which I also published in the *Scottish Journal of Theology*. Since then I have always avoided teaching summer school, using that time (sometimes the only opportunity) to work out my own thoughts and writing.

The department of philosophy and religion at Western Kentucky University (which is said to have been the successor of the earlier department of philosophy and penmanship) was founded in the 1960s as an evangelical department, the idea being that if secularists could use the state university for their ideological purposes, as they no doubt often do, then Christians might do the same thing. Being in the Bible Belt and somewhat insulated from mainstream academic life, Western made it easier than it might have been at most state universities to get away with hiring faculty on the basis of their Christian beliefs. (Western was jokingly referred to as the largest Southern Baptist university in the country, and in the phone call initiating my candidacy for a job, one of the first questions put to me was "Are you an evangelical?") The department head got further protection from having one of our department's biblical scholars become dean of arts and humanities a couple of years after I arrived. While I appreciated the freedom to express my convictions in class, I was unhappy with the deception that seemed to be basic to the situation. The fear that our little island of Christianity would be invaded and swamped by the secular forces all around us made manipulation and lies the administrative policy of choice. Later, at Wheaton College, I discovered that a like fear in a rather different institutional context similarly compromised integrity. There the fear of creeping liberalism also begot tight control from above, effected by a kind of subtle terror on the part of the faculty and students, of the consequences of getting "out of line"—all, of course, in the name of Jesus and his love. It is disappointing to see how evangelicalism, which is supposed to be a Christianity filled with the vitality of personal trusting faith, so often ends with an anxious distrust of everybody, including God.

By 1975 Nancy was down to forty-nine pounds and sometimes unable to rise to a standing position without help. This time she was hospitalized not at Topeka, where she had had therapy, but at Larned State Hospital, where she would receive merely "custodial care." The phrase struck terror into me. Was there nothing to do but make her a charge of the state for the rest of her life, to lock her into some concrete block ward where she would eat enough to "survive" but have no real life? My simpleminded assessment was that she needed, above all, to get away from her parents, yet without being in that hospital. But where would she go? Again I seemed to need to take charge, so I proposed that she come live with me and go to college at Western. She became strong enough during her stay at Larned to make the trip to Bowling Green, and so in the summer of 1975 Jimmy drove her there, and in the fall, a very frail but gradually recovering young woman enrolled in the university. My strategy was to give her a place to live and speak to her as little as possible about food. She did gain some weight and graduated four years later with a 4.00 grade point average. In the 1980s she spent several years teaching English in the Middle East, first in Beirut and then in Kuwait—in each case escaping in the nick of time from impending social disaster.

At New Year's of 1976, Corry Vos, wife of my colleague Arvin Vos, introduced me to her sister Elizabeth Vanderkooy, from southern Ontario. We saw each other quite often during the spring and summer and were married in December. Elizabeth taught sixth grade when I met her and is now a social worker. We have three children: Nathan (1978), Beth (1981), and Maria (1983). My family is the chief source of my temporal happiness and my moral education in these last seventeen years and a dominant occasion of my gratitude to God.

During the eleven years that I taught at Western, I gradually evolved into something of a philosopher. But I think I've been a rather peculiar philosopher, both because of a natural bent and because of my education. The peculiarity is that philosophy is for me an activity of articulating things that in a sense everybody already knows, but then in another sense doesn't know or at any rate isn't very articulate about or very conscious of. Philosophy is a process of clarification, of shedding light on corners of our lives and thus improving them. Its purpose is to make us more conscious of our own existence as human beings. Thus philosophy, as I do it, may be contrasted with the activity of establishing truths, of laying foundations for things (such as morals, theology, science, and the interpretation of texts), of working out and defending theories—say, of showing that we have free will or that God exists or that human beings are or aren't just pieces of meat (or, more modestly, that it is *possible* that we have free will, that God exists, etc.). Of course, no hard and fast line can be drawn between philosophy as proof and philosophy as clarification. In the process of proving that we have free will, one must clarify what our life as agents is like, and sometimes when I'm clarifying a concept—say, the concept of emotion or some virtue concept—the clarification may sound quite a lot like an argument for a thesis. But still, there is a marked difference between a philosopher whose chief purpose is to clarify concepts and one who primarily aims to establish truths.

I'm not indifferent to truth. It is enormously important that Christian teachings be true, and be taken to be true by believers—that is, be believed. If the basic teachings are not true, then much of our distinctively Christian outlook and behavior are in vain; and if we do not believe them, we will soon find that our outlook and behavior become something other than Christian. On the other hand, people's behavior and outlook sometimes degenerate despite their believing the Christian truths (we see this frequently enough among the hyperorthodox), and perhaps Christian philosophy can help here, too. If so, it must be more than just showing the Christian claims to be true; we need an exploration of concepts like freedom, duty, faith, hope, chastity, and truthfulness so as to make clearer what it is to live one's life in a distinctively Christian way.

One might be tempted to call this *pastoral philosophy*, since it so resembles what pastors do (or are supposed to do) in their preaching and counseling and leading of worship. They are not in the business of proving anything, but rather of exploring, in a heartfelt manner and with some precision, the inner workings of the Christian life so that people are better able to see its attractions and glories, to recognize the pitfalls in the way, to diagnose their own spiritual condition, and to distinguish the Christian life from culturally seductive look-alikes. Despite its oddity this can, with historical justification, be called philosophy, because it is something that philosophers have done, especially philosophers like Plato, Wittgenstein, and Kierkegaard, who emphasize the therapeutic character of philosophy. It is philosophy as deliverance—from the cave, from the fly bottle, from the illusion of Christiendom. But it is not just restorative or corrective, as these images suggest; it is also nurturing, growth-provoking, a source of positive insight and wisdom.

To me the attractions of philosophy, from my first reading of Will Durant to the present, were less in the promise that something might be proven than in the hope that something might be made manifest. I seem to see in my present understanding of philosophy (as I practice it—I do not mean to rule out another kind of philosophical activity for others) a reflection and a development of my early tendency to love philosophy for the sense of depth that it lent to life. I interpret the depth more culturally now, for I think it resides in a kind of spiritual residue of our tradition and the language of our tradition. Thus there is Christian wisdom, Buddhist wisdom, liberal wisdom, and so forth; the clarification that philosophy can pursue is always clarification in terms of concepts that arise among human beings pursuing life within some fairly definite cultural forms. What is perhaps surprising is the extent to which the concepts of our moral and spiritual and aesthetic traditions do have depth—that is, they can be "teased" in such a way as to reveal us to ourselves and surprise and edify us. The teasing is what I call philosophy—or at least the aspect of philosophy that I find myself practicing. To me the prime example of a thinker who teases the depth out of the concepts of a tradition for the purpose of spiritual restoration and edification is Søren Kierkegaard. *Fear and Trembling* and *Philosophical Fragments* are chiefly a teasing of the concept of faith, while *Works of Love* is a teasing of the concept of love; *The Sickness Unto Death* does a similar job on the concept of a self. By contrast, it is remarkable how infrequently Kierkegaard sets out to prove anything, or show that something is possible, or lay the foundations for anything.

In 1984 my family and I moved to Wheaton, Illinois, where I now teach at Wheaton College. One attraction of Wheaton is the students. They are, for the most part, quite serious about their studies and capable of pursuing them successfully, and are generally a joy to teach and work with. Another attraction of the assignment was the work it involved in the clinical psychology program of the Wheaton Graduate School. I had studied very little psychology formally, but my work on emotions, Christian spirituality, and the dynamics of the virtues and vices was mapping some of the same territory that personality psychologists and clinical psychologists tread in their concerns with emotions, mental health concepts, explanations of personality failure, accounts of development, and strategies for changing people's behavior and attitudes. The field seemed to be familiar enough for me to be able to contribute something to it and new enough for me to be able to learn something from it, and this hope has, I think, been realized. I have taken my methods of clarifying the virtues and applied them to the psychotherapies (thus clarifying the character ideals implicit in the therapies), so as to display the ways they are similar to Christian thinking and practice concerning persons, and the ways—often subtle and deep—that they diverge from Christianity. This allows us to make fairly subtle decisions about how a psychotherapy is to be modified when we adapt it for Christian use. It also makes us more sensitive to the ways that psychotherapeutic thinking can form us, and "feed" us as persons, and become a substitute for the spiritual nourishment that we should be receiving from scripture, liturgy, and the fellowship of our Christian congregations.

I experience God each day, usually in undramatic ways that I may not even notice unless I am attentive and well attuned. I experience Him in my interaction with students, be it pleasant or difficult; in my relations with colleagues; in my intellectual labors, whether they go smoothly or frustratingly; in my daily prayers; in the special work that I do in the context of my congregation; and in my interactions with my wife and children (perhaps especially these last). In the background of all that I do and think is the sense that Jesus is there, the Lord who commands but also the Savior who has healed the rift between us and the Father so that we human beings can live in confidence and hope despite our horrible, intractable sin. It seems to me that Christian philosophers know God pretty much the way anybody else does, except that they *may* be somewhat more articulate conceptually, and thus may have this *one* special advantage over others which, it seems to me, it is also their vocation to share with others, as they have occasion.

Note

I acknowledge with gratitude the support of the Pew Charitable Trusts in the writing of this essay.

NOT IN KANSAS

ANYMORE

Jeff Jordan

9

Though I do not know how a family in Kansas becomes Southern Baptist, mine did. I was raised a Southern Baptist, and many of my earliest memories are of worship services at the Immanuel Baptist Church in Wichita. Being raised a Southern Baptist is perhaps not all that uncommon, since the Southern Baptist Convention is the largest Protestant denomination in the United States—currently some 15 million strong. (It is hard to say exactly how many Southern Baptists there are because, like McDonald's, the number served increases rapidly.) In many ways, my story of faith and reason is also not all that uncommon. There are no great dramatic conversion experiences in my story, no episodes of apostasy, no period of finding my way back. My story of life and faith is much more a story of a journey, a gradual movement from one kind of faith to another. Early on, my belief took on the veneer one might expect of a Southern Baptist; faith involved Bible studies and a fervent search for the acts of God in every event. Today, while I am still a believer, I am so not in the same way or for the same reasons as before.

Because it is big, the Southern Baptist Convention is a world of its own. It has it own television programs, its own radio programs, its own publishing houses, and its own colleges and universities. This insularity has bred its own subculture. There are Southern Baptist ways of talking and dressing and being in the world. I grew up within that subculture.

My mother was a secretary and my father was a mechanic and owner of a service station, and I was the youngest of three boys. My maternal grandmother, who lived only about a mile away, was probably the major influence in my earlier religious development. Though nearly blind, she often took care of me, since both my parents worked, and she was determined that I would "walk the aisle" and that someday I would be a minister. "Walking the aisle" is the Baptist way of saying that one has publicly declared oneself to be a believer. The high point of a Baptist worship service is the sermon, the proclamation of the gospel. At the end of the sermon, the pastor issues an invitation to those who do not believe to do so. One signifies that one has accepted the invitation by going forward to the front of the sanctuary. By going forward one has, quite literally, walked the aisle. Though I have no memory of a time when I did not believe, at around the age of eight I choose to declare publicly that I was a believer, and I walked the aisle.

My faith at this point was expressed through (and was largely constituted by) prayer and Bible study, community activities, and worship. Much emphasis was put on faith as obedience: believing and doing what the Bible said and obeying one's parents. A personal experience of the divine, sensing the presence of God, was also expected and pursued.

Many of my friends attended the same church as I and, at around the age of fourteen or fifteen, a small group of us would sometimes discuss quasi-philosophhical/theological questions like these: Was the crucifixion really an arduous experience, since Jesus was God? Could Jesus have sinned? Since Jesus was God, to whom did he pray? Of course, we discussed other, more worldly questions as well: Who was better, Jerry West or Oscar Robertson, Wilt or Kareem? and the like.

The most preplexing question that confronted me as a young believer had to do with the Bible. Baptists are said to be a "people of the book." By this is meant that the Bible, and not (at least not in theory) church tradition, historical precedence, or church councils, serves as the guide to doctrine and practice in Baptist thought. Baptists typically regard the Bible as a detailed compilation of precepts and norms that regulate and guide how one should live. In those areas in which there is no detailed biblical norm, there is, Baptists suppose, some sort of general principle that one can use as a guide to decide singular problems or answer questions that arise in the modern age. But as anyone who has read the Bible knows, such an approach to biblical interpretation is extremely fragile. The dual problems of the apparent parity of contrarian views of what the biblical authors intended and the existence of issues never imagined before the modern period threaten the integrity of this approach.

The particular question that preplexed me was, What reading was correct and why? It seemed obvious that there had to be a singularly correct interpretation, but how did one know which one it was? This is, of course, a simple version of a problem that vexes not only biblical scholars but constitutional scholars as well. A virtue of growing up within a textually based religious community is that one encounters this problem early on. Because of this question, I did a lot of reading in the background and nature of the Bible. I read books like *New Testament History* by F. F. Bruce, and Bruce Metzger's *The New Testament,* and *Matthew's Commentary on the Bible.*[1] Much of my reading at this time consisted not of devotional works, but of biblical commentaries and books on the nature of the Bible.

I attended a small Baptist liberal arts college with the intention to enter the ministry. And, naturally enough, it was at college that I took my first philosophy course. It was the start of a love affair with philosophical ideas. It did not take long for me to realize that philosophy, as a discipline, forces a certain level of reflectiveness. The practice of philosophy requires us to take notice of things that might otherwise go unnoticed and unquestioned. I learned that philosophers examine and discuss extremely important and controversial topics that face society, and in doing so they seek clarification and, occasionally, even discover a solution to some of these problems. I found myself attracted to the prospect of somehow entering into a life of philosophical reflection. But for a Baptist, that could easily have been thought highly problematic.

There is a widespread attitude that philosophy and faith are some how incompatible: that one cannot be both a genuine philosopher and a faithful believer. Perhaps the idea is that being a philosopher is supposed to involve a readiness to inquire into the viability of any belief, which amounts to a readiness to give up any belief. A variation of this idea is that while some rather trivial beliefs—$2 + 2 = 4$, or no proposition is both true and false, and the like—are immune to revision, no substantial belief is beyond revision, where a substantial belief is thought of as any belief that would have important implications if true, and concerning which there is some dispute. The philosopher, given this idea, should be willing to put any substantial belief on the block of evidential bidding. And if a belief is on the block, then it is a belief that cannot be resolutely held. It is held only in a tentative way. On either construal of this idea, philosophy requires that no religious belief can be a resolute conviction.

On the other hand, faithful religious belief, especially a mature faithful belief, involves a deep commitment to the object of faith, a commitment that is nearly unreserved and unconditional. So, for the religious believer, there are certain beliefs or certain claims that are not just tentatively held but are decisively thought to be true. These religious beliefs are, except perhaps in the most theoretical sense, beyond the pale of revision. To a degree, faith is an attitude that disregards any need of any further inquiry into the legitimacy of that faith. Indeed, to grow in the faith is to grow in one's firmness of hold on the beliefs of the faith. Yet, if philosophy involves a readiness to give up any substantial belief, and if faithful belief consists, in part, of a decisive assent, then there does appear to be a kind of incompatibility between faith and philosophical reason.

Understood in a certain sense, there is a grain of truth in this attitude. Philosophy does tend to have a moderating effect on one's assent; dogmatists are usually not philosophical. It is quite difficult to be close-minded and, at the same time, to be philosphically reflective. Having said this, however, it is also clear that the idea that philosophy involves putting every belief up for inquiry, or a readiness to give up any substantial belief, is wildly implausible because it's wildly impractical. There are any number of legitimately rational, nonreligious beliefs, not all of them trivial, that are decisively held by many persons and disputed by others. For example, think of the belief that each individual has a nearly absolute moral right to free and unfettered speech; or think of the belief that every human life has intrinsic moral weight and value. These beliefs are firmly and decisively held to be true by many (myself among them), but not by all. I, for one, cannot imagine rejecting either of them, even though they are both notoriously hard to defend. They stand as legitimate counterexamples to the principle that one should be willing to reject any substantial belief. There are beliefs concerning the truth of which one is so convinced that one can properly disregard any purported evidence to the contrary, and do so without being dogmatic, or close-minded, or in the least irrational.

Another common pessimistic attitude concerning philosophy and faith is based on two ideas. The first is that authentic philosophy involves a large dose of iconoclastic rejection of conventional values. This idea, coupled with the second idea, that Christianity is a very conventional value, leads to the result that genuine philosophy involves a rejection of Christian belief. The idea that Christian belief is merely a conventional value traces back to Karl Marx's view that religious belief is an ideology that preserves the status quo of society.

Again, there is much that is true here. Philosophy, in its incessant questioning of common beliefs, often results in the revision and sometimes rejection of conventional values. Nonetheless there are at least two problems with the claim that philosophy is incompatible with Christian belief because the former is iconoclastic, while the latter is conventional. The first problem is that the iconoclasm of philosophy must be seen contextually. If we take into account the conventional context of various beliefs and values, then it seems rather obvious that in the place where philosophers are most to be found— the academy—the conventional values and beliefs are decidedly antireligious. A Christian philosopher is, in most university departments, an exception to a strong convention of secularist values. If context is taken into account, it is the Christian philosopher who iconoclastically rejects the conventional ideological animus toward faith that is so common in the modern university.

Indeed, this result may be generalizable: Though it would be an exaggeration to claim that Christianity constitutes a genuine counterculture movement, it is clear that, while our society might have been sympathetic to religious belief at one time, it is disputable whether it remains so today.

But suppose we concede that Christian belief is a conventional value, in the sense that it is so widespread, even if it is not culturally normative.[2] There is still a second problem with the claim that philosophy must involve an iconoclastic rejection of anything like a conventional Christian belief, in that it assumes that Christian belief is only a conventional belief. It is correct that the philosophical frame of mind often involves one in questioning important common assumptions. But even so, just because a belief is questioned, it does not follow that the belief is false or that it should be relinquished. And if there is no good reason to think a belief false, then there is no compelling reason to reject that belief. The attitude, then, that authentic philosophy necessarily rejects Christian belief is faulty on a number of grounds, not the least of which is the claim that is typically smuggled in: that Christian belief is false. So, without a lot more to go on, the second common attitude concerning philosophy and faith is faulty as well.

During my sophomore year of college, I came across Francis Schaeffer's *How Then Should We Live?*, a work that deals with philosophy from a Christian perspective. In this book, Schaeffer critiques the history of Western civilization, from ancient Greece to modern existentialism, from the perspective of Christian theism (all in less than 300 pages!).[3] Schaeffer was, I think, the C. S. Lewis of my generation. In the next year or so, I read nearly every book written by Schaeffer. No doubt I profited from that reading, though it seems to me today that Schaeffer's work, in the end, is too general and of limited value. Nonetheless, he had a powerful effect on many people of my generation, opening our eyes to the rich interplay possible between Christian faith and the great ideas of philosophy.

I graduated from college with the equivalent of a double major in philosophy and religion. After graduation two major events occurred: I married and I began a program at a Baptist seminary. Seminary was the natural culmination of my intention, formed early on, of becoming a minister. It was not long, however, before I realized that the ministry was not the right occupational choice. When confronted with a question about suffering, for example, I am much more comfortable answering: Well, some philosophers and theologians would say X, while others would say Y, and still others would claim Z. Of course, this is not the sort of answer that is appropriate when one confronts the existential anguish of personal suffering. A more appropriate pastoral answer, however, is neither my primary interest nor one that I would feel comfortable giving.

This was driven home once in a small class at the seminary. We sat one day in a circle, and we were to go around and talk about the various problems we currently faced in life. Well, here I was, twenty-three years old, recently married, healthy, my family well, and while we did not have much money, we were not in dire financial straits (though, of course, we could have used more money). I did not have any serious problems; indeed, I don't think I had any real problems at all. My concerns were with grades, with certain abstract questions of philosophy and theology, and with the fact that the Cubs were once again out of the race early on. As the discussion worked its way around the circle, the person next to me talked about the recent suicide of a parent. When my turn came, I shared the fact that, frankly, I didn't have any problems, especially nothing on the scale of dealing with the unexpected death of a parent. My instructor and my classmates were convinced that I was withholding something, something I was not willing to share. But I wasn't. I was just particularly fortunate to have escaped the all too common misfortunes that afflict so many. I was not long in seminary before I realized that I was not cut out for the ministerial cloth.

Graduate school rather than seminary was a more appropriate place for me. I decided to pursue graduate work in philosophy, and the problem was to decide on the area of philosophy. The two areas that interested me were philosophy of religion, and social and political philosophy. Having taken into account my Baptist background and my theological education in seminary, I finally decided to pursue philosophy of religion, so I went to Purdue to study with William Rowe, whose book, *The Cosmological Argument,* I had read a couple of years before.

It would be a neat flourish if one of the reasons I went to study with Professor Rowe was that I felt that a little ideological balance would be nice: going from seminary to do graduate study with a leading academic atheist. But having read Rowe's book, I was fairly certain that he was, if not a Christian, at least a theist. At the get-acquainted picnic of the philosophy department during my first semester of graduate work, after a few games of volleyball, I discovered that Professor Rowe was in fact an atheist.

Professor Rowe had also been raised a Baptist. Several years earlier, he had attended a seminary with the intention to enter the ministry and, after a change in plans, had gone to do graduate work in philosophy. Though we shared a similar background, I did not find Rowe's atheism any sort of threat. While I had thought about it, I never seriously wondered if I would follow a similar path to atheism—partly because I did not find the arguments for atheism persuasive and partly because I felt that the loss of faith would be a loss of too much that is valuable. We acknowledged our ideological differences more in a humorous way than in any serious debate. The time I spent in graduate school working with Rowe was exciting and profitable, and I gained much from him.

Professor Rowe's primary argument against Christian theism is a version of what is known as the *empirical problem of evil.*[4] Basically, this is an argument that the pain and suffering of innocent beings makes it unlikely that God exists. If there are cases of pointless suffering—pain that does not facilitate some greater good—then there is good reason to think that God does not exist. The problem of evil in its various forms is, clearly, the strongest objection against Christian theism, and Rowe's version is widely considered the most cogent presentation of the problem.

I have been immensely fortunate to have never had any personal experience of great suffering or painful anguish. But the problem of evil was made vividly real once during a mandatory college chapel service. A choir of preschool-age children, each with some disability—some blind, some deaf, others crippled—sang the old hymn "How Great Thou Art." To hear those voices singing about divine greatness seemed so incongruent. I still struggle with the question of whether the suffering of those little ones was inconsistent with the words they sang. I do not think it is; at least, I hope not. In part because—and this is put too briefly—if there is no God, then there will be no time when the blind will see and the deaf will hear and the lame will walk. If there is no God, there is no hope of a time when all will be made right.[5]

Today I am in my fourth year out of graduate school and am an assistant professor of philosophy at the University of Delaware. And today I am still a Christian. Let me set out briefly three broad reasons why I am still a Christian: the reasons are, respectively, intellectual, existential, and prudential in nature.[6]

I should note, first, that my faith is perhaps best described as a hope rather than as a belief. That may set me apart from many contributors to this volume. I hope that the Christian message is true, and I try to act in the light of that hope. While I assent to the propositions of Christianity, I think it best to describe my faith as a hope rather than as a belief because I do not think I have rationally decisive evidence for the truth of Christian claims, and I realize that it is a real, but to my mind not a very likely, possibility that Christianity could turn out to be false. There is a famous passage in the New Testament that is read often at weddings: "so there are these three: faith, hope and love; and the most important of these is love."[7] Usually people focus on the last clause about the importance of love, and faith too is often discussed. Hope, however, is the neglected part of this trio. This is unfortunate, because hope provides a stable and rational basis on which one can erect the scaffolding of faith.[8] That being said, there are reasons for Christian faith.

The first is that there are good intellectual grounds for being a Christian. There are some powerful arguments that can be formulated in support of Christian theism. In particular, I find an appeal to religious experience to be the basis of a strong argument for theism. Though I myself do not have the powerful sense of the divine presence that many credible, intelligent, and perceptive people do claim to have, the fact that there are such persons who report having had these experiences can rationally be taken as evidence in support of Christian theism. In the absence of a good reason to doubt the authenticity or reliability of these experiences, it would be intellectually chauvinistic to dismiss them. And there are other suggestive lines of argument available for the truth of Christian theism as well, from the historical to the metaphysical. Christian theology provides powerful theoretical resources for understanding a wide range of phenomena that any sound philosophy must address.

Secondly, I find the Christian message personally meaningful and significant on an existential, affective level. Christianity, in its traditions and history and liturgy, as well as in its doctrines, adds a rich texture to life, a sense of profundity and drama that would otherwise be missing. Without faith, life would be shallow and thin; Christianity adds a depth to life in that it provides an emotional and spiritual side to existence. Though the metaphor is homey, it may be instructive: Faith is the salt that adds flavor to the commonplace.

There is, of course, another way to make this point, or a closely related one. However shallow ordinary life often seems, a hint of greater depths beneath occasionally breaks through. One catches a glimpse of what may be the enacting of a greater overarching drama. Christianity makes sense of this drama and enhances its impact.

Finally, there is a pragmatic reason for Christian faith. In the 1600s, Blaise Pascal formulated a "wager argument" for Christian belief. The idea, put succinctly, is that if God exists and one believes, one will be in an impressively and immensely favorable position; while if one disbelieves, it is far from clear that one will be in a favorable position. If God does not exist and one disbelieves, one gains very little; but if God does not exist and one believes, one loses little.[9] It seems right that if God exists, faith will be much more beneficial than disbelief. Faith is, then, a necessary first step toward that possible benefit.

The wager strikes me as persuasive—at least, I know of no good reason to think it faulty. But perhaps my response is idiosyncratic because a common response to the wager is that it is inappropriate as a ground of Christian faith. The idea is that the prudential considerations found in the wager seem too narcissistic, too selfish, to be an adequate ground of Christian faith. The wager, if this objection is right, is an immoral calculation of how one might use Christianity to maximize one's gain. But why think of the wager this way? Prudential reasons need not be wholly narcissistic. One can inculcate a belief not only for one's own good, but also for the good of someone else. A parent, for example, might relearn (or learn, as the case may be) some academic subject in order to help her struggling child do his lessons. This sort of prudence is far from mere selfishness, since it is a prudential reason that contains an important regard for the good of others. This kind of prudence seems a reason worthy of Christian faith. And the wager can be formulated in a way that incorporates this kind of prudence.[10]

Hope joined with these reasons constitutes a firm foundation for faith. Philosophy, in addition to its intellectual benefits, provides a means of exploring the topography of Christian hope. Philosophy has put me into an intellectual landscape that is very different in many ways from that of my boyhood. It's clear that I'm not in Kansas anymore. But I'm also not in the wasteland of a shallow world view either. Living between belief and hope, I find the journey exciting and immensely enriching.

Notes

1. *New Testament History* (New York: Anchor Books, 1972); *The New Testament* (Nashville, Tenn.: Abingdon, 1965); the Matthew commentary is published by the Zondervan Publishing Company.

2. According to a recent Gallup poll on religious attitudes, 82 percent of Americans identify themselves as Christian; reported in *The New York Times,* February 27, 1993, p. 9.

3. Published by Crossway Books in 1983.

4. See Rowe's "The Problem of Evil and Some Varieties of Atheism," *American Philosophical Quarterly* 16 (1979), pp. 335–341.

5. I do not suggest that the brief reason given in the text even comes close to solving the problem of evil. The best proposed solution to the evidential problem of evil that I know of is found in William Hasker's "The Necessity of Gratuitous Evil," *Faith and Philosophy* 9,1 (1992), pp. 23–44.

6. There is also a minor fourth reason why I am still a Christian—a cultural reason. Christianity is my heritage in that it was the religion of my family. Being Christian provides historical continuity and, consequently, an identity with which I am proud to associate. This reason is, though, of only minor import.

7. I Corinthians 13:13, my translation.

8. The rational propriety of nonepistemic reasons for belief is a controversial and complex matter. What I have in mind here is something like the situation described in William James's essay "The Will to Believe" in *The Will to Believe and Other Essays in Popular Philosophy* (New York: Dover, 1956), pp. 1–31.

9. For more on the wager, see Thomas Morris, "Pascalian Wagering," *Canadian Journal of Philosophy* 16 (1986), pp. 437–454. Reprinted in Morris, *Anselmian Explorations* (Notre Dame, Ind.: University of Notre Dame Press, 1987), pp. 194–212.

10. For discussions, both pro and con, concerning further issues and objections concerning the wager, see *Gambling on God; Essays on Pascal's Wager,* ed. J. Jordan (Rowman & Littlefield, 1993). See also Nicholas Rescher, *Pascal's Wager* (Notre Dame, Ind.: University of Notre Dame Press, 1984).

10

LOVE OF LEARNING, REALITY OF GOD

Marilyn McCord Adams

Two things have dominated my life from the beginning: a love of learning and a desire for God. In my earliest years, a vivid sense of the reality of God came with mother's milk, with green grass and blue sky. The first home I can remember was my grandfather's parsonage (my father was away in the army air force). In 1943, Grandpa had emerged from early retirement to take a small country parish in western Illinois. He was a preacher in the Disciples of Christ church, a branch of the Campbellite movement. In his generation and in those circles, fundamentalism would have been taken for granted, but his personal flair and pastoral effectiveness won him ecumenical respect even in those pre–Vatican II days, as he became fast friends with the Roman Catholic priest and all the other ministers in town. Sunday morning worship is among my earliest memories. I have a mental image of sitting in the side section reserved for mothers with small children. Even clearer is a Sunday when, at the age of less than two, I decided during a hymn to join my grandfather in the pulpit. He looked down, smiled, patted my head, and said, "My little angel without wings." To me, it is a picture of God's unconditional love and reassurance. What my mother remembered was her keen embarrassment at having to fetch me back to the pew. Later, on return summer visits, I would stand under the colored glass windows beside the organ and sing "Jesus loves me, this I know; for the Bible tells me so" until the postlude was finished. After my grandfather died, when I was three and a half, my aunt took the parish, and lived with my grandmother and great-grandmother in the big Victorian house. I used to accompany my aunt when she went calling—on older parishioners in the afternoon, on families in the evening, sometimes on hospital patients. I loved to listen to the adults, drink lemonade, and eat the cookies they offered. I can't now remember when the conviction formed that I too must be a preacher when I grew up.

In my family, learning was treated with the ambivalence of a scarce but enviable commodity. Of my grandparents, only one (my maternal grandmother) had finished high school. My preacher grandfather quit a few weeks before graduation in a spat with some teachers and had apprenticed himself to a tailor. So far as the Bible was concerned, he was self-taught. The commentaries that lined his book shelves were items of my early curiosity. My soldier father, home for a visit, gave me my first spanking for tearing some of their pages. My grandmother, a Jill of all trades and master of many, whose busy days combined digging and hoeing and fishing, washing and ironing and cooking, improved her mind by memorizing Shakespeare's sonnets as she washed dishes and beat egg whites stiff by hand for her famous angel food cake. Thereby inspired, my aunt became the valedictorian of her high school class and worked her way through a small church college to a magna cum lauda B.A. in the 1920s; my mother came in salutatorian in high school and graduated with a major in Latin from a more prestigious Methodist school. My father's father was an orphan who quit school after the fourth grade and used his wits to make a successful career on the Oklahoma oil fields, until he was killed by a train at the age of thirty-two. Always working to support first his mother and sister, then his wife, my father never went to college, but was for that reason the more determined that his children should have the chance. On the other hand, the demand to outdistance the family record was coupled with the opposite message that such achievement would be disloyal, signal the belief that you were better than your forbears.

Thus, while I at first embraced this family project in the eager confidence that it was my ticket to love and approval, I found myself repeatedly caught in a no-win double bind. When I was no more than two, my aunt arrived for Christmas full of praise for a six-year-old who had recited "The Night Before Christmas" at the church pageant. Not to be outdone, I seized the book upside down and pretended to read the whole thing. If this was added to the family legends of our intellectual superiority, I found it hard to learn the rules. The adults readily commented on the intelligence of others over the dinner table, but I was always reprimanded if I tried to take part. I was offered fifty cents to improve my score in arithmetic and to memorize the Gettysburg Address, but perfect report cards were met with the comment "We don't really care about grades." For my aunt, the best was never good enough. Letters would come back with corrected spelling. When I returned from a university summer science institute for high schoolers with an A+ report, my aunt quipped, "it's too bad you can't distinguish physics from theology," and wouldn't believe that the mathematical sine function was abbreviated as "sin" until I produced an example in the math book. Even when I graduated as valedictorian of my college class, her move was to humiliate me by correcting my manners in front of my friends. There was also the sensitivity of adults to having their own weaknesses and incongruities noticed and exposed. Early on, I was puzzled by their anger and charges of sarcasm at what I had intended as straightforward statements of fact. These accusations were reinforced with injunctions not to contradict my elder's word—a defensive maneuver that I failed to respect, given that many of their contentions were obviously false.

The surrounding small-town culture was still more inhospitable. Once I finished early kindergarten, where I learned to write and read, I couldn't wait to go to school. Often I ran away to first grade and lied to the teacher when she asked whether my mother knew where I was. But the public schools proceeded at a snail's pace, half of each year seemingly devoted to what had been done the year before. In third grade, I was in a "split" room, and so managed to entertain myself by listening to the fourth-grade lessons, which made the next year relatively unbearable. In fifth grade, I took up a new strategy of inventing work for myself. At first, I invested my energy in social studies, poring over encyclopedias. In high school I turned to science, ordering books from the state library on genetics, physics, and so on. Eventually, I resorted to playing hooky. I would get up at 4 A.M. to work, then retire at about 6:30, when my mother rose, and pretend to be sick until she left for the school (where she taught English and Latin). Then I would get up and go back to work at my own pace. Most of the high school teachers evidenced scant intellectual motivation. My interests were regarded as comical or sinister, either way as abnormal. The high school principal became my adversary. When I signed up for a college math course by extension, he refused to let me take five local subjects as well. So I audited shorthand in my study hall and won the prize for the most words per minute at the end of the year. When I explored whether I could graduate in three years, he insisted that four years was the residence requirement. He grumbled when I ordered Marx and Lenin from the state library so that I could study socialism (the economics teacher was subsequently fired for introducing the topic into his economics course). In my senior year, when I refused to give a "canned" speech at graduation, he said he would rather have well-rounded B students than someone like me. And that was the truth. Two things saved my sanity during high school: first, my high school science teacher, who valued the life of the mind; second, a six-week summer science institute for high school juniors at the University of Illinois, where I met other kids who read and questioned with energy and enthusiasm.

My earliest attempts at integrating faith and reason put the latter in the service of the former. In Sunday school, even toddlers had weekly memory verses; "The B-I-B-L-E, yes that's the book for me; I stand alone on the word of God, the B-I-B-L-E" was among our earliest songs. In Christian Endeavor, there were games and competitions to make sure that we knew the order of the books of the Bible, the stories, and their characters. Daily vacation Bible school was great fun, combining singing and crafts with special theme studies. An eager Bible student then, I have never lost my love of the Bible: As an Episcopal priest, it is my favorite subject to teach. In junior high, I took on the adult assignment of reading the Bible straight through and found that the Sunday school syllabus had been expurgated (imagine my surprise at encountering Lot's daughters). I also set out to read all the books in the church library, which gave me my first (and dubious) exposure to philosophy à la Will Durant. My introduction to philosophical puzzlement had come much earlier, however, when at the age of two and a half I was shown a picture of hungry war orphans. I promptly supplied some Cheerios, only to discover that depicted children can't eat real food.

While I was memorizing away, more serious intellectual issues remained at the margins of my consciousness. The Disciples were split down the middle, between the fundamentalists and the so-called liberals, over the logically independent issue of whether congregations should each send their own missionaries or pool their resources in a joint effort. My maternal family was likewise split: my aunt and mother supporting the missionary society, while my great-uncle and second cousins were of the "independents." I was very curious about these debates but was forbidden to bring them up at family gatherings. The matter was even more complicated because the church we attended had a fundamentalist orientation, which translated locally into the concrete quarrels of whether the new RSV was all right or only the King James Version and whether everyone who went to the dozen or so other churches in town was going to hell. At the age of ten, I was put on the spot when my parents gave me a new white leather–bound RSV for Christmas, when the youth leaders had denounced it for changing *virgin* to *young woman* in Isaiah. Eager to please the preacher and his wife, I sided with them in this, as in the literal interpretation of Scripture. When we came to the theory of evolution in sixth grade, I announced that it was incredible because inconsistent with the Bible—to which the teacher made the standard pluralist response: "You don't have to agree with it, but you do have to understand it." Just before I entered junior high, we moved to the next town, where the church was the opposite faction, much to my parents' relief. I took this shift in stride, partly because of my still chameleonlike eagerness to please church authorities and partly because the similarities were greater than the differences. Seventh grade awakened me to Christological controversies when the

Sunday school teacher let it slip that Jesus was not only the Son of God (according to the Arian tendencies of many Disciples) but God. This felt like a conceptual jolt, which the teacher explained was part of growing up, although she did not add much to clarify the terminology. A couple of years later, the Sunday school books introduced us to the documentary hypothesis in a rather matter-of-fact way. But by then my own existential crisis of faith had eclipsed such theoretical problems, only to grasp them as weapons.

A Freudian would, no doubt, be right to observe that my desire for God was confused from its inception with the child's demand to return to the golden years of life with Grandpa. Certainly, good times seemed to fade with my emerging consciousness of the tensions in my parents' home. Changes and crises came thick and fast, with their postwar struggles to find their economic feet; the arrival of my brother; a work-related accident in which my father broke his back and was bedridden for a year, requiring the live-in baby-sitting of my paternal grandmother; and others. Although I cannot now reconstruct the logic, I somehow learned that whatever went wrong was my fault, that I was the troublemaker. The more my badness was pointed out, the more I clung to religion as a life raft, hoping it would help without knowing quite how. Each pious step at church brought ridicule and charges of hypocrisy at home. After all, they taunted, "charity begins at home," "the one who says he loves God and hates his brother is a liar"—"the Bible tells us so." The result was powerful internal conflicts. Clever as I supposedly was, I was clueless about how to get rid of all my "badness"; it seemed to descend on me like a fate. The Bible spoke of repentance and committment. At revival meetings I "rededicated my life to Christ" several times and offered myself for "full-time Christian service" as a missionary to India or the Philippines. But these moves were immediately belied by family conflicts. After years of spiritual direction and therapy, I still think it fair to say that I really did want God, really did want to change. But that was decades before psychology was respectable, much less popular. The adults, the Bible, and the books I read were good at rendering verdicts; but none of us really knew how to ask and answer the questions about how to change.

As I moved into adolescence, matters grew worse instead of better. In all my emotional turmoil, my sense of the reality of God faded to the vanishing point. My cries for help took the form of religious questions—about the relation between Jesus and God, about the Lord's Supper—evolving into full-grown doubts. Eventually, I raised my hand in Sunday school class to ask, "What is prayer anyway? Surely it's more than talking to the wall." Totally unprepared for this, the teacher tried to silence me with, "That was last Sunday's lesson"—whereupon I got up (unintentionally knocking my chair over) and said "All right, dammit, I'm leaving!" That afternoon, she spent an hour in the car telling my mother what a bad person I was for saying the "D" word. I had to face the more terrible fact that I didn't believe anymore. I went down to the basement laundry and tried to think of the worst thing I could do in my rage. "Damn the Holy Spirit! Damn the Holy Spirit!" I muttered, as if in a liturgy to make official my incorrigibly reprobate state, on which significant adults seemed agreed. I wrote my aunt to announce my "conversion" to atheism and my departure from the church. I lost most of my childhood respect for her when she replied by trying to make me feel guilty, stating that such moves would break my dead grandfather's heart. Poverina, she didn't know, none of them knew what to say.

What is there to live for if God isn't real? My answer at fourteen was "Truth." The crisis of Sputnik had to be met with a revival of science education, and the missionary call went out to bright young Americans to accept the challenge. Not surprisingly, I decided to devote myself to science. I remember the first Sunday morning I stayed home from church, studying the structure of grasshopper legs and wondering, How is this going to get you closer to the Truth? My act of faith replied, Never mind; it somehow will. I embraced academic work with religious fervor. Moreover, if truth was God, I had a chance to keep on good terms with Her, aiming to obey the command "Be ye perfect" by getting 100 percent on every test. And this path held the promise of salvation: eventual scholarship and escape from (what was to me) the hell of small-town life to the stimulating pluralism of the university. As John Wesley to prayers, I would rise at 4 A.M. to study. In open rebellion against local culture, I ordered first Darwin and then genetics books from the state library. Longing for sainthood, I shifted my attention to physics, because it was intellectually more difficult for me. This new religion had its drawbacks insofar as it reinforced my alienation, not only from my peers but also from most of my teachers. My allegiance to it thoroughly confused love of truth for its own sake with my desperate determination to survive through intellectual achievements. My soul (and my work) still bear the scars of this idolatry. Yet, on the whole, it was about as constructive a strategy as I could then devise.

Village atheist that I was, I could not bring myself to abandon Christianity altogether. After a few bleak Sunday mornings with my biology books, I began attending the Methodist church. Its salt-of-the-earth minister spent many hours listening to me rehearse the objections to belief in God that are rediscovered by thousands in every generation whose lives get twisted by deep pain and disappointment, during those hours in which miracles still fail to come to them. I sat in the pew Sunday after Sunday, listening to sermons that promised heaven to everyone who would "only believe." But that was the one thing that seemed beyond my power to do. I searched for the real God at youth conferences and summer camps. One camp chaplain assured me that the answers to all my troubles were to be found in Immanuel Kant's *Critique of Pure Reason.* Dutifully I ordered it from the state library and spent summer hours under a tree plowing my way through it, comprehending not a word. (I would have done better to study Greek.) In my junior year of high school, the Methodist minister came up to with a practical solution: He invited me to teach third- and fourth-grade Sunday school, refusing my protest that I didn't believe in God. I began my first exercise in analytical philosophy of religion, endeavoring to decipher what Methodists believed and to present it with clarity. My research also took me into church history. Best of all, it drew me out of my self-imposed slavery to work. My friend taught the first-grade class, and we first begged wooden apple boxes from the grocery store owner and then sanded and finished them into bookcases. We scoured magazines for bulletin board decorations, took trips to neighboring towns for supplies, directed Christmas pageants, and so on. Teaching also exempted me from the high school Sunday school class taught by the school coach, whose topics alternated between the evils of alcohol and the parable of the talents!

One question that tormented me those days was, Why be good if God doesn't exist? The official conceptual scheme of Bible Belt culture said that obligations were owed to God. Since I had tasted and seen Him in the past, that seemed a credible claim. By contrast, the project of doing what the grown-ups wanted, individually or collectively, struck me then as having little merit. Lacking the vocabulary of intrinsic value, I detected an inconsistency in my own position. I was as committed to ruthless honesty as I was to my high-blown search for truth. I undertook to write an essay for the Lincoln's-birthday edition of the school newspaper on why one should be honest even if God doesn't exist. Having excluded theological and contractarian approaches, I thought that evidence as to whether honesty was "good for" the individual was mixed. I found myself quite at a loss to justify the deontological tenacity with which I affirmed the value. At about this time, my science teacher introduced me to Ayn Rand's *Atlas Shrugged,* which seemed to preach a gospel of selfish individualism. Finding no refutations of her arguments, I saw no a priori reason not to act out the contempt in which I held most of my schoolmates and did so in the spirit of moral empiricism. After a while, I found I didn't really like behaving that way and gave it up.

That year I drove with a friend from the summer science program back to the University of Illinois to hear Paul Tillich speak on the dynamics of faith. I reacted with the enthusiasm of a teenager to a rock idol and requested his *Systematic Theology* for a graduation present. I read it and his sermons over and over, feeling sure that they must mean something. Some lines were clear—"accept the fact that you are accepted" (although I couldn't)—while others elude me still. I was smitten with Aldous Huxley's *Brave New World* and T. S. Eliot's "The Hollow Men" and Ibsen's plays. On the senior trip I read Descartes's *Meditations* and returned to the *Critique of Pure Reason.* Amid such ideological confusion, I was finally liberated from high school and headed straight for the University of Illinois.

Hugh Chandler once quipped, "Champaign is better than real pain. Or is it?" Yet to me, at seventeen, it could have been Paris or London. The Big Ten land grant college, teeming with thousands of students, offering courses on more subjects than I dreamed existed, putting on plays and concerts every weekend, and only a couple of miles from the Art Theater that featured Bergman films, was at once liberating, envigorating, and intimidating. Coming as I did from a teetotaling family (my aunt had toured in the 1920s, lecturing against the repeal of Prohibition) and a "dry" county, I was shocked that the pizza place served beer. Yet, because of its value pluralism, I no longer felt like an odd person out because of my intellectual interests. At the same time, since I had bet everything on academics as my vehicle of escape, I was terrified that I wouldn't be able to do the work. I remember contemplating suicide when I couldn't do several of the problems on the honor's calculus test. It turned out that the teacher was giving us the same work as his advanced class and the my 60 curved to an A. I took eighteen to twenty hours a semseter and worked very hard. Because, among other things, my goal was to spend as little time in my home town as possible. I attended every summer session and finished in two and a half years. Since I had three C's and a D in physical education, it came as a complete surprise to me when I came first in my class.

If God did not exist, I had to get at the heart of reality by majoring in nuclear physics—or so I reasoned. But from my arrival on campus, I turned over every stone trying to find someone who could help me believe in God again. Campus religious foundations were flourishing, with Sunday night supper clubs and weekday and evening discussion groups. Neo-orthodoxy was in vogue, and I spent spare moments reading every paperback of Tillich, Bultmann, Buber, and Niebuhr. Along with these came existentialism, and I spent hours in the YMCA coffee shop journaling my reactions to Kierkegaard. If these authors offered a way of being religious—even Christian— without believing as much as I thought was required, this advantage seemed to be bought at the price of reduction. It didn't take long to discover that most of the mainline campus ministers didn't believe in a God as *real* as I remembered. Christian symbols were fine if they were metaphors. But I wasn't looking for a mere metaphor or a permanently eclipsed God. What I wanted was to taste and see again! So far as I could tell, there were three campus groups that believed in a real God: the Newman Center, the Inter-Varsity Fellowship, and the Episcopal Church of St. John the Divine. I knew I could never believe any mere human infallible—which eliminated the first. Nor could I return to the conservative evangelical roots whence I had come. Happily, Henry Johnson, one of the assisting priests at the Episcopal foundation, was doing a Ph.D. in philosophy of education. After-class coffees led to my joining his reading group on St. Augustine, where one could ask and discuss any question. It was "Fr. J" who first confronted me with a vision of the integration of faith and learning, one that I learned to put into practice only years later, with the formation of the Society of Christian Philosophers. I attended the complex high church worship services for about a year before I found myself believing in God again. I was sitting in the library reading Alasdair McIntyre's early (and bad) essay "Visions" (which ridicules the evidential value of religious experience) when my if's, and's, and but's about God ran out. None of my questions had been answered, but I was filled with an overpowering sense of the real presence of God right there in the library. Nor was it a fleeting presence. God remained a given in experience, just as He had been in my childhood, along with sunshine, green grass, and the vast Midwestern skies. I was overjoyed. The Anglo-Catholic approach, with its emphasis on sacrament and ritual, offered one layer of a solution to my long-standing problem of being bad. There was confession and absolution, which made God's forgiveness official. My childhood religion (indeed, the whole culture) had been sentimental: Great emphasis was placed on feeling the right way. By contrast, I was told, participation in the liturgy, fasting on Fridays, and so on counted as genuine steps in God's direction, even before we had managed to get our feelings straightened out. All of this spoke of a God who was willing to work with ambivalence and ambiguity. All the more staggering that He condescended to be really present, consumed by us in the form of bread and wine. I can remember with what excitement I realized that one didn't have to wait from Sunday to Sunday to attend worship; mass was said every day. I had to miss an hour of an ethics seminar to get confirmed on May 14, 1964, by Bishop Albert Chambers, who fifteen years later would join the schism in protest over the ordination of women.

A year into my physics major, I switched to philosophy. The science classes were geared to engineers, while my passion was theory. Professors were not interested in answering philosophical questions raised by undergraduates. I finally bit the bullet when I realized that I was spending all my available time reading philosophical theology. My father couldn't understand it, since I would have been able to make such a good living as an engineer. The truth is that I never gave earning a living a thought, then or since. When I found myself believing in God again, I immediately inferred that I should go into the ministry. The Episcopal church did not ordain women in those days, however, and my Anglo-Catholic friends assured me that I could still be a theologian. They had embraced an Oxford movement approach, which emphasized patristics and even some medieval theology. Nelson Pike, who paid a timely visit to the University of Illinois in the summer of 1963, warned that theology needs methodological discipline. So I decided to go to graduate school in philosophy. The presence of Bill Wainwright, a devout Episcopalian, in the Illinois department provided real encouragement in a faculty dominated by figures openly hostile to religion. During my last year there, the philosophy and math departments teamed up to defeat the proposal to establish a religion department. I got hold of one of their fliers and marched into the chair's office, declaiming it as full of bad arguments. He gave me one of my earliest glimpses into the dark side of professional philosophy when he replied, "They weren't meant to be *good* arguments; they were intended to convince!" When I announced philosophy of religion as my goal, most professors said I would change my mind. Nevertheless, I won my Woodrow Wilson graduate fellowship by telling the interviewers that I wanted to study philosophy, the better to understand the problem of evil and the doctrine of the Trinity. Intent on working with Pike, I set my sights on Cornell. Most of my work at Illinois had been continental or history of philosophy. Despite one bewildering course on Wittgenstein, I had little idea of what some of my teachers were talking about when they warned that Cornell had an analytical department focused on ordinary language.

On the whole, my experience at the University of Illinois had been positive. Intellectually, it had been exciting, despite the fact that its size allowed students to trace a rudderless course. Religiously, faith had found me again. And my Anglo-Catholic mentors and friends had given me a sketch of how to integrate faith with the life of the mind. The fly in the ointment was my old idolatrous desire to please, this time the philosophy teachers who were ushering me into the profession. More generally, my new sense of identity and purpose was fragile; I needed more time to let it stabilize. At twenty, I was too young for what awaited me. My years at Cornell were among the most traumatic in my life, like reentering hell at a still deeper level. The first ring had only robbed me of my religion; the second disarmed me of my principal coping device, my intellectual confidence, and thus brought me closer to despair.

When I arrived in Ithaca, New York, in the fall of 1964, Beatles music was playing in the cafeteria and the campus was gripped by the anti–Vietnam War movement. Although the chaplain was kindly and made an effort to be tolerant, the Episcopal church at Cornell was barely recognizable as a branch of the same communion I had left in Illinois. For most of the congregation, religion was thoroughly politicized: Any interest in individual salvation was denounced as narrowly self-centered; intellectual and theological concerns were judged escapist and socially irresponsible. Some asked why we should bother to teach children the Lord's prayer. Once my consciousness was raised, I, too, was adamantly opposed to our country's policies in Vietnam and caught the infectious cynicism (unfortunately, all too grounded in reality) about our government leaders. To me, it seemed as if Divine perfection could not amount to much if even God had to choose between the good of the whole and the welfare of individual persons; utopia was supposed to be His specialty precisely because it is beyond human power. Religion without a vertical dimension was outside my interest and contrary to my experience. When three couples and I came from Illinois all at the same time and tried to re-create home away from home by starting a patristics reading group, the chaplains were amused and bewildered. We wanted to live out Fr. J's ideal of an integrated world view, but none of us had understood well enough to carry on without his leadership. Church turned overnight, within the space of several hundred miles, from a crucible of creative nuturing into a hostile environment in which I had to be constantly on the defensive about everything, from interest in the salvation of my own "puny soul" (as one sermon put it) to the pursuit of philosophical theology. Nor did matters improve when Bob (by then my husband) and I moved to Michigan in 1968. When the vicar caught me reading St. Augustine before a meeting, he was reproachful: "Why in God's name do you spend time with that?" In Ann Arbor, I was quite active politically. But the antiwar movement was as self-righteous and dogmatic as any nondenominational religious splinter group. Too often, peace masses were spent confessing other people's sins (e.g., LBJ's). Little wonder that we didn't bring peace on earth, when we had such contempt for hawkish opponents. I reacted to this the same way as I had to the social pressures of Midwestern farm towns: according to the maxim "They can't make me conform, but they can make me feel guilty about not doing so." I identified with the rich young ruler who went away sadly because he was too attached to his wealth (in my case, intellectual interests). My inner conflicts and sense of alienation rose to a breaking point, until one weekend in 1971 we drove to Pennsylvania to talk to Fr. J. I asked him why I shouldn't simply leave the church (again). He quipped that I had signed on for life, that no one ever said it would be easy, and he tried to reawaken my sense of vocation as a Christian intellectual. But once again, God seemed to withdraw from my world, far, far away.

In 1964, the philosophy department at Cornell was still in its Wittgensteinian period. Competition between Max Black and Norman Malcolm for control of the realm seemed to have been decided in favor of the latter, and I found the prevailing spirit every bit as rigid and dogmatic as the fundamentalist sects of my childhood. To be sure, the doctrines were different: verificationism and its theorems, antiessentialism, and even a modified rule utilitarianism. I got the sense that questioning these would be a negative reflection on one's intelligence, just as pointing up inconsistencies in the Bible had signaled deficiency in faith. (In retrospect, I find it amazing that early analytical philosophy of religion got anywhere, given the sparse conceptual machinery we were allowed.) Malcolm was a complicated giant, running up the stairs two steps at a time as if he were striding over rows of Nebraska corn. His grades fell into a bipolar distribution, mostly A's and C's (= F's for graduate students), apparently a function of one's departure from his canons of orthodoxy. His course on philosophy of mind from Descartes forward was, ironically, in the continental tradition of rehearsing a history of past mistakes leading up to the Truth as revealed in Wittgenstein. During my time there, two brilliant assistant professors were (in the opinion of many) ruined by a religious conversion to the Wittgensteinian point of view. By contrast, in his seminars, Malcolm would take any opinion seriously—from Leibnizian monads to Platonic forms—and his evidently infinite passionate interest in philosophy stood in refreshing contrast to the posture of other professors who seemed depressed and jaded. Black, too, was multidimensional. He invited students to parties and Thanksgiving dinner, only to cover his social shyness with monologues about Moore and Russell, which we in any event enjoyed. He had long since ceased to prepare for courses and compensated by piling on intense work loads (a paper a week, on which he never made any philosophical comments) and then deliberately humiliating students in class. The atmosphere in the department was highly competitive, and one was apt to be taunted by peers in the lunch line for any stupid remarks that might have passed one's lips in the class before. Consequently, most people learned to keep silent throughout their first year.

In this atmosphere, I took the coward's way out, following my earlier strategy as an atheistic Methodist Sunday school teacher. In philosophy of mind and epistemology, I devoted term papers to critical remarks or to working out the consequences of Wittgensteinian points of view on this or that topic. Alternatively, I retreated to history: A full third of my output was on David Hume. When I was told at the end of the second year that I had negotiated the comprehensive exams with flying colors, I sobbed to Bob, "It's a fraud. It's all a fraud. I don't believe anything I've supposedly learned." I had wanted to write my dissertation on the evidential value of religious experience but ruled this out as ideologically impossible. Still running scared, I reasoned that a historical dissertation could allow me to deal with theological issues without having to assume the full burden of proof for past conceptual schemes. Besides, I was driven back into medieval philosophy by sheer rebellion and the love of detective work when I heard in class that so many medieval ideas just didn't make any sense. Following Nelson Pike's lead, of beginning discussions on the attributes of God with a review of medieval theologians, and picking up the work I had begun with Norman Kretzmann on Ockham's *Treatise on Predestination, Foreknowledge, and Future Contingents,* I decided to write a history of the foreknowledge problem. I stopped when my treatments of Boethius and Ockham summed to 300 pages. Even so, intolerance of metaphysics was so great that my strategy came close to failing. On the day of my oral exam, one committee member charged that I should demonstrate why this topic was acceptable, since Rogers Albritton had recently argued against Richard Taylor that the assumptions that raised the problem were merely "pictorial" and hence strictly unintelligible. I was given a talking-to and let off with the assignment of writing an appendix spelling out differences between the medievals and the ideas Albritton was attacking. I came away with the impression of "passing" by the skin of my teeth, and though I had finished in three years, I felt like a failure.

It took me more than ten years (and promotion to full professor) to recover from the Cornell graduate school experience. For years I asked myself what I had learned that was worth such loss of self-esteem. Not formal logic. Not the history of philosophy. Eventually, I concluded that their advertising had not been false. The Cornell department insisted that philosophy was a method, not a body of knowledge. This was its excuse for an unbalanced curriculum and its rationale for the "problems" section (which might require the student to write on any issue of philosophy) of the comprehensive exams. What I learned was clarity and economy of expression and, above all, to make distinctions. Ironically, these are the strengths most great medieval philosophers had. And they are skills sorely needed when one turns to philosophical theology. Moreover, the very thing that had drawn me to Cornell in the first place was the opportunity to work with Nelson Pike, whose own pedagogical brilliance and commitment to helping students develop their own ideas remain paradigms for my own role as a professor to this day. Best of all, my time at Cornell afforded me the opportunity to meet and marry Bob Adams. This seemed providential to me then, and I count our twenty-five years of marriage as (after Himself) one of God's best gifts to me.

In those days, sexism in the profession was taken for granted. When I applied to graduate school, Norman Kretzmann wrote, "Miss McCord shows no signs of getting married and dropping out of school." Another professor ventured that I would probably end up washing dishes, like all the rest. At the beginning-of-the-year party, the faculty shared its considerable nervousness at having admitted *four* women at once. Max Black opined, "The trouble with women is, if they're married, that's the trouble; and and if they aren't married, that's the trouble!" I pressed for details: What difficulties did they expect? They said, "Well, what if a woman gets pregnant and has to have the baby on the day when prelims are scheduled?" This reminded me of the Sadducees' puzzle about levirate marriage and the resurrection, and I offered the obvious advice: "You could always let her take the exams another day." My solution at the time was to laugh it off, although I remember vowing to sign my articles "M. Adams" so that readers wouldn't know that a woman wrote it. In 1968, Bob and I didn't even consider going on the market together or commuting. He had several attractive offers by the end of October and decided on the University of Michigan. Then Chair Richard Brandt had asked the dean about work for me, but the dean had refused, appealing to the nepotism rule. When Bob was wooed by Perkins Theological Seminary the first year, Brandt used this to pry loose some teaching for me the next year as a visiting lecturer. Eventually, under pressure from the Department of Health, Education, and Welfare, it emerged that there was no written nepotism rule. I was the test case at the University of Michigan for creating part-time tenure-track positions.

With Bill Alston, George Mavrodes, and Bob Adams, the department was flush with philosophy of religion, but I was offered an introductory course and a medieval philosophy course and, beginning with patristic authors, worked my way through the syllabus up to Ockham. My view was that Augustine, Anselm, Aquinas, Scotus, and Ockham were real, first rate philosophers from whom one might learn something different from what Gilbert Ryle had to say. So I tried to give prominence to philosophical issues while taking pains to determine exactly what *their* views were. This project was complicated by the lingering habit of taking the semantic short way with opponents, declaring what one disagreed with unintelligible. Among medievalists, there were other difficulties; historians found my pieces too philosophical, while philosophers were impatient with my attempts to document from the texts. Then there was the more dogmatic brand of Neo-Thomism to contend with. I remember one rejection letter that read: "This is a Platonic problem; Aquinas was an Aristotelian philosopher. Therefore, your paper is unacceptable." (This so-called Platonic problem was quoted from Aquinas himself!) My attempts to unpack medieval theology took me into many other areas besides—Aristotelian hylomorphism, medieval physics, and logic. Yet, my contention was and remains that during that thousand-year period, theology set the syllabus for philosophy; and it is important to see how perennial problems and their solutions permutate under the ontological commitment to the existence of God.

On the whole, being a second-class citizen in the Michigan department reinforced my sense of failure, and combined with the unsatisfactory church situation to leave me frustrated and depressed much of the time. Yet, when the twin offers from UCLA came, I was irrationally reluctant, not recognizing them for the providential gift that they were. In fact, I love Los Angeles precisely because it is so pluralistic. Here *laissez faire* means what it says: Being "square" and loving chocolate and believing that marriage is for life are tolerated, along with jogging shorts, maroon hair, and serial polygamy. Students at UCLA come in all colors, shapes, sizes, and ages, with an impressive variety of gifts and motivations. By now, Los Angeles is the main point of immigration, which blesses us with amazing cultural diversity (and restaurants!). Moreover—let no one convince you otherwise—tenure is a real good and makes a world of difference. I was hired to carry on the tradition in medieval philosophy begun by Ernest Moody, and we were both encouraged (with Rogers Albritton, who shared our interest) to develop a program in the philosophy of religion. I threw myself into my job with enthusiasm and even enjoyed the extensive administrative work on the Committee on Undergraduate Courses and Curricula, carrying the fight against credit for remedial English to the statewide committee.

Nevertheless, although I found California outwardly liberating, I continued to be bound by inner chains. I continued to pour my research energies chiefly into medieval philosophy, partly because that was easier and safer. Moreover, eager to reassure my new colleagues, I construed pluralism in the teaching of religion to imply a sharp division between personal beliefs and course content. I was proud that my philosophy of religion courses were mostly metaphysics and epistemology (although I was equally pleased to have the opportunity to treat philosophical issues in revealed theology in my early medieval course). I felt it was my duty so to teach that no one could guess my beliefs from my lectures. Evangelical students would sometimes ask point blank what my own views were, and I would reply, "I'm an Episcopalian." Not a few came close to saying, "But are you a Christian?" And there was more insight in that query than perhaps they knew. For as the years went by, God seemed increasingly remote. I attended mass almost daily in the Anglo-Christian parish near my home, but it came to seem that God was like the federal government: Like the federal government, He knows all about you; like the federal government, He provides certain goods and services; unlike the federal government, He is supposed to have your interests at heart; but like the federal government, you never meet Him face to face! Yet, I *knew* that God was an empirical entity; I had tasted and seen. I felt I was in a religious rut, but I didn't know what to do. When the Episcopal church finally changed the canons to allow for the ordination of women, I was thrilled. But a look within told me, "You can't be a priest now; you're not even much of a Christian." Theoretical problems loomed large in my mind. Every Christmas I would rehearse with Bob my questions about the intelligibility of Incarnation (the Apollinarian heresy struck me as preferable); each Good Friday, the scandal of the cross. I found the Bible increasingly bewildering, raising more problems than it solved. In retrospect, my polarized approach to faith and philosophy precisely mirrored my soul. My experiences of the reality and goodness of God, and my growing knowledge of the history of theology, had not been integrated with my other life experiences. I suppressed and sublimated as much of my fear and anger as I could by being a workaholic academic. At the deepest levels, I didn't feel that God had saved me from my "incorrigible badness," had not yet calmed the stormy sea of emotional conflict that I carried within.

Allan Wolter, OFM, one of the world's leading experts on Duns Scotus, visited our department in the spring of 1978. I had looked forward to his visit as an opportunity to clarify many difficult points in Scotus's views. The syllabus on Scotus's ethics passed through a question on the human obligation to love God above all and for His own sake. Feeling like the rich young ruler all over again, I commented after class, "I would like to love God that way, but I love philosophy, too, and I don't want to give it up." It would be a decade before I could believe totally that doing philosophy could be *a way* of loving God for His own sake. Wolter's serene integration of faith and philosophy did not escape my notice. One day at the copying machine I found myself saying, "I understand your interest in Duns Scotus, but I don't get it about St. Francis." A few days later a biography of Francis appeared. Reading it, I thought, "I'm the opposite of Francis, but I should be like him." After all, the solution to badness is to embrace its polar opposite. Since then, I've gone to Assisi many times and prayed, "Lord, make me like St. Francis." Only the last time did my prayer change: "Lord, make me love you as much as St. Francis, but let me love you as myself."

School was scarcely out when I ate a double dessert of strawberry ice cream and had the worst stomachache of my life. After ten days of severe nausea, I finally conceded it would be worthwhile to take time out from work to go to the doctor. When initial tests ruled out more obvious hypotheses, he warned darkly that it could be a cancerous tumor. I went to mass that night stunned. I knew, of course, that I would die, but it hadn't occurred to me that it could be that soon. I took stock: I had had educational opportunities, and it was fair to say that I had made the most of them. I had also had religious opportunities. What had I done with them? Several days later, an ultrasound test showed that my malady was only gallstones. But in my midlife crisis, the foundations had already begun to shake. I was overdosed on anesthetic and unable to work for about six weeks after the surgery (I read whole books, of which I couldn't remember a thing). Coincidentally, that fall, a friend in the parish asked me if I would like to join a prayer group she was starting. It didn't seem like my sort of thing, but I was stuck religiously and didn't have any better ideas. We would meditate daily on the lectionary propers for the following Sunday. At our weekly meetings we would share our reactions to these, then have half an hour of silence together and close with prayer-book intercessions. I didn't learn much about prayer, but the Bible came alive for me again. I took to writing little homilies, a predictable one on the text "a prophet is not without honor except in his own country." I also pressed the rector to let me teach a class on Incarnation and atonement, in which I reviewed patristic and medieval positions. It was too academic for my present taste, but it was a start.

Another penny dropped. My father-in-law, then dean of Princeton Theological Seminary, was diagnosed with cancer of the liver. Bob and I decided to spend our 1979–80 sabbatical in Princeton to be near the family and were allotted housing in Payne Hall, the seminary's apartments for furloughed missionaries. At the Central Division meeting of the American Philosophical Association (APA) that spring, Bill Alston mentioned that we should be sure to visit the Episcopal church on the outskirts of Princeton, and said that the rector was an excellent preacher and spiritually the deepest person he had ever met. My experience proved Bill right on both counts. With a Ph.D. in the Old Testament, the rector was a former Mennonite missionary. His sermons drew on those evangelical and biblical roots but transplanted the flower of the Gospel into the setting of medium high church Eucharistic liturgy. To be sure, there was a persistent theme that when it came to religion, scholars didn't know as much as they pretended. But I knew in my heart that this was true; and besides, his academic credentials gave him credibility. More important, he obviously knew the reality of God; his focus on and reverence for Christ were evident and unwaivering. To a degree unprecedented in my experience, he really believed that God was ready, willing, and able to change lives. As my spiritual director for more than five years, he was able to teach me how to put religious experience and theory together with gut-level realities, enabled me to experience the reputed healing power in my own psycho-spiritual blindness and lameness, hear the voice of Jesus say "Peace, be still" to the war in my own soul.

Our work together began after a charismatic prayer meeting. I had carried my perennial questions about prayer with me, had followed Wolter's advice and checked out a textbook on ascetical theology. Every other page referred to the person's "spiritual director." It isn't fair, I inwardly complained, that only people in religious orders get to learn about prayer. Lay people don't get spiritual directors. When I saw the notice of the "prayer and praise" group in the bulletin, I protested, "I can't go to that. What will they do to me?" But I went anyway, figuring I had no right to complain if I didn't take what was offered. In fact, although I clung to my chair for dear life, all they did was sing hymns, talk in a devotional way about a Bible passage, and offer surprisingly detailed intercessions. Afterward, the rector confronted me: "So, tell me about your spiritual journey." I closed an evasive summary with "I came here hoping to learn something about prayer, but maybe I came to the wrong place." He suggested that we should have a talk. I also volunteered, "It upsets me that my father-in-law is dying. I always counted on his generation to be real Christians. Who are people going to 'catch' Christianity from, when people like him are dead?" He said, "Look in the mirror!" When I told him in the first session that God seemed like the federal government, he asked, "Was it ever different? What happened?" His summary diagnosis was, "Your trouble isn't prayer, it's sin. Why don't you repent of your sins?" I was desperate; why not? After that I went to confession every two weeks for about five years. There was the idol of academic ambition, there was my hatred of the Episcopal church for robbing me of my vocation to the ministry, and so on. A few meetings later, he said, "You know, you've got to start believing that this makes a difference." I replied, "But I've got good arguments why God can't change me. It's incompatible with free will!" He laughed and said, "Can a woman be born again after she has a Ph.D.?" My answer to that question is "yes." The metaphor is a good one for the process that covered much the same ground as psychotherapy but integrated it into the context of one's relationship to God. It felt as if I were being dismantled and reassembled. The process was difficult and messy. But I am immeasurably grateful for it; it definitely did, as the cliché goes, "change my life."

Oddly, we didn't often confront the issue of prayer directly. Yet, after a couple of months, I was aware of the reality of God's presence as I hadn't been for years, gentle, pervasive, flowing in and through the community assembled for worship; surprising me as I walked down the street or sat in philosophy lectures. Trying to understand this, I reckon that God is always with us, His defenses ever down. What blinds us to this reality is that ours are up. These spiritual-direction sessions opened me up, removed the barriers that I had put up to detecting the real presence of God. My next question was, "St. Paul tells us to pray without ceasing. But how can one pray and do philosophy at the same time?" The rector gave me *The Way of the Pilgrim,* but his own recommendation was to pray in tongues, because in that sort of prayer "the mind lies fallow." It took months of following the prescription to say "la, la, la" before I did receive that gift, which for me is an utterly nonecstatic experience. As promised, it comes from a different part of the self and can be done while doing philosophy or "under one's breath" at public meetings. I'm grateful to pray beyond what my conscious self knows and can control, for the chance to groan and babble with the Spirit. When he told me it was time to begin saying morning or evening prayer every day, I reported that it was a wonderful experience but it took three hours. He said that the office should be doable in half an hour, but perhaps I was called to be a comtemplative academic. My current study of Anselm is part of my effort to learn how doing philosophical theology itself is a form of prayer.

Vocational discernment involves sorting out mixed motives, the neurotic drives to repeat past solutions from the Spirit's invitation to bold new futures. For example, that first year in Princeton, I was so elated to have found "the pearl of great price" that I was ready to sell everything to buy it. When someone asked whether I thought it reasonable to believe in God, I replied that I didn't know and somehow didn't care. This was misleading. On the one hand, I found my renewed experience of God quite convincing. On the other, I didn't trust myself not to quench it. The war inside between faith and doubt, love of God and accusation, was not over. Because I had given voice to the negative polarity for so long, I deliberately tried to bracket epistemological concerns. When questions arose, habitual and cynical, I moved to silence them with prayers for faith, prayers not to accuse anymore, prayers to love as much as St. Paul, St. Augustine, St. Anselm, and St. Francis. Over the years, faith did grow and accusation fade. But I have never been able to identify with that saying from *The Cloud of Unknowing:* "by love can God be thought and held; by thinking, never!" On the contrary, my experience has seemed to teach that I cannot be confident of holding on to God with either my beliefs or my feelings; if our relationship is going to last, it will be because God is holding on to me. Surface repentance of the sin of academic ambition masked rage at years of self-imposed slavery to my work. There came a time when I, who had always been able to work diligently, was psychologically unable to proceed with my book on William Ockham. Yet, I could not escape my addiction-cum-vocation to analytical thinking, and threw myself into study of the Bible as if to make up for lost time.

Eventually, my stifled sense of vocation to the ministry began to reassert itself. This was threatening, not only for the psychoanalytic reason that it warred with childhood "tapes" on my invincible badness, but also because my spiritual director had opposed the ordination of women, had even gone to General Convention (the national church congress) to vote against it. The Bible, too, seemed to advise against proceeding: "grow where you're planted; stay in the place where you are called." There were motivational questions: Was I merely trying to recover my golden childhood with my dead grandfather? Wasn't it pride that demanded a visible leadership position? So, on the one hand, I would pray for God to show me His will for my life, and, on the other, beg that He would take away my desire to become a priest. I tried hard to listen to the arguments against the ordination of women. But, much as I respected the people who made them and even understood how they came to such a conclusion, nothing inside me had the least inclination to agree; at bottom, my own sense of vocation was too strong. In retrospect, I am sure that my first application to the diocese reflected the strains of these inner battles. I was also quite naive about the workings of the institutional church. Before the bishop, I was much too deferential. I answered the questions on the psychological test with far too much candor, and this combined with the examiner's bias against successful academics (he was later found not to have the psychological degrees he had advertised) to give me a failing grade. My request for reevaluation was first granted and then withdrawn by the bishop. I returned from the Christmas APA meetings to find the perfunctory letter that told me, in effect, not to darken their doors again, to "have a nice life" . . . somewhere else.

The effect on me was apocalyptic. If my home town and Cornell had been hellish, this felt more like annihilation, except that you still had to get up in the morning. I had been a tough customer, put up a good fight; but now, it seemed, the forces arrayed against me had finally won. It took only half an hour to realize that my old crisis strategy of burying myself in work was useless. Floundering, I said to God, "The only way I know to keep up communication right now is to give You a running commentary on how I feel, and it isn't going to be pretty!" Indeed, most of it was pain and rage, spewing forth in blasphemy and accusation. We church people are curiously prudish about open verbal blasphemy. Yet, maximally indecent as it is, the deeper blasphemy with which we caricature the image of God in ourselves and others is virtually inevitable. From time to time, I would look up from such prayers amazed that I hadn't been "zapped" yet. I would look to the cross and apologize, grateful that He was there to absorb the worst I could offer. Someone at the New England religious community where I had gone on retreats voiced my darkest fears when he diagnosed the rejection as Divine punishment for rejecting his advice not to apply. I prayed, "I can believe I *deserve* this and worse; after all, so many authorities have declared me incorrigibly bad. But if You're the kind of person who visits this sort of thing on people just because we deserve it, then life is a desperate nightmare. It would have been better never to have been born." Noticing that I wanted to keep on living, even though it meant moving Mount Everest before breakfast every morning, I concluded, "So you must not be like that. You must think some suffering too bad even for the guilty!" Suddenly, I recognized that I did concede cogency to transcendental arguments after all. This is also how I became convinced that any adequate solution to the problem of evil must portray Divine goodness in such a way as to make each person's life worth living. For weeks, I felt as if I were crawling through a tunnel with no light at the end. Then, one day it hit me that this dark tunnel was all on Jesus's lap. As Good Friday approached, I suddenly recognized the passion of Christ as a remarkable identification with the worst that we can be and suffer. If at moments I could still rage, with the bad thief, "Why do you make Your Son and us suffer?" I eventually tumbled to the inference that if Christ crucified is the clearest revelation of Divine love, then maybe God—even in His Divine nature—suffers, too. Ironically, this experience of being turned down by the bishop was what convinced me that God *is* love unconditional. These lessons proved invaluable a few years later, when my ministry brought me in touch with people whose suffering made my life look like an absolute picnic. Jon Olson, the dean of the diocesan theology school, was a mainstay during this time. Once as I poured out my pain and struggles, he blurted out—what I have taken as a key to solving the problem of evil—"Oh, but suffering is a vision into the inner life of God!"

Although the door to priesthood seemed definitively closed, I was accepted at Princeton Theological Seminary. Bob didn't mind taking time off and I had always wanted to go, so we moved back to Payne Hall for the summer and fall of 1983 and again in 1984. At first, I was just indulging the part of a childhood dream that seemed within reach. Although I was betting that God was not punitive, I was still too stunned by the magnitude of the disaster to want to risk a repeat performance. I prayed and prayed for direction, but instead of imperative heavenly voices, I sensed permission and invitation. It was as if God said, "What do you really want? You have my blessing." I admitted that I wanted to reapply. So I switched to a degree program, arranged to do field work at my spiritual director's parish, and began to build a case. I convinced the seminary to let me enroll in its Th.M. program and focus my work on biblical studies and pastoral psychology. A major attraction of Princeton Theological Seminary for me was the possibility of working with Jim Loder, whose project was the (theoretical and practical) integration of psychology and spirituality. Working with him through Freud, Rogers, Jung, Piaget, Kohlberg, Kegan, Gilligan, and other psychologists was intellectually the most stimulating experience I had had since reading Plato's *Republic* in Max Fisch's course on Greek philosophy at Illinois. I remain grateful for many conversations and for his faith, creativity, and compassion.

My second tour through seminary was complicated by my attempts to get back on board ecclesiastically. I had got the impression that were I to transfer my ecclesiastical residence, my spiritual director would recommend me to the diocese of New Jersey. Summer school had scarcely begun when someone hinted that he was going to stand in my way. My confrontation of the issue began a series of bitter arguments that lasted all summer. Sifting and speculation were futile. It boiled down to the fact that he didn't see a priest in me. And that was that! Rejection by a mentor is always painful. Yet, having hit bottom in my round with the bishop, I knew there was a floor under the depths to which one could sink. In particular, I knew that this floor was the love of Christ. "Oh, I see. You want me to rely on You, not some human authority figure. Well, okay. Our deal was that You were going to make me an *adult* Christian." The stress was tremendous, and I did leave with one incomplete course, which I made up during the succeeding winter quarter back at UCLA.

Striding across the campus to teach introductory philosophy of religion, as I had many years in a row, I was raging inside. I knew the bishop's policy was not to grant second interviews. "Lord, I didn't go through all of this just to go back to fishing," I snapped. "Something's got to change." My first thought was to quit my job and go for a second Ph.D. in clinical psychology. I had overintellectualized for most of my career. Focusing on what makes people tick promised a better integration of intellectual and emotional dimensions. Perhaps providentially, I couldn't find a program in town that would teach me what I wanted to know. The previous winter I had gotten to know David Duncan, who had explored the possibility of my doing some adult education work in his Hollywood parish. On the other hand, I wondered whether one of the bigger parishes might not serve as a better base for a possible reapplication. Praying about this, I recognized that I was too angry to bring off Ignatian indifference, so I proposed what the charismatics call a *fleece*: "Lord, if you want me to work at Beverly Hills, let the priest who used to do the weekday services recognize me." Although we had talked at some length, she missed by a continent, whereupon I gave David a call and began work at Trinity.

However much it divides, the Bible also has a marvelous way of bringing people together. Our Sunday morning class included old-timers (early refugees from the Midwest), Filipino immigrants, and the growing number of gay men who were returning to church in the wake of the AIDS crisis. Each group had its saints, but holiness was most evident in the old-timers, who from time to time would zoom in from some tangential position and say something that the rest of us collectively recognized as "the Word of the Lord." Two had congenital eye problems; the woman prayed and prayed for a cure, and after a couple of years she got it when a new doctor nonchalantly recommended cornea transplants. Nobody else's eyes were dry the Sunday she read the small print Bible with ease. The blessings for Antonio were different: One week he proudly displayed his green card to us and announced that his job with Goodwill Industries had made him self-supporting.

Working at Trinity forced me to confront the relation between homosexual lifestyle and Christian faith. My most recent past mentors had been sure that it was an illness to be cured. But you can't preach what somebody else knows, only what *you* know. And I had to ask myself, what did *I* really know? My answer was, not much about sexuality; it's too hard and confusing a topic. For me, the nature of God is much easier. I did feel sure that God as our creator is in favor of whoever we really are, stands ready to help us grow to our full stature, and is willing to start talking to us about our lives wherever we are prepared to begin. So I preached that. Naturally, as a philosopher, I wanted to *understand,* too. We started a theology and sexuality study group, plowing our way through relevant biblical passages, John Boswell's book *Christianity, Social Tolerance, and Homosexuality,* and several others. My own approach was empirical: I tried to learn as much as I could about how they understood themselves. I asked them what they thought of the Freudian hypothesis that homosexuality reflects a domination of the death wish. What I witnessed among so many was sacrificial love. I also recognized in them a mirror of my own predicament. When you don't fit into the preestablished conventional categories, you look and say, "What's wrong with me?" while others echo, "What's wrong with you?" After a decade or two or three, you hate yourself. That inner conviction of *incorrigible* badness is 90 percent sociological projection. Not all gay lifestyles are helpful, any more than all heterosexual ones are. But the church has contributed to the confusion by sponsoring a taboo mentality toward sexuality generally. Conventional religion has blinded us to the image of Christ in gay and lesbian Christians, to the reflection of the Trinity in homosexual partnership, and so bears responsibility for obstructing their process of discernment. It wasn't long before our people began dying. Preaching the Gospel to people whose gray-green skin tells you that they won't be there in six months creates a pressure to tell as much Truth as one can. I did not have to strain to see Christ crucified in these people. Working at Trinity parish was perhaps the most meaningful experience of my life.

I wanted change, but things had not really been the same since our return from Princeton in 1981, when we gathered the philosophy department Christians into a Sunday night Bible study. Over the years, we have consumed many pounds of chocolate, while chewing our way through numerous books. Any question can be raised, any doubt expressed. Needless to say, we have discussed the problem of evil hundreds of times. Likewise, the goals of the Society of Christian Philosophers had begun to shake my research program. My spiritual director had challenged me to explore how Jesus solved the problem of evil. I groped my way toward an answer in my paper "Redemptive Suffering: A Christian Solution to the Problem of Evil"; things are expressed more clearly in my more recent piece, "Chalcedonian Christology: A Christian Solution to the Problem of Evil."

In 1985, I broke my vow never to become chair of the department. It was a good experience and a lot of work. David Kaplan taught me volumes about how to think through problems from an institutional point of view. My attempts to negotiate conflicts made me keenly aware of how character faults distort clear vision and make fair-minded problem solving difficult. The responsibility made various forms of self-indulgence intolerable luxuries.

That same year, with the help of David Duncan and Jon Olson, I got back on the ordination track, which was now strewn with ironies. When I took the psychological tests again, the evaluator pulled out the old file to compare the two. She said that normally she would conclude that I had lied my way into the new acceptable score, except that my letters of recommendation confirmed it. I suggested that there were two explanations: Either the first test evaluation was defective (which she would not admit), or else the changes in me were miraculous. I allowed as how I was in the right business to believe in miracles. When I finally went through the diocesan interviews, someone commented, "There was never any question about your case." I could imagine God winking!

When I was finally ordained deacon on June 20, 1987, with students and parishioners behind me and colleagues across the room, I felt as if I had been hit by a ton of bricks, as if there were an earthquake in my soul, with strata and layers shifting and realigning, mostly beyond my conscious ken. Etymologically, deacons are servants, slaves of Christ, by canon law, of the bishop. Liturgically, they are privileged to read the Gospel, to preach, to set the Lord's table, and to distribute the bread/Body of Christ. Most of all, deacons are commissioned to work with the poor and sick. After church the next day, we got a call that Michael was violently ill, and I was on my way for the first of many visits to the small, attractive house where he lived with his lover, Dave. Both were in the magazine business—Dave as an editor, Michael as an illustrator. Both were gentle homebodies: Dave loved to garden, while Mike drew pictures for children's books. They had bought the house only six months before Michael received his death-sentence diagnosis of AIDS, which became his hour of temptation. Scared silly, he confessed to the gay priest at our Hollywood church his thoughts of suicide to cut short the sure torture ahead. The priest challenged: "This is your chance to show how brave a gay man can be with Jesus at his side. Choose life." Michael rose to the occasion, stood on the side of God, and fought death with creativity. Forced to retire on disability, he would lie still for days, hoarding energy, then get up one morning and paint all day. He used art to express his feelings about dying young. In his soul portraits, he appears muscular and vigorous, but there are also symbols of grief, and loss, and wounds. In all, he produced about thirty canvasses during his last six months. Doctors at UCLA's Boyer Cancer Center arranged for a one-man show in the cancer ward and encouraged him to have postcards made for use in art therapy. Armed with a touch-tone phone, a shoebox file, and all the charm in the world, Michael created the HeARTfelt project, which produced packets of the cards for distribution in hospitals. Sales of paintings and posters bankrolled that effort, with surplus proceeds going to help other PWA's (People With AIDS). Michael turned around other glum moments by drawing coloring books for children, which he had sent with free crayons to the pediatric wards. His comment was, "Hey, I could lie here and feel sorry for myself, or I could show a little love to somebody else!"

One day when I visited, a friend of a friend came by unexpectedly with a delivery. When she saw Michael at the door, with purplish lesions spreading across his face, she did a double-take. "Do you . . . do you . . . ?" she stammered. "Oh, don't mind my polka dots," he replied. But afterward he was shaken. That was when I read him the passage from Isaiah about the Suffering Servant of God. Some people say that AIDS is Divine judgment on a homosexual lifestyle. In my opinion, they get it backward: AIDS is a judgment on us, exposing our hidden fear of sudden death, our fear of what is different in others, of the polka dotting spreading across our own selves. We are afraid to look at the disfigured or the dying because they are a picture of our own true selves. Michael saw it as one of his missions in life to convince "all those grandmas out there that PWAs are just as lovable and charming as their grandchildren." With this determination, he dragged himself out of bed a few weeks before he died to give a radio interview and to allow the diocese to make a videotape.

Unlike many who suffer and die of AIDS, Michael did not die abandoned. His lover, Dave, already diagnosed as HIV positive, cared for him to the last. Long-time friends and church people gathered round. But his primary source of strength came from God, who appeared to him in visions in the form of a Lady he called "Grace." Michael assured me that he was not drugged, but that she came sometimes during the day, other times at night. The first time he was frightened, thinking she had come to take him to heaven, when he was not yet ready, when he still had more to say. A couple of months later, he wondered aloud whether he had seen too much of holiness to stay much longer.

Two days before he died, I was keeping midnight vigil. He woke up suddenly and said, "I have pains, as if I were giving birth to twins." "What would you name them?" I asked. "Joshua and Elihu," he replied. "Joshua"—whose name, incidentally means "Jesus"—"is my nephew who's been in a coma. Maybe something good will come for him from this." Michael was a poor Bible student, and he didn't know anyone named Elihu, that is, Elijah, who went up to heaven in a chariot of fire. He fell back to sleep. The air was heavy with sweat and urine. His mother was sleeping on the floor at the foot of his bed. I felt I was watching the Christ's passion being re-enacted, as I softly read psalms from the prayer book: "Into your hands, I commend my Spirit . . ." "Depart O Christian soul out of this world, in the name of God who created you, God who redeemed you, and God who sanctifies you. May your rest be this day in peace, and your dwelling place in the Paradise of God."

I dealt with my grief by writing a letter telling Michael's story (as he had given me permission to do). Among those to whom I sent it were members of the New England religious community where I had gone for retreats. I knew they thought the homosexual lifestyle was ipso facto incompatible with faithful Christian practice. But they were also committed to "living in the Spirit"; they regularly allowed the power of personal testimony to override abstract theological theory. So, I was eager to share with them what I had learned from Michael. Perhaps a month later, I received a mail-gram sent on behalf of a woman who had agreed to be a presenter at my ordination to the priesthood, stating that she would not attend; in the letter that followed, she said I bordered on apostasy in comparing Michael's sufferings to Christ's, that he was more like the thief on the cross; she could not recommend me for the *Christian* priesthood. The iron curtain crashed down between us because I had violated the community's taboos. I was hurt and disappointed: Human communities need taboos to keep out what society's categories can't manage, but the Kingdom of Heaven can't fall apart because it is bound together by the Spirit of God. Still, the Church is both human and Divine. We, its members, all have our blind spots; mine are different from hers, but I have them. My consolation is that since each of us is looking to Christ, daily praying to see more nearly as He does, we will all eventually (beyond the grave) agree in Him.

For my ordination to the priesthood, I requested the Feast of Doubting Thomas, as befits a philosopher. In the end, no authority figures came: one bought a cow, the other married and took a trip, and so on. Even the bishop went to Hawaii with the football team and sent another, who had, incidentally, been a philosophy major at UCLA. No one was there who didn't want to be there. We gathered "outside the gates," and God came. The ordaining bishop said he had never felt such a Presence and confirmation of ministry. My friend Jon Olson spoke of the descent of a "gentle Spirit" on me, who have battled all my life. That night unconditional love was not just a theory. I wondered why those people loved me. Later, I reflected that from time to time I had given them five minutes of real attention at coffee hour. Usually, we can't solve each other's problems; it wouldn't be respectful to try. But each of us can, at least once a week, really listen to someone else for five minutes, and this breaks the spell of loneliness and empowers us to go on. Again, we spend all our lives trying to learn to give and receive love. We demand to have it from parents and teachers and mentors and professional superiors. Yet, that night, I knew that love that Jesus promises, His own and the Kingdom family's, of mother, father, brothers, and sisters, with whom I had struggled and cried, broken bread and prayed!

I had to prove I was superwoman to get ordained. This messy story of failure and confusion confirms the obvious truth that it is not so. Yet, I feel sure, I have found my vocation as a scholarly priest and a priestly scholar. It is a great blessing to be able to offer the world's sufferings and joys to be united with Christ on the altar. For me, there is the quiet joy of putting on alb and stole, early on Sunday morning when the sun streams through the stained glass windows, to get the reserved sacrament for the eight o'clock mass. Perhaps because I was deeply convinced that I could not bring good to anyone, I love to bless the children or give them the bread or wine with the words "This is Jesus, and He loves you very much!" Like other priests, I get a "ringside" seat on the miracles, as people share what God is doing in their lives. Not surprisingly, I enjoy rolling up my sleeves and digging into the text at adult Bible study between services. At school, I take special delight in "coming out of the closet" as a Christian philosopher (philosophical theologian) and cheerleading others into doing the same. I have many philosophical interests, but all are focused by my desire to know the meaning of suffering and the goodness of God. Yet, I discover the most about these when I preach because of the Spirit's radical pressure to tell it like it is—with utter candor, how things can seem from a human point of view—and then to tell the old, old story of Jesus and His love.

My tale also makes clear why defensive apologetics is not my cup of tea. It presupposes that all the problems are on the outside and undertakes only to rebut objections raised by someone else; whereas for me, difficulties on the outside set up a war in *my* members, between faith and doubt, desire and hate. None should wonder now why I am a universalist. My experience is that God's love is unconditional and all-inclusive. My fears to the contrary have always turned out to be a projection of the dark side of some merely human authority figures. Badness and evil do infect our human condition, but life could not be worth living if any were incorrigible to God. Perhaps I sometimes hoped that ordination would at last fit me comfortably into a conventional category. Not so! Rather, I begin to appreciate how my life to date has prepared me for the mission fields—not India or the Philippines, according to my childhood fantasy, but at a secular arts faculty of a state university, at the social frontiers of Hollywood or Santa Monica, to those who long for God but can't yet believe that God's love has always been with and for them.

I I

FARAWAY FIELDS

ARE GREEN

William J. Abraham

Many people, when they hear that I was born and brought up in Northern Ireland, respond with a mixture of pity and curiosity. They feel pity because they are aware of the long history of strife and terror in Northern Ireland, and they wonder if I have lost friends or relatives. Unfortunately, this is indeed true. They express curiosity, partly because there is a natural interest in anything Irish and partly because they wonder how anyone could really take Christianity seriously given the connection between religion and conflict that has existed in Ireland for centuries. It is difficult to know how to react to this. Sometimes I am tempted to launch into a quick analysis of "The Troubles," as we affectionately call the strife. Sometimes I want to provide a catalog of the extraordinary goodness of the people I know at home.

Some of these people come from my home church; in the wake of unspeakably horrific events, they have been amazing in their generosity and faith. Sometimes I feel like explaining how well the churches get along together officially. I often want to say, "Well, if you think things are bad with Christianity in our history, imagine what it would be like if we did not have Christianity."

The Christian tradition in Northern Ireland is in a state of extensive disrepair, to be sure. Compared to the rest of Europe, Northern Ireland is nominally Christian. In many ways it is easy to see it as a cultural backwater, for the political and nationalist conflict has forced people to preserve vast tracts of Christian tradition that have long been forgotten elsewhere. Equally, there is a squalid disregard for central elements of the Christian gospel, even though there is much talk about faithfulness to Christianity on all sides. In some cases, what has been handed down has clearly been transmitted in forms that can only be described as religiously abusive. However, having lived extensively outside Northern Ireland, I see the elements of the Christian heritage preserved in Ulster not as a backwater, but as an incredibly rich reservoir of cultural and religious materials. This was not how I initially perceived the situation. In fact, I made up my mind early on to keep the whole thing at arms length. As long as I can remember, I made a stern but unspoken resolution not to become a Christian. More precisely, I was determined not to allow God to have any say in my life.

This was common among many of my friends and relatives. One belonged to the church, but one generally had no intention of paying any attention to its teaching. It was also common to yield for a while to the appeals of the traveling evangelist. The revivalist tradition that began in Ulster in the seventeenth century and migrated to North America via Scotland has returned again in a radically revised form. My own encounter as a child with this tradition is still a vivid memory. I went to meetings after school, and I had a very clear sense of the reality and call of God in my life. I even made a public profession of faith. It lasted all of twenty-four hours. It ended when I had a strong altercation with my mother about who should lock up the hens for the night. I was sure that the obligation to do this fell to my younger brother, so I dropped the fragile faith I had rather than agree to the chore imposed on me. Thus ended abruptly my first conscious encounter with Christianity.

One of the great saving virtues of Northern Ireland is its educational system. Some of our most gifted people become teachers; the economic situation makes this a highly attractive profession. Last year I returned to Northern Ireland to visit my mother in her eightieth year. While there, I went on a pilgrimage to meet some of the teachers who had done so much to kindle a passion for serious study. One of them, whom I had not seen for thirty years, is still introducing a new generation to the joys of learning. She is also radiating as humbly as ever the love of Christ. There is a native sanity in such teachers that prevents them from naively adopting utopian schemes of educational reform. They let the English try it out first and then, if it has value, they borrow without apology.

I had the good fortune to get a scholarship to Portora Royal School when I turned eleven. This opened up a whole new world. One was immediately plunged into a rich liberal education that took one in considerable depth through a whole range of disciplines. I still find it hard to believe that there were times when I could not wait to get to school to continue our reading of authors like Racine and Goethe. Of course, one was also dragged into the daily round of morning prayers, and school assembly, as well as the standard diet of religious education. However, I had long learned how to handle these, and for the most part they were bland and harmless. Years later I came to appreciate how valuable they are in one's moral and spiritual formation. Even now, the Anglican collects for the day are recalled with satisfaction. Moreover, I was deeply impressed with the honesty and intellectual depth of some of my teachers. I recall two incidents. In one case I asked "Faggy" Benson, the rector who taught us Latin and smoked like the proverbial train, about preparation for death. He spoke with quiet conviction. "There is always hope between the stirrup and the ground." The image of God that this expressed captured precisely a notion of mercy that was deeply attractive. On another occasion I recall an encounter with the headmaster, "Percy" Rogers, a bear of a man who had been a student of C. S. Lewis and had a thunderous laugh. I asked what he would recommend to someone who wanted to start a new religion. The answer came very naturally: "Gather a band of disciples, get yourself crucified, and then try coming back from the dead on the third day." In all, then, school was both a wonderful distraction from religious interests and a place where, now and then, one encountered the real thing.

I also encountered the real thing in the Methodist ministers who visited our home. They represented a sacred world that had a deep aura of mystery in it. My family had always been Methodist; both my mother and my father came from Methodist stock. My father had been killed in a dreadful road accident when I was three, so my mother was left to bring up six boys on her own. How she managed this is itself a marvel. Part of her strategy was to keep us in the countryside in the wide open spaces of a small farm, where we had plenty to absorb us. The routine and delight of caring for farm animals, of cutting hay, of gathering apples in the orchard, of fishing in the river, of gathering frogspan, of wandering in lush green meadows—all these, and much else, were more than enough to keep us fully occupied. The English used to think that the Irish raised their pigs in the corner of the kitchen. They were not entirely wrong. In our house, the pet pigs, discarded by a neighbor because the litter was too big for the sow, were reared for a time in tea chests by the fire. This was a prudent way to ensure their survival.

The other part of my mother's strategy was to send us to Sunday school. This in itself was an adventure. The seasons of the year brought their own crop of unique experiences, like climbing the giant chesnut trees before lessons started in order to harvest the most magnificent chestnuts imaginable or walking for miles through ten inches of spotless snow on a shiny Sunday morning. Transportation to Sunday school was supplied by bicycles, which were in short supply. With careful planning, four of us could travel for several miles on one bicycle;

there was one boy on the handlebars, one on the bar, one on the seat, and one on the outer nuts of the rear wheel. Sunday school, in turn, brought visits from the Methodist ministers. Actually, they came with the orphan money from the church that provided shoes and clothing. What amazed me most was not the gifts they brought, crucial as these were to us as a family, but the sense of natural intimacy with God that came through when the ministers got us all down on our knees to pray before they left the house. In addition, I found it astonishing that God should show the least interest in us, either individually or as a family. Yet this was the unspoken assumption that operated in these encounters. The encounters were, of course, fleeting and intermittent, but they were fully welcome and eagerly anticipated on my part.

The overall impact, however, was ephemeral. By the mid-teen years I had become an atheist. Looking back, it would be easy to see this as a normal bout of intellectual measels that would pass with time. This was not at all the case. The issue for me was quite simple: If God was invisible, then God did not exist. Formally speaking, the problem was conceptual: Only those things that were available to the senses were real. God was not available to the senses; hence God was not real. When this began to sink in, I found myself scared. The residual consequences of traditional theism continued to haunt my imagination and my mind. God would ultimately punish me for my unbelief and for my antagonism to the things of the spirit. It was not difficult to rid myself of the feelings this engendered. If God did not exist, then there was no divine agent to exercise judgment on me or anybody else. As our beliefs and emotions usually are logically connected, working this through brought deep peace. I was no longer even concerned that I was not afraid of the change that had crept over me intellectually. The road lay wide open ahead of me, and I was ready to stride forth and follow wherever it might lead. The sense of freedom was exhilarating.

Yet liberty is a two-edged sword. Ironically, the slide into atheism set me free to explore the claims of the Christian tradition. Having become an atheist, the next step was to drop out of the Christian community and stop attending church. This could have been done very easily; one could simply sleep in on a Sunday morning and let nature take its predictable course. Yet it did not happen that way. Deep within, I knew that the decision to leave the church would bring long-term, drastic consequences. It should not, therefore, be taken lightly. I resolved to delay this decision for three months, and then, if things were still the same intellectually, I could leave and let nature take its course. In this there was not a hint of praying the agnostic's prayer, "Lord, if you are there, reveal yourself to me." This was psychologically phony for me. Nor could I countenance even the remnants of Pascal's wager and somehow bet on the existence of God as a better option than unbelief. When I discussed this at length with a friend who later became a policeman, it could not even begin to break the conceptual stranglehold that gripped my mind; besides, it reeked of dishonesty. Nor could I countenance some great leap of faith. This was just nonsense, for I had no way of imagining or conceiving what it would involve. What I could and did resolve to do was to pay careful attention to religious people, to read sporadically in such religious literature as I could find, to focus as best I could on what I heard and encountered, and to give the Christian faith one last run for its money. So I would look over the hymns we were singing, listen to but not participate in religious conversations, and pay very careful attention to the sermons, all the while pretending that I was bored to tears. Above all, I read through J. B. Phillips's paperback translation of the New Testament; this I did late at night, when everyone else had gone to bed and the television had closed down for the evening. All this was high-risk behavior for an immature, very young atheist.

The combined effect of these activities took me by surprise, yet none of them brought about the breakthrough without which I could never have found my way into the faith. The great obstacle that had to be overcome was the conceptual inability even to conceive of the reality of God. I can still see the place on the Sligo Road in Enniskillen outside the Salvation Army Hall where the possibility of theism dawned afresh for me. It was close to the core of what attracted me to the Christian faith.

What captured my imagination very generally was the Christian reckoning with the reality of evil in the world. The issue here is not the standard one of theodicy, of how to reconcile the goodness and power of God with the exis- tence of evil, a matter that has tormented theists of one kind or another for centuries. I have never seen an adequate solution to this problem; in fact, I tend to think that solutions to this issue are generally superficial, and I am convinced that having a solution in hand is by no means a requirement for being an intellectually responsible theist. What I found carrying enormous weight was the extent to which Christianity absolutely refused to blunt the reality of evil by denying it, taming it, pushing it to the margins of existence, covering it up cleverly, and the like. On the contrary, it took the reality of evil so seriously that evil showed up all over the place when one came to expound and explain its teachings and practices. Now this was not what caused the breakthrough; what opened up the heavens was the ability to conceive of the demonic. As I pondered the depth and extent of evil in the world, I had no difficulty whatsoever conceiving the possibility of the influence of a thor- oughly malevolent agent. When this dawned on me, it destroyed in an instant the ontological principle that said that only the visible could be real. Once this was gone, I could reckon with the possibility of the reality of God with a clear conscience. When this was overturned, I was set free to explore the content of the Christian gospel with new freedom.

Intellectually it was pretty much plain sailing from there on. As I exposed myself to the gospels, to the material I sang and heard in church, to the bits and pieces I read and pondered, I began waking up with different beliefs. There was a kind of beginning and end to the process, but I have no idea of the stages in the middle. I started out at the beginning an atheist, and I ended up at the end a convinced believer in Jesus Christ as the Son of God and the Savior of the world. What complicated matters for me was that I knew that if I yielded, if I repented and gave my life to God, I would have to head eventually into the ordained ministry of the church. This was the last thing in the world I wanted to do; my first choice was to become a teacher; I did not want to give myself to a calling whose journey was utterly beyond my ken. So I found myself not just with changed beliefs, but with a radically changed vocation.

Two other factors stand out now as I review the total process. I had to learn what it was to trust the promises of God, and I had to overcome the crippling fear that set siege to me when I contemplated what others would think and say when they discovered that I had become a believer. Both of these were addressed in a mission that was held in my church. On the first evening of the special meetings, I publicly acknowledged that I intended to follow Christ. This was an extremely difficult step to take, but I knew it was totally unavoidable. As a consequence, I talked with a wonderful African-American singer named Jimmy MacDonald, who explained what it meant to relax and take salvation as a gift freely given to us by God. Faith came by hearing, and hearing required a response of trust in the offer given to us in the gospel. New light dawned to round off a process that had begun months before and that opened up a new boundless world. The race had now begun in earnest, and I had no idea where it would eventually take me. As the race proceeded, the fear of what others might think simply disappeared.

The aftercare of my home church was exactly what I needed. One of the pastors provided the loving, gentle mentoring and the intellectual initiation into the faith that fed both my mind and my soul. On one level, the goal was to let my studies and my life as a whole come gently and fully into the arena of the kingdom of God. Conversion in fact opened up all sorts of new questions that left me bored with the study of French and German at school. Only later did I discover that there was a whole world of theology and philosophy that one could enter for oneself. I developed a fascination with some of the issues that came up in divinity classes taught by "Percy" Rogers. Through the radio, we were introduced to the thought of Bishop John Robinson. The ultimate effect of the latter was to inoculate me forever against forms of Christianity that are mostly the rehashing of secular values and convictions in the guise of religious creativity or new reformations. The penultimate effect was to make me aware of a deep conversation about the meaning and truth of Christianity in the modern world. On another level, the goal was to become a member of the church and then later begin the process of work and study that would eventually lead to ordination. This was the normal course for those who had been baptized as infants and now had to own the faith for themselves. At yet another level, I found myself immersed in scripture and in the life and writings of John Wesley. The latter suddenly became vibrantly alive. I cut my theological teeth on the content of his sermons. Years afterward, in seminary, it all became a kind of religious archeology, until it was suddenly reopened through an encounter with a brilliant set of taped lectures given by Albert Outler. After my conversion, it provided a network of concepts, doctrines, themes, puzzles, insights, and loose ends that was inexhaustible. It also opened up a lane into the classical Christian tradition, especially its Eastern Orthodox form, for which I shall be forever grateful.

My first encounter with philosophy was something of an accident. I did not have a clue about what it involved. I took it up as a subject at Queen's University in Belfast, together with psychology, because I had a vague notion that it would somehow be useful when I eventually trained for the Christian ministry. I also had the naive and pious idea that it would do me some good just to encounter the great minds of the past. When I began to find my way into philosophy, it quickly pushed psychology into the back seat of my life. My first teacher in philosophy was Professor W. B. Gallie, who later took a chair in politics at Cambridge. We read Plato's *Republic* and Bertrand Russell's *Problems of Philosophy*. I still consider the latter to be a throroughly unsatisfactory introduction to the subject, not least because it gives the deep impression that philosophy breeds erudite nonsense. Later it was a wonderful discovery to learn that G. E. Moore rejected, as I instinctively did, Russell's conviction that common sense represents the metaphysics of a savage. Gallie, however, rescued philosophy for me by his own embodiment of what it is to be a philosopher and by his fascinating proposal, derived from Plato, that philosophy is fundamentally the criticism of standards. It took a lot of time to get on board but, once launched, there was no turning back. I pursued a joint honors degree in philosophy and psychology for four years, but the psychology did not come close to providing the passion and joy I found in the study of philosophy.

The department in which I trained was remarkably cosmopolitan. The curriculum was of the standard kind, providing immersion in the history of philosophy, on the one hand, and a good grounding in logic, metaphysics, moral philosophy, epistemology, and the like, on the other. The faculty included an existentialist and a wonderfully gracious Idealist, who was not in the least intimidated by logical positivism. All were at home in the analytical tradition that was the norm of the period. Lectures, with one exception, were uniformly good. Tutorials in groups of four or five were excellent. The highlight of our work was a weekly honors seminar that lasted for ninety minutes and ran for the last three years of our training. The whole department, together with all the honors students, participated. Over time one learned, through reading papers and joining in the discussion, the inner logic of philosophy. The standard practice was to take a modern contribution to a philosophical topic and work systematically through the arguments and issues. At times the discussion was heated and frank; it was always civil and courteous.

The great lacuna was the lack of attention given to the philosophy of religion. Here one simply had to fend for oneself, finding a friendly tutor who would provide a bibliography and give initial direction. It was a great day when among the new books in the library, I stumbled across a book by Alvin Plantinga that discussed the epistemology of religious belief as rigorously and thoroughly as those found in the philosophy of science or the philosophy of history. Equally, it was a great pleasure to come across articles in the philosophy of religion when browsing through back issues of the *Proceedings of the Aristotelian Society* or the standard philosophical journals. The implicit message, however, from mainstream philosophy was clear: Philosophy of religion was not to be taken seriously.

My intellectual development as a Christian was, of course, affected by my studies. The initial influence was, I suspect, entirely indirect. I was so absorbed in becoming initiated into the history and forms of philosophy that I scarcely had time to work through the impact the latter were having on my faith. This situation changed dramatically toward the end of the second year. By that time, I had been deeply exposed to the whole gamut of empiricist and rationalist epistemologies that form the backbone of the Enlightenment. Consequently I had to work out what to do by way of response to the deep challenge they posed. The crux of the matter was that working through Hume and Kant undercut any appeal to natural theology as the foundation of my theological convictions. I remember vividly talking to an older student in the Student Union who had come up to the university intent on becoming a Presbyterian minister. He had been required by his church to take courses in philosophy and had taken it up as his major field of study. Reading Hume and Kant had decimated his religious life; when I met him, he had abandoned his faith and was looking to teaching as a future career. We talked at length about my own intentions; toward the end, he predicted that I would undergo a similar crisis of faith. He did not think that I would survive any more than he had.

When the crisis came, I was driven into an intense period of introspection. Part of my predicament was a deep ambivalence concerning the requirements that pressed for attention. On the one hand, I had never really been a convinced believer in natural theology. The classical arguments for the existence of God were intrinsically interesting, but it had never occurred to me that they were essential to the maintenance of the rationality of religious belief. In fact, I doubt if I could have formulated clearly the place they should have in the life of faith. On the other hand, I felt compelled to give some answer to the question of why I believed, so the rejection of natural theology forced me to come up with some kind of justification. It was not enough to fall back on faith, as was the practice of most of my friends at the time. I also had to reckon with a deep skepticism about the whole process itself. It seemed to me at times that, at bottom, a really clever philosopher could come up with a justification for any belief. All one needed to do initially was to take one's convictions back to the ultimate presuppositions on which they rested; so long as one was prepared to make the necessary adjustments at this level, it would always be possible to justify well nigh anything. Immersing myself in the writings of R. G. Collingwood helped flesh out this claim in some detail for me. It was far from easy to identify and work out the intuitions that lay buried among these issues, yet I could not ignore or evade them.

The matter ultimately came to a head in a burst of deeply painful reflection. The choice was whether to abandon my faith or find some way to continue until new light dawned. One issue finally kept me in the faith. Were I to give up the Christian faith, I would have no way to make sense of the figure of Jesus Christ as I saw him mediated in the New Testament. I would have no way to do this if I were to become an atheist again. This judgment was not made in a historical vacuum. I was already well acquainted with debates about the historical value of the gospels, and I had been introduced to the various critical questions that were currently in vogue. These lay in the background as I sought to weigh the full impact of the figure whose life and character came through in a composite reading of the New Testament. I knew that in an instant I could have walked away from the figure of Christ; and I knew also that I could easily either forget the impact of Christ on me or find ways to rationalize my decision. I also knew that it would not be irrational to stay with deep intuitions about the person of Christ. Hence I resolved to stay the course and keep the faith. With this decision behind me, I could return to my philosophical studies with a sense of freedom. I continued my initiation into the field and waited for the time when I could find a more coherent way to resolve the questions of justification that had troubled me with the collapse of natural theology.

Looking back on things now, it is astonishing how long it took for this to get sorted out. I went to seminary at Asbury Theological Seminary. Choosing to go to Asbury was one of the best decisions that I have made in my educational journey. Going to Kentucky was a splendid mixture of romance in traveling to the United States and escape from the violence and seclusion of Northern Ireland. I was capitvated almost immediately by biblical studies and, to some extent, by the history of the church. This was partly a matter of the extraordinary quality of teaching in the field and partly a matter of my pietist prejudices. Philosophy of religion was not taken seriously at that time at Asbury, so I put it on hold. I found overall that there was more than enough to keep me occupied merely in trying to unravel the gospel of Mark, the Pentateuch, and the epistle to the Romans. I have never regretted this concentrated focus on scripture. Overall, seminary provided the opportunity for a deep immersion in the classical faith of the church as mediated through the Wesleyan tradition. I hope the experience represents in some small measure the joys of heaven itself; I suspect it is rare to find a seminary where love for God in a deeply personal sense is so enthusiastically wedded to a commitment to study and service in the church. The worship services remain an indelible part of my memory; the quest for holiness combined with the manifestation of a generous civility might even have made John Wesley happy.

When I got a chance to pursue graduate work in philosophy at the University of Oxford, I relished the opportunity to return to the field. Absence had made the heart grow fonder, and I was eager to meet and study with those whose work had been such a delight prior to my study of theology. Toward the end of my seminary training, two issues had caught my attention. The first was the nature of religious language, and the second was the relation between historical criticism and the internal content of the Christian tradition. I went to Oxford intending to pursue one of these options.

When I arrived at Oxford, I was immediately immersed in a rich philosophical and theological universe. It took the good part of a year to visit all sorts of lectures and seminars simply to make up for blind spots in my earlier training and to get a feel for the extraordinary resources available. One of my difficulties as a student is that I have had very little trouble developing an interest in any subject that can fit even remotely into philosophy or theology. Oxford provided a magnificent environment for fostering my interests. I roamed all over the place, relishing lectures in everything from ancient Israel to modern sociology and participating in seminars in everything from the philosophy of Wittgenstein to the analytical philosophy of history. I was especially surprised on two counts. One was the freedom permitted me as a student. There was absolutely no desire to mold me into a particular school or party. The other was the extent to which philosophy of religion had moved beyond questions about language to classical questions about the justification of religious belief. After taking my bearings for a year or so, I finally settled in to work on the logic of historical inquiry and how this affected Christian discourse about the activity of God in history. This eventually became my dissertation topic and proved to be as demanding and interesting as I had first hoped.

On leaving Oxford, I have worked alternatively in local churches and in the academy. This, of course, creates its own problems and opportunities. One has to take on very different roles, depending on the work at hand. Over the years, I have become more and more convinced of the cruciality of philosophy in making sense of the Christian tradition down through history and in mapping its claims in the modern world. This is often taken to mean that the task of philosophy is to provide a foundation for theology and thus give it intellectual respectability. This is not at all how I see it. In fact, this whole approach to the relation between philosophy and theology is unsatisfactory, as I see it. Much bad theology arises precisely because purely philosophical convictions and arguments of one kind or another are made the rational foundation of faith. If anything is to be the foundation of faith, it has to be revelation and religious experience. Alternatively, theologians hook their wagons to a philosophical horse in an effort to find a suitable partner for the journey. Few things are more exasperating than to find that a theologian presents the ideas of some favored philosophical authority under the guise of the riches of the Christian faith. John Macquarries's use of existentialism comes immediately to mind as a good example. Equally, as instanced in the case of Hegel, in his use of Christian pneumatology, philosophy can easily become thoroughly unintelligible precisely because it takes various fragments of the Christian faith and makes these the foundation of some grand speculative system.

Mature Christians eschew too close a connection between theology and philosophy. The gospel is not the reworking of the latest philosophical proposal to emerge from the prestigious universities. It is rooted in Christ and the work of the Holy Spirit in the church. Down through history, mature believers have made use of all sorts of concepts and arguments drawn from philosophy in order to give a reason for the hope that is within them. At times, various alliances have been worked out that are of enormous historical significance. Becoming a Christian does not, however, commit one to any philosophical school. It is a sign of health, for example, when Christians have at their disposal a wide range of epistemological strategies to make good their intellectual responsibilities in the world. This is exactly our present situation. The revolution in philosophy of religion that has taken place since the 1960s makes it much easier to be a Christian now than it was when I first trained. It does not, of course, make it any easier to love God, or to be humble, or to love one's neighbor, or to care for the poor of the earth, and the like. These have been and always will be a matter of grace and the working of the Holy Spirit in one's life. Nor will philosophy bring an end to terrorism, religious bigotry, or murderous nationalism in Northern Ireland. Philosophy has a more modest role in the life of faith. It can clear away obstacles, clarify crucial concepts and options, lay bare the process of relevant justification, make manifest hidden assumptions, bring to light unforeseen consequences of belief, open up to view contradictions and paradoxes, and the like. These are intrinsically important to creatures endowed with reason, and they have their own place in the fostering of the intellectual love of our great God and Savior.

12

PHILOSOPHY

AND FAITH

Laura L. Garcia

Peter Geach entitles one of his essays "Can a Catholic Be a Philosopher?", and that is the question that has played a central role in my thinking and that in many ways has defined my intellectual life to this point. One could put the same question more generally, as in "Can a committed religious believer be a scholar?", and in this form I think it must be answered by any believer who pursues the life of the mind. Geach puts the question in the order he does, rather than the other way around, because he rightly sees that one is not first committed to the academic life and only secondarily to Christianity; rather, one is first a believer, and the question is whether the scholarly profession fits with that more fundamental commitment. If I had found the answer to Geach's question to be in the negative, I think I would still be a believer. This is the sort of thing that scandalizes nonbelievers, especially those within academe, but that is because they think of religion as merely a set of propositions when it is really closer to friendship.

In any case, Geach's question arose for him only after his conversion to Catholicism, but for me it was bound to be addressed in the order he suggests, since I grew up in the home of a minister and believed in God from my earliest years. My father pastored mainly in nondenominational Bible churches falling broadly within the Calvinist theological tradition. We were taught that the Christian Scriptures were inspired by God and totally reliable, and as children we were encouraged to commit large segments of Scripture to memory. Probably the earliest song I learned as a child was the one quoted by Karl Barth as the most important truth he had learned in his years of theological study: "Jesus loves me, this I know; for the Bible tells me so."

Of course, not every child who is immersed in a religious environment emerges as a believer in the end. In my own case, I think there were two very powerful influences that combined to make the Christian faith my own. One was the example of my parents, who lived in order to serve and who are still two of the most selfless people I know. I suppose that one of the most persuasive arguments in favor of any religion is its ability to transform the lives of those who practice it. That the Christian church has members who bring dishonor on it is no surprise, since degrees of commitment (and of hypocrisy) are a common enough phenomenon even in secular matters, and it would be more surprising still if God were to sanctify people against their will. But those whose commitment to God and to others leads them beyond what merely human compassion would explain stand as a sign, and one far more compelling to most people than any academic arguments for theism or for Christianity.

The second most powerful influence on my own acceptance of a spiritual realm was the natural beauty and grandeur of the Pacific Northwest, where I grew up. The rugged mountains of the Cascade range, with their unapproachable cliffs and wild, raging rivers, and the timeless thundering of the surf along the Oregon coast made a very deep impression on me. I still feel, with Wordsworth, that there are places where it is almost impossible to stand without coming to believe that one is face to face with the divine. My father loved to quote Gerard Manley Hopkins, the nineteenth-century Jesuit poet who I think understood the presence of God in nature better than anyone else. "The world is charged with the grandeur of God," says Hopkins, and that has always seemed to me close to a self-evident truth.

Some will see in this nothing more than a (short and unconvincing) version of the design argument for God's existence, but that is not how I would describe it. Rather, it seemed to me as though I felt God's presence in the beauty of these natural wonders, that I was standing before Him, their maker and their life. I would say the same thing about the example of my parents— that I did not really infer the existence of God or the truth of Christianity from their actions so much as experience the presence of God in them. Philosophers rarely talk about such experiences, because we are taught that only public evidence is admissible and that every conclusion requires a chain of premises to support it; and, of course, if one were trying to *persuade* another person to believe in God, this is just how one would proceed. But from the perspective of the believer, coming to God often seems more like an encounter than like solving a math problem.

Although I was never plagued by grave doubts about the truth of my faith, I came in time to be troubled by the apparent lack of interest among the members of my religious communion in questions of a deeper theological or philosophical kind. During my high school years, my peers and I began to wonder about the coherence between the doctrine of God's mercy and a strong Calvinist reading of the doctrine of predestination, which seemed to make one's eternal destiny a purely arbitrary decision on God's part. We wondered what would happen to those in countries who had never heard of Jesus, and about our own friends who seemed oblivious to religious beliefs and practices. We began to grapple with the problem of evil, and not only as an abstract philosophical issue. If evil was evidence *against* God's existence, what was the evidence in its favor? How do we know that the Bible is authentically from God but the Book of Mormon isn't?

I assumed at first that there were satisfactory answers to these questions, but I experienced continual frustration in seeking to have them addressed by the teachers and youth group leaders in my church. In time I began to be a little afraid that there couldn't be convincing answers to my questions, and that believers might be doomed to chronic intellectual inferiority in the wider marketplace of ideas, holding on to beliefs the truth or reasonableness of which could only be appreciated by those on the inside.

However, while still in high school, I came across two authors who brightened the prospects for combining faith with philosophical inquiry. The first was the late Francis Schaeffer, whose book *The God Who Is There* suggested that Christian presuppositions (as he called them) could be shown to be superior to non-Christian starting points, since the latter always led to some contradiction or some other absurd consequence. Schaeffer exhibited great confidence in the ability of a well-trained Christian intellectual to bring the opponent's view "crashing down on his head," and while I believe he underestimated the strength of the opposition, his confidence in the survival of Christian belief within the wider intellectual field was certainly exhilarating. I also read at this time a small paperback by Arthur Holmes, philosophy professor at Wheaton College, called *Christianity and Philosophy*. Holmes believed that operating from the standpoint of religious faith enabled one to develop a comprehensive world view that would unite all knowledge and experience into a coherent, rationally persuasive picture of reality.

While Schaeffer's work still treated philosophy primarily as an aid in apologetics, and as serving a largely negative function in displaying the many errors of the secular mind, Holmes held out hope for a positive role for philosophy, not just in apologetics or in aiding the systemic theologian, but in exploring the foundations of knowledge and engaging issues not discussed in the Scriptures. If there was such a thing as the "worldly and vain philosophy" warned against by the apostle Paul, there was also such a thing as good philosophy. Further, Holmes was a champion of the claim that all truth is God's truth, so that whatever genuine discoveries were made in science or psychology or biology or philosophy could never contradict a truth revealed by God.

Elated by this vision of the role of the intellect in the life of the Christian community, I signed up for an introductory philosophy course in my first semester of college. The school itself, Westmont College, was a very young interdenominational Evangelical liberal arts college, modeled after Wheaton College in numerous respects, and the faculty all signed a statement of faith. In philosophy the first item discussed was proofs for the existence of God. I was astonished—that my questions were being addressed in a sustained and systematic way, and that so much careful reflection lay behind the arguments. The next issue was the problem of evil, where at first Hume's arguments seemed invincible, until gradually the theistic responses began to undercut the strength of his case against God. I was riveted by these discussions, and never had much doubt from then on that I belonged in philosophy. Whereas before I had sometimes been made to feel suspicious or overly stubborn for seeking answers to my questions, in college the door to the world of ideas was suddenly flung open, and I felt like a child in a new playground.

I consider it a great privilege that so many of my teachers in college and graduate school were themselves committed both to their faith and to excellence in their chosen fields of study. Stanley Obitts, my mentor in philosophy at Westmont, and Professor Holmes, with whom I spent one year at Wheaton, provided powerful models of how to continue faith in God with philosophical depth and rigor. Obitts introduced us by way of their writings to other Christian philosophers, and I came to admire the work of George Mavrodes, Robert Adams, Nicholas Wolterstorff, and especially Alvin Plantinga. Over time I began to have a clearer idea of some of the outlines of the Christian world view that Holmes had described in such a tantalizing way, and to understand the value of truth for its own sake, not simply for evangelization or apologetic purposes.

However, along with the joy of discovering that the life of a Christian intellectual was a genuine possibility, there was also a growing sense of disappointment over the fact that I had failed in the end to achieve the comprehensive synthesis that Holmes envisioned. Westmont required every freshman and transfer student to enroll in a January interim course called "Christian Perspectives on Learning." Here Holmes's educational philosophy shaped our discussions, and we merged with a great sense of excitement and with the expectation that our courses at Westmont would contribute to the realization of a coherent, comprehensive, theistic picture of the world. While many courses fulfilled this expectation admirably, most failed miserably, and in some cases faculty in the sciences found themselves attracted to views apparently completely at odds with Christian teaching. In one particularly lame effort to integrate faith and science, my chemistry professor read a verse from the Bible each class period before getting down to the real business at hand.

Even in philosophy, I felt I had a much better grasp of what I rejected than of the contours of the view I wanted to defend.

In time it occurred to me that building a world view is not the task of a single individual, and that Christians have always drawn heavily on the work of previous generations, who have thought through many of these same issues and articulated a Christian response. We look back to Augustine or Aquinas, and even beyond them to Plato and Aristotle, and so on, to give substance to our own views and to give us clues about how to address contemporary problems and issues that didn't arise from them. However, philosophers in the Reformed theological tradition in which I was raised and educated face some tensions in the effort to embrace these past syntheses of faith and reason because they were produced, for the most part, either by Catholics or by pagans. The Reformed emphasis on the effects of sin and the fall of man on the intellect have made this tradition fairly suspicious of unredeemed intellectual activity and sympathetic to the view that anyone who begins from a false starting point (in atheism or even Judaism) is bound to fall into numerous errors or to miss the truth altogether. One can always go back to John Calvin instead, but Calvin was not a philosopher, so the burden of developing a truly Reformed or Evangelical world view continues to rest on the current generation. I believe Alvin Plantinga has done more than anyone else to advance this project, and that others have made significant contributions to it as well.

I came to feel that the relationship between faith and reason from the Reformed perspective gave too little credit to reason, even reason marred by the effects of sin. When I read Holmes's claim that all truth is God's truth, I expected to find not only that discoveries in science or philosophical speculation would be unable to overturn the faith, but also that some of these findings might be embraced and turned into building blocks to extend and enhance the Christian world view. Instead I found that many within the Reformed tradition remain suspicious of secular culture and of the achievements of the human race outside of those specifically informed by religious values. To use Niebuhr's categories, there was more emphasis on Christ against culture than on Christ transforming culture, and I felt once again that a love of learning for its own sake could not be made wholly legitimate within that tradition. It is true that this suspicion of culture is more pronounced in the fundamentalist circles in which I was raised than in other centers of Reformed faith and practice, but it is pervasive enough to contribute to a definite ethos. I believe this evaluation of culture shows itself even more clearly in the attitude to music and the arts, which are often considered suspect in themselves and omitted from the design and liturgy of many Reformed churches.

To some extent, my conversion to Catholicism in graduate school can be explained by considerations like those just mentioned. The Catholic church retains great confidence in the ability of Christ to redeem the world, and not just to replace it with the kingdom of God. The Catholic view that grace perfects nature means that even the fallen world shows the glory of God and that fallen human beings can produce goodness and truth and beauty that are genuine, albeit imperfect or incomplete. That some truths, even about the moral law and about God, can be known independently of revelation, and that truth and beauty are good in themselves—these are fundamental claims that have always seemed right to me and that are most strongly articulated and defended within Catholicism.

I will make some attempt here to describe the path that led from my very deep commitment to Evangelical Protestantism to the Catholic church, even though this is a difficult project for me, as I think it would be for any academic. One wants to give arguments or evidences that will make such a move look as intellectually respectable as possible, whereas the real causes of one's conversion are often more personal and diffuse, and in the end outside oneself altogether, assuming that faith is a gift.

One difficulty with telling the story of one's own religious pilgrimage is that described by G. K. Chesterton in recounting the story of his conversion (from Protestantism to Catholicism): "I happen to have a strong feeling that this method makes the business look much smaller than it really is. Numbers of much better men have been converted to much worse religions." What one would like to say about one's religion, I think, is that one believes it because it is true, and, of course, there are always many ways of arriving at the same truth. A second major obstacle to telling the reasons for one's conversion has been well described by John Cardinal Newman, also a convert to Catholicism. It is that the deliberations leading to such a decision are so numerous and varied that it is almost impossible to choose one or two considerations as *the* reason(s) for converting, as though the whole matter could be put into a neat syllogism. Consequently, what follows is much more a narrative than an argument, though I think it will seem a familiar story to many who have followed the path to Rome.

I encountered Catholicism for the first time when I arrived at Notre Dame in the fall of 1977 to do graduate work in philosophy of religion. I was drawn there in part because of the commitment of the university to what was at least a theistic world view, and because Alvin Plantinga was coming from Calvin College to teach one course a year in the graduate program, and I was (and am) a great admirer of him and his work. At the same time, I felt a slight sense of dread about spending several years in a Catholic atmosphere, since, in my circles growing up, the Catholic church was viewed with a combination of suspicion, fear, and loathing. During my first week in South Bend, I met a woman in her second year of philosophy studies who became in time a very dear friend. She shocked me early on by confiding that she was considering converting from her Southern Baptist tradition to Catholicism, and I set out to save her from making what I thought would be a terrible mistake. Soon she had me reading Aquinas and Bonaventure, and attending vespers and even mass at Notre Dame's spectacular neo-Gothic Sacred Heart Church, so that I could get to know the enemy, so to speak. The number of Evangelical Protestants in philosophy and theology at Notre Dame was quite large at that time, and we began a lively ongoing debate among ourselves and our Catholic friends on the issues that divided us: justification by faith alone, the role of Church authority, the sacraments, Mary and the saints, purgatory, and the like.

On the intellectual side, I would say that two major considerations led me toward the Catholic view. The first was that I began to have doubts about the Reformation doctrine of justification by faith alone. Another Evangelical friend in the graduate program persuaded me over time that the Scriptures did not support this view, and that many Scriptures suggested just the opposite (the Letter of James, for example). I will not attempt to reconstruct those arguments here. Suffice it to say that I became more and more attracted to the view that God saves us by grace alone, where grace is to be understood as a genuine divine force in our lives that seeks to transform us into the likeness of Jesus Christ, to make us fit for heaven. Faith is a necessary condition for salvation, on this view, but it must be a living faith, informed by grace and leading to a certain kind of life. On such a view, it is possible to reject God's grace, not just by refusing to come to faith but refusing to accept and obey His laws. At the time, I saw this change in my thinking as significant but not particularly as a step in the direction of Rome.

The next major shift in my views focused on the second pillar of the Reformation: the view that Scripture alone is our authority in matters of faith, and that the claims made by tradition or Catholic teaching are strictly optional for believers. One vexing problem was that it was difficult to find in Scripture a clear justification for the view that only Scripture can be the guide of our faith. But I was even more influenced by the recognition that the canon of Scripture could not itself have been decided by appealing to Scripture, so I was forced to acknowledge the authority of the Catholic church in at least that one instance. I also began to wonder how the basic creeds of the church, setting out the orthodox doctrine on the Incarnation or the Trinity, could be defended as settled or permanent without some appeal to the Holy Spirit's guidance in these important matters.

This problem became more obvious to me during a year I spent teaching at Calvin College, since one of the papers everyone was discussing that year was written by a theologian defending social trinitarianism, the view that there are three divine beings who have in common the property of being divine, and who know and will all the same things. My reaction to this view was that, although it solved various thorny theological problems and could be made (with not too much effort) consistent with the Scriptures, it simply was not acceptable because Christendom would view it as heretical. (In fact, such a view was explicitly condemned by the Fourth Lateran Council in 1215; it had been suggested by a certain Joachim in opposition to his teacher, Peter Lombard.) If the Scriptures alone are to be our guide, then it seems incumbent on each person confronted with a new theological opinion to learn enough Greek, Hebrew, biblical studies, and history of the Near East to decide what the Scriptures do in fact teach. And it began to seem implausible to me that God would have left the essential doctrines of the faith so inaccessible to the average layperson and so open to revision. So, on this point as well, I began to lean in the direction of the Catholic view that the apostles (and their successors) have been entrusted with the care and guidance of the church in matters of faith and morals, and that Peter holds a kind of primacy in this mission.

With these two central doctrines of the Reformation beginning to erode in my mind, I gradually slid into a deep personal crisis. One convert has said that what had started for him as an interesting detective story suddenly changed into a horror story, as he began to fear that the Catholic faith he had once despised might actually turn out to be true. Like many in that position, I turned first to the Episcopal church, hoping that I could accommodate my new convictions without leaving the familiar and comfortable umbrella of Protestantism. I also began reading more seriously about the Catholic faith—books by Chesterton and Newman and Thomas Merton, as well as more Aquinas and some of the early church fathers. Probably even more important than the intellectual defense made for Catholic doctrines in such books was the sense I had that these authors, especially Merton and Aquinas, possessed a level of spirituality I had never encountered before, and I was deeply attracted by it.

At about this time, four of us Protestant graduate students in philosophy decided to investigate Catholicism more seriously and directly, and to hear a defense of its teachings from someone who was personally and deeply committed to them. Such a person was more difficult to find at Notre Dame than one might think, but Ralph McInerny of the philosophy department agreed to meet with us and suggested that we read and discuss the document of Vatican II on the nature of the church. These meetings continued for many months, and although at first I felt on absolutely safe ground in my role as critic of Catholic teachings, over time I began to see the plausibility of the case in their favor, including the scriptural warrant for them, and I could anticipate what the answers to my objections would be.

However, just as my resistance to the Catholic view was never purely intellectual, so my eventual attraction to it was not simply an intellectual process. I was impressed not just by the arguments McInerny put forward in defense of his views, but also by his obviously deep and genuine faith. It seemed clear to me over time that here was a man who was deeply Christian and who was much further along the path toward holiness than I was. At the same time, although I still attended the Episcopal church on Sundays, I would often be found at the weekday mass on campus at Sacred Heart church, and I began to be deeply pained at being excluded from receiving communion. I was more convinced of the real presence of Christ in the Eucharist, and I felt an intense longing to receive Him and be united with Him. Just as once I had known the presence of God through the beauty of forests and rivers and the night sky, so now I was drawn to His presence in the sacraments, and in the end I could not imagine my life without them.

Finally, in the fall of 1981, I entered the Catholic church and embraced as my teacher, my mother, and my home what I had once viewed as my mortal enemy. It is difficult to put into words what an agonizing decision that was, as I knew it would cause enormous pain to those who were dearest to me—my family and most of my closest friends. From my own point of view, my conversion was less a matter of rejecting my former beliefs than of coming to embrace them in a fuller and richer dimension, but I know it can hardly be seen this way by the Protestant community. In the end, I can only say that I believe I know the voice of God when He speaks to me, and that this is where He has led me. I think that in any such move from unbelief to faith, intellectual considerations will take one only so far. Ultimately, it is always a matter of hearing the voice of God as addressed to oneself, as calling one's own name, and of choosing to listen and obey.

Although there is, sadly, much that divides the Christian community, there is surely far more that unites it, and I believe that Christian philosophers can work together to continue to develop a theistic world view and to defend philosophical positions congruent with the faith. I hope that my own work in philosophy is at least aimed at the goal Arthur Holmes set out in the book that introduced me to the word *philosophy:* to "incorporate Christian ideas and values . . . into the broader scope of a system that respects also materials and problems which are common to a given culture or to men generically. From this perspective [the Christian philosopher] may speak to his day, seeking as do other philosophers to shed light on the varied problems and changing structures of human experience. He will stand a responsible member of society, sensitive in soul and alert to the bewildering conflicts of an onrushing history. He will come not to be ministered unto, but to minister."[1] That philosophy can be seen in this way as a vocation, as a calling from God, suggests that faith and reason are not only reconcilable but can actually be made to serve each other. Etienne Gilson once wrote an essay called "The Intelligence in the Service of Christ the King,"[2] and like most Christian philosophers, my greatest hope is that that phrase may one day serve as a fitting description of my life and work.

Notes

1. *Christianity and Philosophy* (Downers Grove, IL: Inter-Varsity Press, 1963), pp. 36–37.

2. In *Christianity and Philosophy,* tr. Ralph MacDonald (New York: Sheed & Ward, 1939), pp. 103–125.

13

CONFESSIONS

OF A COLLEGE

TEACHER

Arthur F. Holmes

I got into philosophy by accident. For some years after World War II, qualified philosophy teachers were in short supply, especially for small church-related colleges. So, in the summer of 1950, a spring graduate entering a master's program in theology was offered a one-year teaching fellowship in philosophy. He took it, completed doctoral studies in philosophy, and stayed for over forty additional years rather than becoming a missionary in the Third World, as he had intended.

Why? What sense of mission motivated the change from missionary to philosopher? And why stay for an entire career in one small school?

I had grown up in England, my father a schoolteacher and Baptist lay preacher who became a town council-man and local magistrate, and our family addicted readers. As a ten-year-old, in response to questions about a vocation "when you grow up," I boldly declared I wanted to be a missionary. In school, for a writing assignment about what we might be doing thirty or forty years ahead, I imagined myself a missionary on furlough. The teacher, Miss Rockwood, took me aside to ask if that was indeed my ambition and to encourage me in it.

In secondary school it was history that most turned me on, and I eagerly drew on our public library's resources both for historical novels and as a supplement to school textbooks. Indeed, history surrounded us in Dover; its huge Norman castle, with the French coast in the distance, was clearly visible from my bedroom window. On cycling excursions we habitually visited old churches and explored fortifications raised to fend off Napoleon's invasion. A few miles away was Canterbury, with its magnificent cathedral where Thomas à Beckett was murdered, and Richborough Castle, a Roman fort where I once found a stone arrowhead. In Dover Castle itself there remains to this day the shell of a Roman lighthouse, the Pharos (after which our high school annual was named), and tiny St. Mary's in the Castle has a plaque noting the spot where the Gospel was first preached in England. With the coming of World War II, bedraggled troops evacuated from the Dunkirk beaches crowded our sea front, weaponless, eating food distributed to them by Boy Scouts and similar groups. The prime minister had declared that it would take a miracle to save the army, yet here they were, thanks to a protective fog that blanketed much of their Channel crossing to within a mile of Dover harbor. I have never been able to separate history, past or present, from Christianity. They simply refuse to be compartmentalized.

Religion was hardly my motivating force in those high school years. When the principal suggested I go into teaching, like my father, I responded with a vehement "Anything but that!" My missionary ambitions had given way to the desire for a civil service job with a lot of security and room for advancement. Yet it was the war that brought home to me my need for God. Separated from family as a sixteen-year-old with typical teen struggles, evacuated to a South Wales coal mining valley, working in London amid the terror of night blitzes, then serving for five years in the Royal Air Force, good and evil were real, if sometimes commingled, and with them the sense of God's presence. My parents' example bore fruit when at seventeen I committed myself to living for Jesus Christ. And the desire to be a missionary returned.

My reading took new directions, not only devotional literature but also biblical backgrounds, introductions to theology, defenses of the Christian faith against its critics—what I soon learned to call "apologetics." Barrack-room arguments honed my thinking, and lay preaching opportunities developed communication skills before I reached college as a twenty-three-year-old freshman. I had already devoured C. S. Lewis's *Case for Christianity* and *The Problem of Pain* and C. E. M. Joad's *Recovery of Belief,* even though, in retrospect, I barely understood their lines of thought. College provided a broader and more systematic orientation, and helped me discover my aptitude and possible gifts as a teacher, a missionary teacher.

But where? The moment of truth came when a visiting missionary educator described the kind of work I envisioned on a continent I had never considered. I posed my situation and he said, "Perhaps you need to decide whether God is calling you to a certain kind of ministry or to a geographic location." The penny dropped. It was to be teaching. The location would just be a matter of opportunity. So when opportunity knocked at Wheaton, first a teaching fellowship and then as a beginning instructor, no doubts remained. I would be a missionary educator in America.

Teaching has been the most challenging and satisfying occupation I can imagine. The excitement of ideas, the opportunity for research and writing, the challenge to keep up in one's field, the stimulus of the classroom, the art of pedagogy, the faces of young people opening up to new ideas, the hurdles they have to surmount, the growth we see in a few short years, the roles they go on to play in society, the contributions some of them make in philosophy itself—I can imagine nothing that compares.

As a young teacher, I soon developed two or three main goals. One, of course, was to encourage the faith as well as the learning of my students. Another was to counter the strain of anti-intellectualism that runs through both church and society in America and occurs even in a college community. The third was to make it unnecessary for the college to have to hire someone as ill-prepared as myself. Over the years, these goals grew into a sense of mission in helping prepare future generations of Christian intellectuals to take their place in academia and in society in general.

In regard to the first goal, some of my own teachers had pointed me beyond loose conjunctions of faith and learning. Kenneth Kantzer alerted us to the presuppositions that undergird beliefs and theories of every sort and talked of a Christian world view; visiting theologian Carl F. H. Henry one summer taught a course on "The Drift of Western Thought," which helped me look at the history of ideas from a theological perspective; and John Luchies drew my attention to the "cosmic Christ" of Colossians. Things like this excited me. If Christian beliefs have an integrating role in the world of ideas, then we must learn to see things as the interrelated whole they are, rather than compartmentalizing them. If Jesus Christ is indeed creator, redeemer, and lord of all, then we must cultivate a philosophy that recognizes this and beware of what is simply "according to tradition" (Col. 2:8). So we must scrutinize presuppositions and examine reasons for beliefs, which, of course, is precisely what philosophy best does. And since we all have presuppositions of some sort and think from some perspective or other, we should admit that philosophy is inevitably perspectival and cease thinking of scholarly objectivity as synonymous with neutrality.

This realization developed slowly. In the 1940s and 1950s, introductory textbooks talked of philosophy's two functions: the critical and the systematic. The former seemed of immense value educationally in developing analytical skills and uncovering presuppositions, assessing evidence and critiquing arguments. The systematic function, meanwhile, provided ready-made theories one might consider and the hope of formulating positions consonant with Christianity. Such was the rather simplistic point of view with which I began.

Graduate school at Northwestern University in Evanston, Illinois, was an exhilarating and mind-stretching experience, culminating in a dissertation on realistic theories of perception in early-twentieth-century philosophy. The decision to work in epistemology frankly stemmed from apologetic interests. As an undergraduate, I had been introduced to the "Old Princeton" school rooted in eighteenth-century Scottish realism. As a graduate student, I discovered philosophers like Moore, Russell, Whitehead, and Santayana. A realistic epistemology that guaranteed bona fide knowledge of the natural world would provide a firm basis for doing natural theology. Or so I thought. Gradually the conclusion forced itself on me that the basis for a realist epistemology was more a methodological decision than a logically coercive argument. Descartes had begun by claiming to bracket all his beliefs and proceeding *ex nihilo* to deduce an entire philosophy from the realization that since I think, I must therefore exist. The alternative was to begin *in situ* by taking our natural beliefs for granted and subjecting them to critical scrutiny as the need arises. The latter, I became convinced, was the only practical path to follow and is the way we ordinarily function in any case: We are immersed in reality. So the philosophical question is not *whether* an external world really exists but *what* is its real nature. Natural theology was not going to be as presuppositionless as I had supposed.

Other consequences soon followed. If philosophy is done *in situ* rather than *ex nihilo,* then one need not perform the psychological contortions of trying to bracket religious beliefs and put them out of operation in philosophical matters, as if that were even possible. Objectivity consists not in having no prior attitudes and understandings but rather in making them explicit, tracing their influence, and being willing to scrutinize them. It is more a matter of intellectual honesty than of having no assumptions. So when a former college classmate teaching at a state university asked that I respond to an article on "The Dangers of Theism in the Classroom," I wrote:

> Dr. Robertson evidently refers to the naive obscurantist rather than the historic theist whose faith stimulates him to reason. It is an unfair caricature of the theist, one which ridicules his academic honesty, to picture him as occasionally titillating his students with consideration of ideas contrary to theistic principles, as excluding scientific attitudes from the spheres of morality and religion, as suppressing if not effacing the intellectual independence of the student, and as indoctrinating rather than educating.... The theist approaches life's tasks as a sacred stewardship of God-given opportunity and ability. The teacher who is a dedicated theist should therefore be dedicated to broadening horizons, stimulating inquiry, and encouraging critical thought.[1]

The theist, I argued, is no more obscurantist than the psychologist whose naturalistic premises influence his or her work, provided that they both are open, aboveboard, and self-critical about it. Every scholar in every discipline has assumptions, both methodological and substantive.

For ten years I explored some of the methodological diversity in twentieth-century thought, until it became evident that assumptions of some sort or another are invariably at work. Philosophy, I concluded in *Christian Philosophy in the Twentieth Century,* is not an impersonal activity but consciously or unconsciously reflects the perspectives of people immersed in the realities of history and their own experience.

At the time, I had not yet read Kuhn's *The Structure of Scientific Revolutions,* nor had the discussion of hermeneutical theory yet surfaced. Had I read Kuhn, parallels between the histories of philosophy and science would have become evident, for in addition to changing paradigms, Kuhn recognizes normal scientific work of a more detailed nature that takes an overall paradigm for granted. Similarly in philosophy, within the variety of perspectival traditions (such as theism and naturalism), a great deal of detailed philosophical work goes on that takes a perspective for granted while still being more or less influenced by it, along with a great deal of healthy dialogue across perspectival traditions.

So my theological background came into play in articulating Christian perspectives. I thought of the less theoretical orientation of the Hebrew mind and its "wisdom" literature—the biblical book of Ecclesiastes, for example—rooted in the struggles of faith and life. I thought of St. Paul's address to the Athenian philosophers and how he appealed to Stoic ideas. I still ponder the Logos of the fourth gospel and its elaboration in the theology of the church fathers in response to the challenge of Gnosticism. Biblical religion plainly brings significant resources to philosophical reflection.

But this *perspectival* view had far broader application than to philosophy alone. A philosopher can hardly devote years to teaching and advising undergraduates, helping to shape a department, and serving on institutional committees without thinking about the goals and processes of education. Not only the acquisition of knowledge and understanding but also its transmission, it seemed, would naturally involve the operation of perspective. The aims of education, then, should include an awareness of world-view perspectives of both past and present that have influenced and still affect our culture, along with the development of critical skills necessary for analyzing and evaluating them. The student must learn to uncover and critique assumptions, trace unstated implications, think through the validity of personal and others' beliefs, and integrate faith with learning.

My second goal was therefore to counter anti-intellectualism. There are always those who call liberal learning impractical or who think that intellectual endeavor threatens piety. In my experience, the opposite was true: I found that understanding enlarged my faith and enriched my devotion to God, just as that devotion motivated me and faith guided me in philosophical work. So I adopted a dual strategy. On the one hand, I made a point of addressing the issue both in class and outside, orally and in writing, both with specific reference to philosophy and in more general terms, while pushing my students in nonthreatening ways to think for themselves. On the other hand, I committed myself to showing in my own life that there need be no conflict between rigorous intellectual and genuine Christian devotion. We are called to intellectual stewardship in service to God and society, called to bring "all our being's ransomed powers."

My third goal involved building a department that would regularly send students to graduate school. I was the second or third graduate in the 100-year history of our college to earn a doctorate in philosophy. Back in the 1950s, most small Christian colleges had departments of religion and philosophy, often without philosophically trained teachers. So I found myself teaching philosophy in a department composed mostly of biblical scholars and theologians, and in the early years taught a potpourri of courses across all these fields. The philosophy offerings were largely in philosophy of religion and the history of philosophy, so a more rounded curriculum had to be developed. Even when a separate philosophy department was established, some faculty continued to straddle theology. But a separate image was developing, and some of our best graduates were going on to first-rate graduate programs even though the department was virtually unknown.

Two incidents illustrate this. I was, of course, active in professional associations and served on the program committee of our state organization. At a lunch meeting one day the chairman of that committee, himself department chair at a large university, turned to me and said, "Tell me more about that student of yours who has applied to our grad program. We would rather take a student of someone we know than of someone we don't know." The student was admitted, the first of several who went to that school.

At another meeting I was approached by a Yale professor who spotted my name tag and said, "Holmes, I've been waiting to meet you. I've been trying to figure out what makes graduates of schools like Wheaton and Calvin such good philosophers." He had one of ours in class, as it happens (one who contributed to this book), but he went on to say that he had gone incognito to Calvin College and tried to figure out the place. Two things struck him: A defined theological heritage enabled students to recognize a conceptual problem when they saw one, and an intellectual community fostered hard thinking. I suggested a third factor: the motivation to intellectual inquiry that Christian faith brings.

My three goals were, of course, interdependent, and all three are essential if further generations of Christian philosophers are to help make Christianity a significant influence and a viable option in the world of ideas. In the late 1960s, when Martin Luther King's cadences were still ringing in our ears, I spoke in our college chapel on the educated Christian's mission in this world and said something like the following:

> I, too, have a dream. I dream of a hundred of our philosophy majors, rigorously educated, going on to

the best graduate schools and then strategically located
in colleges and universities across the land. I dream of
the impact they could make on people and on the history of ideas. I dream of those who go into other profes-
sions, who will bring Christian perspectives to bear
throughout the disciplines, and in law and business and
medicine and throughout our society.

I tried to articulate this kind of mission for the educated believer in other
Christian colleges as opportunity occurred, and wrote about it for a general
audience in *The Idea of a Christian College,* laying particular emphasis on the
integration of faith and learning. In *All Truth Is God's Truth,* I picked up on
the church fathers' claim that the ultimate source of all possible knowledge is
both thanks to God, and centers on him as Creator and Incarnate Lord. The
mandate to pursue truth in whatever field, then, cannot be inhibited either by
anti-intellectualism or by secular/sacred dichotomies.

Historically, two purposes dominate discussions of Christian learning. For
the medievals it was a contemplation of the works of God, each of which in
its distinctive role and all together in their magnificent symphony exhibit the
perfections of their Creator. For the moderns, in the spirit of Bacon's "knowledge is power," it became a means to service that improves the human condition and helps to further the purposes of God in this world. Philosophy, for
me, has been both of these things, and that is what makes Christian philosophy such a worthy "mission."

Some philosophers are fortunate to have their philosophical work determine what they teach. For me the reverse has been more the case: Teaching
has largely directed what my philosophical work will be. Teaching led me to
explore similarities among scientific, historical, moral, and religious knowledge, and to see that all knowledge in every department is interpretive, and so
perspectival. It was student concerns about the relation of faith and reason
that led me to explore philosophical methodologies of the twentieth century
and to argue that all philosophy is perspectival. It was teaching historical
courses (combined with the historical sense of my youth) that made my way
of doing philosophy a historical dialogue. It was students' moral dilemmas
during the Vietnam War and the activist 1960s that drove me into applied
ethics. If this has somehow come together in helpful ways, I can only thank
God's good providence in the life and work of a child who never grew up to
be what he wanted. Or did he?

Note

1. "The Theist and His Premises," *Basic College Quarterly,* IV, 4 (1959), 5.

14

FROM JERUSALEM

TO ATHENS

Brian Leftow

I am a philosopher because I am a Christian. To many intellectuals, this probably sounds like saying that I am a dog because I am a cat. Dogs hate cats, and otherwise polite philosophers have said to my face, with vigor, that "Christian philosopher" is a contradiction in terms. Cats are not fond of dogs, either. Christian friends have often reminded me that Luther called reason a whore. Well, reason *is* a whore. It will serve any master who can pay its price. But a whore was first to the empty tomb on the day of the Resurrection. Reason will serve God if given the chance; philosophy can be a work of Christian service. And Christian belief (I want to suggest) is far more a help than a hinderance to serious intellectual work.

My being either a philosopher or a Christian came as a surprise to my family and myself. I was born Jewish and grew up in a Jewish/Italian neighborhood in Brooklyn, New York. I'm not sure that this really counts as spending my youth with two distinct ethnic groups. Outsiders can rarely tell (non-Hasidic) Brooklyn Jews and Brooklyn Italians apart, and specialists debate whether they are two species or just variants of one. In my neighborhood, I think, the main difference was that the Jewish families skipped religious services on Saturdays and the Italian families did so on Sundays.

My parents sent me for six years to after-school classes in Hebrew, the Old Testament and so on, at an Orthodox synagogue. The rabbi thought I had the makings of a rabbi (what would he think of me now?) and tried to persuade my parents to send me full-time to a yeshiva, a Jewish school that would have put me on the road to the rabbinate. My parents refused. They are not practicing Jews themselves. They did not give me a Hebrew education to make me religious, let alone to make me a rabbi. They just wanted to ac-quaint me with my ethnic roots. This culminated in a bar mitzvah in which I chanted a portion of Hebrew Scripture well enough to bring tears to the eyes of the old men in the synagogue. There was just one problem: Nobody ever told me what the words I sang meant. My Hebrew was not good enough for me to make it out, so I never knew.[1] This sums up a religious education that left me wholly secular in mindset, or almost so. I did pick up a vague idea that there was probably some sort of God, and He probably had put me here to do something. I had no idea what, though. I remember thinking that for all I knew, the whole point of my life, the whole reason God made me, would be to kick a rock into a particular place, so that someone else would trip over it years later and set some complicated historical event in motion.

Brooklynites of the World War II generation have a common migratory pattern, probably encoded genetically: Having hatched and fledged in New York, they move to New Jersey in midlife, then retire to Florida. My parents reached New Jersey in 1970, when I was of high school age. There I met Christians for the first time, including some whose lives seemed to me hard or even tragic. The father of one family, in particular, had had an accident at work some ten years before and had almost died. The family lost all they had paying the hospital bills to save him. He came out of it brain-damaged and disabled. The family then cared for him at home. Daily they struggled to get by financially and coped with his varying health and behavior. I had to think that his presence was depressing and always reminded them of what they had lost. So I once asked why they did not institutionalize him. The mother replied, "I took a vow—'in sickness or in health'." For her, that was that.

Despite their difficulties, I found the Christians I met often cheerful and usually kind, particularly to me. They had something. I didn't know what it was, but I liked it and began to get curious about Christianity. Now a lot of things were happening at the time. I was an adolescent and doing my share of rebelling. I was attracted to non-Jewish girls and dating one. (Dating *shiksas* was a twofer: good company *and* it ticked my dad off.) Though it was the 1970s chronologically, it was still the 1960s in spirit. (In the same way, the

1950s really ran through about 1963.) So the questioning of received wisdom (being Jewish) was in the air. Still, these were not the reasons Christianity started to appeal to me. I could easily have rebelled, dated a pretty girl, and appeased the *zeitgeist* without ever giving God a thought. Christians intrigued me. They dealt well with problems I doubted I could have handled, and so many of them were so *nice*. I wanted to be like that. It occurred to me that the only real difference between us was that they were Christians and I was not. So, as I said, I got curious about Christianity. I went to a local pastor to inquire.

At the time, I had a part-time job with irregular hours, washing dishes at a Howard Johnson's. This left me free to come and go without raising my parents' suspicions, so I spent perhaps six months reading the New Testament on the sly and sneaking out to talk it over with the pastor. After a while, the book seemed to make too much sense not to be true. I found myself believing it. It wasn't so much a matter of accepting the basic factuality of New Testament stories (though I did, and later acquaintance with biblical criticism made me doubt not the veracity of the New Testament but rather the wits of the critics). What drew me was the philosophy in Christianity—its view of the world, its vision (founded in the person of Jesus) of what sort of person is truly good, and the Christian grasp of how hard it is to become that sort of person. The book that truly got to me was Romans. It spoke to me about human evil, the way our deepest selves struggle against our best intentions, and I felt a shock of recognition: This is it! This is *me!* Nobody else gets this right! Some liberal theologians seem to think that talk of sin drives people away from Christianity ("so negative, after all"). To me, the traditional Christian view of sin was attractive because it was obviously true.

Descriptions of the moral life are not pure phenomenology (not that I knew that word then). They are tinged with the writer's perspective, the way the writer views the world. If the writer gets the description exactly right, that is a pretty good reason to think that the writer's world view is true. If you see things as they are from the place where you're standing, you're standing in the right place. I came to believe in God because only those who believed in God saw good and evil as they are—or so it seemed to me then and still does.

I started wearing a small cross on a chain under my shirt—partly because I was starting to think that Christianity was true, partly as a hidden act of teenage defiance. It was a good one. Even Jews with no formal religious beliefs tend to think of converting to Christianity as going over to the enemy. One day I was bending over in our garage, putting gas in the lawn mower, and the cross fell out of my shirt. My father came into the garage.

"What's that?"

"A cross."

"Give it to me."

"I won't."

He grabbed for it, and we started to wrestle. We fell to the ground. My grandfather came into the garage then. He looked at my father.

"What has he got? Is it drugs?"

"NO. IT'S WORSE."

My grandfather had a heart attack and collapsed. My father stopped fighting and rushed to him. (That is why I still have the cross; my father was a lot bigger than I was.) My grandfather pulled through, and when the hospital released him, he spent six weeks recuperating in our house before he was strong enough to go home.

During that time he pleaded with me repeatedly, in tears, not to wear that awful thing or (God forbid) to convert. He reminded me of all that "the Christians" have done to Jews. He told me that "the Christians" would never accept me, that they'd always call me *kike* and *sheeny* behind my back. He was scared for me, scared that someone he loved would become a stranger, scared that his own flesh would repudiate things he loved most. This was agonizing. I loved my grandfather. He was a big, happy, street-wise bull of a man, strong and tough. Now I had almost killed him, and here he was, suddenly frail, crying, begging me to do something for him, something small, something easy, something that would make up for what I'd done to him.

Somehow, I didn't. I don't remember enough of my state of mind to say just why. A lot of what I do recall is shameful. I was and am just plain stubborn. I was deep into every adolescent's fight to set up a self that his parents have not defined and scared of what would happen if I backed down. I was vain and afraid my girlfriend would think me a coward. I can be callous, and that may have come into play, and God forgive me if it did. Was that all of it? I hope not. I don't *think* it was. I think there was something else. I just kept feeling that the things my grandfather was telling me were bad were *good*. If a thing appears true to you, you can't *make* yourself think it false: Try getting yourself to believe that you don't see a book in front of you right now. I don't know what weighed most with me. I do know that God can put even bad motivations to good use.

I think the Jewish idea that "Christians" are the enemy arises partly from a false analogy. "Jewish" names both a religion and an ethnic group. Jews use "Christian" in the same dual way, leading to such oddities as statements that Christians put Jews in the gas chambers at Auschwitz. Christians did no such thing—or if any did, they hated themselves. *Gentiles* did it. You can be a Gentile but not a Christian or a Christian but not a Gentile. German churches were full of Gentiles who were not Christians. Being in a church does not make you a Christian. As Corrie Ten Boom put it, if a mouse gets into a cookie jar, that doesn't make it a cookie. But they don't teach these subtleties in synagogues. It doesn't help that the Gentiles who ran the Spanish Inquisition were wearing church robes, either.

Anyway, I found myself thinking that Christianity told the truth about God and the world. Not long afterward, I was baptized. My parents discovered this by accident months later. We then spent a long time yelling at each other. I was a high school senior then, and so thinking about career options. I wanted to do something for God, and like many another new convert, I thought the way to do that was to be a minister. My parents said they would not finance this. (Can you blame them?) Either I studied to be a doctor or lawyer, or I was on my own. I didn't want their money anyway. So I left home to work my way through a small Christian college, whose tuition was low enough to make this possible. I did not communicate with my parents again for three years.

I didn't have all the money for my first semester's tuition. The college came up with an "emergency scholarship" for the difference—which I found out much later had come from my parents. But after that, it was up to me (with a little help from my friends). I worked nights and weekends, twenty-five hours a week, first at a local burger palace, then as a janitor in a local church. During summers I held down two jobs, putting in at least sixty-five hours a week at minimum wage. I spent one college break house sitting for a professor, others visiting friends, one or two sleeping in a church basement. (I had nowhere else to go.) But all this was peripheral. My coursework excited me, my friends were great company, and I felt I was living *for* something. Those years were the happiest of my life.

Over this time, my Christian friends gently and gradually got it through to me that Christ had a claim even on the parts of my life I wanted most for myself. This bore in particular on my family. Left to myself, I would gladly have had nothing more to do with them. I didn't feel much missing in my life, and it would not be easy to heal the breach between us. But a Christian is not left to himself. My parents and I started speaking again the summer before my senior year. They paid for my senior year.

By then, I knew I was not going to be a minister. But I found that I particularly liked one part of a minister's task, that of thinking about the nature of God and the implications of my faith. My coursework had introduced me to philosophy as a way to do this. Becoming a philosopher seemed a natural next step. It let me think through my beliefs full time.

Thus it was Christianity that brought me to philosophy. I think this was a natural way to come to philosophy. Certainly many great philosophers have taken just this route: for example, Anselm, Duns Scotus, Bonaventure, Aquinas, Kierkegaard. (Looking to other Western religions, al-Ghazzali and Maimonides leap to mind.) Some today think that a genuine philosopher must be a skeptic, particularly toward religious belief. Were this so, Aquinas would not count as a philosopher. Some today think that philosophy well practiced has skepticism at least as a natural by-product. Were this so, Aquinas's work would not count as good philosophy.

Giving Aquinas and other medievals as examples of people who philosophized because of and out of their faith courts this sort of reply: "Well, Aquinas and that lot didn't know any better. They lived in an age of faith, without the illumination of science. (Kierkegaard had the benefit of our scientific culture, but, hey, he was unstable anyway.) Today, though, no truly sophisticated or educated person can hold religious beliefs, and no person who is neither educated nor sophisticated can be a real or a good philosopher." This is a silly thought, even though I could cite serious philosophers who have put it into print. Most bigoted thoughts *are* silly. But let me be silly enough to answer it. Recent surveys show that more than half of American scientists are theists. Many of these scientists say that it was their scientific work that led them to belief. Evidently "the light of science" shines on different conclusions for different people. I myself have met literally hundreds of Christians with Ph.D.s from the world's best universities. Could Yale, Harvard, Cornell, Oxford, and so on keep their reputations if their Ph.D.s were routinely uneducated and unsophisticated?

Dismissive talk of an "age of faith" reveals a bill of goods that Enlightenment historiography has sold us. From 400 to 1500 A.D., almost all Western philosophy was associated with some religious tradition. From 500 on, after the death of Greco-Roman paganism (for which late Platonism served as theology), the traditions were Christianity and Judaism, with Islam coming on stream in the 700s. Now consider the names that histories of philosophy give the 500–1500 period. The label *Dark Ages* needs no comment. The label *age of faith* is meant to contrast with *age of reason*. Given this pairing, there is little doubt which sort of age is best. Reason knows. Faith just believes, unseeing. Even the innocuous term *Middle Ages* has a hidden freight. Calling the 500–1500 period merely *middle* denies it a distinctive character of it own. It defines it as between *other* periods, its chief significance being in separating them. It thus suggests that the 500–1500 period is a less important period that comes between the good stuff.

The standard names for other historical periods reinforce this message. Standard histories have it that a *Renaissance* succeeded the *Middle Ages*. A renaissance is literally a rebirth or resurrection, with all the positive connotations these terms bear. If first there was cultured, enlightened, rational Greco-Roman civilization, followed by period X, after which the good things of Greco-Roman civilization were "reborn," then during X those things were dormant or dead. So the natural complement of *Renaissance* might be *Age of Sleep* or *Dead Ages*. *Enlightenment,* of course, comes after darkness, and dispels it. So *the Enlightenment* has not the relatively innocent *Middle Ages* but the loaded *Dark Ages* as its natural contrast.

There *is* an easy nonpejorative name for the 500–1500 period. One *could* call it the *Age of Religious Philosophy,* thus noting that all the philosophy that went on was in explicit, positive dialogue with Judaism, Christianity, or Islam. But this name (suggested by Harry Wolfson) is never used. This may be because most philosophers prefer pejorative names for the period or because those who would call the phrase *Christian philosopher* a self-contradiction find *religious philosophy* similarly jarring. But another reason may be that this name does not fully distinguish the medieval from the classical period, since most classical philosophy was done from an explictly religious world view as well.[2] Still, this very shortcoming of the name makes a point. There just *is not* the radical breach between classical and medieval philosophy that talk of descent into a Dark Age (followed by a renaissance of the classical) implies. The religious tradition involved changed, much of the record of Greco-Roman philosophy was lost, and purely political upheaval kept philosophical production low for part of the period. But the

Middle Ages understood the philosopher's project just as most classical philosophers did, as an effort to understand a world that was taken to include the divine.

If we view philosophy in its real historical context, it is not Christian but secular philosophers who have made a radical break with philosophical tradition. If working within a religious tradition means that Christians who think as Christians do not produce "real philosophy," then Platonism, Neo-Platonism, Stoicism, and Spinozism aren't real philosophy either. In fact, by this criterion, there was almost no real philosophy before Hume, save for classical Skepticism and some strands of Epicureanism,[3] and there have been no real Jewish or Arabic philosophers. (Heaven help whoever makes the latter claim in these Politically Correct times.) Until the 1700s, almost all philosophers drew more or less explicitly on some religious tradition. Apart from Skepticism and perhaps Epicureanism, purely secular philosophy—if it exists—is a recent innovation. As such, it has no claim to set the meaning of the term *philosophy*. That was around long before the secularists. So "Christian philosopher" is no contradiction. In fact, someone who moves from explicit Christian faith to philosophy is just bringing the subject back to itself.

There is room to wonder whether any philosophy ever has been purely secular, that is, had no religious roots. Socrates, whose work shaped philosophy as we know it, understood his life in philosophy as a religious mission.[4] Even Epicurus sought to give mortals an analogue of the tranquility he saw in the gods.[5] Tillich argued powerfully that such apparently secular philosophies as Marxism and Nazism actually rest on and express "ultimate concern," an attitude indistinguishable from religious devotion. Perhaps at some level, philosophy is *always* the theology of some ultimate concern. For all philosophy is written in the service of a particular world view and set of values. Almost always, something in a thinker's world picture or values calls forth a nearly religious awe or attacts a supreme, quasi-religious loyalty. This is true even of the naturalism, materialism, or scientism that are the self-proclaimed orthodoxy of today's academic philosophy. For these too have beliefs about what deserves awe or devotion, though they are rarely articulated. Catch the naturalist in a reflective mood, feed the naturalist some beer if necessary, and you may hear sentiments like these:

> Humanity matters most, and philosophy ought to just help make our sorry years a bit more bearable.

> Justice matters most, and what gives our brief lives worth is devoting ourselves to realizing it in a classless society.

> Truth matters most, and we redeem ourselves from our utter insignificance by serving it.

> The universe dwarfs us, and the best thing we
> can hope for is to understand and accept our
> place in it and feel (as we are) a part of nature.

Naturalists do have such thoughts, though they rarely utter them. They draw them from Stoics, Epicureans, Spinoza, or Marx. These arguably are propositions of the atheist theologies that naturalists live by.

Thus there is a strong historical tie between religious belief and philosophy. The tie continues among explicitly religious philosophers and (arguably) under the strange guises of atheistic quasi-religions: I would argue that both theist and atheist write in the service of their faith. I do not think this is a coincidence or a historical fluke. As I suggested above, I think the connection between religion and philosophy is *natural*.

One studies philosophy because one wants to know or more fully grasp the answers to certain questions.[6] Thus the turn to philosophy comes from the desire for truth or understanding—the love of truth—not from disillusion with the search for these.[7] A skeptic is disillusioned with the search.[8] A skeptic is a lover who has been burned. The skeptic trusted some authority or belief and then came to think it false. Trust someone who is not trustworthy, and you do get burned. Get burned often enough, and you do grow wary, weary, and cynical, and start to think you've seen through it all. but if you happen to trust someone who truly deserves your trust, you may find no reason to turn sour. If you have found none yourself, why *act* sour? True, others *have* thought themselves deceived. They advise wariness. But are they the best advisors? The divorced are not the best source of marital advice. Act as they say, live in the expectation of hopeless marital discord and breakup, and you will probably bring about the breakup you fear. The only way to *be* happily married is to believe that you can be and take the risk of trust.

Philosophy means "love of wisdom." Etymologically, then, philosophy is a form of love. A philosopher is someone who lives out a love of truth. Those who think that philosophy must lead to skepticism seem to think that love of truth must be disappointed.[9] But why believe this if you have not yet found it to be so? Those who think that philosophy must begin with skepticism seem to think that you can only love what you do not believe you have. But were this true, marriage would be impossible. As a Christian, I came to philosophy believing that I knew certain large philosophical truths—for example, that there is a God. I came loving those truths, and so wanting the pleasure of more fully understanding them. If you do not have what you love, your love takes the form of desire. If you do have what you love, your love is still desire—but to desire what you have is just to enjoy it. If you lack what you love, you seek it. If you have what you love, you revel in it. You look at it again and again, more and more closely. You try to grasp it ever more deeply. You savor the familiar parts and relish each new facet that shows itself. What could be more natural? This, I think, is why Christian faith, and more generally religious belief, naturally leads to philosophy.

A Christian philosopher lives out a love of Christian truth. Doing philosophy can be a way to live out this love, because doing philosophy need not make one a skeptic. Philosophy well practiced does develop critical skill. It shows up the holes in one's arguments and the objections to one's beliefs. But it is one thing to be a critic and another to be a skeptic. One can rationally believe that Christianity is true *and* that there are objections to it—even some to which one does not have a wholly satisfying answer. All that one has to do is admit that one does not fully understand either Christianity or much else. Philosophy certainly should inspire *that* thought. One can wholeheartedly love a spouse whose flaws one knows. One thing that helps is knowing at least some of one's *own* flaws.

I believe that the Christian faith tells me the truth about God and the world in broad outline. For me, philosophy is an effort to fill in the details and resolve the difficulties my beliefs face. I think out my faith, and I think out of my faith. As I've already noted, some deem this intellectually illegitimate. These say that even if Christian faith accounts for one's interest in philosophy, and even if this is a natural thing, a genuine, serious, intellectually honest philosopher must check all religious beliefs at the gate to Athens. I think this view misunderstands both philosophy and Christianity. But this view does arise from a legitimate concern.

I went into philosophy intending to remain a Christian. I believed that there is a God, for instance, and I intended not to give up that belief. It is fair to ask whether one can both intend this and be intellectually honest. Can a committed theist consider arguments with an open mind? Or must a theist pretend not to be a theist in order to judge arguments fairly?

I suggest that philosophers have as much right to resepct their theism in doing philosophy as to respect their belief that, say, there are material objects. We all do believe that there are material objects. Yet we cannot *prove* that there really are things such as tables and chairs. We could be wrong to believe in material objects, and we know this. As we do, we take arguments against material objects' existence seriously. But this does not mean that we set aside our belief in material objects when we consider such arguments. We are sure that material objects exist, and we respect this surety by the attitude we take to arguments that material objects do not exist. For we approach such arguments with the attitude that though they could in principle persuade us, our job is to find their flaws.

This attitude is quite rational. For it seems true to us that material objects exist. The bare fact that this seems true is good reason to expect a flaw in an argument against material objects. For one thing, if material objects exist, there are no deductive proofs that they do not. There is no deductive proof that $2 + 2 = 5$, just because it is not true that $2 + 2 = 5$. So if it seems to us that there are material objects, this is reason to think that any apparent deductive proof that there are none has a hidden flaw.

Now an argument can be rationally compelling (i.e., give strong reason to adopt its conclusion) without being a deductive proof. But if material objects exist, this is good reason to think that there are no rationally compelling arguments that they do not. We hope (and live by the hope) that being rational is the best policy for attaining truth. Accepting rationally compelling arguments is one part of being rational. So the more rationally compelling arguments there are for false conclusions, the less reason there is to think that being rational is the best policy for attaining truth. So if we are rational to hope that being rational will lead to the truth, we are rational to hope that every seemingly compelling argument for a false conclusion really has a flaw.

Thus, if "there are no material objects" seems to us a false conclusion, it is rational to hope that seemingly compelling arguments for this conclusion have flaws. If it is rational to hope for such a flaw, it is rational to seek such a flaw. Again, it is rational to hang onto the truth if one has it. So it is rational to seek to hang onto beliefs that seem true. Thus, if it seems true that material objects exist, and a successful argument against material objects would deprive one of this belief, it is rational to actively seek a flaw in arguments that material objects do not exist. Further, the better our reasons to think that there *are* material objects, the more reason we have to *expect* a flaw in arguments against material objects.

Seeking a flaw need not involve intellectual dishonesty. For it is one thing to seek a flaw, and quite a different thing to find it. As long as we do not invent flaws that are not there, we are honest. Thus, one can be intellectually honest and yet respect in one's thinking one's belief in material objects.

Belief in God is quite like belief in material objects. For belief in material objects is basic to our thinking. If I give up belief in material objects, I must give up belief in tables, chairs, and human bodies, or else change my concepts of these things and no longer take them to be material objects. For I now think of chairs as material objects. That is, I now take it that "there are chairs" entails "there are material objects." So if I deny material objects, I must either reject "there are chairs" or so change my concept of a chair that "there are chairs" no longer entails "there are material objects." Thus, if I give up belief in material objects, I must either drop or reinterpret almost every belief I have.

Belief in God is basic to theists' thinking. If I gave up belief in God, I would have to change radically my views of the nature and content of morality, the large-scale nature of the world, human destiny, the meaning of life, the kinds of explanations events can have (e.g., as acts of God), and so on. I would also have to reinterpret most of my beliefs. For to a theist, "there are chairs" entails not only "there are material objects" but also "there are creatures." Ceasing to think of chairs as creatures (and so as having a creator) is at least as large a shift as ceasing to think of them as material objects. So just as a believer in material objects is rational to seek a flaw in arguments against them, a theist, facing an argument that there is no God, is rational to seek a flaw in it and expect to find one.

To respect one's theism as one does philosophy is just to approach anti-theistic arguments this way. Theistic philosophers do not treat theism as immune to argument. We respect our theism by approaching anti-theist arguments as those who believe in material objects approach arguments against material objects.

Commitment to retain theism in one's philosophy is like commitment to retain belief in material objects. It is not impossible to find reasons to give up either. But it is entirely rational and can be entirely honest to resist doing so. If commitment to material objects does not unfit one to do fair, honest philosophy, why should commitment to theism?

One possible answer is that there are personal, emotional, and moral dimensions unique to the theist case. Christian commitment, for instance, is not just abstractly intellectual. It is passionate. It involves hopes, ideals, self-discipline, and personal sacrifice. Passions can tempt one to intellectual dishonesty. Further, the more hope and effort one invests in a religious belief, the more it would hurt to find that belief false, and the more foolish one would feel. So depth of Christian commitment can also tempt one to intellectual dishonesty—for example, weighing anti-Christian arguments unfairly. There is no passion, hope, or effort in our belief in material objects. We do not invest ourselves in this as we do in a religious belief.

Again, becoming a Christian involves intending to stay a Christian, just as marrying involves intending to stay married. Being a Christian or a spouse is a lifetime project. If one does not stay married, one fails in the project one undertook. Losing one's faith in the face of an argument can feel like a similar failure. Martial commitment has a moral dimension. In marrying, one makes serious promises. It is a deep moral failure to break these promises. To be unfaithful in marriage is shameful. To be unfaithful as a Christian can feel at least as shameful. Desire to be faithful can push one to take anti-Christian arguments less seriously than one should. There is no question of shame or failure about giving up belief in material objects.

Let us push the marital analogy a step further. Like intending to stay married, intending to stay a Christian is intending to stay in a faithful, loving relation with someone who loves you. Both marital and Christian commitment involve commitments to *think* a certain way, because thinking this way is necessary to keep this relationship going. A marriage is a friendship. It is impossible to keep a friendship going if you think nothing but ill of your friend. So intending to keep marital friendship going involves intending to think well of your spouse. If your spouse does not deserve such thoughts, this threatens to involve large-scale self-deception. Christian faith is a marital friendship with God (Ephesians 5:31–32). Like other friendships, it makes demands on our thinking as well as our doing. (Of this more anon.) So, too, as with other friendships, the possibility of self-deception exists. There is no similar pressure to deceive ourselves about material objects.

For these and other reasons, it can seem improper or dangerous to intend to keep believing in God as one does philosophy. Thus it can seem that a Christian can do intellectually respectable philosophy only by not intending this, and so only by abstracting from Christian commitment in doing philosophy. But even so, I now argue, the intent to remain a faithful Christian is compatiable with intellectual honesty.

Commitment to continue being a Christian includes intending to keep on holding certain beliefs. This is a bit like the commitment we make to love, honor, and so on when we marry. On reflection, it can seem strange to promise to love. For love is (partly) a feeling, and feelings (so we think) are largely beyond our control. They just happen to us. We call some of them passions just because we are passive to them. But some things that just happen to us, things to which we are passive, are things we cannot directly control. If whether we love is not under our direct control—if we cannot directly affect whether we love—it is puzzling how we can truly and seriously promise to love. For I cannot truly and seriously promise to make it the case that the Milky Way contains more than 10 billion stars, just because there is nothing I can do to affect this.

Now, intending to believe is a bit like promising to love. For belief, like love, is not directly under our control. As I said before, try to believe that you do not now have a book in front of you. Do you even know how to *try* this? If we cannot control our believing, it is just as puzzling how we can intend to continue believing something as it is how we can promise—or intend—to keep loving someone.

One can truly, seriously promise to love only to the extent that whether we love is under our control. But we *can* affect whether we love. Love is not just a feeling. Part of what it is to love someone is to treat that person a certain way. Doing that is wholly in our power. Further, the feelings involved in loving someone are also, to a large and surprising extent, under our *in*direct control.

To love someone and continue to do it requires a certain directing of our thoughts and attention. If I sit and think about my wife, it is up to me to decide what I think about. I may choose to dwell on her many virtues, her smile, her kindness, and the way it has expressed itself in nice things she has done for me. If I do that, I will probably feel warm and grateful, and when I see her at home at the end of the day, I will likely be almost as nice to her as she deserves. On the other hand, I may choose to dwell on any annoying habits or character flaws she may have (not that she really has any), on any grievance, real or imaginary, or on the worst disagreements we've had. If I do that, I will get angry and sullen, and will probably storm in the door and start an argument. It is all up to me, and if I think negatively often enough, I won't have much of a marriage left.

In promising to love my wife, I undertake to direct my very thoughts to that end—to dwell most on what is good in my wife and (as far as I can) think only charitably on the rest. Now, of course, it is not really in our power to believe whatever we choose. A man could not really make himself believe that his wife is faithful to him in the face of a great deal of evidence to the contrary. But if his evidence about her faithfulness were genuinely ambiguous, he would be faithful to his commitment to love his wife only if he did his best to construe it charitably, and to direct his thoughts about the evidence, as far as he *honestly* could, to finding flaws in the hypothesis that she is unfaithful.

Intending to remain a Christian in philosophizing is something like intending to believe the best you can of your spouse, as long as you can do so honestly. This is not an ideal parallel. It makes sense to say, "Is my wife cheating? She may be, but it's not clear, and I can't believe she'd do that to me," but it makes no sense to say, "Is God nonexistent? He may be, but it's not clear, and I can't believe He'd do that to me." But there is a parallel to this extent: Commitment in either case does not require us to evaluate arguments or evidence unfairly. It merely dictates the attitude and expectation we bring to them. It dictates that we *look for* flaws in arguments against the existence of God and expect them to be there. If our beliefs are true, there will be flaws to find in any case against God—or against one's spouse. So if we are convinced that our beliefs are true, it is perfectly rational to assume that flaws will be there and to seek them.

Love, commitment, and invested effort do create a temptation to intellectual dishonesty. Few men *want* to believe that their wives are cheating. So too, if we love the Christian picture of the world we carry about in our heads, we will be loath to give up any part of it. But love can also make you want to be the best person you can be for the sake of the one you love. This applies particularly in God's case. Loving someone involves identifying that person's interests with your own. God's interest in each of us is our own moral and intellectual perfection. If so, love of God works *against* intellectual dishonesty. Further, accepting a Christian world picture may well include accepting the existence of a hell. Intellectual dishonesty is a sin. It is a form of lying. Belief in hell is not an inducement to sin.

Does love make one irrational? If loving a friend makes one strive to maintain one's belief that the friend's character is good, that can be morally admirable: We count it a flaw to believe ill of one's friends easily. It's an interesting question whether the moral or the intellectual virtues *ought* to win out if the two conflict, or whether the two ever really can conflict. But in any event, there is no conflict in the Christian case. If one has good reasons to accept Christianity, one also has good reasons to hold on to it even when an argument temporarily seems to tell against some part of it. *Some* commitment to hold on to a belief in the face of initially counterweighing evidence is necessary to hold on to almost any truth. This is particularly so in philosophy, where almost any truth faces fairly impressive counterarguments.[10] If Christianity is in fact true, a good reason to hold to Christianity is a good reason to hold on to truth until the evidence comes to square with it. There is nothing irrational—or dishonest—about holding on to a position one has had good reason to adopt in the hope of finding flaws in an argument against it—at least for a good while.

So, the least one can say about the passionate part of Christian commitment is that it need not unfit one for doing honest philosophy. If love of God is love of one who wills our intellectual and moral perfection, one can say more: Christian passion is a spur to the highest intellectual standards. This has a paradoxical consequence. For it implies that my loyalty to God and to what God wants for me could in principle lead me to reject belief in God. Suppose that I find a crushing anti-theist argument that turns out to be utterly beyond reproach. In this case, if my desire to be what God wants me to be enjoins intellectual honesty, my very desire to please God would lead me to reject God. Christian authors have not shied from this paradox. Aquinas once wrote that if an erring conscience tells one that it is wrong to believe in Christ, one does evil to believe in Christ: Conscience's moral authority is so great that even Christian faith against conscience is evil.[11] But to Aquinas, conscience has its authority precisely because its dictates have the force of God's commands.[12] So, if (as I believe) intellectual honesty is just a facet of honesty in general, and if honesty is one thing conscience commands, then if Aquinas is right, the Christian commitment to intellectual honesty is great enough to lead a Christian (in principle) to reject Christianity. I do not know how one could prize honesty more.

Perhaps, though, it is not the passion or commitment in Christian faith that makes some think that Christians must check their religious beliefs at the gate to Athens. Perhaps it is instead the fact that Christian belief carries *wide-ranging* philosophical implications. As this is so, some may think, surely Christian faith will lead one to prejudge the outcome of *too many* philosophical debates unless one explicitly ignores it.

Christians do come at a variety of debates with an expectation of what the truth will turn out to be. Christian beliefs give me positions on some key philosophical issues: On some things, I have philosophical views before I start to do philosophy. But this is not unique to Christians. Atheists too often have many strong philosophical views before they take up philosophy. The passion with which some atheist philosophers argue is not purely a function of how good they think their philosophical case is. Again, most philosophers have strong ethical views long before they examine their views' philosophical merits, and in doing philosophy, they strive to preserve these views. Let me briefly examine (what I think are) the Christian givens. Most, I think, are of genuine benefit to philosophers and other serious intellectuals.

Christians believe that God made us and our world. For this reason, Christians' philosophical givens include the following:

1. There are truths independent of human opinion. (For God created a definite world. It is as He made it. So there are truths about it, the truths He intended in making it. Again, God's beliefs are not just matters of His opinion *or* ours. God's perspective isn't just another point of view.)
2. Our basic cognitive faculties are reliable, at least as originally created, and over some range of ordinary experience. (Christianity doesn't *entail* this. But why would God set us up to err?)

Christians believe that God sent Christ to save us from our sins. For this reason, the Christian givens include the following:

3. There are real, objective moral facts. (Our sinfulness is not a matter of opinion; Christ died for it.)
4. We are morally responsible for our actions. (If not, Christ had nothing to save us from.)

Are (1)–(4) handicaps to philosophers? Most people, Christian or not, believe (1)–(4) before philosophy gets to them. So, if believing (1)–(4) is a handicap, it is one nonbelievers share. If prephilosophical commitment to (1)–(4) disqualifies one from being a philosopher, almost nobody has been qualified, from Socrates and Plato on. But (1)–(4) seem, on the contrary, to be ideal spurs to intellectual effort. For instance, belief that there is real, objective truth to be had is one large reason to pursue philosophy. Does belief in (1)–(4) promote intellectually dishonesty? I don't see why believing that there are real, objective wrongs one could do would incline one to these particular wrongs. Nor can I see why believing that truth is independent of one's opinions would make one tend to substitute one's opinions for the truth. On the contrary, (1)–(4) seem to be clear incentives to careful, honest thinking. For they tell us that there is real truth for such thinking to grasp, that we can be really wrong if we are not careful, and that honesty is a real virtue.

The most basic Christian given is this: A Christian comes to philosophy holding that God exists. This given dictates a Christian's attitude to the traditional philosophical effort to prove or disprove the existence of God. For me, this debate is not an attempt to determine the truth about God. I have no serious doubt what the truth is. Rather, for me, this debate is part of epistemology. Its subject is not whether God exists but whether the proposition "God exists" has a particular status, that of being provable or supportable by argument. This latter question is interesting but finally academic, which is why Christian philosophers can sleep at night. I tend to think of the existence-of-God debate this way: I'm sure that God exists, even if I can't give a good argument that He does. If one can prove God's existence, atheism is irrational. So as I see it, the real stake in the debate is not whether God exists but whether atheists are rational. Why should Christians lose sleep over this? At most, for atheists' benefit.

The debate over God's existence is a football game that has gone on at least since Plato. As each generation hones the arguments pro and con, the ball moves up or down the field—that is, as discussion continues, the general philosophical community adjusts its opinion of just how strong the two sides' cases are, and this revised opinion seeps out into the culture at large, affecting broader attitudes toward the rationality of belief in God. Aquinas gained ten yards for the theist side. Kant threw it for a ten-yard loss. Christian theists, in particular, have some obligation to care how the game goes to the extent that people's opinion of the general intellectual respectability of Christianity affects their likelihood of coming to believe it. It is the same obligation Christians have to care about the salvation of everyone. It is not an intellectual obligation but a religious one.

Belief in God gives a Christian reason to hang on to (1)–(4), for as I've shown, God's existence and actions are what give Christians their special reasons for (1)–(4). But everyone has a *lot* of reason to hang on to (1)–(4), and yet (1)–(4) remain philosophically contestable, and even those who favor them can consider the case against them honestly. Further, if belief in God favors (1)–(4), then if (1)–(4) promote intellectual virtue, belief in God does so precisely *by* favoring (1)–(4). So, it seems that the Christian givens are for the most part not unique to Christians, and are more boon than bane for the intellectual life.

Beyond disposing one toward (1)–(4), Christian faith leaves one fairly open to philosophical alternatives. Christians ought to be cautious in drawing further philosophical consequences from their faith. For we may not understand the content of the faith aright. In Galileo's day, some thought that the proper interpretation of Christian doctrine required belief that the earth is the center of the solar system. We now know that this is not required precisely because we know that it is not true. If we commit ourselves unwisely to a certain doctrine as "the" philosophical implication of Christianity, we may cause others to stumble. For it we say that Christianity implies what non-Christians have good reason to think false, this gives non-Christians good reason to conclude that part of Christian belief is false.[13]

Christians can be confident that the ideal, accurate interpretation of all Christian doctrines will be compatible with the claims of an ideal philosophy. If Christian claims are true, true philosphical claims will in the end be compatible with Christianity. So the basic constraint I operate with as a Christian philosopher is that my philosophical position be compatible with the proper interpretation of Christian doctrine. As I may not know this yet, this constraint is not narrow. The fact that I do not necessarily know the best interpretation of the things I believe dictates that I be cautious in drawing philosophy from specifically Christian premises.

What if the best philosophical arguments support positions that seem at odds with Christianity—for example, by supporting the denials of some of (1)–(4)? What if I seek flaws in these arguments and do not find them? this may be because I don't understand either Christianity or philosophy as I ought. Perhaps the arguments seem best because I am reasoning badly. Perhaps I am wrong after all in thinking that Christianity requires all of (1)–(4). Perhaps I need to nuance my understanding of (1)–(4). In any event, it is rational to live with inconsistent beliefs, at least for a while, if one has strong reason to hold both and one cannot see which belief errs. So at worst, a Christian may say, with the Latin Averroists, "the Faith says one thing, and The Philosopher, without its illumination, says another." This is an intellectually honest position, albeit an uncomfortable one. But hope is a Christian virtue, and any Christian who faces this prospect can reasonably hope to find a way out of it. There is just one body of truth. Its parts are mutually consistent, since they are all true together. If Christians believe aright, Christianity is one part of that body. If it is, it is compatiable with the rest of the truth.

I have said that I am a philosopher because I am a Christian and want to understand better the things I believe. But there is also a connection that runs the other way. I became a Christian because I admired some Christians and asked why they had the qualities I admired in them. In asking this, I was asking what are really philosophical questions: What must I do to be good? What *is* goodness? The writer best known for finding in Christianity the answers to such philosophical questions is St. Augustine. The answers I found turned out rather like his; I close by recording them.

What is goodness? Being good is being like God. It is turning toward God. We are basically mirrors. We reflect into the world whatever we turn ourselves toward. If you aim at money, the world will see only money when it looks at you. If you aim at power, the world will see only power when it looks at you—and will run for cover or use you. If you aim at fame, you turn toward others to have them look at you. But when they do, they do not really notice you—they just admire a reflection of themselves *in* you. If you simply love yourself, you are a mirror just reflecting itself, and the world will see nothing when it looks at you. Good people reflect God's goodness. They are turned toward God, whether they know it or not. All they have of goodness is an influx from God, whether they know it or not. Those who look at them see the likeness of God. Mirrors do shine, but they shine with a borrowed light.

What must I do to be good? If being good is being like God, those who strive to be good must seek to be Godlike. How can human beings know what it is to be Godlike? What does Godlikeness look like in a human life? I was and am persuaded that in Jesus Christ, God showed us this by revealing His nature in human flesh. (Could a God who cares about human goodness do less?) If God comes to us in Christ, the best route to goodness is to meet Him there.

Notes

1. Nor could I understand the Hebrew liturgy I sang at the many Sabbath services I attended as part of my education. I suppose this is another likeness between some Brooklyn Jews and some pre-Vatican II Italian Catholics.

2. As pagan Greco-Roman philosophers were polytheists, a more distinctive name for the 500–1500 period might be *Age of Monotheistic Philosophy.*

3. Socrates seems to have had strong religious beliefs; see, for example, Gregory Vlastos, *Socrates, Ironist and Moral Philosopher* (Ithaca, N.Y.: Cornell University Press, 1991), pp. 157–178. Plato clearly did. Aristotle argued the gods' existence, though his full religious views are unclear. Epicurus's views are matters of debate, and some Epicureans probably were atheists. But arguably, Epicurus believed in the existence of gods; see, for example, *Letter to Menoceus* 123, in B. Inwood and L. Gerson, eds., *Hellenistic Philosophy* (Indianapolis: Hackett, 1988), p. 23. The views of Socrates, Plato and Epicurus diverge markedly from the Greek religion of their day. But their thinking about religion arose within the Greek religious tradition and took shape as a critique of (major) parts of that tradition. Unlike Hume and the Skeptics, this

critique left Socrates, Plato, and (perhaps) Epicurus with positive religious beliefs that had some significant content in common with their tradition. So while their views are not orthodox Hellenic religion, it seems fair to say that they worked within the Greek religious tradition.

4. See Plato, *Apology*.

5. See *Letter to Menoceus* 135, in Inwood and Gerson, p. 25, and Plutarch, *Against Epicurean Happiness*, 1091B-C, in A. A. Long and D. N. Sedley, eds., *The Hellenistic Philosophers* (New York: Oxford University Press, 1987), p. 144.

6. On most accounts of knowledge, one knows a proposition P just in case P is true, one believes P, and one's belief in P has the right kind of backing. (Much recent debate about knowledge has been about what the right kind of backing *is*.) So one might turn to philosophy in order to *know* the answer to a question if (a) one has no idea what the answer is, and wants an answer, or if (b) one believes that the answer is a proposition P, and believes P, and wants to give one's belief that P the status of knowledge. Many who philosophize in order to back or understand their beliefs better are seeking to know truths they so far only believe, even if they do not explicitly think of it this way. If one's belief that P already counts as knowledge, or philosophy cannot turn it into knowledge, or one does not in any way care whether it is knowledge, one still may turn to philosophy (c) just to more fully grasp or penetrate what one believes. Christians often pursue philosophy for type (b) or (c) reasons. So do others. For instance, some people come to philosophy out of a burning conviction that certain social practices are unjust and that widespread beliefs which back these practices are false, and a desire to unmask these practices and debunk these beliefs. They come, that is, believing that a proposition P is false or that a practice P* is unjust, and seeking to "prove" P's falsity or P*'s injustice (and/or convince others). Either is a type (b) or (c) reason to do philosophy.

7. Those whom political passions bring to philosophy may say that they come to seek justice. But their political beliefs often look like atheist faiths their philosophizing serves, they "seek justice" in part because they love certain beliefs (e.g., that a particular practice is unjust, that a different practice would be more just, and that justice is worth pursuing), and they "seek justice" by philosophy rather than violence or politics because they want to understand and spread understanding of what they see as just and unjust.

8. Of course, skeptics *have* found what skeptics think *are* truths—for example, that the senses deceive us, that philosophy cannot produce reliable knowledge (save about its own incapacities), or that religion is the opiate of the masses. Skeptics may well love these truths as hard-won products of philosophical toil. But these probably were not the truths that wooed the skeptic into philosophy; the skeptic neither believed them beforehand nor hoped to validate them through philosophy. The skeptic is likely disillusioned about his or her *prior* beliefs or hopes.

9. Or at least that love of nonskeptical truth must be.

10. Consider, for instance, the philosophical claims that "numbers exist" and "it is not the case that numbers exist." One of these claims must be true. But there are impressive arguments for and against each. So, whichever true is true despite impressive counterarguments. This is so with many other pairs of contradicting philosophical claims.

11. Evil *per accidens,* in Aquinas's terminology. See Aquinas, *Summa Theologiae* I–IIa, 19, 5.

12. Aquinas, *Disputed Questions on Truth,* 17, 3; 17, 5; 17, 5 *ad* 3.

13. For instance, many Christian thinkers seem to feel that Christian belief in an afterlife requires belief in an immaterial, immortal soul. But belief in such a soul is controversial among philosophers. So it is worth noting that almost everything Christians believe about the afterlife can be true even if there are no souls. Christian beliefs about life after death center on the hope of a *bodily* resurrection. It is at least arguable that God can resurrect me even if I have no immaterial soul.

15

THERE WAS

A WIND BLOWING

George I. Mavrodes

Tom Morris invited me to write an essay "from the heart," something about my own life as a Christian and an academician in the field of philosophy, perhaps a "spiritual–intellectual autobiography," as he put it. I can try.

When I set myself to that project, thinking about what my life has been like up to now, three themes seem initially to stand out. One of them is expressed in a saying attributed to Jesus in one of the Gospels: "The wind blows where it chooses, and you hear the sound of it, but you do not know where it comes from or where it goes. So it is with everyone who is born of the Spirit" (John 3:8, New Revised Standard Version). I may not fully understand that saying and the analogy in it. But what it suggests to me now is the theme of how little we known of our own spiritual biographies and how much is hidden. It suggests that to me, I suppose, because that makes sense in the context of my own experience. In large part, that is how my own life seems to me. I have the feeling that much of what was most important in it is obscure to me, dimly seen, if at all. And that is so for what I think of as the most overtly spiritual elements of that life, as well as the merely (?) this-worldly. When I look back, it seems to me that there was a wind blowing there, a wind of divine love (and maybe other winds as well). But when and how it began, and how those winds twisted together—well, I don't know all that much about it.

A second theme crops up in "The Myth of Er," the story that ends Plato's *Republic*. That story seems to be a sort of parable (perhaps not entirely unlike Jesus's parable of the rich man and Lazarus), a parable whose purpose is to stress the importance of choosing one's life carefully. But Plato also introduces into the story another element, perhaps curiously un-Platonic. Er sees a crowd of souls who are about to be born into the world. But first, they must choose the life they will lead from among a large assortment offered to them. The selection, however, is not infinite—some types of life may be in short supply. And then, before the souls choose, another being appears. A "prophet" he is called in Benjamin Jowett's translation and also an "interpreter." He throws into the crowd of souls a shower of numbered counters—lots—and each soul picks up whatever lot falls near him. Those numbers determine the order in which the souls choose their lives. And the order of their choosing makes a difference, because those who choose late do not have as wide a selection as those who came earlier. Some lives are no longer available.

What is that prophet doing in the story of Er? It seems to me that he represents the theme that there is something significant in human life that is neither necessity nor choice. It is chance.

I know that the notion of chance has not gotten a very good press in much of Christian theology and philosophy. But I'm not convinced that its bad reputation is fully deserved. (I think, for example, that the argument that nothing can happen by chance because everything is foreknown by God is a fallacy. I believe that everything is indeed foreknown by God, but the divine foreknowledge determines neither the events nor the manner of their occurrence. That, however, is a long argument, and this is not the place for it.) I suspect that Plato was on to something important when he brought in that prophet with his handful of lots. There seem to me to be chance elements in my life. But the question of how to integrate that suspicion fully with the elements of my Christian conviction is not now resolved for me.

The third element is perhaps best described as a certain kind of "feeling," but in the sense in which a feeling is not simply, or even mainly, an emotion. It is rather a kind of conviction, a kind of belief, having attached to it a certain quality, a coloration, that gives it a peculiar and powerful grip. Such a feeling makes the context in which most other beliefs, and emotions too, live or die.

For myself, I have often been gripped, and sometimes puzzled too, by a sense of the *goodness* of things, of being surrounded everywhere by something that is good. C. S. Lewis, who perhaps saw into his own life more deeply than I do into mine, called his autobiography *Surprised by Joy*. I have often been, and still am, surprised by goodness. People who know me know that I have had disappointments and sorrows, and also that in my life there are many things badly done and others wrongly done. Despite those things, it seems that I have often found myself (and lately more often than before) with a sense—a conviction—of being surrounded by something good that I can hardly grasp, perhaps a love to which I can so far respond in only the most rudimentary way. And maybe the "despite" in the preceding sentence is not exactly right. For this sense of a goodness and a love in the world sometimes seems to come, to me anyway, in a way that envelops the other elements and does not merely push them aside. Maybe it "supervenes" upon them and makes them a part of something new and different.

I know that in thinking of my experience in this way, I am making use of ideas that are not original with me. They are largely drawn from the Christian faith—ideas like those of the goodness of God, of the Divine love for the whole creation and for every individual in it, of redemption and forgiveness, and of hope and a new life. But that kind of thing seems to me to be a regular and common feature of human experience. The kinds of experience that we can have depend in part—only in part, but there really is that part dependence—on the ways we have of thinking about our experience, of bringing it into consciousness. And none of us invents a whole intellectual life from scratch. A few of us invent a little, but mostly we try the ideas that are presented to us and gradually choose those that seem to make the most sense out of what happens to us and what are the deepest convictions in us. At least, so it seems to me. And, for better or worse, that is what I too am doing.

Well, so much for that. How did I come to where I am now? Our home, when I was growing up, was not especially religious. My father was a refugee immigrant to the United States, an ethnic Greek from Turkey. He was nominally Greek Orthodox, but he had almost no noticeable interest in the church or anything connected with it. My mother had grown up as a Catholic in Ireland, but in the United States she drifted into Protestant circles. For a while, she and I attended a Presbyterian "home mission" Sunday school held in a two-room adobe schoolhouse in the Rio Grande Valley south of Albuquerque, New Mexico. It was there, I think, that I made my first entry into the Christian faith.

I say "I think." That is because there was no crisis, no traumatic conversion experience in which my life was suddenly overturned. Or at least, there was no such experience that I now remember. In the Gospel of John, Jesus is reported as saying that "no one can see the kingdom of God without being born from above" (John 3:3). During my late teens and throughout the first part of my adult life, almost all of my church connections were with churches that emphasized the "born-again" experience. But I myself could not point to a particular time at which that had happened to me. That naturally generated some tension—mostly within me. But it is in that same conversation that Jesus also draws the analogy to which I alluded earlier, the analogy between the new birth and the wind. Some shifts in the wind are readily noticed, and people who live through a hurricane or a tornado will probably not easily forget the onset of those storms. But there are also times when we look back and say to ourselves, "There must have been a change in the wind back there, but I guess I didn't notice it all that much at the time. Just the same, I seem to be on a different course now." I think that happens in life too, or at least in some lives. And that is how I have come to think of my own beginning in the Christian faith.

My undergraduate college career involved three institutions—the University of New Mexico, New Mexico State College, and (for my last two years) Oregon State College. And during that time, especially in my junior and senior years, that earlier shift in the wind turned into something stronger, something that actually began to make a difference to me.

At Oregon State I got into a great church—at least, it was great for me— First Baptist of Corvallis. The pastor, a man named Hart, seemed to me to combine deep personal spirituality with intellectual honesty and achievement. He was a fine preacher and also a fine teacher of the Bible. I learned a lot from him—more, I'm sure, than I can now identify in detail—and his example encouraged me to go on to learn on my own. And it was in that church that I was baptized.

During those two years, I also began thinking about some philosophical problems related to the Chritian faith—about philosophical attacks on the Christian view of the world and of human life, about Christian apologetics, and about Christian philosophy more generally.

I think that Oregon State, when I was there, had no program in philosophy. At any rate, I didn't do any formal work in philosophy during my undergraduate career. But I did read, on my own, some contemporary Christian philosophical writers, people such as C. S. Lewis, Edward John Carnell, and Carl F. H. Henry. I also began reading some classical philosophers who had a lot to say about religious topics. I can remember trying to muddle through Anselm, Descartes, and Hume. And I was finding, more and more, a desire to get into that conversation myself.

I don't now recall whether, at that time, I was clearly considering philosophy as a possible professional career. At any rate, I don't suppose that question was a major preoccupation of mine as an undergraduate. But I was powerfully attracted by the substance of philosophy, especially as it related to the Christian faith. I was more interested in that than in most of the courses I was taking. I don't remember really being worried that philosophers would refute the faith, or that Christianity might turn out to be fundamentally false after all. I know there are people like that, and I don't disparage those concerns at all. But that is not, so far as I can remember, what happened to me. I didn't have that particular kind of *angst*. But I did think that there ought to be a philosophical response to the philosophical skeptics, and I thought that such a response could be an important part of the evangelistic armory of the church.

To a somewhat lesser degree, I think, I was also interested in how we could use philosophy to improve and deepen our understanding of the Christian faith. But it seems to me that this interest was not, at that time, as strong as the apologetic interest.

I got my bachelor's degree at Oregon State (in food technology!) as World War II was winding down, and I immediately enlisted in the navy, serving for a little more than a year, all of it ashore in the United States. I continued to read philosophy, and by the time I got out of the navy, I had tentatively decided to try for a career in philosophy. Just how I came to that decision, I don't now remember. Maybe in this case too, the beginning was too slight to be much noticed.

At any rate, since I was mostly interested in the religious—indeed, in the Christian—implications and connections of philosophy, I thought I should do some theological study first. So I enrolled at a small theological school, Western Baptist Seminary in Portland, Oregon. Western was strongly oriented toward preparing students for the pastoral ministry. I never did have any serious expectation that I would do that kind of work, so perhaps Western was not the best possible choice for my purposes. But, all in all, I had a useful time there, getting some background in theology, some biblical study, church history, and so on. And at Western I took my first formal philosophy course, the only one that was offered. Stuart Hackett, just beginning his own teaching career, was my first professor in that subject, and I've continued a friendship with him, and with his wife Joan, down to the present.

Looking back to that time in the seminary, three philosophical incidents now stand out. First, I remember a long classroom discussion in which I defended Anselm's ontological argument. Hackett, more aligned with Aristotle, Thomas, and Kant, rejected it. So far as I can recall, that discussion (like a great many others in the history of our discipline) ended without much change of conviction on the part of the participants.

Second, there was the time when Hackett, I, and one or two other students drove down to Stanford to go to a meeting of the American Philosophical Association. It was my first philosophical convention. Hackett gave a paper there, but I don't remember it at all. Probably I had heard the argument earlier. I do remember another paper, though I long ago forgot the author. I suppose he was a logical positivist. Anyway, he maintained that what looked like statements about God were not true, and they were not false either. They just didn't have any meaning at all. I knew something about atheism and its arguments, and about agnosticism, but I guess I had never heard the positivist view before, and the verifiability theory of meaning was news to me. At the time, of course, that unfamiliarity was a symptom of the sketchiness of my own knowledge of the contemporary field. At any rate, I could hardly bring myself to believe that I was understanding the lecturer correctly. I came away thinking that it was the most incredible thing I had ever heard a professor say.

The third incident foreshadowed a concern that has extended throughout my professional career. It was catalyzed by another seminary student who knew of my philosophical interest. He had a friend who was an atheist, and he invited the two of us to his home for a meal and conversation. I was eager to make a rational conversion, so I unloaded on the poor unbeliever an argument that I thought was really strong: a version of C. S. Lewis's moral argument for the existence of God. I was stunned when I saw that the argument was apparently having no bite at all. When the evening ended, the friend was, so far as I know, no closer to theism than when we first met. Maybe that was, for me, the beginning of a long reflection on the role of argument in religious affairs and in human life generally. That concern, somewhat broadened to cover other elements sometimes included under the rubric of "reason," has been one of the main elements in my own philosophical work.

After finishing in the seminary, I worked in Portland for a couple of years. At the same time, I took some undergraduate courses in philosophy to prepare for admission to graduate school. Some of that work I did in night classes at Portland State University, and the rest was by correspondence from various American universities. (I don't think I've ever known of another academic philosopher who did a substantial part of his or her undergraduate work by correspondence. Are there any?) I then started graduate work at the University of Oregon, which at that time had only an M.A. program. After a year there and part-time study for another year, I was admitted to the Ph.D. program at The University of Michigan, and I was awarded a teaching fellowship.

There was only a little graduate work in philosophy of religion at Michigan (and there isn't much now, either). My own transcript doesn't show any course in that subject, though I think I did audit a seminar given by William Alston. Nevertheless, that was the area I wanted for my own work in philosophy, so I wrote a dissertation in it. The general topic of that dissertation—the human experience of the Divine—has continued to be a major interest of mine down to the present.

My first job after earning the Ph.D. degree was at Princeton University. After a year there, I returned to take up a position at The University of Michigan. I have worked there for the rest of my professional career, except for a few fellowships and visiting appointments at other institutions. So most of my education, and almost all of my career as an academic philosopher, have taken place in secular colleges and universities.

Many Christian academics who work in secular institutions struggle with the question of how to integrate their faith with their scholarly work. I suppose that this is, in some sense at least, less problematic in philosophy than in most of the disciplines, and perhaps easiest of all in the philosophy of religion. Since the subject matter of my philosophical work is overtly religion, I suppose I can hardly be blamed for bringing religion into it. And so, almost all of my own work has been generated by my faith, by the problems that it raises, by the ways in which it has been challenged and criticized, and by the challenge that it, in turn, poses for the dominant secular culture. I have been able, by and large, to do the work I love, and to think about and write about the things that really interest me and that drew me into this profession. I can sympathize with Christian colleagues who wonder how to make their work in chemistry, mathematics, or other disciplines distinctively Christian. But my own experience is not of much help to them. In their case, the connections (if they are there at all) are obscure and hidden. In my own field, some of those connections, at least, are fairly obvious.

Throughout most of Western intellectual history, a concern with the problems raised by religious faith and life has been a major element in philosophy. But interests ebb and flow. When I was beginning in philosophy, the philosophy of religion seemed to be a rather minor and old-fashioned piece of intellectual furniture. Using a different metaphor, it was a sort of backwater, just beginning to stir again. But throughout the last thirty years or so, there has been a continuous growth of interest in this field, and now it is again a fairly prominent part of the philosophical scene. I've been fortunate in being able to work with, and learn from, many of the philosophers who have contributed, from the side of Christianity, to this resurgence—people such as William Alston, Alvin Plantinga, Richard Swinburne, James Ross, Nick Wolterstorff, Robert Adams, Marilyn Adams, and many others. Those people have made my field of philosophical work an exciting one for three decades. I'm glad to have been, and still to be, a part of it.

16

FAITH SEEKING

UNDERSTANDING

Merold Westphal

It was love at third sight.

During my senior year in high school my English teacher decided, I know not why, that I should read Plato's *Republic*. She set it up as a special project for me, which I attacked with vigor but without much success. Lacking someone to help me see what was going on in the text, I easily worked my way through its minefields without triggering any explosions of insight. My seduction by philosophy did not begin with love at first sight.

Still, when I got to college, I immediately signed up for an introduction to philosophy course. This time I had some help, and I fared a little better. There was more confusion than comprehension on this second date, and though I was intrigued by what was going on in these strange texts, I was not infatuated. It was not love at second sight either.

Still, at the end of that semester, I talked a young woman I had dated off and on into taking a philosophy course (we celebrated our thirty-first anniversary in the summer of 1993), and when fall came, I signed up for a year-long course in the history of philosophy. My sophomore year was a heavy one academically; I was taking eighteen hours of coursework. But I soon discovered that I was spending about half of my time on the history of philosophy and the other half on the other fifteen hours. And I soon began to notice that although I was a history major, my bookshelf looked more like that of a philosophy major. I had fallen. It was love at third sight.

It was my good fortune that Art Holmes, a contributor to this volume, played the role of Cupid in this seduction. Long before I read Rorty, I learned from him that philosophy was a conversation that spanned the centuries; and long before I read Gadamer, I learned from him that texts were the embodiment, not the entombment, of tradition, and that as such, they addressed their readers with claims that put the readers and their world in question.

Art Holmes was a Nietzschean, though he would not have put it quite this way. I mean simply that he affirmed, with Nietzsche, both that our thinking is inescapably perspectival and that the goal of objectivity was to be pursued, not by trying to escape perspective in a Platonic flight from the body or a Cartesian flight from history and tradition, but in a conversational multiplying of perspectives.

All of these insights were placed in the context of the most important thing I learned from Art: that for the committed Christian believer, philosophy could be faith seeking understanding. Long before I came to philosophy, I had come to a Christian faith that was the center of my life. It provided my metaphysics and my ethics, though I didn't use that language to talk about it. Although I had grown up in a Christian family, my faith had become a personal commitment enacted in a life of regular worship and of daily prayer and Bible reading. I was a Sunday School teacher and choir director before I became a philosopher. I sang the four-part harmony of gospel quartets before I learned the fourfold theory of causality in Aristotle.

The encounter of such a young believer with philosophy is often traumatic, precisely because philosophical texts are not so much objects to be studied as subjects that put their readers in question. This trauma is especially likely to be violent and destructive in the case of those whose faith has been shaped by the anti-intellectual fundamentalism in which I grew up. My father never really understood what philosophy was all about, but he had been taught that it was nothing more than the enemy of faith, a sophisticated form of rebellion against God.

My mother, more intellectually gifted than my father, had come to the same conclusion on her own, thanks to a professor at Barnard College who shamelessly ridiculed religious believers in his classes. He convinced her that the relation between faith and philosophical reason was an unqualified either/or, but having won the battle, he lost the war. For she threw away her Phi Beta

Kappa key and went to Bible school to prepare for missionary work in China. (I owe my life to the mosquito that gave her malaria, sending her home to meet and marry my father.)

To their dying days, neither my father nor my mother was able to reconcile my philosophical vocation with the fact that I continued to profess the faith, to be active in the church, to pray, and to teach our children the faith. Instead of rejoicing that there were Christian philosophers quite unlike the one who had almost cost her her faith, my mother comforted herself with Proverbs 22:6: "Train up a child in the way he should go, and when he is old he will not depart from it." She continued to hope that eventually I would abandon philosophy and come back to the true faith.

I was reminded of all this recently, when I noticed a bumper sticker on my way home from work. It read: "God said it; I believe it; that ends it." I wondered if I had taken a wrong turn and somehow ended up at the buckle of the Bible Belt. But a quick look around assured me that I was on the Throgs Neck Bridge, suspended between the Bronx and Queens, well within the city limits of New York. I asked myself what it is that gets ended in this way, and, given my background it was not hard to figure out. The function of the hermeneutical theory so succinctly put is to terminate conversation and critical reflection. By terminating conversation with those who do not share one's specific interpretation of the faith, one pretty much terminates the possibility of critical reflection on the truth, meaning, and relative significance of the various components of one's theology, rendering one's current understanding of the faith final for all intents and purposes. Ironically, the quest for certainty that motivates this posture is anything but philosophically innocent. It is more like a cross between Plato and Descartes dressed up in its Sunday-go-to-meetin' clothes.

It is just because my own faith was originally nurtured in this pious hostility to conceptual reflection, unknowingly but deeply infected with modernity's neurotic need for absolute certainty, that the most important thing I learned from Art Holmes was that philosophy could be faith seeking understanding. If one does not assume from the outset, with my parents and my mother's professor, that faith and philosophical reflection are inherently antagonistic, the possibility of discovering another relation remains open. It was precisely that opening that has been Art's greatest gift to me and to so many others. I am happy to say that as I write these words a *Festschrift* in his honor, appropriately entitled *Christian Perspectives on Religious Knowledge* (Grand Rapids: Eerdmans, 1993), is in press.

Toward the end of my senior year, I was accepted for graduate study in philosophy at Yale. I have always assumed that my having won a Woodrow Wilson Fellowship played an important, even decisive, role in that admission, for my undergraduate department was an entirely unknown quantity to the department at Yale. The interview that led to the fellowship is an important part of the story of my vocational entrance into the academy. Due to a corker of a blizzard, compounded by a flat tire and a trunk frozen shut, I was over an hour late for the interview. I figured I was doomed but discovered that I was one of only a few who made it at all.

The four interviewers placed me in a rather uncomfortable situation. I was at the center of a semicircle, while they sat at 9, 11, 1, and 3 o'clock, respectively. I couldn't face all of them at once, and had to turn my back on 9 o'clock to talk to 3 o'clock. They seemed entirely uninterested in philosophy, and for quite a while we talked only of the trip through the Middle East I had taken the previous summer as part of my job in a travel agency. Suddenly, out of nowhere, came the question, stated in the indicative: "I suppose if Catholics had written the Bill of Rights, we wouldn't have religious liberty in the Constitution."

I knew immediately what the questioner was up to. He was worried that my training in a conservative Protestant college might have left me with a sectarian narrowness that would get in the way of serious graduate study. Perhaps he was aware that the unabashedly pro-Nixon posture of our college president in the 1960 election had not been free of anti-Catholic bias against Kennedy. I replied, "I don't know what the Bill of Rights would look like if it had been written by Catholics, but I do know that the first colony to practice religious toleration was the Baltimore colony, founded by Roman Catholics."

Although we continued to talk about a variety of matters for a while longer, it was clear that the interview was over at that point and that it had been successful. This was a double moment of truth for me. First, I realized that my undergraduate experience, which would hardly be described as latitudinarian, had actually been a broadening and stretching experience. Among the few colloquial German phrases my father passed on to me from his farm days in northwestern Minnesota was *die verdammte Katholische,* spoken as a single word, referring to "them" as the damned Catholics. My teachers had helped me to see the world more openely than either my father or our college president were able to see it. I had begun to see that the walls erected to keep "us" safe could function as blinders, and that I didn't need to cling blindly to them lest I see something dangerous.

Second, I learned that the secular academy was not incorrigibly biased against those with religious faith. In spite of their nervousness about my religious training, my interviewers had not prejudged me. They had taken the trouble to find out who I was and to take me as I was. I learned to expect the academy to practice the openness and toleration it preached. That expectation has not always been fulfilled, and I have encountered rather blatant antireligious bias here and there, but happily for me, that came only after my graduate experience. I found Yale to be a genuinely liberal place. I was more fortunate than my mother in this regard, though in retrospect, I am tempted to believe that under the guidance of divine providence, her bad experience played an important role in making my good experience possible.

In those ways, Yale was a wonderfully pluralistic place to study philosophy. The faculty may not have loved one another very much, but they were splendidly diverse, and the ethos among the graduate students (assisted, no doubt, by the structure of the comprehensive exams) was to take it all very seriously and to build a broad base. So I worked hard under the likes of John Smith, Paul Weiss, Wilfrid Sellars, Russ Hanson, Rulon Wells, and Dick Bernstein.

IN RETROSPECT, I think I would have to say that I became a Kantian in graduate school, though whether it was because of or in spite of my unusual introduction to the serious study of the first *Critique,* I can't say. I had the rare experience of getting all the way through it, though not in a single semester. My first course, taught by Wilfrid Sellars, was typical in that it only covered the first (smaller) half of the book, through the Transcendental Analytic. It might well have been entitled "Kant's Theory of Mental Acts," for every class produced a blackboard full of small circles (representing mental objects) to which were attached little squiggles (representing mental acts). What it most reminded me of was my junior high sex education class, with diagrams of eggs under attack by sperm.

The following year, John Smith taught a course that was, perhaps by design, the perfect complement. It began with the Transcendental Dialectic, and we read the entire second (larger) half of the book. Out of this double dose I emerged something of a Kantian, for one of the first essays I published was a piece in *Kant-Studien* defending Kant's theory of the thing in itself, and one of my most recent essays, written for the Holmes *Festschrift,* is entitled "Christian Philosophers and Copernican Revolution," which argues that the former should be friendly rather than hostile, as so many are, to the latter.

My dissertation was on Hegel's *Phenomenology of Spirit,* which culminates in the claim to surpass Kantian finitism in the historical emergence of spirit's self-consciousness as Absolute Knowledge, bridging the gap between subject and object, thought and being, self and other. I found the argument important and intriguing but not convincing.

More important, I found that the issue was deeply theological. My reading of Kant had shown me that the distinction between appearances and things in themselves was the distinction between the world as it appears to us and the world as it appears (or would appear) to the mind of a divine creator. Insofar as Hegel's Kant critique did not thematize this issue, it avoided any direct contact with Kant's theory. At the same time, it offered an alternative account in which the distinction between the human and divine minds was a distinction between two modes of the human mind. The resulting dilemma is quite simple. Either, as appearances suggest, the divine, absolute mode of human thought has not been achieved, in which case Kantian dualism and finitism have not been surpassed; or, appearances to the contrary notwithstanding, that mode of human thought has been achieved, in which case "we" have somehow become absolute, history has reached its culmination, and modern society is the long-awaited Kingdom of God.

For me the appearances to the contrary withstood, and I found myself siding with Kant against Hegel's claim to have surpassed him and, in the process, to have given a philosophical transcription of a deep truth of the Christian faith. Kantian thought seemed to me a far better expression of the biblical theme of the radical difference between the divine and the human as creator and created, and of the apostolic reminder of the epistemological consequences of this difference, that we hold whatever truth we possess in "clay jars" or "earthen vessels" (2 Cor. 4:7) and that we see "in a mirror dimly" or "through a glass darkly" (1 Cor. 13:12).

In other words, my journey through the Kant–Hegel debate had been one of faith seeking understanding, of finding in Kantian theory a philosophical vocabulary for a view of things already implicit in my religious faith. Was this just a matter of theological premises dictating philosophical conclusions? It seemed to me (and still does) that Kant had the better of the philosophical argument, but I will not try to claim that when I entered graduate school, I simply shed my religious identity and encountered the great texts of German idealism as an abstract thinker who was neither a believer nor an unbeliever but some kind neutral, pure intellect. I didn't think then and I don't think now either that we ought to try to do that or that, if we were to try, we would be able to perform this self-denying ordinance, this dehumanizing of ourselves. So I am not eager to deny that my religious faith played a role in my choosing Kant over Hegel.

But I do not think the process is very well described as "just a matter of theological premises dictating philosophical conclusions," and this for two reasons. First, while Kant's finitism matched nicely with certain elements of my theological background, it fitted very badly with others. Both my informal and my formal (undergraduate) theological training had placed great emphasis on biblical revelation as indispensable for our knowledge of God and of ourselves. One of my teachers had been fond of saying that the Bible is the "divinely revealed misinformation about God," making the essentially Kantian point that biblical revelation comes to us in human language and that it enables us to think humanly, but not divinely, about God. But another of my teachers claimed that what we know about God through biblical revelation, though it may be quantitatively less than God knows, is qualitatively on a par with God's own self-knowledge. While my new-found Kantianism helped me to understand the former motif in my faith, it required me to abandon the latter.

This latter motif was no small part of the faith I brought with me to philosophy. Ironically, as previously mentioned, the fundamentalism that prided itself on remaining biblical in the face of "the corrosive acids of modernity" had been, as Hegel (yes, Hegel) helped me to see, powerfully shaped by the Enlightenment and its quest for certainty. Its biblicism often took a foundationalist form that differed from the secularism it attacked only on the question of whether the first principles of thought come from reason or revelation, but shared without question an essentially rationalist view of the status and role of those first principles.

The relation between my faith and my philosophy, it seems to me, was circular. My faith disposed me toward one philosophical theme rather than another, but that theme, in turn, reacted on my faith and caused me to reconstrue it. I was beginning to learn (1) that the religious world I had grown up in was often a world of myth, in Camus's sense of the term, a world of all answers and no questions; (2) that bumper sticker theology cannot convincingly bring an end to conversation and critical reflection on the truth, meaning, and relative significance of the various components of one's theology;

and (3) that the task I had set for myself under the rubric of faith seeking understanding was likely to be the task of a lifetime.

There is a second reason why I don't think my experience is very well described as "just a matter of theological premises dictating philosophical conclusions." My Kantianism opened a kind of philosophical Pandora's box that was enlarged and, one might say, exacerbated the circular movement between faith's preunderstanding and philosophy's self-examination. One who has seen the force of Kantian finitism, inspired as it is by an essentially theistic view of the world, cannot simply dismiss other expressions of finitism, even when they are quite differently motivated. Thus I have found it necessary to take seriously such theories, often motivated by unbelief and just as often perceived as threats to the life of faith, as Nietzsche's perspectivism, Heidegger's hermeneutical circle, and Derrida's deconstruction based on *différance*. If there is ultimately a theological rationale for my serious exploration of these powerful secular forms of finitism—variations, if you will, on a Kantian theme—it is clear that this is possible only where there is a willingness to be put in question. However imperfect is my practice of this willingness, I have come to see it as an essential ingredient in faith as a virtue.

Faith's self-understanding is likely to be changed in the process. My own faith has continued to be central to my being-in-the-world, but it has not been a fixed and final point impervious to reinterpretation. Faith in the unchangeableness of God does not entail the unchangeableness of faith itself, for faith is not so much my holding on to God as it is my willingness to let God hold on to me. Such faith includes the trust that in this process one's relation to God will be deepened rather than destroyed, and that has been my experience. I don't have the world on a string (or God in a box), as I did when I first came to philosophy. But I am convinced that I understand both God and myself better because of these losses. What Jesus said about finding our life through losing it has many meanings, one of which, in my experience, pertains to the life of the believer engaging in philosophical reflection (Matt. 10:39, 16:25). We have a similar experience when we discover that human relations, such as marriage, are so much richer when we abandon the effort always to be in control.

VERY EARLY IN my teaching career I got a real plum, the opportunity to teach the Kant seminar. But at the last minute I was asked to teach Kierkegaard instead, for which I was dramatically less well prepared. It turned out to be Providence rather than preparation that paved the way, for the seminar was an exhilarating experience and the beginning of a process of reading, reflecting, teaching, and writing that continues to the present day to shape and challenge both my life and my thought.

I couldn't easily summarize all I have learned from Kierkegaard. Probably the most pervasive theme has been that of sin as an epistemological category. For Kierkegaard as for Kant, the distinction between human and divine thought is fundamental. The claims (explored by his various pseudonyms) that faith is absurd, paradoxical, contradictory, madness, and so forth, are all dramatic attempts to highlight the radical divergence between what makes sense when God is figured into the equation and what makes sense when God is left out. If the latter insists on calling itself Reason, Kierkegaard asks, why not identify faith as the Paradox in order to avoid the master illusion of Christendom? That would be the illusion that one still lives the life of faith even after God has been effectively eliminated as an independent agent in the language games and social practices that constitute both one's world and one's self.

For Kierkegaard's epistemology as for Kant's, the difference that really makes a difference is that between the divine and the human. But they view this difference differently. Kierkegaard does not deny the finitude that is the heart of the Kantian analysis; but he subordinates it to a more radical rift between ourselves and God, our sinfulness, which he understands as our desire to domesticate God to the point of being useful without being a nuisance. He points out the workings of this desire, not just in our behavings but in our believings as well. Hence the contrast between "humanly understood" and "divinely understood."

I found in Kierkegaard a powerful expression of the noetic effects of sin, a theme already familiar to me from St. Paul (Romans 1) and Calvin. Once again, faith was shaping my philosophical journey; but, once again, there was a retroactive movement as well. My Christendom was a blend of conservative Protestantism, the *Reader's Digest,* and a Republicanism that wasn't sure of the patriotism of the moderate wing of the party. It might be summarized as complacent conservatism across the board. It was not by any means complacent about the world in which we lived, threatened as it was by Rockefeller Republicans, Democrats, and communists. But, like Kierkegaard's Christendom, it was complacent about its own beliefs and practices, whose heavenly good housekeeping seal of approval was never in doubt and never to be doubted.

There were many experiences that challenged this complacency: an historian friend with a very different understanding of Christian faith, my first direct encounters with urban African-Americans (including welfare families, Black Panthers, and pentecostal Christians), the social and political turmoil of the late 1960s and early 1970s in both its civil rights and anti-Vietnam War moments, and my own discovery of the Hebrew prophets. These experiences proved decisive in giving me a very different understanding of my faith from the one I started out with. It is not that my complacent conservatism was devoid of defenses in the form of strategies whose function was to turn such experiences into confirmations of itself. What made me "vulnerable" to these experiences was in large part the constant reminder from Kierkegaard that the thinking of sincere Christians was not immune to the corruptions of the fall. I was no longer able simply to identify the Christian world view I had inherited with the truth of God. Once Kierkegaard had become the occasion for a shaking of the foundations, significant parts of that edifice came tumbling down like the walls of Jericho.

My politics moved a lot further to the left than my theology. But the form of both changed, along with the content. Having learned the hermeneutics of finitude from Kant et al., and the hermeneutics of suspicion from Kierkegaard et al., I discovered that the confidence of finality I have been calling complacency was not the appropriate mode for holding to any politics or theology. I don't mean to say that I was instantly cured of all intellectual arrogance, only that my new certainties were constantly challenged to submit to the kind of cross-examination that had overtaken the earlier ones. I was learning that the life of belief is a journey, and that "living happily ever after," noetically speaking, comes at the end of the story and not in the middle.

Kierkegaard et al.? Just as the theistically inspired finitism of Kant opened the door for me to the secular postmodernisms of Nietzsche, Heidegger, and Derrida, so the Christianly inspired suspicion of Kierkegaard opened the door for me to the secular "masters of suspicion," as Ricoeur has called them— Marx, Nietzsche, and Freud. The process described in the previous paragraph has its philosophical origin in Kierkegaard, but that point of departure was broadened and deepened by intensive study of the other three. They proved to be my worst friends, the kind everyone needs—to tell you what you best friends won't tell you, about your bad breath and dandruff. I found them to echo in the context of modernity the kind of critique originally directed by Jesus, the prophets who preceded him, and the apostles who succeeded him to those who saw themselves as the covenant people of God. These great modern atheists helped me to discover a dimension of the biblical message I had not noticed much before.

So it is that one of the strange results of my experience of faith seeking understanding is that my latest book, *Suspicion and Faith: The Religious Uses of Modern Atheism* (Grand Rapids: Eerdmans, 1993), is a sustained appeal to the Christian church to take the religion critiques of this unholy trio seriously rather than simply trying to refute or discredit them, to read them as a kind of Lenten spiritual exercise in self-examination. It seems to me that their deeply hostile and unflattering accounts of the personal and corporate life of Christians is all too true all too much of the time. I don't think it is the whole truth, as they are inclined to suggest, but the best way to show this, I think, is not to argue against their theories but to submit to their discipline and relearn to live the life of faith in ways less vulnerable to their critiques. If there is more to the life of faith than self-deception in the service of self-interest, the best demonstration of this is not proof but practice.

THERE HAS ALWAYS been a strong element of pietism in my religious life. Orthodoxy, in the sense of thinking rightly about God, oneself, and one's world, so far as one is able, has been and continues to be important to me. But this has never been antithetically related to the experiential dimension of faith. For me, believing has always been linked to seeing God at work in the world, not least in one's own life, and to hearing God's voice speaking words of comfort, direction, reproof, and so forth. I've never understood this to be restricted to one hour a week on Sunday morning (important as public worship is to the life of faith), but rather as something to be woven into the warp and woof of daily life. For this reason, a daily practice of prayer and Bible reading has been part of my Christian identity BP and AP (before and after philosophy became a part of my identity).

Against this background, Pascal's distinction between the God of the philosophers and the God of Abraham, Isaac, and Jacob has always seemed to me to have a point. I could not worship a God to whom I could not pray, and prayer, for me, presupposes a God personal enough both to speak and to hear. (If it is possible, as I have found it possible, to pray to the One than whom a greater cannot be conceived and who cannot be conceived not to exist, this is no doubt due to the fact that it was in prayer that Anselm discovered these formulas.)

While the experiential orientation of my faith originally was personalistic in the sense of individualistic, it has come to include a collective dimension as well. Partly from my experience of team spirit as an athlete and sports fan and partly from my growing philosophical realization (in which Hegel has played an important part) that we are not selves all by ourselves or even just in one-on-one situations, I have come to view experience as having both I and we as its subject, not always easily distinguishable. Correspondingly, the corporate dimensions of the religious life have become more important to me. The petition "Forgive us our debts" no longer parses for me simply as "Forgive me my debts, and forgive him his debts, and forgive her her debts," and so forth. So, while the experiential pole has been constantly present in my religious life, it has not been fixed or static.

When this side of my faith has sought understanding, it has found itself drawn to phenomenological approaches, those that, in the words of Paul Ricoeur, let the believing soul speak. Quite early on, I developed a philosophy of religion course oriented more to description than to argument. It was built around the question What does it mean to be religious? By bracketing the question of truth (but not because it is unimportant) and focusing on the question of meaning, and by asking about the meaning, not of a proposition, but of a way of life or a mode of being-in-the-world, this course distinguished itself sharply from traditional philosophy of religion courses focused on proofs for the existence of God and objections to them, including the argument from evil and responses to it. I didn't consider such courses inappropriate; I just found this other way of doing philosophy of religion more in tune both with my ongoing work in the so-called continental traditions in philosophy and with the pietistic dimension of my faith. (Had my philosophical orientation been different, I might have explored the experiential side of my religious life by seeking to develop arguments designed to show that the claims in religious experience talk are not inherently irrational. But I would never have written a book as brilliant as Bill Alston's *Perceiving God*.)

I understood the question What does it mean to be religious? to be something like Thomas Nagel's famous question, What is it like to be a bat? The working assumption was not that the religious life is as far removed from the normal undergraduate's experience as is bat life, though in some cases that would not have been entirely wide of the mark. The assumption was rather that regardless of the degree to which our own life is religious, we can listen to the believing soul as he or she tells, in various ways, what it is like to be religious, and we can conversationally bring what we hear into touch with our own experience to see where we find it familiar or strange, inviting or repelling, compelling or insipid, and so forth. Needless to say, much of what we read was not found in either the standard philosophical canon or the standard philosophy of religion literature. I quickly discovered that to listen to the believing soul in this way was not simply to hear the echo of my own voice, but to encounter another whose dealings with the divine were sometimes similar to but often quite different from my own.

This course gave rise eventually to a book, *God, Guilt, and Death.* In three important ways, this book gives witness to my own journey of faith giving itself over to reflection. Methodologically, the subtitle is of crucial importance: *An Existential Phenomenology of Religion.* The approach is phenomenological in the descriptive, experiential, meaning-oriented senses already mentioned. But phenomenology, in its original Husserlian form, was an attempt to make philosophy into rigorous science, and I was neither religiously nor philosophically sympathetic to such a project. For me, the point of letting the believing soul speak was to encounter possibilities rather than to establish certainties. While I had qualms about the term, I could find none better than *existential* to signify this difference of purpose. Like Socrates, I had come to view philosophy more in terms of opening oneself to questions than in terms of giving apodictic answers, just as I had come to view faith more as opening oneself to God than as finding final formulas about God. (Incidentally, *Suspicion and Faith,* mentioned briefly above, is the methodological complement to this book, in which the believing soul, who had first been allowed to speak more or less without interruption, is subjected to hostile cross-examination.)

Second, there is the main title of the book. When I first proposed it, my editor said, "Let's get sex in there somewhere and make it a best-seller." I suggested that we would have an interesting title if we substituted sex for any of the three key terms. Since then I've received considerable criticism about the title, usually from those who have not read the book. But it points to some of my most exciting discoveries (1) about the meaning of guilt and death in relation to human identity, (2) about the intimate linkage between the two, and (3) about the virtually universal centrality of these issues as questions (though the answers are widely divergent indeed) to religious experience in contexts far beyond the biblical tradition that was my point of departure.

The exploration of this latter point involved me in extensive study in the history of religions, living and dead, East and West, and so forth. In this way the question What does it mean to be religious? has become the question What does it mean to be a Buddhist?, What does it mean to be an animist?, What does it mean to be an ancient Egyptian priest?, What does it mean to be a Sioux sage?, and so forth. Thus the search for understanding of my own faith has brought me into conversation with religious texts, traditions, and experiences very different from my own. Reflections on the significance of these encounters could be the subject of an entirely separate essay.

Finally, there is the discovery that surprised me most. As a concern with solving the problem(s) of guilt and death, religion is clearly interested and, we might say, self-centered. My dealings with the divine are motivated by and directed toward gaining what the Apostle's Creed identifies as "the forgiveness of sins, the resurrection of the dead, and the life everlasting." Across an enormously wide variety of traditions, religion is understood as having some form of this instrumental character.

But at the same time, I found the ever-renewed protest against reducing the religious life to its instrumental character, making it vulnerable to Satan's question, "Doth Job fear God for nought?" (Job 1:9, KJV). In response to the persistent question What's in it for me?, whose prevalence in American religion today may make the churches as secular as the secular humanisms against which they rail, there arises again and again the reply, Some practices are justified simply by being appropriate. I have come to call this dimension of the religious life *useless self-transcendence*. Here piety is useless in the sense of not having its value as a means to some end; and it is self-transcendence, not because it relates to the Transcendent (which can be an entirely ego-centered project), but because it involves a decentering of the self that always aspires to be the center of the world.

To speak of useless self-transcendence is to talk like a philosopher. To that charge I plead guilty. But this language comes back to me as the meaning of Jesus' summary of the law as the commandment to love God and to love one's neighbor as oneself (Matt. 22:34–40). In a strange way it gives me a certainty, in a world of reflection where certainties are rare, of something I have never doubted, namely, that this norm, whether in the language of the Hebrew Bible that Jesus was quoting or in the language of phenomenological reflection, is the deepest meaning of my life. Since even a minimal grasp of this notion is sufficient to dispel all illusions that one has fulfilled it, I have found this certainty to be a persistent enemy of complacency.

The concept of useless self-transcendence is not an argument for the rationality of religious belief. But it is a challenge to every rationality, sacred or secular, that functions to make the human self or the human community the possessor and dispenser of Truth. At the same time it summarizes, perhaps better than anything else, what my faith has found as it has sought understanding, namely, that faith is the task of a lifetime. The present narrative ends here, but the story it has tried to tell goes on. As those who know me best will gladly attest, God isn't finished with me yet.

17

WHEN THE TIME

HAD FULLY COME

Spencer Carr

This essay is a bit of an interloper in this volume, I am afraid. In the first place, I am not a professional philosopher. I am, as I like to say, a recovering philosopher, for although I did study and even teach philosophy for a while, for the last fifteen years I have been making an honest living as an editor in scholarly publishing.

Second, I am a newly (re)converted Christian, so I am very much more at the beginning of the project of working out the issues of faith and reason than are the other contributors to this book. Indeed, several of the essays in this volume, which I had the chance to read in manuscript form, have been influential in my first tentative steps in this direction. Nevertheless the problem has loomed large in my life for a long time, as will become clear.

MY EARLIEST CHURCHLY memory is of my mother, my brother, and me arriving one fall Sunday morning at a deserted and locked church. Bewilderment
gave way to chagrin as it dawned on us that we had failed to turn our clocks
back for the end of daylight savings time and had arrived too early for the
services. It was not to be my last spiritual misfire.

I recall later a period during which Mother sent my brother and me to
Sunday school. At my instigation, we can be sure, my brother and I took to
spending the time high in the branches of a large tree, from which we could
see the church letting out so that we would know when it was time to return
home. This worked well for several weeks before our teacher remarked to
Mother that she missed seeing the boys at church. Though I do not remember
it, I am told that the punishment for this was immediate, severe, and definitely
corporal. To Mother's credit, she decided that if she herself didn't care to
attend church, it wasn't fair to continue to insist that her children do so.

Despite these tentative efforts, more culturally than spiritually inspired,
religion was simply not a part of our life. There was, for example, not even a
token Bible in our home.

THESE EARLY FLIRTATIONS were with the Methodists, but religion first became
important to me in high school when I fell in love with a Baptist girl and
started attending that church. The Baptists seemed to take their religion more
seriously than did the Methodists in our town, and for various reasons I was
ready to respond.

Partly, I suspect, it was adolescent rebellion. I was an awfully "good" kid,
responsible and hard-working, and it isn't easy for such a youth to find a
good way to rebel against his parents. Others smoked, drank, drove fast cars,
and stayed out all night. But conservative Christianity worked just fine for
me; it drove my folks nuts. And when I announced that I planned to become a
missionary or a minister, it was "Where have we failed?" time for my poor
parents.

In retrospect, I think that I was also rejecting a set of values that I had
picked up, one emphasizing success, not to say perfection, in all endeavors.
While I still felt driven at some level to be the best at everything I did (and our
town was small enough that I could come close enough to this ideal to mask
its insanity), church was a repose that stressed the possibility, nay the necessity, of failure, forgiveness, and ultimate worth despite the failure.

Although I cannot at this remove be completely sure of the quality of my
spiritual life, I know that this was a serious commitment. Bible study, prayer,
and church camp were all important to me. *Mere Christianity* became like
second scripture, and I remember reading the sermons of nineteenth-century
preachers from a book my minister loaned me. I sang in the choir, taught
Sunday school to junior high students, and delivered a sermon to the congregation on Youth Day.

The church was not relentlessly fundamental, but neither was it enlightened. I remember asking our minister who wrote the Book of Job. He had to go look it up, and I was informed the next Sunday that it was Moses. I don't remember whether I was skeptical.

My best friend during those years was my girl friend's father, a fine man who combined a fundamentalist faith with liberal social and political views, as well as what I remember as unfailing generosity and good cheer. For some reason I remember one particular conversation in which Bob denounced beauty pageants as demeaning to women, one view among many that marked him as a bit of an eccentric. So far as I know, Bob hadn't read any early feminists; he spoke from a natural sensitivity and generosity, and he was not afraid of unusual or unpopular ideas. Later, he sold his (at best) marginally profitable five and ten cent store to attend seminary. He spent the last years of his life as pastor of a small country church in Washington State. I know they were the happiest years of his life, and I am confident that they were good ones for that church as well.

But in the meantime I had fallen away. Bob had predicted this. He always told me that my faith was overly intellectual, that it was based upon arguments and reasons that would always prove vulnerable to other arguments, other reasons, other intellectual fashions. It took just a year away at college to prove him right.

I arrived at Occidental College as a pretheological philosophy major, and I remember clearly that I was a philosophy major rather than a religion major simply because I felt that a religion major was not sufficiently respectable. I had no idea what philosophy was, but it sounded good and impressed people. This was just one of many decisions in a pattern of choosing a path with an eye to impressing others rather than to what best suited my own interests or talents, and I eventually paid heavily for it.

The first philosophy course I took was an anachronism even by the mid-1960s. It was in all its essentials an immersion in logical positivism. The teacher wielded the verifiability principle, the analytic–synthetic distinction, and other positivist paraphernalia against all things metaphysical, superstitious, and religious. At the time it seemed a breath of fresh Ayer; the professor enjoyed it hugely, and it was infectious; it was probably the most popular course on campus. (Sadly, three years later this exceptionally likable man and gifted teacher was dead by suicide.)

My religious belief was not up to this powerful conception of philosophy; indeed, the only students who were able to resist seemed to do so by compartmentalizing faith and reason. I couldn't do that, and decided to put away what I took to be the childish things of faith. I do not remember how suddenly this happened or just how I came to this decision. I do remember telling the college chaplain that I was withdrawing from the campus religious community and, in what may have passed for counseling in his vocabulary, his only reaction was to call me a horse's ass.

I paid the consequences of a year's depression and withdrawal from most of life. Narrowly avoiding flunking out (and exposure to the Vietnam War draft), I did learn to play a good game of bridge during this time, and I also learned how to drink.

I CAME OUT OF IT, of course, and went off to graduate school committed to atheism. (I recall years later donating a copy of Russell's *Why I Am Not a Christian* to a local library.) This aggressive secularism was certainly reinforced by the intellectual milieu at the University of Michigan, where a religious sentiment would be greeted with just slightly less condescension than, say, an endorsement of Heideggerian metaphysics. There were Christian philosophers, of course, even among the graduate students, so I am unclear how much I may be projecting my own attitudes onto the department as a whole.

Now that I am once again a Christian, the academic prejudice against believers of all kinds, the very prejudice that I once exemplified in spades, strikes me as simply bizarre. It is worth pondering why it is so easy, or even necessary, for academic secularists to attribute disagreement over religion to ignorance or, where that is not plausible, to emotional or even moral weakness. (See Peter van Inwagen's essay in this volume for some fine reflections on this.) Do I exaggerate? Recently, one young philosopher friend of mine confided that she was converting to Judaism, but she swore me to secrecy about it, fearing that her colleagues might learn about it before her tenure decision.

After graduate school, life occasionally turned hard, and in my case, the major crisis was my failure to find a full-time, permanent teaching position in a difficult job market. By this time I was happily married to my college sweetheart, who, to my great good fortune, was enormously patient and generous to her periodically unemployed husband. But by the mid-1970s, I needed more help in dealing with these failures, and while I turned to therapy for a short time, mostly I turned to alcohol.

Eventually, and given the strains, inevitably, my wife and I divorced, and I abandoned my hopes for a scholarly career and made a start in the publishing industry. In many ways, most of them irrelevant to the themes of this essay, I didn't start to grow up until these difficult years of travel, loneliness, forced self-reliance, and business pressures.

Philosophy stood me in good stead in my new career. At the beginning, the analytic training enabled me to write memos about textbook markets that impressed my superiors and led to early promotion to acquiring editor at a major university press. Later, I found that a nose trained for philosophical questions let me converse intelligibly with people in almost any discipline, even those I knew least about. I might not be able to follow, say, an economist's exercise in general equilibrium modeling, but it was usually possible to steer the conversation to a related philosophical issue, where I would be on more familiar ground.

Finally, it turns out, I am sure, that I am a better academic editor than philosopher. One of my weaknesses as a graduate student (and in preparing for the job market) was dilettantism. Rather than settling in and making some small area my very own, I kept being distracted by other topics, other fields. Once I saw, or thought I saw, the general shape of the question or set of issues, I lacked the discipline or the interest to see things through, to see how they worked out in the details. But for an academic editor, dilettantism is not an occupational hazard; it is a job requirement.

There is no tenure in the publishing industry (I miss the summers off, too), and I have worked now for three scholarly presses, acquiring books at one time or another in sociology, economics, geography, political science, philosophy, women's studies, legal studies, and, most recently and most pertinently, religious studies. I enjoy the work immensely, and I treasure both what I have learned and the wide range of friends I have found in all these fields.

BUT BY THE WINTER of 1991–92, I came to realize that I needed help. I was trying to come out of a depression from a relationship that had ended unhappily, and these struggles revealed certain things to me. Most important, I finally accepted that on my own I was not going to be able to lead my life the way I wanted to lead it.

I was especially dissatisfied with the fact that I continued to drink heavily. There are many ways to abuse alcohol. Mine was to put professional responsibilities first and then just to drink as much as possible consistent with those responsibilities. I could refrain from drinking when I had a good reason to do so, but if there was no special reason to refrain, I indulged. I should say that if I was not able to *recognize* a reason, I indulged. For it is only a slight exaggeration to say that the only reasons that ever mattered were those related to business, so the impact of my alcohol abuse was that for many of these years, I had almost no life outside of work. It was all I could do to handle a job that typically demands fifty or more hours a week and my drinking habit as well.

But I knew that this was unhealthy in all kinds of ways, and I felt that I had to find a way to handle my life better. And I began to see that underlying this problem was another one: that I didn't care enough about other people, other values, or myself to see any of this as a reason to stop drinking and attend to them.

It was just at this time that I was asked by my publisher to establish a new line of books in religious studies. So I began to read widely on religious topics at just the time that I felt I was looking for a new way to order my life. As usual, I liked the philosophy best. I used to be astonished that undoubtedly intelligent and talented philosophers might be religious believers; now I was delighted to read the rich literature of analytic philosophy of religion.

How many Christians can say that their most meaningful inspirational reading has been analytic philosophy? (How many would *want* to? I can hear someone asking.) But I was not reading the Bible at this time, and analytic philosophy played a crucial role in leading me to seriously consider religious faith for the first time in thirty years. When I wonder why, I suspect that one reason is a sense of relief that if these people, these fine minds, can be committed to a religious faith, then surely I can have leave to be. I do not like this insight much (it shows how far I have to go to leave behind my childish intellectual insecurity), but I fear that it is right.

Recognizing that I was in trouble and encouraged by these religious writings, mystical as well as analytical, I asked for help. And I was helped. I prayed for God to ease my mind, and I felt eased. I asked for help to control my desire to drink, and gradually I found that help. I asked for help to overcome the insecurities and defensiveness that separated me from others, and I began to feel more open, more loving toward the people around me.

These changes did not happen all at once, nor am I presently in any danger of being mistaken for the reincarnation of St. Francis. But there was no denying a clear change of direction in my life.

Does this mean that I felt God working in my life? In a situation like this, there are always skeptical doubts, fears that what one is feeling can be explained away perfectly naturally without reference to God's agency. But, when I entertained such doubts, I asked myself, what more do you really want? What you prayed for, you have received. Can you really ignore that? Is that playing fair or even being honest with yourself? What kind of sense would it make to accept this short fix and to take the less demanding, but discredited, path of reverting to trying to handle life again on your own terms? No, I really had to continue this journey of exploration.

So I began to read the Bible and to shop the local churches, looking among those Protestant denominations closest to the experiences of my youth. I alternated for a time among Presbyterian, Methodist, and Baptist churches and found much to like in each of them, but to my considerable surprise I have landed in an Episcopal church and in a tradition quite different from what I have known. I am impressed by the fact that my Episcopalian friends there say that we are to use four criteria in arriving at belief: scripture, tradition, reason, and experience. For one needing all the help he can get, this seems most useful. If I were to try to sketch the relationships among these four sources in my own case, I would say that I tend to begin with experience and to apply reason to scripture and tradition to understand and interpret the experience. I am grateful that, despite my initial concerns about possible demands for orthodoxy, my church seems content to let me work out the emphases and interpretations of Christian doctrine that seem best for me.

BACK TO FAITH and reason. The largest difference between my current faith and that of my adolescence is that now I find faith resting most solidly, as I have said, on the wonderful *experiences* I have had and continue to have.

Life has a different quality for me now. Not all the time, but often, and more and more. There are times when I feel a powerful sense of love and goodness spreading over and through me. The sense of well-being, of contentedness, the acceptance of both others and myself, can become almost palpable. I believe that this is God allowing me glimpses of what life with him is like.

I can remember how I used to have a genuinely misanthropic streak. I would pass people on the street whom I had never seen before and suddenly be struck with the most inexplicable conviction that these people were contemptible. It is embarrassing to recall how freely I would project my own self-contempt onto these innocents. I would fix on some aspect of their appearance or demeanor and construct some picture that would justify despising them. The spell would immediately be broken if I came to know them or even to interact with them. But so long as they did not have to be dealt with directly, I could form such feelings.

Today, in what is probably the strongest phenomenological evidence for the change wrought in me, I pass these same strangers and experience strong feelings of warmth and affection for them. I can almost think that they can feel the sympathetic emanations radiating from me. Similarly, in the rituals of church services, in solitary prayer, and in Christian community, I experience a wholeness, a sense of participating in and being in communication with something much larger and better than myself.

So in dealing with faith and reason, I begin with experiences like these as being in some sense basic. My project must not deny these experiences but rather make sense of them.

There are reductive accounts of religious experience, of course, but these mostly appeal to people who do not actually have this sort of experience and so do not have to make sense of its power. It is these experiences, interpreted by reason in the light of scripture and tradition, that lead me inexorably, joyously, to acknowledge the existence of a transcendent being of wonderful power and love.

I have grown up in a Christian culture, however contaminated it may be, and I am for the most part very much at home with its traditions. So it is natural and easy for me to interpret my experience of such a being within a Christian context. But there is no doubt that had I grown up Jewish, in the Arab world, or in India, I would seek, and find, my interpretation in one of the other great religious traditions. I cannot believe that God honors those who reach out to him from the Christian tradition above those who reach out to him from the Jewish, from the Islamic, or from any other tradition. (I am much influenced by John Hick's writings here.) He may even choose to honor New Age metaphysicians, though I find this harder to accept.

The Christian tradition is fascinating, endearing, enriching, and frustrating, and I am grateful for the efforts of those Christian philosophers who explore the boundaries of Christian doctrine, the range of interpretations and possibilities of belief. I rejoice when I see a way to understand a particularly hard doctrine that makes it more acceptable to reason.

I do not know where I will come out (if indeed I ever "come out" anywhere) on questions of, for example, the Incarnation, atonement, or the Trinity. I suspect that with time my faith will grow so that I will come to accept more and more of a traditional Christian theology. But for the time being, I see this as less important, and I find it easier to bracket questions like this as mysteries that may or may not become clearer one day.

Finally, I am struck by Bill Alston's reflections (in this book) on the importance of timing in coming to God. As an adolescent I was surely not sufficiently formed to be ready to become a mature Christian. I do not know that I needed to wait thirty years to take up the task, but perhaps this was necessary. My early religious experience may perhaps be encapsulated in my first memory of having been locked out of the church for having arrived too early. "Not so fast," I can imagine God saying. "You're not ready for this yet."

When I think this way, I cannot but wonder what it all would have meant if perhaps I had not survived long enough to find my way back to God. A little bad luck at a couple of moments in my life, and I would have died outside the Christian faith and without any religious faith at all. What would this have meant? Could that have been God's plan? I have no idea what to say about this except that between faith and reason there is a lot of room for mystery.

Note

I wish to thank Bill Alston, Tom Morris, and my colleague Mary Kay Scott for helpful suggestions on an earlier draft of this essay.

18

THE MIRROR

OF EVIL

Eleonore Stump

There are different ways to tell the story of one's own coming to God. Straightforward autobiography has its merits, but, paradoxically, it can leave out the most important parts. I want to tell my story in a roundabout way that will, I hope, show directly what for me is and always has been the heart of the matter.

For reflective people, contemplation of human suffering tends to raise the problem of evil. If there is an omnipotent, omniscient, perfectly good God, how can it be that the world is full of evil? This response to evil is normal and healthy. I have discussed this problem myself in print and tried to find a solution to it. But there is another way to think about evil.

Consider just these examples of human suffering, which I take from my morning newspaper. Although the

Marines are in Somalia, some armed Somalis are still stealing food from their starving neighbors, who are dying by the thousands. Muslim women and girls, some as young as ten years old, are being raped and tortured by Serb soldiers. In India, Hindus went on a rampage that razed a mosque and killed over 1,000 people. In Afghanistan gunmen fired into a crowded bazaar and shot ten people, inncluding two children. Closer to home, the R. J. Reynolds company is trying to defend itself against charges that it is engaged in a campaign to entice adolescents to smoke. The recently defeated candidate for governor in my state, as well as lawyers and doctors employed by the state as advocates for disabled workers, are charged with stealing thousands of dollars from the fund designed for those workers. A high school principal is indicted on charges of molesting elementary and middle school boys over a period of twenty years. A man is being tried for murder in the death of a nine-year old boy; he grabbed the boy to use as a shield in a gunfight. I could go on—racism, rape, assault, murder, greed and exploitation, war and genocide—but this is enough. By the time you read these examples, they will be dated, but you can find others just like them in your newspaper. There is no time, no part of the globe, free from evil. The crust of the earth is soaked with the tears of the suffering.

This evil is a mirror for us. It shows us our world; it also shows us ourselves. How could anyone steal at gunpoint food meant for starving children? How could anyone rape a ten-year-old girl? How could anyone bear to steal money from disabled workers or get rich by selling a product he knows will damage the health of thousands? But people do these things, and much worse things as well. We ourselves—you and I, that is—are members of the species that does such things, and we live in a world where the wrecked victims of this human evil float on the surface of all history, animate suffering flotsam and jetsam. The author of Ecclesiastes says, "I observed all the oppression that goes on under the sun: the tears of the oppressed with none to comfort them; and the power of their oppressors—with none to comfort them. Then I accounted those who died long since more fortunate than those who are still living" (4:1–2).[1]

Some people glance into the mirror of evil and quickly look away. They take note, shake their heads sadly, and go about their business. They work hard, they worry about their children, they help their friends and neighbors, and they look forward to Christmas dinner. I don't want to disparage them in any way. Tolkien's hobbits are people like this. There is health and strength in their ability to forget the evil they have seen. Their good cheer makes them robust.

But not everybody has a hobbit's temperament. Some people look into the mirror of evil and can't shut out the sight. You sit in your warm house with dinner on the table and your children around you, and you know that not far from you the homeless huddle around grates seeking warmth, children go hungry, and every other manner of suffering can be found. Is it human, is it decent, to enjoy your own good fortune and forget their misery? But it's morbid, you might say, to keep thinking about the evils of the world; it's depressive; it's sick. Even if that were true, how would you close your mind to what you'd seen once you'd looked into the mirror of evil?

Some people labor at obliviousness. They drown their minds in drinking, or they throw themselves into their work. At certain points in his life, Camus seems to have taken this tack. He was at Le Chambon writing feverishly, and obliviously, while the Chambonnais were risking their lives rescuing Jews.[2] Jonathan Swift, whose mordant grasp of evil is evident in his writings, was chronically afflicting with horror at the world around him; he favored violent exercise as an antidote.[3] The success of this sort of strategy, if it ever really does succeed, seems clearly limited.

Some people believe that evil can be eliminated, that Eden on earth is possible. Whatever it is in human behavior or human society that is responsible for the misery around us can be swept away, in their view. They are reformers on a global scale. The moral response to suffering, of course, is the Good Samaritan's: doing what we can to stop the suffering, to help those in need. Global reformers are different from Good Samaritans, though; global reformers mean to remove the human defects that produced the evil in the first place. The failure of the great communist social experiment is a sad example of the problems with this approach to evil. Every good family runs on the principle "from each according to his ability; to each according to his need." The extended human family in Eastern Europe intended to run on this principle and turned it instead into "from each according to his weakness; to each according to his greed." Ecclesiastes sums up the long-term prospects for global reform in this way: "I observed all the happenings beneath the sun, and I found that all is futile and pursuit of wind; a twisted thing that cannot be made straight, a lack that cannot be made good" (1:14–15).

And don't reason and experience suggest that Ecclesiastes has the right of it? The author of Ecclesiastes says, "I set my mind to study and to probe with wisdom all that happens under the sun . . . and I found that all is futile . . . as wisdom grows, vexation grows; to increase learning is to increase heartache" (1:13, 14, 18). This is a view that looks pathological to the hobbits of the world. But whether it *is* pathological depends on whose view of the world is right, doesn't it? A hobbit in a leper colony in a cheerful state of denial, oblivious to the disease in himself and others, wouldn't be mentally healthy either, would he? Ecclesiastes recognizes the goodness of hobbits. The author says over and over again, "eat your bread in gladness, and drink your wine in joy; . . . enjoy happiness with a woman you love all the fleeting days of life that have been granted to you under the sun" (9:7, 9). But the ability to eat, drink, and be merry in this way looks like a gift of God, a sort of blessed irrationality. For himself, Ecclesiastes says, "I loathed life. For I was distressed by all that goes on under the sun, because everything is futile and pursuit of wind" (2:17).

So, some people react with loathing to what they can't help seeing in the mirror of evil—loathing of the world, loathing of themselves. This malaise of spirit is more likely to afflict those living in some prosperity and ease, inhabitants of the court, say, or college students on scholarship. If you've just been fired or told you have six months to live or have some other large and urgent trouble, you're likely to think that you would be happy and life would be wonderful if only you didn't have *that* particular affliction. Given the attitude of Ecclesiastes, it's not surprising that the book was attributed to Solomon, who was as known for wealth and power as for wisdom.

The misery induced by the mirror of evil is vividly described by Philip Hallie in his book on Le Chambon.[4] Hallie had been studying cruelty for years and was working on a project on the Nazis. His focus was the medical experiments carried out on Jewish children in the death camps. Nazi doctors broke and rebroke "the bones of six- or seven- or eight-year old Jewish children in order, the Nazis said, to study the processes of natural healing in young bodies" (p. 3). "Across all these studies," Hallie says, "the pattern of the strong crushing the weak kept repeating itself and repeating itself, so that when I was not bitterly angry, I was bored at the repetition of the patterns of persecution. . . . My study of evil incarnate had become a prison whose bars were my bitterness toward the violent, and whose walls were my horrified indifference to slow murder. Between the bars and the walls I revolved like a madman. . . . over the years I had dug myself into Hell" (p. 2).

Hallie shares with the author of Ecclesiastes an inability to look away from the loathsome horrors in the mirror of evil. The torment of this reaction to evil is evident, and it seems the opposite of what we expect from a religious spirit. It's no wonder that some people think Ecclesiastes has no place in the canonical Scriptures. To see why this view of Ecclesiastes is mistaken, we have to think not just about our reactive attitudes toward evil but also about our recognition of evil.

How does Hallie know—how do we know—that the torture of Jewish children by Nazi doctors is evil?

By reason, we might be inclined to answer. But that answer is not entirely right. It's true that our moral principles and our ethical theories rely on reason. But we build those principles and theories, at least in part, by beginning with strong intuitions about individual cases that exemplify wrongdoing, and we construct our ethical theories around those intuitions. We look for what the individual cases of wrongdoing have in common, and we try to codify their common characteristics into principles. Once the principles have been organized into a theory, we may also revise our original intuitions until we reach some point of reflective equilibrium, where our intuitions and theories are in harmony. But our original intuitions retain an essential primacy. If we found that our ethical theory countenanced those Nazi experiments on children, we'd throw away the theory as something evil itself.

But what exactly are these original intuitions? What cognitive faculty produces them? Not reason, apparently, since reason takes them as given and reflects on them. But equally clearly, not memory: We aren't remembering that it is evil to torture children. And not sense perception either. When we say that we just see the wrongness of certain actions, we certainly don't mean that it's visible.

At this stage in our understanding of our own minds and brains, we don't know enough to identify the cognitive faculty that recognizes evil intuitively. But it would be a mistake to infer that there is no such faculty.5 It's clear that we have many other cognitive faculties that similarly can't be accounted for by the triad of reason, memory, and perception. We have the abilities to tell mood from facial expression, to discern affect from melody of speech. We have the ability to recognize people from seeing their faces. When I see my daughter's face, I know who she is, and not by reason, memory, or perception. There are people who suffer from prosopagnosia. In them, reason functions well, and so do memory and perception; they perform normally on standard tests for all those faculties. Furthermore, the links among reason, memory, and perception also seem intact. Prosopagnosics can remember what they've perceived and thought; they can reason about what they remember and what they're perceiving. Nonetheless, they can't recognize people they know on the basis of visual data acquired by seeing their faces. So it is plain that reason, memory, and perception no more exhaust the list of our cognitive faculties than animal, vegetable, and mineral exhaust the list of material objects in the world. That we have no idea *what* faculty has been damaged or destroyed in prosopagnosia obviously doesn't mean that there is no such faculty. Furthermore, there is no reason for being particularly skeptical about the reliability of such peculiar cognitive faculties. It seems to me that our cognitive faculties come as a set. If we accept some of them—such as reason—as reliable, on what basis would we hold skeptically aloof from any others? So I think it is clear that we have cognitive faculties that we don't understand much about but regularly and appropriately rely on, such as the ability to recognize people from their faces.

Our ability to recognize certain things as evil seems to me like this. We don't understand much about the faculty that produces moral intuitions in us, but we all regularly rely on it anyway.6 The vaunted cultural relativity of morality doesn't seem to me an objection. The diversity of moral opinions in the world masks a great underlying similarity of view;7 and perhaps a lot of the diversity is attributable not to moral differences but to differences in beliefs about empirical and metaphysical matters. I think, then, that we have some cognitive faculty for discerning evil in things, and that people in general treat it as they treat their other cognitive faculties: as basically reliable, even if fallible and subject to revision.

It also seems clear that this cognitive faculty can discern differences in kind and degree. For example, there is a great difference between ordinary wrongdoing and real wickedness. A young Muslim mother in Bosnia was repeatedly raped in front of her husband and father, with her baby screaming on the floor beside her. When her tormentors seemed finally tired of her, she begged permission to nurse the child. In response, one of the rapists swiftly decapitated the baby and threw the head in the mother's lap. This evil is different, and we feel it immediately. We don't have to reason about it or think it over. As we read the story, we are filled with grief and distress, shaken with revulsion and incomprehension. The taste of real wickedness is sharply different from the taste of garden-variety moral evil, and we discern it directly, with pain.

What is perhaps less easy to see is that this faculty also discerns goodness. We recognize acts of generosity, compassion, and kindness, for example, without needing to reflect much or reason it out. And when the goodness takes us by surprise, we are sometimes moved to tears by it. Hallie describes his first acquaintance with the acts of the Chambonnais in this way: "I came across a short article about a little village in the mountains of southern France. . . . I was reading the pages with an attempt at objectivity . . . trying to sort out the forms and elements of cruelty and of resistance to it. . . . About halfway down the third page of the account of this village, I was annoyed by a strange sensation on my cheeks. The story was so simple and so factual that I had found it easy to concentrate upon *it,* not upon my own feelings. And so, still following the story, and thinking about how neatly some of it fit into the old patterns of persecution, I reached up to my cheek to wipe away a bit of dust, and I felt tears upon my fingertips. Not one or two drops; my whole cheek was wet" (p. 3). Those tears, Hallie says, were "an expression of moral praise" (p. 4); and that seems right.

With regard to goodness, too, I think we readily recognize differences in kind and degree. We are deeply moved by the stories of the Chambonnais. People feel the unusual goodness of Mother Teresa and mark it by calling her a living saint. We sense something special in the volunteers who had been in Somalia well before the Marines came, trying to feed the starving. We don't have a single word for the contrary of wickedness, so 'true goodness' will have to do. True goodness tastes as different from ordinary instances of goodness as wickedness does from ordinary wrongdoing; and we discern true goodness, sometimes, with tears.

Why tears, do you suppose? A woman imprisoned for life without parole for killing her husband had her sentence unexpectedly commuted by the governor, and she wept when she heard the news. Why did she cry? Because the news was good, and she had been so used to hearing only bad. But why cry at good news? Perhaps because if most of your news is bad, you need to harden your heart to it. So you become accustomed to bad news, and to one extent or another, you learn to protect yourself against it, maybe by not minding so much. And then good news cracks your heart. It makes it feel keenly again all the evils to which it had become dull. It also opens it up to longing and hope, and hope is painful because what is hoped for is not yet here.[8]

For the same reasons, we sometimes weep when we are surprised by true goodness. The latest tales of horror in the newspaper distress us but don't surprise us. We have all heard so many stories of the same sort already. But true goodness is unexpected and lovely, and its loveliness can be heartbreaking. The stories of the Chambonnais rescuing Jews even on peril of their own imprisonment and death went through him like a spear, Hallie says. Perhaps if he had been less filled with the vision of the mirror of evil, he would have wept less over Le Chambon.

Some people glimpse true goodness by seeing it reflected in other people, as Hallie did. Others approach it more indirectly through beauty, the beauty of nature or mathematics or music. But I have come to believe that ultimately all true goodness of the heartbreaking kind is God's. And I think that it can be found first and most readily in the traces of God left in the Bible.

The biblical stories present God as the glorious creator of all the beauty of heaven and earth, the majestic ruler and judge of the world. But Rebecca feels able to turn to Him when she doesn't understand what's happening in her womb, Hannah brings Him her grief at her childlessness, and Deborah trusts Him for victory in a pitched battle with her people's oppressors. Ezekiel presents Him at his most uncompromisingly angry, filled with righteous fury at human evil. But when God commands the prophet to eat food baked in human excrement as a sign to the people of the coming disasters, the shocked prophet tells Him, "I can't!", and almighty God rescinds His command (Ez.4:12–15). When His people are at their repellent moral worst, God addresses them in this way: "They say if a man put away his wife and she go from him and become another man's, shall he return to her again? . . . you have played the harlot with many lovers; yet return again to me, says the Lord" (Jer. 3:1). And when we won't come to Him, He comes to us, not to rule and command, but to be despised and rejected, to bear our griefs and sorrows, to be stricken for our sake, so that we might be healed by His suffering.

There is something feeble about attempting to describe in a few lines the moving goodness of God that the biblical stories show us; and the attempt itself isn't the sort of procedure the biblical narratives encourage, for the same reason, I think, that the Bible is conspicuously lacking in proofs for the existence of God.[9] Insofar as the Bible presents or embodies any method for comprehending the goodness of God or coming to God, it can be summed up in the Psalmist's invitation to individual listeners and readers: Taste and see that the Lord is good.

The Psalmist's mixed metaphor seems right. Whether we find it in the Chambonnais or in the melange of narrative, prayer, poetry, chronicle, and epistle that constitute the Bible, the taste of true goodness calls to us, wakes us up, opens our hearts. If we respond with surprise, with tears, with gratitude, with determination not to lose the taste, with commitment not to betray it, that tasting leads eventually to seeing, to some sight of or insight into God.

Hallie left his college office and his family and went seeking the villagers of Le Chambon. He concluded his study of the Chambonnais years later this way:

> We are living in a time, perhaps like every other time, when there are many who, in the words of the prophet Amos, "turn judgment to wormwood." Many are not content to live with the simplicities of the prophet of the ethical plumbline, Amos, when he says in the fifth chapter of his Book: "Seek good, and not evil, that ye may live: and so the Lord, the God of Hosts, shall be

with you." . . . We are afraid to be "taken in," afraid
to be credulous, and we are not afraid of the darkness
of unbelief about important matters. . . . But perplex-
ity is a luxury in which I cannot indulge. . . . For me,
as for my family, there is the same *kind* of urgency as
far as making ethical judgments about Le Chambon is
concerned as there was for the Chambonnais when
they were making their ethical judgments upon the
laws of Vichy and the Nazis. . . . For me [the] awareness [of the standards of goodness] is my awareness of
God. I live with the same sentence in my mind that
many of the victims of the concentration camps uttered as they walked to their deaths: *Shema Israel,
Adonoi Elohenu, Adonoi Echod.* (pp. 291–293)

So, in an odd sort of way, the mirror of evil can also lead us to God. A
loathing focus on the evils of our world and ourselves prepares us to be the
more startled by the taste of true goodness when we find it and the more
determined to follow that taste until we see where it leads. And where it leads
is to the truest goodness of all—not to the boss of the universe whose word is
moral law or to sovereignty that must not be dishonored, but to the sort of
goodness of which the Chambonnais's goodness is only a tepid aftertaste. The
mirror of evil becomes translucent, and we can see through it to the goodness
of God. There are some people, then, and I count myself among them, for
whom focus on evil constitutes a way to God. For people like this, Ecclesiastes is not depressing but deeply comforting.

If we taste and see the goodness of God, then the vision of our world that
we see in the mirror of evil will look different, too. Start just with the fact of
evil in the world, and the problem of evil presents itself forcefully to you. But
start with a view of evil and a deep taste of the goodness of God, and you will
know that there must be a morally sufficient reason for God to allow evil—
not some legal and ultimately unsatisfying sort of reason, but the sort of
reason that the Chambonnais would recognize and approve of, a reason in
which true goodness is manifest. People are accustomed to say that Job got no
answer to his anguished demand to know why God had afflicted him. But
they forget that in the end Job says to God, "now I see you." If you could see
the loving face of a truly good God, you would have an answer to the
question why God had afflicted you. When you see the deep love in the face of
a person you suppose has betrayed you, you know you were wrong. Whatever happened was done out of love for you by a heart that would never
betray you and a mind bent on your good.[10] To answer a mistaken charge of
betrayal, someone who loves you can explain the misunderstanding or he can
show his face. Sometimes showing his face heals the hurt much faster.

If a truly good God rules the world, then the world has a good mother, and
life is under the mothering guidance of God. Even the most loathsome evils
and the most horrendous suffering are in the hand of a God who is truly
good. All these things have a season, as Ecclesiastes says, and all of them

work together for good for those who love God—for those who are finding their way to the love of God, too, we might add.[11]

Nothing in this thought makes evil less evil. Suffering remains painful; violence and greed are still execrable. We still have an obligation to lessen the misery of others, and our own troubles retain their power to torment us. But it makes a great difference to suppose that the sufferers of evil, maybe ourselves included, are in the arms of a mothering God.

Although, as Ecclesiastes is fond of saying, we often cannot understand the details of the reason why God does what He does in the world, when we seen through the mirror of evil and taste the goodness of the Lord, we do understand the general reason, just as Job must have done when he said, "now I see you." Like a woman in childbirth, then, as Paul says, we feel our pains of the moment, but they are encircled by an understanding that brings peace and joy.

And so in an Alice-through-the-looking-glass way, the mirror of evil brings us around to the hobbit's way of seeing things at the end. "Go," says Ecclesiastes, "eat your bread in gladness and drink your wine in joy; for your action was long ago approved by God" (9:7). If God is mothering the earth and if its evils are in His hands, then you may be at peace with yourself and your world. You can be grateful for the good that comes your way without always contrasting it with the ghastliness elsewhere. This road to quiet cheerfulness is the long way to the goal, but perhaps for some people it is also the only way there.

Nothing in this view, of course, is incompatible with a robust program of social action. "Send your bread forth upon the waters; for after many days you will find it," Ecclesiastes says. "Distribute portions to seven or even to eight, for you cannot know what misfortune may occur on earth" (11:1–2). If you are moved by goodness, then you will want to ally yourself with it, to diminish evils in the world, to alleviate suffering. Those who love God will hate evil, the psalmist says (97:10). There is no love of God, I John says, in those without compassion for the world's needy (3:17). A good part of true religion, James says, is just visiting "the fatherless and the widows in their affliction" (1:27).

The spirit with which you respond to the evil around you will be different, though, if you see through it to the goodness of God on the other side. Someone asked Mother Teresa if she wasn't often frustrated because all the people she helped in Calcutta died. "Frustrated?" she said, "no—God has called me to be faithful, not successful." If God is the world's mother, then Mother Teresa doesn't have to be. Quiet cheer and enjoyment of the small pleasures of the world are compatible with succouring the dying in Calcutta in case the suffering ones are in the hands of a God who is truly good. Maybe that's why the Psalmist follows his line "Taste and see that the Lord is good" with "blessed is the man that trusts in him."

Even our own evils—our moral evils, our decay and death—lose their power to crush us if we see the goodness of God. The ultimate end of our lives is this, Ecclesiastes says: "the dust returns to the ground as it was, and the lifebreath returns to God who bestowed it" (12:7)—to God who loves us as a good mother loves her children. In the unending joy of that union, the suffering and sorrow of this short life will look smaller to us, as Paul says (Rom. 8:18).

244 I   God and the Philosophers

Nothing in this view of our relation to God makes *joie de vivre* seem any less crazy; sin and death are still real evils. But tasting the goodness of God makes seeing the world's evils and our own compatible with joy in the Lord.

I think the Psalmist is speaking for people who take this long way round to peace and cheer when he says, "I have taught myself to be contented like a weaned child with its mother; like a weaned child am I in my mind" (131:2).[12] How can a child who is being weaned understand the evil of the weaning? What he wants is right there; there is nothing bad about his having it—it costs his mother nothing to satisfy him; the pain of doing without it is sharp and urgent. And so, for a while, the child will be overwhelmed by the evil of his situation. But sooner or later in his thrashing he will also see his mother, and that makes all the difference. His desire for what she will not give him is still urgent, and the pain of the deprivation remains sharp. But in seeing her, he feels her love of him. He senses her goodness, and he comes to trust her. As Isaiah puts it, he sucks consolation to the full in another way (66:11). That is how he can be both weaned and also resting peacefully by her side.

And doesn't it seem likely that he comes to see his mother as he does just because he finds the evil of weaning intolerable? How much did he see her when his focus was himself and what he wanted, the comfort of the breast and the taste of the milk? The evil of the weaning, which seems to separate him from her, in fact drives him toward recognizing her as a person, and a person who loves him.

For Hallie, for the author of Ecclesiastes, and for me, too, the ghastly vision in the mirror of evil becomes a means to finding the goodness of God, and with it peace and joy. I don't know any better way to sum it up than Habakkuk's. Habukkuk has the Ecclesiastes temperament. He begins his book this way: "How long, O lord, shall I cry out and You not listen, shall I shout to You, 'Violence!' and You not save? Why do You make me see iniquity, why do You look upon wrong? Raiding and violence are before me, Strife continues and contention goes on. That is why decision fails and justice never emerges" (1:1–4). But he ends his book this way. He presents the agricultural equivalent of nuclear holocaust: the worst sufferings imaginable to him, the greatest disaster for himself and his people. And he says this: "Though the fig tree does not bud, and no yield is on the vine, though the olive crop has failed, and the fields produce no grain, though sheep have vanished from the fold, and no cattle are in the pen, yet will I rejoice in the Lord, exult in the God who delivers me. My Lord God is my strength" (3:17–19).

This is the best I can do to tell my story.[13]

Notes

1. I am quoting from the new Jewish Publications Society's translation. With the exception of quotations from Jeremiah 3 and Psalm 34, all quotations from the Hebrew Bible will be from this translation. The suffering of the Jews during the Holocaust reflects all the worst misery and all the deepest wickedness in the world,

and so it seemed appropriate to use the Jewish translation of the Hebrew Bible in an essay on suffering.

2. One of the first things Camus wrote in his diary on arriving in Le Panelier, the village on the outskirts of Le Chambon, was "This is oblivion" (quoted in Herbert R. Lottman, *Albert Camus* [Garden City, N.Y.: Doubleday, 1979], p.276). During his stay in Le Chambon, he was writing *The Plague* and his play *Le Malentendu,* as well as making notes for *The Rebel.* Apparently, several of the names in *The Plague* are borrowed from the people of Le Chambon (Lottman, op. cit., p. 290).

3. This included not only strenuous riding and walking but also "hedging and ditching"; See David Nokes, *Jonathan Swift. A Hypocrite Reversed* (Oxford: Oxford University Press, 1985), p. 341.

4. Philip Hallie, *Lest Innocent Blood Be Shed* (Philadelphia: Harper and Row, 1979).

5. By talk of a faculty here, I don't mean to suggest that there is one neuro-biological structure or even one neurobiological system that constitutes the faculty in question. There may be many subsystems that work together to produce the ability I am calling a cognitive faculty. Vision seems to be like this. It is entirely appropriate to speak of the faculty of vision, but many different neural subsystems have to work together properly in order for a person to be able to see. It may also be the case that some of the subsystems that constitute a faculty have multiple uses and function to constitute more than one faculty. This seems to be the case with vision, too. Our ability to see apparently requires the operation of some subsystem of associated mem-ory, and this subsystem is also employed in other faculties, such as our ability to hear. The wild boy of Aveyronne, whose subsystem of associated memory was no use for dealing with urban sounds, was originally believed to be deaf and was brought to an institute for the deaf in Paris.

6. In claiming that we have a faculty that recognizes moral characteristics, I am not claiming that nurture and environment play no role in shaping our moral intu-itions. It is difficult to make a principled distinction between what is innate and what has an environmental component, as philosophers of biology have helped us to see. And there are clear examples of characteristics that most of us strongly believe to be genetically determined but that nonetheless require the right environmental or cultural conditions to emerge. The human capacity for language is such a case. It seems clearly innate and genetically determined. And yet, as the few well-documented cases of feral children show, without human society and nurture at the right ages, a person will be permanently unable to acquire a language.

7. Perhaps this isn't the best case to illustrate the point, but it is one of my favorites. In his public remarks during the period when he was rector, Heidegger tended to make statements of this sort: "Do not let principles and 'ideas' be the rules of your existence. The Fuehrer himself, and he alone, is the German reality of today, and of the future, and of its law." Cited in Victor Farias, *Heidegger and Nazism,* trans. Paul Burrell [Philadelphia: Temple University Press, 1989], p. 118. After Germany lost World War II, when the French moved into his town and confiscated his property because he was on their list as a known Nazi, he wrote an indignant letter to the commander of the French forces in his area. It begins this way: "What justice there is in treating me in this unheard of way is inconceivable to me" ("Mit welchem Rechts-grund ich mit einem solchen unerhoerten Vorgehen betroffen werde, ist mir unerfind-lich"). Cited in Hugo Ott, *Martin Heidegger. Unterwegs zu seiner Biographie* (Frank-furt: Campus Verlag, 1988), p. 296.

8. Alvin Plantinga has suggested to me that not all tears have to do with suffering;

there are also tears of joy, at the beauty of music or of nature, for example. But I am inclined to think that even tears of joy of that sort have to do with suffering. As C. S. Lewis maintained in *The Pilgrim's Regress,* and as Plantinga also recognizes, the vision of certain sorts of beauty fills us with an acute if inchoate longing for something—the source of the beauty perhaps—and a painful sense that we don't possess it, aren't part of it, now.

9. Arguments for God's existence certainly have their place, but for most people that place is after, not before, coming to God. I have explained and defended this attitude toward arguments for God's existence in "Aquinas on Faith and Goodness," in *Being and Goodness,* ed. Scott MacDonald (Ithaca, N.Y.: Cornell University Press, 1991), pp. 179–207.

10. Answers to the question of why God permits innocents to suffer admit of varying degrees of specificity. Theodicies typically provide fairly general answers. So, for example, Richard Swinburne's explanation of God's permitting natural evil is that the experience of natural evil gives people knowledge about how suffering is caused and so gives them the options necessary for the significant use of their free will. Although I don't share Swinburne's view, I think that his account does constitute an answer to the question of why God permits innocents to suffer from natural evil. It tells us that God will allow one person S to suffer in order to provide a benefit for a set of persons that may or may not include S, and that the benefit is the significant use of free will, brought about by knowledge of how to cause suffering. Nonetheless, Swinburne's account omits a great many details; it doesn't tell us, for instance, exactly what sort of knowledge is produced or precisely how the suffering conduces to the knowledge in question. And it obviously has nothing to say about the suffering of particular individuals; that is, it doesn't tell us what individuals were benefited and how they were benefited by the suffering of this or that individual innocent. Similarly, in seeing the face of a loving God, Job has an answer to his question about why God has afflicted him; but like the account of evil theodicies give, it is only a general answer. It lets Job see that God allows his suffering for his own spiritual or psychological good, out of love for him; but it doesn't tell him precisely what the nature of that spiritual good is or how it is connected to Job's suffering.

11. In other work, I have argued that God uses suffering to further the redemption of the sufferer. Some people find this claim highly implausible. So, for example, in a recent article, "Victimization and the Problem of Evil: A Response to Ivan Karamazov" (*Faith and Philosophy* 9 '1992], pp. 301–319), Thomas Tracy notes "the stunning counterintuitiveness" of this claim (p. 308). His own preferred view is this: While God does want His creatures to be intimately related to Him, God sometimes lets an innocent person suffer not for some good accruing to her but rather just for the common good, or for the good of the system. I find it hard to understand in what sense the claim that suffering conduces to the redemption of the sufferer is supposed to be counterintuitive, since most of us have few if any intuitions about the redemption of other people and what conduces to it. On the other hand, if Tracy's line is meant just to suggest that this way of looking at suffering seems to stand our ordinary views on their head, then his line seems right but unworrisome; what would be surprising is if a Christian solution to the problem of evil didn't turn our ordinary views upside down. What seems to me truly counterintuitive is Tracy's suggestion that we could have a relationship of deep trust and love with a person who, we believed, had the power to alleviate our suffering but was nonetheless willing to let us suffer undeservedly and involuntarily in the interest of the common good. For a vivid illustration of the deep distress and resentment people feel toward those who respond to their trust in this

way, see, for example, the description of communist marriage in China in Jung Chang, *Wild Swans. Three Daughters of China* (New York: Simon and Schuster, 1991), esp. pp. 145–146, 176, 298.

12. The pastor of the South Bend, Indiana, Christian Reformed Church, Len vander Zee, whose sermons are so full of wit, wisdom, and learning that they are more worth publishing and reading than much that appears in the journals in the field, preached an insightful sermon on this passage and the problem of evil in 1992. If that sermon were published, it would be a foolish oversight not to cite it here; as it is, the closest I can come to citing it is to say that his sermons are available from his church office.

13. I am grateful to my husband, Donald Stump, and to my friends William Alston, Alvin Plantinga, and Peter van Inwagen for helpful suggestions on an earlier draft of this essay. I am also deeply indebted to my two teachers: John Crossett, whose efforts on my behalf made this essay possible, and Norman Kretzmann, whose thoughtful collaboration has made all my work, this essay included, much better than it would have been otherwise.

19

TRUTH, HUMILITY, AND PHILOSOPHERS

George N. Schlesinger

I shall attempt to recount—with an imprecise description at best—the transition from an intensely religious community to a radically differently motivated community consisting of mainly secular philosophers. I shall try to outline the contrast between a community devoted to the study of the vast sacred literature, composed of students in the Talmudic academies, bent on fulfilling the verse "This book of law shall not depart out of your mouth, but thou shalt meditate it day and night" (Joshua 1:8), a community I once belonged to, and the fundamentally different kind of community, consisting of relatively free-thinking academics.

One might think that the best way for me to proceed would be to contrast the methodologies, the ways of reasoning, characteristic of these different schools. It might be fascinating to depict the almost impassable gulch separating the two areas of study and the special obstacles encountered in an attempt to cross from one domain of inquiry to another so far removed in content and style of argumentation. However, I am not up to the task of giving a brief yet intelligible summary of the major intellectual features of the two disciplines concerned.

There are two reasons for this. First, as we know, in philosophy, unlike even the most rigorous other disciplines, there exists virtually no popular literature to offer a nontechnical yet authentic account for the perusal of the intelligent layman. In other branches of study it is possible to reproduce, intelligibly, interesting results without describing the strenuous way they have been arrived at. For example, there is a theorem that if a map is to be colored in such a way that no two countries with a common boundary have the same color, then regardless of how many hundreds of countries are to be represented and regardless of how convoluted their boundaries may be, four colors will always suffice. A few years ago, a proof of this theorem was published that ran over 150 pages. Naturally, a popular writer will not try to reproduce the extremely involved proof. But then most readers find the description of the theorem on its own fascinating enough.

The essence of analytic philosophy, on the other hand, is the production of arguments, not results (which, anyway, are not very exciting). Imagine that next year, at a huge conference of philosphers from all over the world, unanimous agreement is reached that universals are real, that bare particulars exist, and that there are negative as well as positive facts. The public in general would ascribe little significance to these findings. No newspaper would be likely to report the proceedings of the conference, except perhaps the fact that philosophers have found something to agree on.

Now, Talmudic reasoning happens to be in many ways even more intricate and insurmountable than that to be found in analytic philosophy. It should suffice to mention that the very term *Talmudic* is commonly used to indicate a tortuously finicky, convolutedly labyrithine casuistry. This is by no means due to religious prejudice; it is a consequence of its inaccessibility to minds used to much less painstaking practical reasoning, with its vaguely defined concepts and its tendency to omit many intermediate steps required by rigorous reasoning.

THUS, INSTEAD OF comparing methodologies, I shall attempt to sketch the basic difference in intellectual attitudes, in the emotional climates prevailing in these two types of colleges. This will not be easy, as most of my readers will find the spiritual world I am about to try describing far removed from their own experiences, and it will be hard to render palpable what motivates those who devote all their time to study what Longfellow—taking what at the time was a highly unconventional attitude—called "That book of gems, that book of gold / Of wonders manifold." Yet it is absolutely necessary for me to attempt it, not merely because the subject is so far removed from most people's minds but because of what Josh Billings once said. His famous quip was, "The trouble with most folks isn't so much their ignorance, as knowing so many things that ain't so." I believe that there is no other subject where this is as true as in the context of religion. There are, of course, those who know that religion is a search for a father substitute; that it is generated by wishful thinking; that it is an opiate. But then, even among its practitioners, there are many who do not know where religion ends and superstition begins, and others for whom it is a convenient way of camouflaging their self-serving actions. As Marlowe put it, "Religion / Hides many mischiefs from suspicion."

But, putting these extreme attitudes and ideas aside, let us ask what most people who are sympathetic, and are to some extent acquainted with religious faith, would designate as the most indispensable and unique factor, one that is central to all genuinely religious attitudes, one that shapes all the sentiments and colors all the thoughts of the truly pious. Is the answer the belief that the soul is eternal? That all our acts and thoughts are under constant scrutiny? Or that everything is for the best in this best of all possible worlds?

Such thoughts do indeed constitute elements in the mental world of the pious. But I should like to pursue a more fundamental point. What single human characteristic is a necessary ground without which no piety can prevail, a characteristic recognized also in the secular world to be desirable, but by no means the most exalted and indispensable human quality? I shall devote the next section to an elaboration of this characteristic, but first, I shall conclude this section with one of the best-known and little-understood Talmudic stories.

In Tractate Shabbat 31b, it is related that a heathen came to Hillel, asking, "Convert me on the condition that you teach me the whole Law while I stand on one foot." Hillel accepted him and said, "What is hateful to you do not do to your fellow: that is the whole Law; all the rest is interpretation. Go and learn."

There are at least two problems with this passage that commentators have grappled with over the centuries:

1. In Leviticus 18:18 it is written, "you shall love your neighbor as yourself." The commandment is not merely worded differently but also makes a stronger demand than Hillel: Positive love is required, and merely avoidance of hurting others. What made Hillel disregard the biblical formulation and offer his own instead?

2. Judaism is replete with all sorts of commandments that do not seem to have anything to do with one's behavior toward one's fellowman—for example, the numerous dietary laws. How can these be regarded as implied by or even as related to the injunction against wronging other people?

After the next section, we shall be able to see that Hillel succeeded in formulating with utmost brevity the most central and essential principle of Judaism.

(a) In Judaism, humility is regarded as the most highly cherished human trait. The idea that this particular characteristic is the noblest of all virtues may be traced back as far as the Bible. Reading about the events involving Moses, we learn that he displayed through his actions a wide range of virtues. Yet only one is singled out for explicit mention: modesty. "Now the man Moses was very meek, more than all the men on the face of the earth" (Numbers 12:3).

One of the most revered authorities, Maimonides, advocates the "golden mean"—nothing too much or too little. He makes, however, one exception: Modesty has no limit—the more the better.

It may strike one as odd that humility—the presence or absence of which in a given individual benefits or harms others relatively little—should be regarded as the supreme form of moral rectitude. There are good reasons to condemn and be wary of individuals who are cruel, violent, vindictive, dishonest, and so on, as they constitute a threat to one's well-being. On the other hand, while we may find the manifestation of excessive conceit irritating, even a person utterly devoid of all modesty seems to present no serious menace to the material or mental comfort of others.

However, one's surprise at the high value ascribed to humility is probably due to an insufficient understanding of the true nature of this virtue. As mentioned earlier, there have been many attempts, more than those with respect to any other virtue, to capture the essence of this slippery topic of ours. Let me cite some of the better-known ones.

1. It has often been said that a modest individual is not merely one who refrains from boasting; we also expect that he will understate his true worth.

This view does not stand up to close scrutiny. It is difficult to reconcile oneself to the idea that speaking falsely should be morally obligatory, and that it should constitute a necessary element in the noblest of human characteristics. It seems more likely that belittling oneself dishonestly amounts to something undesirable, namely, false modesty.

2. Humility has sometimes been said to demand the realization that no matter what heights one has reached, one is still infinitesimal in comparison with God.

Undoubtedly, it would be utterly foolish for any human being to fail to realize his nothingness before heaven. It seems, however, that merely avoiding being utterly foolish is not the pinnacle of moral accomplishment.

3. In the June 1989 issue of one of the leading philosophical periodicals, the *Journal of Philosophy,* Professor Judith Driver, in her essay "The Virtues of Ignorance," suggests that modesty is "underestimating one's worth." Note: not understating, which implies falsehood, but underestimating, which amounts to an honest mistake.

Strangely enough, this recent suggestion harbors more difficulties than the earlier ones it proposes to replace. First, we might ask, should we admire an exceptionally skillful heart surgeon who is convinced that he is incapable even of treating properly an ingrown toenail? Surely, such an individual would be responsible for the death of many whom he could have saved. Second, we are bid to emulate virtuous individuals and strive to acquire qualities similar to theirs. How is a person supposed to go about outsmarting himself, and sincerely adopt false beliefs about his skills and achievements, whatever they might be?

Furthermore, if we accept the view that in the context of humility there is no limit as to where to stop, for the humbler the better, how are we to picture the ideally modest person? Is it reasonable to depict him as someone who in every respect completely misjudges himself?

4. Owen Flanagan, writing in the same journal in 1990, criticizes Driver's position and advances instead what he calls the *nonoverestimation account*. He claims that a modest individual is required only to not overestimate his accomplishments and worth.

Closer inspection makes one wonder whether Flanagan's condition is either necessary or sufficient. It may not be necessary: If someone lays claim to an accomplishment that he mistakenly believes to be his, he would not necessarily be charged with lack of modesty. Flanagan's condition may not be sufficient either: An individual incapable of talking about anything else but about the few things he has (truly) accomplished is surely deficient in modesty.

The above was a rather superficial and quick dismissal of four views. My excuse is that all I wanted is to show was that there are unique difficulties in explicating the notion of humility. Unlike compassion, generosity, or honesty, which are fairly well defined even in a common dictionary, the nature of this particular virtue, however important it is said to be, is still a subject of much controversy.

(b) I believe that the assertion of any false or true statements about one's worth and accomplishments, or the harboring of correct or incorrect beliefs about them, plays no substantial role in determining the degree of humility an individual may exemplify. Instead, humility is a function of the attitudes a person has toward certain facts and of the significance he attaches to them. It has to do with what an individual's attention is focused upon, the extent to which his mind keeps dwelling on various human merits, talents, and achievements. As a first step toward the clarification we need, let me suggest what may be the first axiom in the study of humility:

> A person exemplifies modesty if and only if he does not cherish any of his moral or intellectual endowments or accomplishments more—just because they are his—than comparable ones of other people.

What basic character trait would ensure the kind of attitude implied by our axiom? It would seem that someone who has acquired a large dose of disinterestedness, though he may be fully aware of all his accomplishments, does not focus on these any more than on other people's achievements. It would be a person who has broken out of the narrow confines of his self and whose concerns are other-directed. Consider an immensely talented individual who has made unparalleled contributions to our understanding of nature and is correctly regarded as one of the greatest physicists in the history of science. When his work is viewed in an overall perspective against a comprehensive background of the sum total of the various scientific as well as literary, musical, and other artistic creations, his contribution's significance to the enrichment of our lives will have shrunk considerably. It, after all, constitutes only a fraction of a percentage of the entire harvest of human genius. From an objective point of view, even an individual's most remarkable handiwork is but a single element in the vast mosaic produced by creative people throughout the generations that should command our interest. Thus, modesty amounts to the tendency to adopt the objective perspective. A truly humble person will come close to distributing his attention evenhandedly, and consequently will dwell only briefly and infrequently on what is notable specifically about himself.

(c) Rabbi I. Z. Meltzer was arguably this century's most prominent Talmudist and leading expert on the writings of Maimonides. People flocked to his weekly lectures in Jerusalem, which were replete with brilliant arguments and deep insights and never failed to arouse great intellectual excitement among those present. He was also highly revered for his piety and goodness. He was peerless in his modesty.

In the mid 1940s a scholar published in *Sinai*—a journal devoted to Jewish studies—an essay in which he argued at length that Rabbi Meltzer's monumental work on Maimonides contained many errors and inconsistencies and was based on insufficient scholarship. I remember quite clearly the uproar this caused among the scholars of the city. After a while, a senior student of Rabbi Meltzer came to inform him that after intense research he was able to refute all the allegations that had been made against his mentor, and was able to show that the great teacher had committed not a single error. The student also indicated that he was about to send a copy of his findings to the editor of the journal, *Sinai*. To this, the rabbi's swift reaction was, "You are to do nothing of the sort! You probably are not aware that the author of the polemical essay has regrettably undergone a series of misfortunes, as a result of which he has lately become deeply depressed. Surely, I cannot allow you to deprive a man, in such a deplorable state of mind, of whatever joy and satisfaction he may have derived from being able to refute some of my theses."

The train of thoughts that led this great man to his magnanimous decision may only be conjectured. He was likely to have believed that by permitting his critic to have the last word, no real damage was caused. Those who are truly interested in the matter are unlikely to be deceived about the scholarly issues involved. They may be assumed to be able to go and study the relevant passages carefully, and to be able to distinguish between right and wrong. On the other hand, the opinions of those who are not very interested do not make a great difference. At the same time, the incident offered a good chance to lift the spirits of a suffering individual. And that was of overriding importance.

The main point for our purpose is that this incident illustrates the manifestation of true modesty. The fact that Rabbi Meltzer's prestige was at stake played no crucial role in his reasoning. From a disinterested or objective point of view, it was one factor among several others, which were judged to be of greater importance.

(d) A pious individual is supposed to live a God-centered life. The practical implication is that such an individual will try to adopt God's perspective when comparing the significance of the variety of aptitudes and achievements, and when judging the order of significance among the many wants, ambitions, and longings to be found in the world. He will not keep harping on his petty concerns, for important though he may be in God's eye, he is but one of many Divine creatures. Thus, he who is conscious of having been formed in God's image, and thus is anxious to emulate His ways, is likely to distribute his interests over a wide spectrum of needs and causes. He will respect the hopes and strivings of others, and will share their joys and sorrows. Thus the virtue of other-directedness, the core of humility, is the ultimate source for all other characteristics that involve an impartial concern for worthy ideals and causes, and that require sympathy for the well-being of others. Righteous moral behavior is grounded in an outlook that is close enough to the objective perspective and, therefore, ranks sentiments, accomplishments, needs, and aspirations in accordance with their actual, inherent order of importance.

(e) The question raised at the beginning of this section was: Is it just to regard humility as the supreme virtue when the absence of it, unlike the absence of other virtues, does not constitute a serious threat to the welfare of anyone? By now we should realize that the mind of the humble, which has soared above the confines of the self and consequently has gained an objective perspective, provides an indispensable prior condition for righteous behavior. Thus, modesty occupies a central position among all the precious human qualities as it supplies the requisite solid basis for all the other virtues.

(f) It goes without saying that investigations fueled mainly by self-serving motives are likely to produce results that exemplify features that will maximize their surface value. Truth may or may not be one of the major features. On the other hand, for self-forgetful individuals, who view reality from an impartial standpoint, an honest search for the objective truth is bound to be the sole factor animating their endeavors.

Rabbi Aaron Cohen, one of the deans of the seminary in Jerusalem where I studied, was, I believe, the greatest mind I have ever had the privilege to observe at work. His disciples came to regard him as a living refutation of the principle that nothing travels faster than light: Rabbi Aaron's mind obviously did! Once, he happened to come across a Talmudic problem that greatly disturbed him. Day after day, he devoted all his energies to figuring out a way to escape his puzzlement. Eventually, he came up with a brilliant idea that seemed to everyone to be a perfect solution. A few days later, he discovered that an identical solution had already been suggested by a highly regarded Talmudist more that 100 years earlier. Rabbi Cohen was overcome with joy:

"So I did not toil in vain. I owe great gratitude to the Almighty Who has enabled me to hit upon an idea that fully concurs with the idea of such an unquestioned, universally revered authority."

At the time, given the cultural climate in which this incident took place, none of us present found anything in it to be astonished at. Now, looking back on it, I find it remarkable. It is not easy to think of many secular academicians who are likely to take this attitude under similar circumstances. A more typical reaction would be to deplore the time wasted on trying to find a solution to a problem solved long ago by others.[1]

WE MAY RETURN now to the incident, involving Hillel, referred to in the second section. Hillel must have realized that a person may be commanded to perform, as well as to refrain from performing, certain acts, but he cannot be told that he must feel or refrain from feeling in this or in that way. How then is one to understand the biblical commandment to love one's neighbor? If A has a deep hatred of B, can he suddenly begin to love B simply because he is so commanded? It is, however, possible over an extended period of time to condition oneself, through the modification of habits and patterns of behavior that are bound to result in the transformation of one's mental attitude. Thus A may actually loathe and despise B, but if he makes it a strict habit never to be unpleasant to B and ensures that all his practical conduct is as it would be if he loved B, then by the testimony of many contemporary psychologists, A will end up with a changed attitude and eventually acquire positive sentiments toward B. Thus, Hillel was offering the heathen a practical piece of advice on how to set out on a course that would lead him eventually to the state of mind envisaged by the Bible.

Hillel's statement concerning the required behavior toward others is an auxiliary proposition that he uses to demonstrate a deeper proposition. Ultimately, the state of mind of the truly pious is one filled with the love of God, as it says in Psalms 42:3: "My soul thirsteth for God." How does one inculcate in one's heart a longing love, and a yearning for nearness to the Creator and sustainer of the universe? Surely by the kind of behavior modification just mentioned. By carrying out all the commandments of the Law, for many of which we know not the reason, yet we carry them out because they are the will of God. We keep behaving toward Him as a lover behaves toward his beloved.

Thus Hillel was trying to explain to the heathen, who was asking for a succinct description of the essence of Judaism, that it was to devote one's life to attain a state of mind described by Maimonides as loving "the Lord with a great and very strong love so that one's soul shall be tied to the love of the Lord, and he should be continually enraptured by it, like a love-sick individual.[2] Hillel also informed the man that such sublime sentiments can be implanted in one's heart by doing the will of God, that is, by observing the Law. Thus he gave a brief indication of what the main purpose of the law is.

Concerning the question "and what precisely are these laws," he merely said, "Go and study."

Maimonides also explains that a person who lives a God-centered life is bound to wish to emulate Him: "The way of life of such an individual . . . will always have in view lovingkindness, righteousness, and judgment, through assimilation to His actions."

The pious individual is supposed to raise himself to a level at which all trivial and unbecoming concerns are seen in their properly reduced size. He is bound, therefore, to adopt an impartial view, the kind of view attributed to God Himself, as it says in Deuteronomy 10:17: "For the Lord your God . . . is not partial and takes no bribes." In a similar fashion, a God-centered individual, who refuses to yield to the blandishments of his narcissistic appetites, tends to make unbiased, correct value judgments. But God's love of other individuals is, of course, no less than that. It is an utterly impartial love. The core of human impartiality is adoption of this kind of impartiality.

I SHOULD EMPHASIZE that the substantial majority of people regarded as religious, even among those who have set out to dedicate their lives to serve as teachers or professional promoters of spirituality, fall far short of the exalted state of mind outlined in the last two sections. There is no need for me to elaborate on the presence of pretensions, intolerance, holier-than-thou attitudes, and superstitions mistaken for pious acts. Indeed, even among those who have made an honest, strenuous, and prolonged effort, not everyone has succeeded in liberating themselves from the fetters of their ego and reaching a state of genuine, impartial attitude.

At the same time, it is essential that we realize that it is the handful of such spiritually sublime persons that set the tone; it is they who are highly influential, and who shape the climate of opinion and the emotional atmosphere that prevails in the major Talmudic academies. It is only those who are generally known to be godly minded who are revered and regarded by all as paragons to be emulated—often, of course, without much success. Scholarship, even of the highest order, if divorced from intense piety, elicits no admiration. In my experience, those who exerted an influence on the students' value judgments and aspirations were never merely great minds who bedazzled with their vast intellects, but were also venerable models of piety. And, of course, any student, though he might have been an intellectual prodigy, who was seriously neglectful in his religious conduct was sent packing.

Now we have come to a radical contrast between the two intellectual communities we are dealing with. It is unquestionably true that moral values are held to be of crucial importance in the secular world. There are plenty of irreligious people whose behavior accords with very high ethical standards. I found the late Herbert Feigl—who was a militant atheist (in the kindliest sense possible)—one of the most caring, compassionate, generous, tolerant persons I have ever had the privilege to know. But his magnanimity had little to do with his being a philosopher. One could have easily pictured Herbert as a musician or an investment banker, but not without his princeliness. Thus, we may admire a philosopher for his noble personal qualities, but these qualities will have no effect on our evaluation of him as a philosopher. We all find that self-renunciation, big-heartedness, meticulous honesty, and the like are most laudable characteristics, but they do not feature in the training of philosophers, nor do they play any role in the criteria whereby philosophical proficiency is measured.

DAVID HUME WAS unquestionably a decent and compassionate individual. Adam Smith, in a letter to William Strachan (November 1776), writes about Hume:

> Upon the whole, I have always considered him, both in his lifetime and since his death as approaching as nearly to the idea of a perfectly wise and virtuous man, as perhaps the nature of human frailty will permit.

At the same time, it has also been said about Hume that his

> vanity to show himself superior to most people, led him to advance many axioms that were dissonant to the opinion of others . . . all to show his preeminency. (George Nicholl in *Edinborough Magazine,* 1782)

Nicholl should not be taken as slandering Hume; Hume himself was candid enough to admit that the chief aim of his intellectual exertions was self-promotion. In *My Own Life,* Hume explicitly says that his ruling passion is the "love of literary fame." Posterity judges Hume one of the greatest philosophers in history. The question of what motivated Hume in his writings has played no role in this judgment.

The fact that moral integrity is not an organic part of secular studies has concrete repercussions. The journal *The Behavioral and Brain Sciences* conducted a symposium on the journal review process, the outcome of which gave rise to serious concern among its readers. The discouraging results indicated that scholarship, precision, validity of argument, correctness of results, and originality are by no means the only criteria in deciding the fate of a paper. Among the many other determinants on which an article's acceptance for publication hinges are considerations like whether the author is well known, or at least located at a prestigious institution. In addition, editor–author friendship and old-boy networks play an important role in editorial decision making. Furthermore, when everything else is equal, the more brilliantly original a paper is, the less chance it has for acceptance. D. F. Horrobin writes:

> most scientists follow the crowd when it comes to recognition of brilliance. . . . Ordinary scientists consistently fight against or ignore the truly innovative.[3]

Horrobin was editor of a medical journal and was referring to experimental science, where the criterion of truth is supposed to be far more straightforward than in philosophy. Nevertheless, of course, it is easily recognized that when a paper proceeds along unfamiliar lines, it requires an honest readiness to do much harder work: to examine it carefully to see whether its strangeness is due to its pathbreaking novelty. As an experienced editor, Horrobin concludes that not many are prepared to go through the painstraking process that total integrity demands.

IN VIEW OF THE many extraneous factors that enter into editorial decisions, J. Scott Armstrong, an editor of the *Journal of Forecasting*, has advanced what he calls an "author's formula," consisting of a set of rules that authors may use in order to increase the probability of their work's acceptance for publication.

> Authors should (1) not pick an important problem, (2) not challenge existing beliefs, (3) not obtain surprising results, (4) not use simple methods, (5) not use full disclosure, (6) not write clearly.[4]

Dr. Armstrong, of course, intended his advice for the ordinary scientist whose problem is how to get published. His formula is quite suitable for the majority of philosophers as well. However, famous philosophers, whose competence is unquestioned, face different problems. Their manuscripts are bound to be accepted anyway, and in most cases they are solicited as well. Their objective is to produce exciting material to keep the philosophical community's interest engaged and have their writings under continuing study and discussion. The set of rules applying to them have to be different.

Years ago, I was present when a highly respected philosopher was asked for his opinion about the claim that weird theses and arguments are from time to time advanced by philosophers on the assumption that asserting the precise opposite of what everyone regards to be the plain truth amounts to bold inventiveness. The discussion was prompted by the appearance of an essay by David Stove in *Encounter* (June 1985) that contained witty and devastating criticism of those he called the "four contemporary irrationalists" in philosophy of science, namely, Popper, Lakatos, Kuhn, and Feyerabend. Stove's main point was that these people belong to the group of philosophers who reckon that by standing ideas on their heads, they will succeed in making our work appear exciting enough to attract attention to our unduly neglected discipline.

In responding, the eminent philosopher whose opinion was sought explained, while maintaining a perfect poker face, that in philosophy it is hard to get to the top and even harder to stay there for long. Subsequently, he offered the following prescription for enduring philosophical stardom: Publish at fairly regular intervals papers that will strike the reader as virtually pathbreaking in their astonishing originality. To actually have original ideas may[5] be a sufficient but by no means a necessary condition for the purpose. A more common and effective method is simply to advance a mind-boggling thesis implying that the truth does not in the least resemble what hitherto everyone took for granted. One of several methods to render the outrageous plausible is to follow the statement of your thesis with qualification after qualification until it is whittled down to such extent that, in the end, it is impossible for anyone to articulate the difference between it and the thesis it was supposed to replace. It is also essential to introduce a certain amount of opaqueness into your paper, not only to ensure that a potential critic will be at a loss in formulating the thesis he would like to attack, but also because, to many people, "clear, and easily understood" is synonymous with "superficial or trivial." However, great care should be taken with the fuzziness with which one endows one's paper. It has to be subtle enough to make its source undetectable and highly suggestive, to provide ample scope for the imaginative reader to ascribe a variety of unstated profundities to the text.

Clearly, the above characterization requires some qualification if it is not to remain merely a caricature. Among other things, it should be mentioned that genuine scientific results may also strike one as outrageous, such as Non-Euclidean geometry or some of the highly counterintuitive results of quantum mechanics and relativity theory. But there is a radical difference between such initially strange hypotheses, which ultimately unify and simplify phenomena, and those that set out with some wild ideas not because objective reality demands them, but merely because of their provocative, eye-catching flashiness.

It is interesting to read what Wittgenstein thought of the matter. Erich Heller writes about Wittgenstein:

> He could not but have contempt for philosophers who "did" philosophy and, having done it, thought of other things: of money, of publication lists, academic advancement, university intrigues, love-affairs or the Athenaeum—and thought of these things in a manner which showed even more clearly than their product that they have philosophized with much less than their whole person. (*Encounters*, p. 378)

It is significant that Wittgenstein—for whom philosophy was a consuming passion—while demanding that one philosophize with one's "whole person,"

does not also insist on the philosopher's having certain essential moral qualities, like perfect honesty and a commitment to a single-minded, impartial
search for the truth.

IT IS IMPORTANT to point out that, contrary to what one superficially might
have thought, the existence of efforts fueled by ulterior motives, like the
passion to get into print, the desire to play one-upmanship, the ambition to
bedazzle the reader with technical virtuosity, and the determined attempt to
sweep us off our feet by advancing entirely unexpected, counterintuitive
theses, is not likely to cause long-lasting damage to our discipline; it is even
likely to prove beneficial to it.

Let us first remind ourselves that it was hundreds of years ago that Cicero
said, "There is no nonsense but some philosopher has said it." Unquestionably, the amount of nonsense is greater in philosophy than in most academic
disciplines. The reason, of course, is not that proneness to error is a malady to
which philosophers are specially susceptible. It is simply that any extended
piece of formal reasoning provides indefinite scope for going wrong. Formal
arguments are, of course, employed elsewhere too, such as in physics and
mathematics. However, in physics and mathematics, errors are much easier to
spot. In the former, experimental evidence may indicate when a false move
has been made. In the latter—unlike in philosophy—it is clearly spelled out
which assumptions we may and may not make.

Nevertheless, in the long run, errors tend to be detected in philosophy too.
What Dr. Johnson said in a different context applies here as well:

> The irregular combination of fanciful invention may
> delight for awhile by that novelty of which the com-
> mon satiety of life sends us all in quest; but the plea-
> sures of sudden wonder are soon exhausted, and the
> mind can only repose in the stability of truth.

Our minds are equipped, to some extent, with sensors to help us overcome
the tendency to be infatuated by fanciful inventions. Sound intuition provides
a fairly effective mechanism for the eventual rejection of most inauthentic
philosophical propositions. In general, when something strikes us as counterintuitive, there are two possible explanations. One is that we relied on
illegitimate inductive reasoning. For example, the proposition that a whole
may not be bigger than any of its parts sounds highly counterintuitive, yet it is
true in the case of infinite sets. Our strong initial wish to reject the proposition is based on our vast experience with finite sets, where the whole is always
larger than its parts. Thus, we are tempted to extrapolate to infinite sets that
are radically different from the familiar ones. The second possible explanation is that through our intuition we have been alerted to the presence of a

faulty piece of reasoning; thus, we should try locate it precisely and provide an article description of the mistake committed.

Furthermore, one may ascribe positive value to ingeniously contrived fallacies: They serve as superior puzzles through which to sharpen our wits. According to Wittgenstein, philosophy is not a body of doctrines but an activity the main purpose of which is to expose all the sentences of metaphysics as nonsense. Since his time, of course, metaphysics has staged a strong comeback. Still, the activity of exposing nonsense, the discovery and correction of erroneous arguments, remains an important, constructive part of philosophy.

However, to the individual who is supposed to engage in unraveling conceptual intricacies, to inspire students with the love of grappling with ultimate questions, to that individual the issue of motivation makes a fateful difference. As a mental exercise, playing chess or constructing ingenious crossword puzzles is as strenuous and invigorating as struggling with analytic problems. But to free oneself from the prison of the prejudices derived from common sense and, in the words of Bertrand Russell, to acquire that which "keeps alive our sense of wonder by showing familiar things in an unfamiliar aspect," is, of course, granted only to unrelenting, honest conceptual toil. He who engages in philosophy not purely for philosophy's sake; he who grants a role to extraneous elements like reputation and fame in his investigations, will eventually have his vision blurred and is likely to loosen his grip on the truth in general, ending up with an inaccurate picture of reality as a whole. Hence, while an individual's actual objectives in doing philosophical work have little effect on the ultimate shape of our highly resilient discipline, it has an incalculable impact on his personal development, character, integrity, and on the depth of fulfillment deriving from his life's work.

NOW WE COME to the part I would like to make as brief as possible. It is the part where, according to our editor's wishes, we so to speak bare our souls, or in any case make a personal statement about our spiritual journey in life. My own journey may in a significant sense be said to have been uniformly downhill. I am not referring to basic ethics or common decencies. What I have in mind are those stratospheric virtues I have outlined before: I can no longer honestly claim to have a realistic chance to recapture even the mere urge of possessing them.

Yet the effects of my earlier vocation cannot be said to have vanished without leaving a trace. For example, when writing a paper or a book, there are certain thoughts that rarely enter my mind. I hardly ever ask myself: Is this a fashionable topic? Is the flavor of my arguments such that they are unlikely to offend the tastes or cherished prejudices of many potential readers? Have I introduced enough ambiguity into my theses to foil attempts to refute them? And so on. Let me hasten to add that this has nothing to do with moral purity. My work habits are simply a matter of conditioning, which, in spite of the inevitable penalties that go with them, I cannot help. I find doing philosophy excruciatingly hard as it is; if I were to impose on myself extra constraints arising out of pragmatic consideration, constraints in opposition to my second nature, I would find the burden intolerable.

Notes

1. A dramatic illustration of the truly cherished goals of some contemporary scientists may be found in the fascinating story of the double helix.

2. *Mishneh Torah,* Hilkhot Teshuvah, x.

3. "Peer Review: A Philosophically Faulty Concept Which Is Proving Disastrous for Science." *The Behavioral and Brain Sciences* 5 (2), 1982, p. 218.

4. "Barriers to Scientific Contributions: The Author's Formula," op. cit., p. 167.

5. Whether it is sufficient depends on the prevailing climate of opinion. For example, in the sixteenth century, a claim that a perpetual motion machine was invented would have been found highly seductive. But Galileo's genuine, novel claim about Jupiter's moons was found repugnant.

20

THE OVEREXAMINED LIFE IS NOT WORTH LIVING

David Shatz

I am an Orthodox Jew and have been so all my life. I did not choose Judaism but was born to parents who, while modern in dress, educational ideals, and occupations, were Orthodox; and so my early life was permeated with Jewish observances, while my education took place in schools that combined a secular curriculum with a traditional Jewish one. I attended a yeshiva elementary day school in Monsey, New York, then studied at the high school administered by Yeshiva University in New York City, went next to Yeshiva University for my B.A., and finally culminated my Judaic training by receiving rabbinical ordination in a three-year program at the university's affiliate theological seminary, while simultaneously going for an M.A. degree in philosophy at another local university. In contrast to two other sorts of institutions—religious schools that eye secular curricula with suspicion and contempt and Jewish universities that are secular in character—Yeshiva University (YU) maintains that traditional Jewish study and commitment to the full range of Jewish law must be combined with worldly wisdom and broad exposure to secular culture. Indeed, YU is unique among Jewish institutions of higher learning by virtue of this driving ideology, which it captures in the slogan "Torah u-Madda"— roughly translated as "Torah and general knowledge." Consequently, when I began to pursue my Ph.D. in philosophy at Columbia, it was the first time I had been free of a formal commitment to a dual curriculum. Up to the age of twenty-four, every day of my formal education—eighteen years' worth, often eleven hours a day—had included intensive exposure to Jewish sources, with study of Talmud and Jewish law embracing more hours than secular subjects and constituting around 80 percent of Jewish studies after the early grades.

You might now expect the next sentence to read "And then the roof fell in." But it didn't. Obviously, as time moved on, the demands of professional life and of enlarged domestic responsibilities—not to mention personal deficiencies in motivation and stamina—shoved the idea of six to eight hours of Talmud study a day beyond the pale of realistic possibility. Nonetheless, neither graduate school in philosophy nor a career in the field did much to change my overall religious orientation and practice. I have always belonged to Orthodox synagogues and attended them regularly; for many years, in fact, I've cultivated avocations as the regular Torah reader in my synagogue (this involves chanting the weekly biblical portion) and occasional cantor. (The humorous side of a philosophy professor's leading the climactic prayer for forgiveness on Yom Kippur has not escaped the congregation's notice.) My wife is a rabbi's daughter—a descendant, on both her father's and mother's side, of distinguished Hasidic families. My children, like other American teenagers, are tuned in to entertainment, sports, and politics; but they attend religious schools, pray the prescribed three times a day, study religious texts intensively, and observe the precepts of Jewish law piously and meticulously. We have never tried any other way of life. In a nutshell, my upbringing and lifestyle have been basically uniform, without the on-again, off-again quality described by some of the other contributors to this volume.

I wish I could boast that my continuance in my religious lifestyle is the result of some grand synthesis of religion and philosophy on the order of that envisaged by Maimonides; or, alternatively, that it testifies to my being a Kierkegaardian knight of faith. But the immediate explanation, I'm afraid, is more prosaic and far from self-congratulatory. I didn't come to religion, I merely managed to hold on to it in conducive circumstances. My familial, educational, and social lives were so much built around Judaism; the social context in New York, with its impressive Orthodox population and its abundance of personalities, synagogues, and houses of study, was so friendly to the status quo; and the atmosphere at my place of work was so congenial to my inherited ways that holding on psychologically was easy. My present academic appointment is at Yeshiva University, where I enjoy the unusual luxury of presenting myself to my students exactly as I am, without having to explain myself or apologize, and where, unlike so many of my Orthodox friends who feel themselves the odd one out in their work environment, I can enjoy a pleasing continuity between my personal and professional lives.

Leaving the fold thus never made an appearance as a serious option, because my very identity was so tied up with my faith and religious practice. And I cherished the "halakhic" way of life (i.e., life in accordance with Halakhad, Jewish law) despite—or maybe because of—its many demands. Religious observances, while multifarious and laden with myriad technicalities, impart structure to daily life, give rhythm to the calendar, inject warmth into family celebrations, and create solidarity during times of sadness and crisis. Most important, the many laws governing routine activities serve, in a classic but pointed phrase, to "sanctify the mundane." Study of Jewish texts, furthermore, excited my mind. These attractions and benefits, on which I shall elaborate later, might have looked different had I found myself in some far-flung and God-forsaken community where everyone around me thought differently and where temptation lurked in every cranny. But in the actual world, given the acute sense of community I enjoyed, there seemed to be (in William James's phrase), no "live options," no real competitors, to my established way of life. On top of that, my personality is somewhat allergic to change—adjustments intimidate me—and so a conservative course in life seemed a foregone result.

Some of my conservatism has also to do with the educational philosophy in which I was reared. In Chaim Potok's novels—Potok, by the way, is a Yeshiva University graduate—protagonists experience powerful tensions between their traditional Jewish upbringing and exposure in later life to broader horizons. And in Potok's novels the characters rebel, or at a minimum undergo profound and wrenching conflict. But rebellion and conflict often emerge precisely when one's early education takes place in an atmosphere that is extreme and denigrates secular studies totally. Open the window just a bit later in their lives and expose them to some of the finer things in culture, and those same people who had been conditioned to think of secular studies as vapid, alien, and dangerous sometimes feel they've been cheated, their talents stifled, their true calling unactualized. When one is taught from the outset, as I was, that secular studies are of value and can coexist with Judaism, when one hears this, moreover, trumpeted as ideology, as I did, one *might*, of course, rebel as conflicts become evident, casting doubt on the ideology's optimism; but another result can be a refusal to see oneself as mired in either-or situations—one hopes for a resolution down the line. That others with comparable backgrounds and training have not held on but have instead felt conflicts to be insuperable doesn't alter *my* realities. In *my* case social identity, psychological boons, the inspiration of role models (more on this later), the power of ideology, and innate aversion to change proved a strong enough bond, and I suspect that in the cases of others who turned out differently, psychological and sociological forces were likewise conspiring—albeit to produce a contrasting result.

Birth, upbringing, tradition, education, and community are focal categories in analyses of religious commitment that flow from Jewish law, Jewish thought, and Jewish experience. There is a definite fit between these analyses and my biography. Indeed, typically, so goes my impression, "born" Orthodox Jews, while they interpret events in light of their belief in divine providence, nonetheless report few or no specific episodes of experiencing God's voice or immediate presence, few or no direct personal revelations, which sustain them in their faith. My own history, stressing as it does contingency over choice, community over individuality, study over personal revelation, is therefore not unusual among my coreligionists and may be quite representative of a large population. (I make no comment here on converts to Judaism, who may represent a contrasting category).

BUT HOW DO I FEEL about this narrative? My preceding description might seem doubly shameful: It testifies to no great spiritual strength, and it amounts to a philosopher's *mea culpa* (or to use the Hebrew, "*al het*"). Philosophy—in the spirit of Bacon's methods and the opening lines of Descartes's *Meditations*—is supposed to root out the prejudices we acquire in our youth and from our peers. If so, why didn't a career spent pursuing truth and rationality dislodge any psychological and social forces that were keeping me in the fold? Why didn't being so aware of the contingency of my upbringing make me worry about the epistemological merits of what I believed? Didn't I violate professional norms?

Naturally, I have been asked these questions often in my life, and from two different points of origin. Nonreligious academics ask—if not by words, then by their glances—"Shouldn't philosophy have affected your lifestyle?" Members of my religious community ask me—again, often by their glances—the reverse: "How can a religious Jew study this stuff and survive spiritually?" Behind such questions lie immense presuppositions and expectations about what effect philosophy "should" have on religious belief. By and large, these presuppositions remain unarticulated and unexamined by the people who make them. Yet they persist, and their tenacity, in large part, is what motivates this anthology and will make its contents and direction surprising to many.

I am inclined to think that questions about how one can be both religious and a philosopher rest on some misconceptions. These include misconceptions about the state of philosophy today, about the impact of philosophy on life's big questions, and about the urgency of purging prejudice from one's being in order to number oneself among the true professionals in our discipline. There are, on the contrary, several ways in which a professional philosopher can shut out philosophy from his or her religious life—with or without conscious rationalization—all the while maintaining professional integrity; and there are also ways in which a philosopher can let philosophy enter religious life without emerging scathed by the intrusion. I don't mean to say that bifurcation is praiseworthy; I do mean to say that the lives of many religiously committed philosophers cannot be understood without first appreciating to the fullest the *potential* that exists for defensible, rationalizable bifurcation. And I would describe my own process of intellectual maturation as a struggle to break down the walls of a bifurcation that I could, if necessary, legitimate intellectually and for a long while did; as a quest for a meaningful way of integrating my professional and personal commitments.

The answers I would have given to the questions at hand (about how I could be a religious philosopher) at certain stages in my career are not identical with the answers I'd have given at other stages. As a result, the reader may detect some contrasts or even inconsistencies among the answers I catalog below. But let me nonetheless lay out the total territory—the several ways in which one could, if so motivated, separate philosophy from life or, alternatively, find it congenial. I now recognize the limitations of these tactics and will explain them in due course. Even so, all have played some role at some point in my own narrative, and there is something to be learned from them, I think.

1. *Specialization:* If a philosopher doesn't want to examine his or her religious beliefs with professional tools, philosophy offers many "safe" fields that constitute neutral ground; they don't need to be connected to religion at all. The age of academic specialization and, to be frank, narrowness has made segregation possible: You can specialize in epistemology, philosophy of language, logic, history of philosophy, philosophy of science, and, yes, *even* metaphysics, and yes, *even* ethics, without the slightest intrusion of religiously sensitive material—unless you want the intrusion, in which case there are numerous ways you can invite it. Many of the problems I address in professional life have nothing immediately to do with religion. A philosopher friend of mine once asked facetiously about a colleague: "How does he reconcile substitutional quantification with Judaism?" His point, here expressed humorously, was that if you specialized in substitutional quantification, you didn't have to grapple with God. Just as mathematicians, scientists, and computer experts can avoid religiously charged questions if they want to, so can a professional philosopher.[1] And I know some people of my faith who do exactly that. They violate no professional norm in the process. If anything, the contrary holds. Professional norms for a time viewed philosophy of religion as "soft" philosophy, unsuitable for the truly serious. Due to my graduate department's particular emphases, I did no work in philosophy of religion for many years, and specializing elsewhere served me for that time as a defense against thinking too hard about my beliefs and lifestyle.

2. *Internalization:* An assumption that lies behind the questions we religious philosophers get asked is that philosophers internalize the conclusions that their intellects draw—and live by them. David Hume taught us otherwise. Hume was fascinated by the divorce between philosophy and practical life. In my study, he said, I come to appreciate that I lack adequate grounds for all sorts of things I take for granted in my life—the regularity of nature, the reality of the physical world; yet when I exit, those intellectual infirmities have not the slightest influence on my belief system. A philosophical skeptic,

someone who casts doubt on our grounds for these and other common beliefs (e.g., belief in other sentient creatures, belief in the trustworthiness of memory), cannot *live* his skepticism, Hume holds. (Here Hume is rejecting the contrary view of the ancient skeptics.) Even in his study, in fact, Hume isn't really a skeptic: He doesn't doubt he's putting pen to paper, and doesn't wonder whether the paper will abruptly pop out of existence. That nobody is *really* a skeptic—*even* while philosophizing—becomes clear if you watch what we philosophers do, not what we say. When a philosopher publishes an article called "Why There Are No People" (an actual title!), he invites a joke: Whom does he think he's writing for? Whom will he blame if he gets turned down for tenure?

Think of another specialization in philosophy: ethics. Many philosophers can rehearse arguments to show that ethics is relative, that it is subjective, that it is biologically determined, that it is contingent on tradition and upbringing. And they don't generally know how to rebut *all* those arguments. Some may actually endorse *intellectually* one or more of these bugaboo theses. But do they internalize them? Do they take leave of ethical behavior or of their particular moral beliefs because of it? Or consider the old conundrum of political philosophy: Why must we obey the laws of the state? Philosophers who find no compelling argument for obeying government do not necessarily use this as a license to flout the law or to look sympathetically at those who do. Determinists can be just as ready as everyone else to excoriate wrongdoers, even if they can't articulate a theory of responsibility that is consonant with determinist assumptions. Again, there are philosophers who find ingenious ways to show that death need not concern us; how they weather a gloomy medical prognosis remains to be seen. In the sphere of religion, proofs for the existence of God don't always sway people into belief (the ontological argument of Anselm is notorious for not converting those who think it is sound); intellectual solutions to the problem of evil, however formidable, often fail to soothe the gut-level feeling that a perfect God would not allow evil; and, by the same token, objections to a theistic position don't always translate into abandonment of belief, because other forces shape us. So, even if philosophy were to deliver its conclusions about religion, it would not be astonishing if professionals did not internalize them.

My point so far has been descriptive only; philosophers, I've said, don't *in fact* internalize philosophical arguments. Hume's point, however, was probably normative as well as descriptive. Hume taught us, in effect, that it is a *vice* to be too rational, to hold out for rigorous arguments in *all* walks of life. Only a mad person would want to conduct his or her life with complete, Spock-like logicality. We are possessed not of minds alone, but of hearts, emotions, needs, instincts, and habits; and we inhabit social contexts. Obviously, without the use of reason, anarchy enters; still, in most areas of belief and practice, we don't—and shouldn't—let *philosophical* worries get to us. When the subject isn't religion, people joke regularly about the sterotypical philosopher whose head is in the clouds and who worries about intellectual puzzles that no one else gives a thought to—or, to repeat, *should* give a thought to. But then we get to religion, and here I detect a double standard. Suddenly, if our philosophical ruminations don't profoundly impact on our lives, if we live without the two synchronized, we're accused of being hypocrites and irrational. True, Hume was speaking of beliefs everyone shares, "natural beliefs"; and religion, in our age, no longer fills that bill. Also, the beliefs Hume spoke of were irresistible, which religious belief is not. But try to explain *why* his point should work only for universally held and irresistible beliefs; the plain fact is that we allow ourselves a considerable degree of nonrational influence when we engage in the business of forming a metaphysics and a world view. I shall say more later about what experiences keep one wedded to religious belief.[2]

In my early years in the field, throughout the 1970s, I found it particularly easy to resist internalizing philosophy. The regnant analytic approach to philosophy had curiously distanced itself from real religious life by insisting on putting everything in its characteristic idiom: technical, dry discourse, inaccessible to all but the philosophically trained. A clever student of mine, having sat through a long, complex technical series of arguments and objections I had dutifully presented in logical notation, once put this question to me with only partially mock astonishment: "Do you mean to tell me that the existence of God might depend on the scope of a quantifier?" A certain cynicism set in as one followed the literature. No sooner had one become convinced that—to put it in professional jargon—"(3c) follows from (27a), assuming the correctness of (19")" than a subsequent issue of the same journal appeared where one learned that "unfortunately, (16) is not as evident as might appear, vitiating the inference from (18) to (19)." It is not just that the notion grew that every position and argument could be refuted with sufficient ingenuity, so that no individual argument could be cause for panic. After years of thinking and writing in this genre—and enjoying it, I confess—I got weaned off the habit when it hit me that philosophy had lived for nearly two and a half millennia with hardly anyone—including the greats—expressing ideas that way. When I coedited a text on philosophy of religion in 1982 and searched the literature for accessible articles to reprint (I'll skip explaining the providential way this project fell into my hands), I was amazed at how few pieces could be grasped by the uninitiated. Does all this really have much to do with religious life, I wondered? If you saw somebody trying to resolve a spat with a spouse by putting pen to paper and setting up numbered premises, you'd find it a crazy way to settle things, and maybe would also brand it as a tactic for fleeing the real issues. Only in philosophy does this sort of exactitude win an imprimatur; elsewhere, we find it stultifying, obsessive, and immature. There was no reason to carry this mindset into life in general and religious life in particular. Religious people who look at philosophy sometimes find themselves put off at what strikes them as mind games that have no hold on what it *feels* like to be religious—no existential grip. Worst of all, those thinkers who *were* touching chords in religious people, who were drawing on religion as it is actually lived, were being scoffed at as mere "theologians." The unkindest cut of all, presumably.

In light of this, I wonder whether my extensive exposure to Talmud was what led me to like the philosophy I studied as an undergraduate and to whet my appetite for more. Subtlety, rigor, complexity; dexterity at deciphering difficult texts; the mongering of distinctions and counterexamples—all these are nurtured in both Talmud study and analytic philosophy. Philosophy, in other words, catered to my talmudically trained mind. But beyond that lay something else. In studying Talmud, one was immersed in a world that need have no effect on practical life. Some tractates deal with institutions no longer standing—sacrifices and high courts, for example—and even in tractates that dealt with applicable laws such as Sabbath, holidays, prayer, blessings, dietary laws, mourning, marriage and divorce, the particular discussions and debates in the Talmudic text were freighted with fantastic cases (used to clarify legal principles) and with theoretical objections that had no effect on the practical law. In other words, in Talmud you learned to tolerate irrelevance and unreality and to let intellectual gyrations satisfy you for their own sake. Indeed, "study for its own sake" was an ideal to be aimed at; pragmatic irrelevance was to be consciously cultivated. To put it better: The world of Talmud is *a* world, real, vibrant and woven into the fabric of religious existence, but it is populated by abstract entities, classifications, principles, and situations. The same carefree willingness to forego practical application, to luxuriate instead in the motions of the mind, to move about in an abstract universe—a sine qua non for grappling with Talmud—was also a sine qua non for studying philosophy and truly loving it. "Study for its own sake" is an alluring ideal indeed.

The tactic of saying that philosophy, however passionately pursued, didn't have to affect life served me well for a while. Its utility declined when academic philosophy of religion became conscious of psychological, human dimensions of religion it had previously ignored and related itself to deeper aspects of ordinary life. But the aforementioned obstacles to internalizing philosophy probably played a role at a pivotal stage of my development.

3. *Prejudice:* My questioners assume that philosophers ought to be especially ashamed of the prejudices they acquire from their youth. Now we do indeed take question, criticism, and dialogue more seriously than perhaps any other specialists do. But we all have our prejudices. When is a problem interesting and when is it not? When is a reply to an objection contrived and ad hoc, and when is it intuitively satisfying? Often your answer depends on your training and prior conviction. That is one reason why some people find themselves thoroughly satisfied with arguments that others find preposterous, while their opponents remain insensitive to and unmoved by objections that those people think devastating. Then also there's the (alleged) halo effect some complain about: Work in certain journals is more likely to be admired than work in other journals; work by people in school X is more likely to be appreciated than work by people in school Y; and the like. (The frequent insistence on blind review of submissions to journals and conferences surely concedes some of these worries.) But if philosophers are not immune from prejudices, then might there also be other forms of prejudice? Couldn't athe-

ists be as much a product of their upbringing and environment as theists are? What about personal circumstances, like an unhappy home? Did every *atheist* philosopher I knew have a reasoned argument in hand? Did each of them know how to reply to, say, the clever theistic moves of Alvin Plantinga? I saw no reason to accept a double standard.

My ability to live with philosophical assaults on religion was enhanced, not threatened, by the nasty attitude to religion that prevailed while I pursued my doctorate. Although by then few philosophers held any more to logical positivism—the view, once the rage, that religious statements are meaningless—its legacy was palpable, its grip still strong. And this led many departments to regard philosophy of religion as not worth attending to. Nobody in these departments "did" philosophy of religion. The assumption I read into that fact was that there were no interesting controversies in the field because religion had no philosophical merit. All this called to mind Russell's complaint that religious motives (along with ethical ones) "have been on the whole a hindrance to the progress of philosophy, and ought now to be consciously thrust aside by those who wish to discover philosophical truth."

That was the party line. But then I'd read something by a good mind sympathetic to religion, and I'd see instantly that the supposedly decisive objections were poorly formulated and easily met; the questions were still open after all. This led me to think that philosophers were just being prejudicial. If more philosophers had deigned at that time to treat religious claims more seriously, it might have led us theists to take their objections more seriously. As things were, philosophers seemed to be taking cheap shots and missing; philosophers didn't notice the extent of the partisanship because there were too few believers working in the field. Rumor had it that some journals would never publish a religion article; and I heard speculation that acceptance was easier for hostile than for friendly pieces. (For all I know, both this perception and vehement denials of its accuracy were themselves products of prejudice!) Sure, the pro-theistic philosophers were bringing their own prejudices in too. But knowing that others were culpable took the sting out of any charges of prejudice leveled at the religious.

Some years ago, I was asked to referee a paper in the philosophy of religion that took a pro-theistic stance. After much thinking and weighing, I decided to recommend against acceptance: The author's point seemed insufficiently argued, I felt, and even if it was right, it had been made already in the literature in different form. My identity as a referee was, of course, unknown to the author. A while later, the editor of the journal sent me, apologetically, a letter that he had received from the paper's author and that the author had insisted I see. The letter angrily took issue with my evaluation—and charged that the referee was obviously biased against theism! I relate this not to commend myself for my objectivity; in truth, the incident only attests to the degree of compartmentalization a philosopher could achieve, and anyway, subscribing to theism does not require accepting *every* argument offered on its behalf. My critic may have thought, though, that only those unsympathetic to religion could criticize a pro-religious paper. If so, at least we agreed that prejudice existed in the academy. Here then was another reason to bracket philosophical anxieties about religious belief: for you never knew when you were being suckered or browbeaten unfairly. (Of course, this response works best when you find a particular argument appealing while your adversary does not, so it necessitates your having an argument to begin with. I think the argument from design provides a lovely example for this purpose.)

4. *The state of philosophy:* So far, I haven't touched on how philosophy could actually prove friendly to religion. However, over the past ten to twelve years, another response has come into focus as trends have shifted in the philosophical community. We live in an age of ideological pluralism. No methods are privileged; even science is just one slice of culture, not a supreme judge and jury. In the wake of Thomas Kuhn's *Structure of Scientific Revolutions,* scientific theories are not the bastions of objectivity people thought they were. In this atmosphere, religion now claims parity with other views and approaches. Some even argue that religion can set its own standards; let other disciplines and contentions stand before its tribunal, rather than the other way around.[3] Also, it is fashionable in philosophy today to recognize a "social" dimension in the justification of belief. You are justified in doing or believing something provided that the practice or belief is appropriate given your community's standards. If your religious community is your dominant one, then, if your beliefs and actions are justified by *its* standards, they are "justified," given this social account. (I realize the situation gets complex when you belong to *both* a religious *and* an academic community; that's why I stress dominance.)

There's more. When we're dealing with large-scale ways of looking at the world, "methodological conservatism" is now recognized as good rational practice; the mere fact that you already believe something gives you a reason to keep believing it. You can be the most rabid critic of Quine's behaviorism, but surely you don't expect Quine to suddenly drop his view of human psychology just because someone has posed a strong-sounding objection at some conference. He's too invested in it. If he'd dropped his lifelong belief just because someone came up with an objection, it's not just that you'd be surprised; to a certain degree, you'd think Quine was irrational. We all begin our inquiries somewhere, with a large complex of presuppositions and convictions. We should be open to change, but all change is gradual. As one philosopher (Gilbert Harman) has put it: We strive to "maximize coherence and minimize change."

Philosophy today also teaches that no theory of the world is perfect—intellectual maturity requires living with objections. As a Yiddish expression neatly puts it: "A person does not die from a question." Finally, philosophers are more open than ever before to the realization that their bread and butter—to wit, arguments—doesn't coerce listeners. Philosophical expositions furnish them with new *perspectives,* not knockdown weapons of persuasion. What someone called the *scorched earth* approach to philosophical argument is giving way to a more accepting attitude to rock-bottom disagreement.

So, to some extent, the very *expectation* that philosophy, as it exists today, would undermine religious life betrays ignorance of what's going on in academic life; it rests on an outmoded stereotype. A lot of pro-traditional recent work in the philosophy of religion plays off of this kind of focus on epistemology and on the nature of philosophical argument. Now I don't want to grant this response more punch than it deserves—there are times when it downright irritates me. I am not terribly gratified at defending my point of view by saying to opponents of religion, "Look, you're in the same boat as regards a lot of things you believe." And I've never seen a good answer to the following challenge: If *I* can claim immunity from criticism on the grounds that justification is social, that starting points enjoy special protection, and the like, can't *anyone* in *any* community do likewise? If so, do I really want to allow that—to legitimize any and every world view? Surely there's no *other* philosophical position I'd care to defend just by pointing up the difficulties of proving anything whatsoever or by positing the *basicality* of that belief in my *noetic structure* (these terms are borrowed from Plantinga's recent attempts to reinstate Reformed epistemology.). Still, any realistic look at how philosophers assess religion has got to take notice of the contemporary pluralist, "postmodern" consciousness. And that's a key part of the answer to the questions I get asked. Moreover, Alasdair MacIntyre and Charles Taylor, eminent philosophers both, have argued forcefully not only that world views and moral commitments must arise in the context of tradition and community, but that *religious* communities deserve pride of place.

I haven't even introduced yet the fact that natural theology, which attempts to prove basic religious doctrines, is making a vigorous comeback. Top-flight people who have forged their stellar reputations in mainline, "hard" fields like epistemology, metaphysics, philosophy of language, and philosophy of science, are theists and argue proudly for it. Now citing authorities who hold a position is hardly a way to make a philosophical point, particularly when the views of those authorities are hotly disputed. Even so, clearly philosophy isn't the devil it once allegedly was, and a religious philosopher can exude greater tranquility and confidence today than at any other time in recent decades.[4]

5. *The challenge of other fields:* All this leads to another question: Why pick on philosophy? Writing in *The American Scholar* in 1979, Kenneth Seeskin of Northwestern noted: "such disciplines as science, history and mathematics culminate in a body of accepted beliefs. . . . But it would be hard to find any accepted beliefs that originated with philosophy." True to this assessment, the toughest challenges to religion today, or at least orthodox religion today, come from empirical disciplines: history, archaeology, biblical scholarship, neuropsychology, genetics, artificial intelligence, and the like. When it comes to these challenges, philosophers have a luxury that religiously inclined specialists in those other fields lack: They can profess that they don't know enough about the state of empirical affairs to form an intelligent judgment on whether those fields threaten their views. More important, though, philosophers are also very adept at undermining the credentials of other disciplines; give them a view, and they'll find a way to destroy it. Confronted with challenges from the empirical world, philosophers might even emerge as

cool heads, pleading for restraint and methodological caution. Disagreements between scholars, frequent changes in the orthodoxies of other fields, foundational issues about the basis for accepted methods—all these, a philosopher might say, promote a rational skepticism about the claims put forward by scholarship, lending succor to the religious position. The people in the other fields, on the other hand, commit professional suicide if they move to the meta level at which they question the very foundations of their disciplines; to steal a quip of Russell's, imagine a tailor running through the streets yelling, "There are no pants! There are no pants!" It is high time for the hackneyed identification of philosophy as *the* nemesis of religion to give way to the indictment of other suspects in other professional associations, and for the potential for philosophy to defuse some of these cultural challenges to become widely recognized.

The notion that there's something *especially* incongruous about being a philosopher and being religious is, then, a holdover from an earlier era. The climate may change back again soon, so in flux is the discipline. But in today's environment, not seeking proof for everything and learning *not* to capitulate in the face of objections and difficulties can be a mark of sophistication.

TAKING ALL THIS together, it's clear that a philosopher has multiple routes to either rationalize not bringing philosophy and religion together, or to convince himself or herself that relations between the two domains are congenial, at least compared to the relations between religion and other disciplines.

With the heightened self-awareness that comes with middle age, I recognize elements of immaturity and unseemly defensiveness in each of the strategies I've outlined for explaining how one can be a religious philosopher. Some of the responses involve not really dealing with the issue but evading it; this applies to response 1, "specialization," and response 2, "internalization." Other responses ask, in effect, "Are you any better?" (this applies to response 3, "prejudice"); or else they amount to complaining "Hey, he or she is doing the same thing" (this applies to response 3 and 5 "the challenge of other fields"). I've already expressed some discontent with response 4. All of these moves, then, fall short of being fully satisfying. And so it's natural for me, as time passes, to grow uneasy about making them, and to seek in lieu of them a meaningful integration of two worlds I could keep separate. But how does one do that? What form can integration take?

More on this anon. Bifurcation, however, has other sources, to which I now turn.

SO FAR I'VE SPOKEN about being religious despite being a philosopher. I haven't yet considered the second half of the problem: being a philosopher while being religious. Here the challenge has been not to justify my religious beliefs in the face of philosophy, but to justify my pursuit of philosophy in light of the religious ideals put forth in my tradition.

If the thought of a religious philosopher strikes you as oxymoronic, then the thought of an Orthodox Jew in academic philosophy must strike you as stranger still. Christianity has a strong philosophical tradition, especially conspicuous in Catholicism. In Catholic schools people are trained on philosophical texts; those texts are part and parcel of the curriculum. But in Orthodox Judaism the most hallowed texts are not philosophical but legal. The corpus of Jewish law is vast and staggering; its base is the imposing sixty-three tractates of the Talmud, which are written mostly in Aramaic and which deal with topics both relevant and irrelevant to contemporary practice: holidays, divorce, theft, sacrificial offerings, court proceedings, Sabbath observance, ritual purity, oaths, ethics. And the actual text of a Talmudic discussion, formidable as it may be, is just the starting point. There are mountains and mountains of legal commentary and codes, and as you get older and more experienced, you are expected to do more and more climbing. The texts themselves are often linguistically terse and conceptually complex, so it is all very challenging. Yet the educational system prizes not erudition alone but cleverness too; the challenge is not merely to master the texts but to create—to ask good questions and devise good solutions. In some circles, Bible study is deemed "soft" by comparison to legal study, and therefore is marginalized or thought of as something that requires formal instruction only in the early stages of education. The test of your mettle, at least in the classical "Lithuanian" approach, is your Talmudic ability and facility in the legal codes; study of these, significantly, is referred to by the simple term "learning." The educational curriculum of Orthodoxy is geared to producing, if not legal giants, then professionals of all types who will be competent to deal with legal texts and who every day of their lives will devote time to study in deference to religious duty. God is experienced primarily through His words, through a text, not through philosophical reason and not by personal mystical revelation.

As I explained earlier, Talmud and philosophy are to an extent congenial; the two domains call for similar qualities of mind. And I would be dense not to see how greatly Talmud study both attracted me to philosophy and has helped me in pursuing arguments; returning the favor, philosophy, I believe, makes my mind sharper when I turn to a Talmudic discourse. Creativity is valued in both as well.5 Having said this, I still have to urge that in Judaism, the personal ideal of Talmud study inhibits assigning other things a significant role in the process of internalizing beliefs and values. Talmud study is not just part of your training, it is a lifelong commitment, no matter what your profession; as far removed as it may often seem from real life, it is supposed to dominate your time away from work and from domestic responsibility. "This book of the Torah shall not depart from your mouth; you shall meditate upon them [words of Torah] day and night" (Joshua 1:8); "you shall teach them to your children; you shall speak of them—when you dwell in your house and when you travel, when you go to sleep and when you awake" (Deuteronomy 6:7). Torah study is a primary religious experience. God is experienced through the words of Torah scholars, and it is through study that we simultaneously link ourselves to the Jewish collective across time and keep the tradition alive. (The Hebrew word for "tradition," *mesorah,* actually derives from the root "to give over." Learning and teaching are inextricably bound.)[6]

Accordingly, many Orthodox professionals—prominent economists, scientists, lawyers, doctors and professors—rise at 5 A.M. to study before services, sneak in a *shiur* (class) or private study at the workplace, and at night go to the study hall to labor until late. There's no such thing as having mastered an area and earned the right to get on to something else: "One who has learned 100 times cannot be compared to one who has learned 101 times." Pressured by ideals like this, where is there room for philosophy, save at best as a 9 to 5 (for professors, 1 to 4!) living? In many schools the philosophical works of Saadya Gaon or Maimonides are studied mainly as diversions when one needs a break from the exhausting activity of Talmud or, at most, as ancillary supplements. So, whereas Christians who want to be exposed to religious texts are likely to turn to philosophical ones, Orthodox Jews are not.

Despite the parallels between Talmud study and philosophy that I noted before, it is, I think, a result of the structure of Jewish education that there are very few Orthodox Jews in university philosophy departments, and in many cases whatever philosophy they do has only a tenuous connection to internal religious life. Your theological needs, many feel, are met by the Talmudic text. Therein lies a complete spiritual world. To be sure, some of the key movements in Judaism—medieval rationalism, for example, or, else Kabbalah—arose as reactions against an exclusive preoccupation with Talmud to the detriment of broader spirituality. Philosophy and Kabbalah help Jews put flesh on their belief system, indeed create much of that system. Still, speaking sociologically rather than prescriptively, broad conceptions of spirituality and appreciation of philosophy's potential contribution are far more the exception than the rule.

Time allocation is not the sole issue. Much of Jewish tradition is downright hostile to philosophical pursuits because of their historical association with heresy. I realize that the Christian church has its own history of hostility to secular doctrines, the most recent segment of which is the controversy in America over evolution in schools. Still, I have often felt that because Jews need to protect themselves as a tiny people in an intellectually threatening milieu, the conflicts between philosophy and religion—or, for that matter, history and religion, science and religion—were especially threatening to them, those conflicts coming as they did from the outside world. And so Jews needed to band around a common text that was unique to them and could set its own standards rather than answer to an externally imposed one. The few stunning exemplars of philosophy who have been produced from mainstream, legalistic Judaism have sometimes met with suspicion or even enmity. In medieval times Maimonides sought an integration of law with philosophy, producing, on the one hand, a mammoth and monumental code of law that represented the first-ever topically organized assemblage of Jewish law, and, on the other, the *Guide of the Perplexed,* his philosophic magnum opus and a landmark of the Middle Ages. Maimonides (and others) even posited a religious *obligation* to study philosophy; for Maimonides, the "*mitzvah* of Talmud Torah" (commandment to study Torah) *includes* the study of philosophy. Yet Maimonides was perceived by many as overly bold, and his stature as a legal authority made it even more imperative for those who felt threatened by philosophy to limit his influence as a thinker. To this day, Maimonides has been the subject of revisionist biography that seeks—indefensibly, in my opinion—to dismiss the nature and extent of his commitment to philosophy and restore the image of the pure legal scholar, even while academics sometimes go to the other extreme of belittling his commitment to law and Torah study. And so it has been with other legal giants who cast their net wide; their biographies are sometimes mirrors of the biographers. In any case, Jews dedicated to the standard Orthodox curricular emphasis typically have no room in their day for philosophy. Notwithstanding the genius of Maimonides or, to mention a latter-day giant, Rabbi Joseph Soloveitchik, most minds have not proved capacious and quick enough to excel in both or hospitable enough to assign value to both. All of this contributes, of course, to the neglect of philosophy among Talmudists. And it ultimately marginalizes the role of philosophy—even *Jewish* philosophy—in the religious lives of many committed and highly educated Jews. I do not think I fully escaped this effect in my education, even with commitment to a dual curriculum and even with an ideology committed to the synthesis of Judaism with general culture. For to a significant extent, the individual must take the initiative in achieving integration.

I HAVE SPOKEN at length about the extent to which being a religious philosopher, especially an Orthodox Jewish philosopher, brings with it or even requires a feeling of bifurcation. And I have also explained that as I grew older, I became increasingly aware of what was happening and more conscious of the forces that were producing bifurcation. In the wake of this realization, I sought a way of breaking down the walls of bifurcation. In a pinch, I could reach my goal by fixating on the postmodern consciousness I elaborated on earlier, a consciousness that could grant a license to religious commitment (albeit, as I said before, only as part of a broad license that for parity's sake would then have to be granted to many horrendous world views). But in my own life I think I have finally overcome bifurcation in a different way: not by bringing reason and religion together on every point, but by utilizing philosophical methods, categories, and distinctions to clarify my tradition and to reveal layers of richness that would otherwise have eluded me.

To some extent, this means appreciating philosophically interesting material in Judaism on classical philosophical conundra: attributes of God, evil, free will, morality and divine commands, weakness of will, immortality, belief and the will. Analytic training has helped me clarify biblical narratives, comprehend Talmudic positions, and sort out arguments by Jewish thinkers from

Philo to Maimonides to those of today. In this way, I feel my belief system enriched and deepened. Reciprocally, Jewish knowledge has served to contribute vital suggestions to my personal reflection on current debates in philosophy. Thus, contemporary philosophy both illuminates and is illuminated by religious resources, and I have found groups of kindred spirits with whom to share this endeavor. In the process, I have learned that authoritative thinkers of the tradition have been prepared—within limits—to reinterpret teachings that strike them as philosophically problematic, furnishing both a general method for reconciling philosophy and religion and important reformulations of specific doctrines. Many views held by people at the popular level—for example, that all suffering is punishment for sin—were rejected by major thinkers and indeed by sages of the Talmudic period. A commitment informed by the philosophy that has preceded looks quite different from one not thus informed.

When I have not been doing straight philosophy, the issues that have occupied me most in recent years are those that grow out of the confrontation between Judaism and modernity. What are the prospects for transposing an ancient system of law to modern circumstances without violating its essence? How does the Jewish political tradition react to contemporary dilemmas inherent in setting up a state in Israel with a quasi-religious character? What is the place of autonomy in Judaism? What is the meaning of idolatry in contemporary society? How does Judaism assess democratic ideals? What can be done to assuage conflicts between modern liberalism and Jewish moral principles? What have the effects of secularism been on Jewish life, and how does Jewish tradition regard the more positive aspects of secularism—technological and medical advances, for example? It is stimulating for me to see, for example, how Ronald Dworkin's or Robert Bork's theories of American law illuminate the nature of Jewish law and the notion of precedent that is so central to it; how theories of reference and approaches to scientific thinking help clarify the nature of belief in God; how communitarian views of political existence clarify Jewish ones, and vice versa; how Jewish and secular systems of medical ethics converse with each other. All the projects I have described reflect the ideal on which I was nurtured, "Torah u-Madda." Secular philosophical tools are brought forth to illuminate an ancient tradition and to appropriate the tradition in a distinctive way; at the same time, philosophical ideas are illuminated and refined by that tradition. Thereby, integration, not bifurcation, has finally become the keynote of my *intellectual* work.

And yet, at a deeper level, integration has its limits. Bifurcation is encouraged, and internalization of philosophy frustrated, by still another hard fact of life: Things that affect and move us in real life, that give our existence texture and richness, resist philosophical defense and in fact are at odds with a philosophical perspective. I see no way to deny this. Here are a few examples.

Models: Models, to lift yet another of Russell's famous witty phrases, have all the advantages of theft over honest toil. When you have a model, you can content yourself with reasoning as follows: This person is brilliant and erudite, so this person must have figured it all out; since *he's* this way, why need *I* sweat over whether it can be done? I had several major models while growing up, living examples of how religion and culture could be fused. Collectively they saved me from having to carve out an articulate rationale for being religious. Now to a hard-nosed philosopher, citing someone else who does or believes X goes no way toward explaining why believing or doing X is a justified course. Someone has got to have an argument for believing or doing X, and the argument should be what counts, not the charisma or IQ of the people who believe or do X. But in flesh-and-blood life, models shape us, and in the presence of a vivid and impressive one, philosophical grappling pales into irrelevance.

For students of Yeshiva University, no one can surpass Rabbi Joseph B. Soloveitchik, who passed away in the spring of 1993 at the age of ninety, and with whom I studied in the late 1960s and early 1970s. Scion of a great family of Talmudists, Rabbi Soloveitchik's analytic brilliance in handling a Talmudic text was arguably the greatest in generations, and he ceaselessly inspired thousands of students in America over the past half-century. His powers of exposition were magnificent, and his rare combination of genius, passion, clarity, and flair made it possible for people to sit and listen to him—with rapt attention—for four or five hours on end. But what made him truly unique was that, apart from vast Talmudic erudition and astounding creativity, apart from an intense impassioned love for Torah study that infected all around him, Rabbi Soloveitchik was also a philosopher. He received a doctorate from the University of Berlin and was thoroughly conversant with the philosophy, science, and literature of his time. He published relatively few works in religious philosophy (relative, that is, to other theologians), but what he did publish showed, first, wide cultural awareness and, second, a depth of feeling that was unusual to behold in such a rigorous intellect. Here was a man who knew as much European philosophy as anyone I had met (albeit not analytic philosophy) and yet, when all is said and done, was one of the greatest men of faith I had ever seen. Rabbi Soloveitchik indeed had little patience for conflicts between biblical scholarship and religion or between science and religion; he focused instead on the psychological state of the contemporary believer—on how the modern consciousness has left the religious personality lonely and alienated. To belittle or dismiss that which this great mind had embraced seemed inconceivable. Surely his deep spirituality and unwavering faith did not reflect weakness of mind or deficiencies in erudition. The best tribute I know to Rabbi Soloveitchik came from a well-known philosopher who studied Talmud with him nearly five decades ago. This philosopher is no longer Orthodox, but he has remarked many times that "after having had Soloveitchik, I could not be intimidated by anyone else's intellect."

Nor is Rabbi Soloveitchik the only great Talmudist to be so erudite and reflective. One of his sons-in-law, Rabbi Aharon Lichtenstein, earned a Ph.D. in literature from Harvard and published a book on the Cambridge Platonists, yet chose to spend his life teaching Talmud and now heads a yeshiva in Israel. A master of language and a stimulating thinker, besides being a stunning Talmudist, Rabbi Lichtenstein is well versed in general culture, and he has argued eloquently that exposure to culture refines one's spiritual sensibilities and is encouraged by Judaism. I can name other bright minds too—well known scientists, historians, philosophers, linguists, biblical scholars, experts on artificial intelligence, and psychologists—who, if not quite as immersed in Talmud, are people of faith, committed to Torah study, and devoted to halakhah. One little synagogue in my neighborhood boasts the nucleus of a good university—a distinguished physicist, a linguist who made *The New York Times,* a prize-winning medieval historian, and several chairs of departments from music to Judaic studies. Knowing of the existence and availability of such people not only eases the burden of being religious in a secular world, it positively inspires. But again: not by furnishing a decisive philosophical argument. On the contrary, I now realize that some models may be what they are because they have not channeled their reflections in the directions in which the challenges lie or else have not been really tough-minded about certain issues. Yet their impact remains.

Intellectual excitement: Teachers and spiritual leaders do not generally influence us by proving points; they do so by exciting our minds, by making texts and concepts come alive. (This was my experience in philosophy too. Sidney Morgenbesser, whose philosophical brilliance is astonishing, has had an enduring influence on students like me more by making philosophy intensely exhilarating than by pushing particular positions.) As a teacher myself, I can attest that the sheer rigor and imagination of classical Jewish texts is part of what inspires students to study more and more. Amazingly, many gifted young men and women today defer entering law school or medical school—and sometimes even accepting lucrative invitations from law firms—to study religious subjects for an additional year or two. No material incentive motivates their choice. Large numbers of Jews enroll in adult education programs in non-degree-granting institutions. They study *lishmah,* "for its own sake." While their choice reflects, above all, religious commitment, part of that commitment is sustained by the intellectual invigoration that study provides.

In an earlier period, I went through a similar process of being energized by my tradition. A pivotal figure was an extraordinarily talented rabbi named Norman Lamm, who served the congregation in which I spent my teenage years. Rabbi Lamm attended Yeshiva College, graduating as a chemistry major and a top-flight student of Rabbi Soloveitchik, and then turned to the pulpit. Combining a dynamic delivery, adroit turns of phrase, intellectual substance, and a great feel for homily, he was a mesmerizing master of the sermon; in his hands it became an art form. My father was such a devotee of the sermons that he had the rabbi send him a typed version after each Sabbath, and we reread these with the excitement you experience when you finally get hold of a recording of that song you loved but whose tune you couldn't remember well enough. For a while, I even wanted to have a pulpit myself. Dr. Lamm is now president of Yeshiva University, and as I sit through the soporific tones at other colleges' ceremonies, I prize his oratorical prowess still more. What he provided me with in my teenage years (and thereafter continued to provide through his many writings on Jewish thought and law) was a conviction indispensible to my later life: that Judaism could excite and energize the mind, and that its ideas can be expressed with eloquence and power.

Which counts more: vividness, excitement, and intellectual engagement— or analytic proof? My own vote is for the former (though I perhaps am overdrawing the dichotomy). When a Jewish text comes alive in the hands of its masters, the religion's teachers and preachers, you feel yourself part of a living tradition and indeed in conversation with august authorities in centuries past. It is the experience that counts; these texts touch me at the deepest recesses of self. No, I don't have a full-dress account of where inspiration and excitement shade off into the text-centered fanaticism of a David Koresh. But this is not a reason for me to be wary of religious excitement; as an autobiographical matter, I find the love of Jewish texts more engaging than abstract explorations into their philosophical validity.

Inspiration: Intellectual excitement is one source of my love for my religion; another is the inspired lives of my religion's devotees. Recently I attended a talk given by an Orthodox woman who has been bound to a wheelchair from childhood. She is married—to a blind man—and remarkably, they are raising a family. She spoke about the Jewish concept that "this, too, is for the good"; she explained how life had done her good turns by means of *ostensible* "coincidences," which in truth, she felt, were signs of God's intervention. By means of her theology, she had turned adversity into inner strength and advantage. The thought of contesting her "invisible hand" interpretation with philosophical arguments seemed so offensive as to be unthinkable. Anyone who would impugn her perspective would only be reflecting their own lack of spirit. If that evening someone had furnished me on the spot with a dazzling philosophical solution to the problem of evil, that would have done less for me as a person than this single autobiographical expression— which from a philosophical standpoint seemed so simplistic.

There are couples I know, friends and coworshippers, who have children with saddening disabilities: Down's syndrome, Tay-Sachs disease, cerebral palsy. Their powers of spirit are extraordinary. On the one hand, they view their circumstances with complete honesty about the initial numbness—the "why me?" reaction—and about the magnitude of the problem of coping. Yet, at the same time, they view their situation as an opportunity God has granted them for moral growth—as a chance to shower love, care, and responsibility on another human being. Survivors of the Holocaust saw their families butchered and brutalized before their eyes, losing parents and siblings and children to the Nazi machine. Of the survivors whom I know, many have drawn from their religious belief the strength, trust, and resolve to persevere and even to live productive, well-adjusted lives.

I can hear the voice of the philosopher arraigning me on a fallacy: "In all these instances, what one is admiring is the people who exemplify such spirit; it does not follow, nor is it true, that all such admirers admire also the *content* of the world views being expressed. Indeed, insofar as there are no atheists in foxholes, we fully expect religion to be useful as an emotional crutch. So do not confuse evaluating a perspective philosophically with evaluating the experience of seeing or hearing it expressed by someone with a certain kind of history; you mix up focusing on ideas and focusing on people. As long as we keep these objects of evaluation distinct, we can avoid being attracted to 'simple' views of providence while simultaneously admiring greatness of spirit."

I am not convinced that this argument does full justice to the situation. First of all, the mere fact that we admire the people means that we recognize virtues besides philosophical rigor. And in any case, there is a real issue here as to *how* ideas themselves are to be evaluated. Religion provides a coherent view of life, one that galvanizes people to moral action, infuses them with strength of character, and gives them perspective on their own troubles. Life would be poorer without that perspective. Is rigor the only criterion by which to judge a perspective? Or is it appropriate only in certain settings?

I cannot overstate how surprised I am by my own admiration for providence-filled interpretations of life. Of all the ideas preached by religion, the one that has brought on it the most ridicule from both philosophers and the person on the street is the notion of Divine providence. God is lampooned as the Father who art in Heaven who distributes lollipops and spankings according to our deeds. When I was a little boy, I took this idea with the utmost literalness; if the New York Yankees blew a double-header, I must have done something really bad. As I grew up, I sought within tradition a different picture of how things operate.

The ridicule to which the simple view is subjected stems from at least six sources. First, in human experience, goods and evils don't get distributed according to the pattern one would expect on the basis of the religious model. Second, the notion that God causes many events in everyday life seems out of step with a scientific world view. Third, religious ethics becomes infantile and heteronomous; you blindly obey because you'll get zapped if you don't. Fourth, you allegedly become self-centered, imaging that all that happens revolves around you. Fifth, you allegedly become helpless and dependent. Sixth, you become callous toward evil, because all is supposedly for the good.

I discovered in Maimonides a captivating idea: that although there is reward and punishment in the universe, we are living a lower form of spiritual existence if we place this idea at the forefront of consciousness. Maimonides bids us to abandon an anthropocentric perspective even while believing in providence. A description of how he carries out this balancing act is beyond my purposes. But surely there is something inspiring about the idea that trust in God does not require belief that He will supply your material needs, but instead requires a steadfast resolve to do His will no matter what life brings you or—phrasing it differently—to deem His will the "good" of your life. And yet, despite my personal attraction to Maimonides's view, those who *do* see events as directed toward their personal interests often tend to be the most benevolent and the most conscious of evils around them. If strong belief in providence yields a self-centered reading of events, it isn't self-centered in any negative sense. In this world view lie the seeds of greatness of spirit. It deserves a place in religious life, even if only as part of a perpetual dialectic, the other pole of which is a Maimonidean outlook that transports us beyond our own interests.

Religious commitment has also had striking effects on the conduct of religious youth. Many young men and women elect to spend their summers caring for others as counselors in an upstate New York camp for special children. Competition for counselor positions there is stiff, eloquent testimony to the value that benevolence and kindness have for these youth. Without question, a secular person could also make altruism and care for others a primary good in life; nevertheless, religious values exert a palpable added impact. Is this impact a philosophical basis for a theistic argument? I doubt it. Is it a reason to value being part of a religious community and to share in its outlook? I think so.

Community: I have just returned from the funeral of a friend of mine, a member of my community, who died abruptly at the age of forty from a heart attack. At the service, people spoke lovingly of his warmth and his selflessness. As is standard at funerals, they related the circumstances to key phrases or ideas in the Talmud, the biblical portion of the week, or the laws governing the season in which his death took place (it was the season for mourning the destruction off the Temple). They compared the situation to others described in the Talmud; they found parallels between him and ancient models. It was all beautiful and moving; and it enabled the hundreds of attendees to begin speaking about, dealing with, and adjusting to a loss that had left them numb and speechless. Yes, of course, people wondered how God could allow a man in his prime, a man without a jealous streak in his body, a man who was incredibly giving, cheerful,, and gregarious, to be snatched from a wife and children without warning. And we still wonder. I know enough about Jewish theology to know that Judaism does not believe that if a person died, he or she must have sinned; and the Book of Job tells me that there is no perfect nexus in the world between deed and destiny. Yet apart from this intellectual resolution by means of "texts," I really wonder what the tribute would have been like were it not for the rich evocative imagery and literary gold mines that brought us together in spirit.

Contingency: I mentioned earlier that philosophers are sometimes troubled by the contingency of religious commitments; were we born in a different place, born to parents whose convictions were different, or educated differently, we'd have turned out differently. Consequently, in forming our beliefs, we need to filter out the results of upbringing and engage in purely rational reflection on what to believe. As already noted, this idea is on shaky turf today, since it is widely recognized that our traditions and environments are inescapably parts of what we are. But Judaism takes this still a step further; it *celebrates* contingency by insisting that one's accident of birth imposes special obligations. We are obligated to carry on a tradition. The destruction of European Jewry and its centers of Torah study during World War II has intensified this feeling, creating a powerful sense in the next generation that we must preserve the tradition in which our ancestors died and must not (in theologian Emil Fackenheim's phrase) give Hitler a posthumous victory. The establishment of a Jewish state heightens the Jew's sense of identity and makes turning away from the people of Israel an act of betrayal. To be sure, Judaism comes in many forms, of which Orthodoxy is but one, and I have no need here to digress about the differences between the denominations. But I would be surprised if any Jew of any religious denomination denied that the contingency of his or her Jewishness had an effect on commitment. But contingency, again, is precisely what the philosopher points to as a reason to *abandon* commitment.

Is it really possible to integrate these religious perspectives with a philosophically detached "assessment" of their "epistemological merits"? My point has been: no. My commitment is not rooted in the (naive) notion that reason vindicates my beliefs. It is rooted rather in what Judaism provides me with: intellectual excitement, feeling, caring for others, inspiration, and a total perspective that is evocative and affecting. I have no doubt that people of other faiths and of other denominations in Judaism gain parallel benefits from their commitments. For all I know, secularists find secularism appealing for many of the same reasons I find my religion appealing. But then they can surely respect why I would hold on to a way of life that furnished those benefits. If I love my family, you can't argue me out of it just by telling me I *could* also learn to love a different family, or would have had I been born into one.

Philosophy has its place among the truly enjoyable, challenging, and edifying endeavors in our culture. But it is not the arbiter of all we think and do; what we do in our study and what we do in the rest of our lives are often not commensurate, because the study is the smaller room in life.

Without question, the essay that has stayed with me the longest is William James's "The Will to Believe." James's argument was that "our passional nature not only lawfully may, but must, decide an option between propositions, whenever it is a genuine option that cannot by its nature be decided on intellectual grounds." Notoriously, James has been accused of giving license to wishful thinking and fanaticism, and I've taken pains to admit both that I don't want to license just any view and that I do not have a principled way of licensing some things and outlawing others. But in choosing between living with this uncertainty about how to draw lines and discarding passional attractions altogether, the former seems the more human and appealing course.[7]

Notes

1. These remarks are de facto, not de jure. On the de jure level, it is well worth pondering Alvin Plantinga's view in his autobiography, written for James Tomberlin and Peter van Inwagen (eds.), *Alvin Plantinga* (Dordrecht, Boston, Lancaster, Pa.: Reidel, 1985):

> Serious intellectual work and religious allegiance, I
> believe, are inevitably intertwined. There is no such

> thing as religiously neutral intellectual endeavor—or
> rather there is no such thing as serious, substantial,
> and relatively complete intellectual endeavor that is
> religiously neutral. (p. 13)

This is an attractive position, though one must add, as Plantinga does, that "it isn't always easy to see how to establish it, or how to develop and articulate it in detail." I can certainly think of illustrations of Plantinga's bold claim.

2. There is an issue I need to bracket here. In the case of commonsense belief, we have no evidence *against* what we believe; whereas we do have evidence *against* religious belief, one may argue, namely, the existence of evil. My response to this would entail a fuller discussion of evil than I want to undertake here, but it suffices to say that philosophers have articulated well a set of value judgments that could make the existence of evil understandable in a world created by a benevolent God. Moreover, as I say, some religious philosophers do not internalize the problem of evil either!

3. To give an example from recent work on theodicy: Atheists argue: "Since there is unjustified evil, there is no perfect God. Theists can retort: "You put the argument backward: Since there is a perfect God, all apparent evil is justified evil." Who can prove which starting point is better?

4. In fact, philosophy may never have been the devil until the Enlightenment. Prior to that, philosophers nearly always believed in God and religion, and it was primarily the details of their beliefs (about creation, for example, or divine foreknowledge) that led to assoication with heresy. The fact is striking that Descartes "solved" the fundamental problem, "what justifies us in our beliefs," by appealing to a God who guaranteed the reliability of our cognitive faculties. George Berkeley's philosophy affords yet another instance of a great philosopher utilizing religious belief to solve a major philosophical problem. The separation between philosophy and religion has been rather brief.

5. Though paradoxically (as George Schlesinger notes in his essay), a creative and original theory in Talmud gets *real* standing when one finds some important legal authority who said the same thing. In contrast to academia, having been beaten to the punch is an occasion for delight, not disappointment. There are few better illustrations of how intellectual creativity and autonomy are fused with—as Schlesinger notes— humility. Josef Stern has also pointed out that whereas in philosophy a good question about a position will often be taken to refute the position, a good question about a position taken by an eminent authority in Talmud will often be followed up by a modest comment that "the subject needs further examination."

6. For a masterly and fertile articulation of the ideal of Torah study, see Rabbi Aharon Lichtenstein's article "Study," in *Contemporary Jewish Religious Thought*, ed. Arthur Cohen and Paul Mendes-Flohr (New York: Scribners, 1987), pp. 931–38.

7. Although the one subject on which I fancy myself the world's greatest expert is my own life and outlook, I cannot but acknowledge that I have benefited greatly from comments by Shalom Carmy and Josef Stern on an earlier draft of this narrative.